EDWARD IV, ENGLAND'S FORGOTTEN WARRIOR KING
HIS LIFE, HIS PEOPLE, AND HIS LEGACY

iUniverse books may be ordered through booksellers or by contacting:

iUniverse
1663 Liberty Drive
Bloomington, IN 47403
www.iuniverse.com
1-800-Authors (1-800-288-4677)

Because of the dynamic nature of the Internet, any web addresses or links contained in this book may have changed since publication and may no longer be valid. The views expressed in this work are solely those of the author and do not necessarily reflect the views of the publisher, and the publisher hereby disclaims any responsibility for them.

Any people depicted in stock imagery provided by Thinkstock are models, and such images are being used for illustrative purposes only.
Certain stock imagery © Thinkstock.

ISBN: 978-1-4917-4633-2 (sc)
ISBN: 978-1-4917-4634-9 (hc)
ISBN: 978-1-4917-4635-6 (e)

Library of Congress Control Number: 2014915829

Printed in the United States of America.

iUniverse rev. date: 1/21/2015

EDWARD IV,
ENGLAND'S FORGOTTEN WARRIOR KING

HIS LIFE, HIS PEOPLE, AND HIS LEGACY

DR. ANTHONY CORBET

CONTENTS

INTRODUCTION

English history immediately preceding the time when Edward IV became king of England in 1461 was dominated by the last stages and the continued effects of the Hundred Years War in France. This had begun in 1337, when King Edward III had claimed the French throne, and lasted intermittently until 1453. When Charles IV, King of France, died in 1328, he had no male heirs, so his cousin was made king of France as Philip VI; he was followed by King John II, Charles V and Charles VI. Despite the Salic law in France, which prohibited inheritance through females, King Edward III claimed the French throne by right of his mother, Queen Isabella, the sister of King Charles IV.

The long war can be divided into three phases: (1) the Edwardian War, meaning the ascendancy of Edward III (1337–60), (2) the Caroline War, meaning the ascendancy of the French King Charles V (1369–89), and (3) the Lancastrian War (1415–53). The first phase was eventually punctuated by English victories such as Sluys in 1340, Crecy in 1346, and Poitiers in 1356. The new king of France, John II, was captured at Poitiers and held prisoner in London. In the Treaty of Brétigny of 1360, France ceded to England large territories in the south-west and also Calais in the north. France agreed to pay a huge ransom for King John. Despite the peace between 1360 and 1369, the English were still involved in regional wars in Castile, Aragon, and Brittany. Generally, they fared poorly.

In the second phase of the Hundred Years War, events again did not turn out so well for England. The dauphin Charles (later Charles V) was regent for the imprisoned King John II. When John II died in captivity, the dauphin was crowned as Charles V, King of France, in 1364. Thereafter, in 1369, began a sustained effort to push the English out of France. The French followed the strategy of not engaging in large battles. Instead, they constantly harassed the English forces, frequently with considerable success. Most of France was restored to French control by 1389; only Calais remained in English hands. There was not much English activity after 1389; Edward III had died in 1377, and his grandson Richard II showed little interest in continuing the war in France. But in 1399, Richard II was overthrown and forced to abdicate in favour of the Lancastrian kings.

The Lancastrian phase of the Hundred Years War began with Henry V's great victory at Agincourt in 1415 and continued with the English conquest of much of northern France and much of south-west France. But during the reign of Henry VI, the French, under Charles VII, progressively regained control, much to the chagrin of the English people. Widespread discontent with the Lancastrians resulted in the War of the Roses, which began in 1455 and lasted until the fall of the Yorkist dynasty in 1485. This book recounts the fall of Henry VI and the rise and fall of the Yorkist kings of England, beginning with Edward IV and ending with Richard III.

William Shakespeare wrote famous plays with titles *Henry VI* and *Richard III*; the great good successful king who ruled between those two sad reigns was largely ignored as only a minor player. One protracted series of disasters, in the case of Henry VI, or one short huge disaster, in the case of Richard III, obviously made for better dramatic plays than Edward's solid mercantile activity, with steady creation of national wealth and prosperity. King Edward IV's reputation deserves to be restored to reflect something nearer the truth. This is especially so if his steady military triumphs in the civil war are also taken into account.

The book is divided into three parts. First is the story of King Edward IV. Second is a discussion of his legacy, the events which followed his death, including the deposition of his son King Edward V, and the usurpation by his brother King Richard III. After Edward died, his marriage to Queen Elizabeth Woodville was declared invalid, and his many children were declared not legitimate and unable to inherit. Not surprisingly, Richard III's usurpation had a miserable effect on the legacy of Edward IV. Here, it is argued that the usurpation was not warranted and was illegal. The last part of the book describes the people who were intimately involved with King Edward IV. There is some degree of repetition, but it is useful to have their mini-biographies gathered in one place.

PART ONE

The Story

CHAPTER 1

The Struggle for the Crown

The Birth of Edward IV in 1442, and His Disputed Legitimacy

Edward IV was born on 28 April 1442 in the French town of Rouen during the Hundred Years War. His mother was Cecily Neville, a great-granddaughter of King Edward III. Edward IV's father was Richard Plantagenet (1411–1460), the third duke of York, a great-great-great-grandson of King Edward III. Edward IV was tall and handsome. Because of this, he was known when he was younger as the Rose of Rouen.

Assuming that Edward IV was born at forty weeks' gestation, it has been calculated, according to logs kept in the cathedral at Rouen, that Edward's father may have been away from home at the time of his son's conception ("Britain's Real Monarch," 2004). The duke was on military operations at Pontoise, near Paris, from 14 July to 21 August 1441, but the calculated date of Edward's conception is 4 August 1441, which might suggest that Edward was illegitimate ("Edward IV of England," 2014). French historians have even suggested who the biological father might be, but this should be regarded with considerable suspicion. If Edward was born at thirty-seven weeks' gestation, then the calculated date of conception is 25 August 1441. This likely coincides with the time soon after Richard's return from Pontoise, which might suggest that he had a happy reunion with Cecily. An infant that is gestated for thirty-seven weeks is often vigorous, suckles well, needs only simple nursery attention, and weighs only a pound less than a forty-week infant. Many authorities consider thirty-seven weeks to be full term, which throws considerable doubt on claims that Edward IV might have been illegitimate. His mother never publicly admitted to any illegitimacy, and his father did not deny that Edward was his son and legal heir, which made Edward legitimate under English common law. Considering the possible errors in the above calculations, it is not unreasonable to consider that Edward may have even been born at thirty-seven and a half weeks' gestation, very near full term, even by the strictest standards.

However, Edward's baptism was muted and private, unlike the lavish baptism of a later son, Edmund, for whom the cathedral in Rouen was thrown open to the public. If Edward was born at thirty-seven weeks' gestation, then perhaps some evidence of frailty was apparent and caution was suggested to his family. When he was older, Edward was tall and well built, unlike his short, spare father. The claim of illegitimacy was made by other members of the family, including two of Edward's younger brothers, Richard and George, and his cousin Richard Neville. But this was a dysfunctional family, and all had seriously doubtful motives at the time. It was even alleged that Edward's mother, while angry with him over his later, secret marriage, threatened to expose him. Such an admission by Proud Cis, however, would have been extremely unlikely.

In her last will and testament, as described by Arlene Okerlund (2005), Duchess Cecily made it clear that Richard, Duke of York, was the father of Edward IV. Cecily stated as follows: "I, Cecily, wife unto the right noble prince, *Richard late Duke of York, father unto the most Christian prince, my Lord and son, King Edward IV,* the first day of April in the year of our Lord 1495, make and ordain my testament in form and manner ensuing" (emphasis added). It is not likely that Cecily would have lied in her last will; she could have simply ignored the problem if there was one. Sceptical historians have not settled the question, but the claim of all subsequent English monarchs through Edward's eldest daughter, Princess Elizabeth of York, has never been seriously challenged. Therefore, the course of English history has confirmed that Edward IV was a legitimate son. The case against Edward IV is absolutely unproven. Accusations of illegitimacy were very common in the Middle Ages and, in the absence of scientific knowledge, often difficult to refute. But this accusation in the case of King Edward IV has little to support it.

The Tragic Reign of King Henry VI, 1422–61

Henry VI was the son of King Henry V and Catherine of Valois. Catherine was a daughter of the French King Charles VI (see Appendix A). When Henry V died of dysentery in 1422, the new King Henry VI was only nine months old, so John, Duke of Bedford, the oldest brother of Henry V, was regent for the considerable English possessions in northern France. Humphrey, Duke of Gloucester, another brother of Henry V, was Lord Protector of England while Bedford was in France (see Appendix B). It was apparently intended that Gloucester should defer to Bedford when Bedford was in England. In practice, the chancellor, Bishop Henry Beaufort, retained most control over English affairs. It could be said that Bedford was regent of England and France and that Gloucester was deputy in England when Bedford was in France (Weir, 1995).

John Bedford had some initial military success in France, notably with his decisive victory at the Battle of Verneuil in 1424, but he did badly with the emergence of Joan of Arc as commander of the French forces in the years before 1430. However, in 1431, Joan of Arc was captured, tried as a witch, and martyred by being burnt at the stake. Bedford died in 1435, exhausted by his efforts. With the First Treaty of Arras in 1435, France and Burgundy made peace with each other. Since Burgundy had previously helped the English, from that point onwards, English fortunes in France progressively declined.

Following the death of Bedford, Richard, Duke of York, was appointed lieutenant in France for a two-year term. He arrived soon after the fall of Paris to French forces in 1436 and seems to have concentrated his efforts in Normandy. With the help of John Talbot, the earl of Shrewsbury, and some of Bedford's captains, Richard drove the French forces out of the province. He had notable success with the recapture of Fecamp and held on to the Pays de Caux. His term was extended for another two years. As the London government did not pay him for his considerable expenses, York refused to continue when his term was up. He went back to England at the end of 1439.

But in 1440, the duke of York was again appointed lieutenant in Normandy for a term of five years, which was later extended another two years, to 1447. His task was to negotiate a satisfactory peace with the French. Although promises had been made, again, his expenses were not covered. In 1443, William de la Pole, the first duke of Suffolk, the king's favourite minister, sent John Beaufort, the first duke of Somerset (see Appendix D) with a force of eight thousand men to Gascony to help restore order. York was unhappy with this arrangement, as it detracted from his own efforts in Normandy by taking money and resources. Somerset failed miserably in Gascony, returned to Normandy, and died in England in 1444, possibly by suicide. Also in 1444, Suffolk brought an embassy to France and negotiated an agreement with King Charles VII. There had developed in English politics a paralyzing schism over the war in France. The boy King Henry VI; Cardinal Beaufort, an uncle of the first duke of Somerset (see Appendix D); and the duke of Suffolk together headed the Peace Party. Humphrey, Duke of Gloucester, and Richard, Duke of York, were in favour of continuing the war in France and headed the War Party, consistent with the deathbed wishes of King Henry V.

With the Treaty of Tours in 1444, the English and French agreed to a two-year truce, to start in 1445. This was later extended in several stages to mid 1450, so, during this period (1445–50), there was a pause in the fighting. Under terms of the treaty, Henry VI agreed to marry Margaret of Anjou, a niece by marriage of Charles VII (see Appendix A). England agreed to surrender the province of Maine to the French, a surrender which, when it became known, proved very unpopular with the English people. In return, the English were allowed to keep the Aquitaine in south-west France, a not inconsiderable concession when considering the deteriorating military situation. But what made the agreement so unpopular in England was that there was to be no marriage dowry. In return for the hard-won province of Maine, England would receive a penniless French princess. The people considered this to be a very bad bargain. In 1445, Henry VI married the beautiful but wilful Margaret of Anjou, who thus became the queen consort of England. It was not until 1448 that Maine was finally surrendered to France after much angry controversy, which only worsened the great friction between England and France. Charles VII used the prolonged truce to greatly improve his forces and plan a final military offensive against the English occupation; in particular, he greatly improved his artillery to counterbalance the deadly English longbow.

In 1447, Suffolk appointed Richard, Duke of York, to Ireland as Lord Lieutenant and replaced him as lieutenant in France with Edmund

Beaufort, who was the second duke of Somerset (see Appendix D), a great-grandson of Edward III, and a possible heir to the childless King Henry VI. In practice, York did not go to Ireland until 1449; he stayed in England to attend to his own affairs. He considered the appointment to be the Peace Party's device to exclude him from English politics.

The government in England was extremely unpopular. Complaints centred on excessive taxation, profligate government spending, low wages, corruption in the judicial courts, maladministration in the counties, and poor progress in consolidating the affairs in France. The king's advisors looked after their own interests rather than those of the whole country, accumulating considerable wealth at the expense of the naive and overgenerous King Henry VI.

In January 1450, the Lord Privy Seal, Bishop Moleyns, was lynched by an angry mob in a dispute over naval wage payments. This was a reflection of widespread disorder. There followed in June 1450 the rebellion of Jack Cade, who led a large force of disaffected English yeomen, mostly from Kent. They captured and executed Lord Say, the Lord High Treasurer of England. After much chaos and a pitched battle on London Bridge, the king's army finally killed Jack Cade and ended the insurrection by July 1450. There followed many short trials. At least thirty-five rebels were beheaded in the infamous Harvest of Heads.

In the meantime, the truce of 1445, with its several extensions to 1450, was broken by the English when they occupied the Breton town of Fougères in March 1449. This operation was carried out by the second duke of Somerset, the newly appointed lieutenant, and had been sanctioned by Suffolk. Charles VII declared war in July 1449. His newly reorganized military forces flourished, but Somerset proved a poor choice as the English commander. Brittany was lost by 1449; Normandy was lost by 1450; Guyenne, with its capital at Bordeaux, was lost by 1451; and Gascony, with its capital at Bayonne, was lost by 1453. These constant English defeats signalled the end of the Hundred Years War. The Battle of Formigny on 15 August 1450 was a catastrophic disaster for England. Suffolk was blamed, tried in Parliament for treason, and sent into exile. On the way to Burgundy, he was captured at sea and brutally beheaded by angry English partisans. England was flooded with unpaid and destructive soldiers returning home after the disastrous losses in France. As a result, disorder and brigandage in England were widespread.

The Rebellion of Richard Duke of York; the Armed Confrontation at Dartford in 1452; the Battle of Castillon in 1453; and the Madness of King Henry VI

The English people were furious about all of these events, especially the loss of Normandy. Richard, Duke of York, returned from Ireland and marched on London with a large number of troops and with enormous public support. In a direct confrontation with the king in his chambers at Westminster Palace on 29 September 1450, the duke of York demanded the resignation of Somerset and many of his corrupt associates. Parliament was called. It passed an Act of Resumption, which called for the return to the Crown of much of the property distributed so generously by the king to his favourites. The duke of York, acting with Parliament, appeared briefly to gain control. On 1 December 1450, Parliament impeached Somerset for his military failures in France. He was taken to the Tower. But almost immediately, Queen Margaret rejected Parliament's decision and had Somerset released. The House of Lords, always suspicious of York, supported the king, so the duke had to back down. By May 1451, York's opponents were back in charge of English affairs. Then, Parliament, at the instigation of a member named Thomas Young, a supporter of Richard, Duke of York, requested that the king settle the issue of his heir. The king refused, had Thomas Young sent to the Tower, and then dissolved Parliament on 31 May 1451. With Parliament gone, the duke of York retired, humiliated, to his seat at Ludlow in the Welsh Marches.

By then, York had realized that the king would not allow any government reform unless he was forced. On 3 February 1452 at Shrewsbury, York issued a manifesto stating that the troubles in England would not cease until the corrupt Somerset was permanently removed from the government. The duke of York then mustered troops and marched towards London. The king and queen raised a royal army and marched out of London on 16 February 1452 to intercept York as he approached the capital, but York evaded the king. Near London, on 29 February 1452, York drew up in battle order at Dartford on the south side of the River Thames. The royal army followed and reached Blackheath on 1 March 1452. The next day, they advanced close to the duke of York's position. It seemed that civil war was about to erupt. The two armies were very large by the standards of the time, each about twenty thousand men, but most of the peerage remained on the side of the king.

Neither side wanted a battle, so at negotiations it was agreed that if York dismissed his army, then the king would have Somerset imprisoned. Naively, York carried out his part of the agreement and dismissed his army, but the queen, yet again, immediately ordered the release of Somerset. During further negotiations at Blackheath, the duke of York, surprised and angered to find Somerset still present in the king's tent – and with his own Yorkist military support gone home – was effectively taken prisoner and was only released after he had promised never again to rebel against the king's government. York was fortunate not to be executed for treason, but the council feared to move against him because of his strong public support, especially in London. For the second time, the duke of York retired, humiliated, to Ludlow. The king issued general pardons and tried to restore his relations with York. On 12 August 1452, he visited with the duke in Ludlow, but there was no agreement. For another year, York remained excluded from power.

In late 1452, John Talbot, the earl of Shrewsbury, with a comparatively small force, sailed to the duchy of Aquitaine and occupied Bordeaux on 17 October 1452. After the elapse of the winter season, the English captured many of the surrounding towns and there was a temporary restoration of English confidence. But then the government in London procrastinated and failed to provide sorely needed reinforcements for Shrewsbury. On 17 July 1453, the French used their improved cannons to decisively defeat the English at the Battle of Castillon. The heroic earl of Shrewsbury was killed. This disaster effectively ended the Hundred Years War, but it meant that civil war was near in England.

King Henry VI was entirely and appropriately blamed for this disgraceful humiliation of England at Castillon. Possibly as a result, the king suffered an attack of insanity, probably a form of depressive schizophrenia inherited from his maternal grandfather, King Charles VI (see Appendix A). During this time, Queen Margaret gave birth to a prince and heir, Edward of Westminster. The queen and the council hid the king's incapacity for as long as they could, especially as they could not get the king to recognize the newborn prince as his own son, an important point in the English common law. In early 1454, the council could delay no longer. Richard, Duke of York, was made Lord Protector. He once more had Somerset imprisoned in the Tower. York did well as Lord Protector and initiated many of the needed reforms, but there was not sufficient time for them to have proper effect.

The Appearance of Richard, the Sixteenth Earl of Warwick, and the First Battle of St Albans (1455)

The king recovered from his illness in early 1455, took back his powers, and restored Somerset. With the loss of his office, the duke of York, still intent on removing Somerset, decided on force of arms. York was supported by Richard Neville, the fifth earl of Salisbury, a great-grandson of Edward III, and by Richard Neville, the sixteenth earl of Warwick, a son of Salisbury and therefore a great-great-grandson of Edward III (see Appendix E). At the Battle of St Albans on 22 May 1455, York was victorious, the king was captured, and Somerset was killed. This was the opening conflict in the War of the Roses. Many other Lancastrians also died, including Thomas, the eighth Lord Clifford, and Henry Percy, the second earl of Northumberland. In addition, Humphrey Stafford, the eldest son and heir of Humphrey Stafford, the first duke of Buckingham, was severely wounded and died later (see Appendix F). The duke of York allowed Henry VI to continue as king, presumably because he was satisfied that Somerset was permanently removed. York was clearly not yet ready to claim the throne, as he still hoped that he could reform the government under Henry VI. The duke of York secured appointment as constable of England and ran the government in the name of the king. In late 1455, the king was ill for a second time. York was again made Lord Protector, which was a more powerful office than constable. Although the king recovered by early 1456, York remained Lord Protector and a leader in the government. But it was in name only, as he was unable to control the hostilities within the council. His influence waned rapidly.

Preparations for War; the Battle of Blore Heath (1459); the Battle of Ludford Bridge (1459); the Flight of the House of York; Warwick Invades England; the Battle of Northampton (1460); and the Act of Accord

In 1456, the king ordered multiple exemptions to the Act of Resumption, much to the relief of the Lancastrians, who stood to lose much of their ill-gained property. Humphrey Stafford, the first duke of Buckingham (see Appendix F), who replaced Somerset as the king's favourite, followed a conciliation policy and managed to maintain the king's peace for a while. But people in London were tired of Henry VI. When a riot occurred in the city, the queen sent troops to suppress it, but then the citizens forcibly prevented a royal judicial court from investigating the cause of the riot. They considered an investigation to be the prerogative of the City of London, not of the Crown. Later in 1456, Queen Margaret, furious with the citizens of London, moved the royal court out of London and set up in Coventry, where the king had more local support and York had less. There followed a standoff between the rival parties as they each recruited political and military support.

The queen negotiated with Scotland for support against York, which made the English people even angrier. The Scots under King James II threatened to invade England and made raids across the border, but York successfully repulsed them. It is true that Richard, Duke of York, began to use his family name of Plantagenet to emphasize his descent from Edward III and his claim to the throne (see Appendix C), but his primary aim still remained to reform the English government, not to overthrow the king. However, the queen and her Lancastrian supporters thought otherwise; they persuaded the king that York did aim to secure the crown for himself. Still clinging to his declining power as Lord Protector, York organized the appointment of Richard, Earl of Warwick, as the captain of Calais, a post which Warwick was to fill with great success, much to the later regret of the queen.

Still in 1456, the king and queen called a meeting of the Great Council at Coventry; the Yorkist lords attended briefly but then withdrew, very distrustful of the queen. The king was persuaded to dismiss all of the Yorkist members of his government, including the Lord Protector, the duke of York. The duke's first protectorate had been in place from 1454 to 1456, with interruptions. The queen negotiated with Charles VII, the king of

France, her uncle by marriage, for assistance to fend off the duke of York. In August 1457, French troops under Pierre de Brézé raided and burned Sandwich on the Kent coast. For this, the people were furious with the government and especially with the queen. Unable to raise a sufficient army to support the unpopular government, the queen introduced conscription for the first time in English history, a move which even further outraged the English people.

The king called a peace conference at Westminster, but it was not successful. In February 1458, in a public show of friendship at St Paul's Church, on the occasion commonly called Love Day, the magnates processioned arm in arm to the church; this deceived nobody, except possibly the king. The younger lords, Clifford, Northumberland, and Somerset, demanded compensation for the death of their fathers at First St Albans. At the orders of the king, York, Salisbury, and Warwick paid financial compensation to the survivor estates. Distrustful of the king and queen, the Yorkist lords returned home – York to Ludlow Castle in the Welsh Marches, Salisbury to Middleham Castle in Yorkshire, and Warwick to Calais.

Warwick had taken to plundering foreign merchant ships in the English Channel, an activity which bordered on piracy but which was very popular with the English people. In May 1458, Warwick successfully attacked the ships of Castile and the Hanseatic League, which aggravated the Lancastrian government because no war had been declared and they had to deal with the diplomatic protests. The queen tried unsuccessfully to remove Warwick from his post in Calais and replace him with Henry Beaufort, the third duke of Somerset, who had succeeded his deceased father. Warwick was attacked in the royal kitchen by supporters of the queen. When he heard of his impending arrest, Warwick fled to Calais. When orders came for him to relinquish his post at Calais, he returned to England and challenged the council. As he left the chamber, he was again attacked by Lancastrians, but, once more, the earl escaped back to Calais.

The queen now began raising an army, both volunteers and conscripts, in preparation for war. The Yorkists launched a ferocious propaganda offensive, attacking the queen and even suggesting that her son, Edward of Westminster, was either illegitimate or a birth-room changeling. With Salisbury in Yorkshire to the north, York on the Welsh border to the west, and Warwick in Calais, the Yorkists were divided. From Calais, Warwick landed at Sandwich with a small, well-trained force and headed for Ludlow. From Middleham, Salisbury also attempted to meet the duke of York at Ludlow, but the queen intercepted him and attacked. At the Battle of Blore Heath on 23 September 1459, Salisbury was the victor over the Lancastrian James Tuchet, the fifth Baron Audley. Salisbury and Warwick were subsequently able to join with the duke of York at Ludlow.

Then, the queen and Henry VI prepared for battle again and won the Battle of Ludford Bridge on 12 October 1459. But York escaped to Ireland, and Salisbury and Warwick, together with York's eldest son and heir, Edward, the seventh earl of March, escaped to Calais. This Edward would soon be King Edward IV. The Yorkist leaders at Ludford Bridge deserted before any large-scale battle could erupt, given that their forces were severely outnumbered, especially after Warwick's lieutenant, Sir Andrew Trollope, switched to the side of the king. In addition, there was a general reluctance on the part of many Yorkists to fight against the king on the open battlefield. This battle was more likely a minor skirmish, but it was nevertheless an important strategic victory for the House of Lancaster. The royal army sacked the township of Ludlow, much to the discomfort of the duchess of York and her young children, including six-year-old Richard, later the Yorkist duke of Gloucester and, still later, King Richard III.

By late 1459, a bill of attainder was passed in the Parliament, which was known as the Parliament of Devils, against York, Salisbury, and Warwick, which meant immediate reversion of all estates to the Crown and execution of the men if they were captured. But the attainders were a mistake. With this crucial event, the only option for the House of York was to invade England and overthrow the king. The Lancastrian government appointed the third duke of Somerset, Henry Beaufort (see Appendix D), to replace Warwick in Calais, and the earl of Wiltshire to replace York in Ireland, but neither could take up his appointment because of solid Yorkist resistance. Somerset occupied Guînes Castle and, from there, sortied against Calais, but without success.

The Lancastrians built transport ships at Sandwich in order to further attack Calais, but the audacious Warwick waited for the ships' completion and then captured them for his own use in 1460. The Yorkists took the local Lancastrian commanders, Lord Rivers and his son Anthony

Woodville, back to Calais, where the Woodvilles were famously berated for fighting against the Yorkist lords. This hostile encounter reflected the antipathy which was to develop between Warwick and the Woodville family. Warwick's big issue seemed to be the Woodvilles' lack of "the noble blood," of which the Woodvilles were to hear much in the future.

Warwick sailed to Ireland to confer with the duke of York about the next possible steps to be taken. On the way back to Calais, the earl avoided the duke of Exeter's fleet, which was out looking for him. Lord Fauconberg and Sir John Wenlock, deputies of Warwick, then captured Sandwich to establish a Yorkist bridgehead. Then, Salisbury and Warwick, accompanied by York's eldest son, Edward, the eighteen-year-old seventh earl of March, landed at Sandwich in Kent and recruited a large invasion force. They occupied London and marched into the Midlands in search of the king.

The Yorkists defeated the royalist forces at the Battle of Northampton on 10 July 1460 and captured Henry VI. The earl of March, the future Edward IV, led the Yorkist left battle with great distinction, pressing ahead in driving rain, leading the way through mud and water. Even at this early stage, Edward's practice in battle was to lead from the front. The Lancastrian cannon could not be used because the rain had soaked the gunpowder. Edward would be known for always having good fortune in battle. In front of Edward, a part of the king's army under Lord Ralph Grey of Ruthin laid down its arms. Thus assisted, the Yorkists climbed over the defensive earthworks and pressed hard on the king's right battle. Then, quickly, Warwick's men in the centre battle and Fauconberg's men on the right rushed over the earthworks. The Lancastrian forces were routed. Humphrey Stafford, the duke of Buckingham (see Appendix F); John Talbot, the second earl of Shrewsbury; and Thomas Percy, the Lord Egremont, lay dead at Henry VI's tent. The Yorkist lords paid homage to the unharmed king.

In the new government after Northampton, more Yorkist than before, George Neville, the bishop of Exeter, the brother of Warwick, was chancellor of England. Henry Bourchier was treasurer, and Robert Stillington was keeper of the privy seal. In August 1460, taking advantage of the trouble in England, James II of Scotland captured Roxburgh Castle, but James was killed when the barrel of a cannon exploded near him. He was succeeded by the nine-year-old King James III.

A few months later, after leaving Ireland, the duke of York landed in Cheshire, marched into London, and laid claim to the throne at Westminster Hall, arguing his ancestral line from the third son of King Edward III, namely Lionel, Duke of Clarence (see Appendix C). This was, at first, not well received by the lords, as they worried about the oaths of loyalty they had sworn to the Lancastrian king. After weeks of negotiation, Parliament passed the Act of Accord of 31 October 1460, in which it was agreed that Henry VI should continue as king for as long as he lived. But the act also established that York and his line were the heirs of Henry VI – and for the present, that Richard, Duke of York, was again to serve as Lord Protector. The king, under immense pressure and probably not knowing what he was doing, gave his assent to the settlement. But as the earl of Warwick had Henry VI locked up in the Tower, the duke of York and the earl of Warwick were de facto rulers of England. The king's seven-year-old son and heir, Edward of Westminster, was effectively disinherited.

The Claim to the Throne of England by the House of York

King Edward III, who reigned from 1327 to 1377, had six sons. In order of birth, they were as follows: Edward, the Black Prince, who died the year before Edward III died, namely 1376; William, who died at one year of age; Lionel of Antwerp, the duke of Clarence (third son); John of Gaunt, the duke of Lancaster (fourth son); Edmund of Langley, the duke of York (fifth son); and Thomas of Woodstock, the earl of Buckingham and, later, the duke of Gloucester (sixth son). The Black Prince (first son) had a boy who succeeded King Edward III as King Richard II in 1377. Richard had a troubled reign and was forced to abdicate in 1399. His throne was usurped by Henry Bolingbroke, the eldest son of John of Gaunt, the duke of Lancaster (fourth son). As shown in Appendix C, the descendants of Lionel, the third son, were the rightful kings of England if Richard II was lawfully deposed.

The House of Lancaster

John of Gaunt, Duke of Lancaster, the fourth son of King Edward III, died in 1399. John had a son by his first wife, Blanche of Lancaster. This son, Henry Bolingbroke, the new second duke of Lancaster, usurped the throne with an army in the field later in 1399. Henry, Duke of Lancaster, killed King Richard II in prison, probably by isolation and slow starvation at Pontefract Castle, and had himself crowned as King Henry IV. The new king, regarded in history as a usurper, had a troubled reign filled with repeated rebellions. When Henry IV died in 1413, his famous son was King Henry V, who, in turn, was succeeded by his less than famous son King Henry VI in 1422 (see Appendix B).

The House of York

Lionel, Duke of Clarence, the third son of Edward III, had a daughter, Philippa, who married Edmund Mortimer, the third earl of March. They had a son, Roger Mortimer, the fourth earl of March, who died in 1398, before the usurpation events of 1399 (see Appendix C). Roger Mortimer had a son, Edmund, the fifth earl of March, who died in 1425, and a daughter named Anne Mortimer. Anne married Richard Plantagenet, the earl of Cambridge, a younger son of Edmund of Langley, the duke of York, the fifth son of King Edward III. Anne Mortimer was eventually, in 1411, the mother of Richard Plantagenet, who became the third duke of York and, later, the sixth earl of March. Richard claimed the throne after the Battle of Northampton in 1460. The duchy of York inheritance came through another, older son of Edmund of Langley, namely Edward of Norwich, the second duke of York, who died at Agincourt in 1415. It should be noted that this York inheritance was not the direct line of inheritance to the throne of England. Rather, the direct line was through Philippa and the Mortimer House of March.

Deviation in the Line of Succession to the English Throne, and the Correction

The rightful heir to the throne at the time of the usurpation in 1399 and the death of Richard II in 1400 was Edmund Mortimer, the fifth earl of March, the son of Roger Mortimer, the fourth earl of March. The boy Edmund was then only eight years old, but nobody made claims for him since he was so young. Edmund Mortimer, the fifth earl of March, died in 1425, and Richard, the third duke of York, the son of Anne Mortimer, the new sixth earl of March, inherited Edmund's claim to the throne, which he ultimately asserted in 1460 after the Battle of Northampton. But with his death in the same year, Richard transmitted the claim to his eldest son, Edward, the seventh earl of March, who, later in the following year, took the throne and became King Edward IV. Although some continue to claim that Edward IV usurped the throne, Parliament had agreed that Edward had a good claim to the throne and invited him to be king. The members considered that King Henry VI had broken the terms of the 1460 Act of Accord.

The immediate Lancastrian line was all male, whereas the Yorkist line included females, Philippa Plantagenet Mortimer and Anne Mortimer (Plantagenet), and was more complex. But England had never accepted the Salic law followed in France, which prohibited transmission of claim through females. However, King Stephen was king in 1135 through his mother, Adele, the daughter of King William the Conqueror; and Henry II was king in 1154 through his mother, Matilda, the daughter of King Henry I. The claim of every Plantagenet king since Henry II and until Edward III was through that same woman, Matilda.

In 1399, the Yorkist claim through Lionel of Clarence, the third son of Edward III, was the stronger one, as it was based on the accepted law of primogeniture, which favoured the oldest surviving child – by custom, usually the eldest son, but not always. However, in a world dominated by males and with a Henry Bolingbroke army in the field, the House of Lancaster prevailed with Parliament in 1399. And it should be remembered that in those days of early English nationhood, some may have considered that the French custom of Salic law should be followed. The final arrangement proved controversial. Later rather than sooner, it resulted in the civil war known as the War of the Roses. It would not be until 1460, in the Act of Accord, that Parliament decided the matter of inheritance in favour of the Mortimer line, which had been married into the House of York.

Since then, the transmission of claim through females has never been challenged again in English history. King James I inherited the English throne through Margaret Tudor, the sister of Henry VIII. King George I inherited the English throne through the youngest daughter of James I, namely Elizabeth Stuart, and her daughter Sophia. Reigning English queens have included Mary I, Elizabeth I, Mary II, Anne, Victoria, and Elizabeth II. In retrospect, the case for York appears to be closed, but it did not seem so obvious in 1460. And besides, the House of Lancaster had rights of occupancy for the sixty-one years of Lancastrian rule since

1399. At a later time in history, the House of Lancaster held a red rose as its emblem. The House of York held a white rose. This was made famous by the painting of the apocryphal confrontation of the two factions (Payne, 2013), which was described by William Shakespeare in *King Henry VI*.

It should be noted that the House of York was really the House of Mortimer, descended from Philippa, the daughter of Lionel, Duke of Clarence, the third son of Edward III. The House of Mortimer added the duchy of York from the descendants of the fifth son of Edward III, Edmund, Duke of York. As is often suggested, the duke of York, the fifth son of Edward III, strengthened the claim of the Mortimer line, but this was not necessary for the legitimacy of the Mortimer claim to the throne. Following the usual custom favouring the male line, the House of Mortimer was merged into and became the House of York (as shown in Appendix C).

During the reign of King Henry IV, there was constant trouble, conspiracy, and rebellion. During the reign of the powerful King Henry V, there was much less trouble at home. Most of the fighting occurred during the successful invasion of France. But with the advent of the boy king Henry VI and with government by what amounted to a regency, the old disagreements emerged on the surface and opened the way for the House of York to revive its claim in 1460.

Brief Note on the History of the Duchy of Lancaster

It is interesting and of some importance to note the peculiar origin of the Duchy of Lancaster. The first creation was in 1351, when Henry of Grosmont, the fourth earl of Lancaster, was made the first duke of Lancaster by King Edward III. Henry Grosmont died in 1361 with no male heir, but he had a daughter named Blanche of Lancaster.

The second creation of the duchy was in 1362, when Edward III made John of Gaunt the duke of Lancaster after he married Blanche of Lancaster, the daughter of Henry Grosmont. John of Gaunt's son, Henry IV, was the next duke of Lancaster in 1399. He declared the Duchy of Lancaster to be part of the monarch's inheritance, to be held irreversibly attached to the Crown. Henry V was the next duke of Lancaster, with the duchy held as part of the monarch's inheritance. Henry VI also held the duchy as part of the Crown inheritance. In 1461, King Edward IV made the arrangement permanent, with the duchy merged into the estate of the reigning monarch, whoever held the position. In other words, the Duchy of Lancaster was attached irreversibly to the Crown. Thus, Edward IV held the Duchy of Lancaster, which contributed greatly to his income. It has remained part of the monarch's inheritance to this day. Queen Elizabeth II presently holds the Duchy of Lancaster as a Crown possession.

The Death of Richard, Duke of York, at the Battle of Wakefield (1460)

The Act of Accord of 1460 was anathema to Queen Margaret Anjou, especially given the exclusionary treatment and disinheritance of her son, Edward of Westminster. After Northampton, she had fled first to Wales and from there to Scotland, and obtained help from Mary de Gueldres, the regent for King James III. In the meantime, in response to the queen's urgent requests, the king's supporters from the West Country and from the northern counties mustered near the town of York and began to raid some of the northern York estates. The Lord Protector sent his son Edward, the seventh earl of March, to the west, while he himself went north, leaving Warwick to look after London.

At the Battle of Wakefield on 30 December 1460, a third of King Henry's large army under Henry Beaufort, the third duke of Somerset, advanced on Sandal Castle, where York was quartered. The remainder of the king's army was concealed in the surrounding woods. York failed to see this arrangement and underestimated the size of the opposing forces; he advanced out of the castle and was badly defeated in the open by forces vastly superior to his own. York was not a good military commander. He should have had more scouts out in the surrounding country to get better intelligence, and he should have waited in the safety of Sandal Castle for his eldest son, the seventh earl of March, the future Edward IV. The Lord Protector; his second son, Edmund, the earl of Rutland; and his brother-in-law, the earl of Salisbury, were killed at Wakefield. Their severed heads were displayed after the battle on the gates at York. A macabre paper crown was placed on the duke of York's head, in order to mock his claim to the English throne. Queen Margaret Anjou was not present at Wakefield but was in Scotland gathering reinforcements for the Lancastrian cause.

The Battle of Mortimer's Cross (1461), the Second Battle of St Albans (1461), and Queen Margaret's Failure to Occupy London

With the disaster at Wakefield, Edward Plantagenet, the seventh earl of March, who was in the Welsh Marches, was now the Yorkist claimant to the throne. He quickly defeated the king's forces under Jasper Tudor, the Lancastrian earl of Pembroke, at the Battle of Mortimer's Cross on 2 February 1461. Jasper Tudor entered England from South Wales, moved east, and was intending to combine with the main Lancastrian forces as they advanced south after Wakefield towards London. But the Yorkists were waiting and intercepted him. As was to be his usual custom, Edward had his scouts out in the countryside and placed his forces in good position. Edward did not adopt a defensive posture behind the south-flowing River Lugg as he was advised, but drew up on the west side, the same side of the river as the Lancastrians, in order to assert the attack. This would have been a big problem if his army had needed to escape, as there was only a single small bridge across the river. But Edward's mode of operation was always the same: attack and seize the advantage early.

Before the battle, three suns were observed in the sky. Edward told his troops that these represented God the Father, God the Son, and God the Holy Ghost and was a wonderful omen for his spectacular victory. Edward subjected the Lancastrians to a ferocious longbow arrow-storm attack. To escape the hail of arrows, the Lancastrians advanced underneath, but the Yorkists stopped them. Then, Edward attacked in the centre, and there followed vicious hand-to-hand combat. The Lancastrians were routed. Owen Tudor, the father of Jasper Tudor, was captured and executed after the battle, but Jasper Tudor, the earl of Pembroke, and John Butler, the earl of Wiltshire, escaped. Lancastrian losses were considerable; it is estimated that up to four thousand men were slain.

At the age of eighteen years, Edward was already a great military propagandist as well as a fine military commander. The three suns were a parhelion related to the refraction of light by ice crystals in the atmosphere; the three suns became the Sun in Splendour, the heraldic emblem of the soon-to-be-established triumphant King Edward IV.

In the meantime, after Wakefield, the queen's victorious army, led by the third duke of Somerset and reinforced with violent Scottish troops, advanced south on a wide front, plundering and pillaging the English countryside. Margaret had not been able to pay her Scottish soldiers, so she had agreed that they could plunder England, but only south of the River Trent. For a queen of England, this was disgraceful leadership. The Lancastrians under Henry Beaufort defeated Warwick at the Second Battle of St Albans on 17 February 1461, just north of London. As in the case of the First Battle of St Albans, the second battle occurred within the township of St Albans. Warwick arrayed his army defensively in the north end of St Albans, but the queen's army, advancing south, diverted to the west at night, moved around Warwick, and attacked from the rear in the south end of St Albans. Warwick had also failed to send out scouts to detect the Lancastrian move; he was outmanoeuvred and badly mauled. But Warwick made an orderly withdrawal of his surviving forces to the west, intending to join with Edward, earl of March, at Chipping Norton in the Cotswolds. The Yorkists left the hostage King Henry VI behind, sitting under a tree, and the queen ordered the execution of the two Yorkist knights who continued faithfully to attend him. Margaret was not noted for her recognition of chivalry or for her generosity.

Although the way was now open for the queen to enter London, she did not do so, which was a disastrous strategic mistake on her part. She knew that the citizens of London hated her. Her Scots were plundering far and wide, causing fear and consternation. London had strong Yorkist sympathies. The queen had brought hated alien troops into England, which was tantamount to treason. So, London closed its gates. The citizens were tired of the unfortunate King Henry VI and hated his French queen. The Lord Mayor sent three gentleladies– Jacquetta Woodville, the dowager duchess of Bedford, a close friend of Margaret; the widow of the first duke of Buckingham, Anne Neville; and also Lady Elizabeth Scales – to plead with Queen Margaret to spare the city of London from the Scots. While Margaret hesitated and eventually retreated north, Edward, united with Warwick, moved rapidly into London to a tumultuous welcome. Edward was acclaimed by a large crowd on St John's Field at Clerkenwell, and Parliament proclaimed him as King Edward IV. It was reasoned that Henry VI, thanks to his queen, had violated the terms of the 1460 Act of Accord. Warwick may have helped Edward gain the throne, thus earning his famous title of Kingmaker, but his role has been exaggerated, especially as he had recently been so badly defeated at Second St Albans. A more powerful factor was the presence of Edward, a young, attractive prince whose handsome appearance and winsome charm embodied all expected of a medieval king.

CHAPTER 2

The Early Reign of King Edward IV

The Triumph of King Edward IV and the Battle of Towton (1461)

There was a large and dangerous opposing army still in the field. King Edward IV did not hesitate; he understood that his newly won crown was not safe because there could not be two kings of England. He and his supporters marched north in search of the Lancastrians. On the eve of Palm Sunday, 28 March 1461, there was fought a major skirmish at Ferrybridge, where the Yorkist army planned to cross the River Aire as they advanced north. Lord FitzWalter was sent to secure the bridge, but the Lancastrians under John, the ninth Lord Clifford, killed FitzWalter and captured the crossing. Then, Edward sent Lord Fauconberg upstream to cross the river at Castleford. The Yorkists put the Lancastrians to flight and killed the fleeing Lord Clifford at Dinting Dale, just south of Towton.

The Battle of Towton on 29 March 1461 was fought on Palm Sunday in atrocious weather, with snow and fog obscuring the field. It was the largest battle ever fought on English soil and certainly the most bloody in terms of dead and wounded on both sides. Edward had decided that there was to be no quarter given. Somerset had the larger army, perhaps forty-five thousand men, against thirty-five thousand for York – and well over half the peerage of England turned out for Henry VI. The Lancastrians held the high ground on the north side of the battlefield, and the Yorkists advanced from the south. But the new king had the advantage of his great personal front-line leadership, his splendid courage, and his already much fabled good fortune. He and his troops had the strong wind behind them. His archers had the much longer range, while Somerset's archers could not reach into the wind. Plus, the snow blew in their faces. Lord Fauconberg had the Yorkist archers fall back out of range and then race forward and shower the Lancastrians with their own arrows, which had fallen short. Threatened by the merciless longbow arrow-storm attack, the Lancastrians advanced downhill from their position of advantage and engaged the Yorkists in horrendous hand-to-hand combat. As Edward slowly gained the advantage, John Mowbray, the third duke of Norfolk, arrived with fresh reinforcements at a crucial time in the afternoon and tipped the scales decisively for York. King Henry's army broke and fled, and there followed a massive slaughter in the Bloody Meadow as the fleeing Lancastrian army tried to cross the frigid stream known as the Cock Beck, on the west side of the battlefield. Those who managed to cross were cut down during the ferocious cavalry pursuit. The Lancastrian army was virtually destroyed. Estimates of the dead ranged from fifteen thousand to thirty thousand, most on the Lancastrian side. Henry Percy, the third earl of Northumberland; Randolph, Lord Dacre; John, Lord Scropes; and Sir Andrew Trollope were killed in the battle. The earls of Devon and Wiltshire were captured and executed a few days later. But Henry VI, Queen Margaret, Henry Beaufort, the third duke of Somerset, the duke of Exeter, and many other Lancastrians escaped north to Scotland. Many Lancastrians then acknowledged Edward as the rightful king, including Richard, Lord Rivers, and his son Anthony Woodville, who both later received pardons. We shall hear more of them soon. The memory of this catastrophic defeat would linger long in the North Country, just as the memory of Mortimer's Cross lingered long in Wales.

Edward's spectacular formal coronation was held on 28 June 1461 in London, where support for him was strong. Edward was king, but Warwick was the power behind the throne, at least while the nineteen-year-old Edward IV learned the trade and found his footing. At the first Parliament of the new reign, which met on 4 November 1461, George Neville was confirmed as chancellor of England, and Sir James Strangeways was elected as speaker of the House of Commons. An act of Parliament established the title to the throne of King Edward IV. The new king's twelve-year-old brother, George Plantagenet, was made the duke of Clarence; the new king's nine-year-old brother, Richard Plantagenet, was confirmed as the duke of Gloucester; and Lord Fauconberg was made the earl of Kent. Commissioners were appointed for every county to initiate legal reforms. In particular, indictments in the sheriff court could be referred to the Justice of the Peace court in order to speed up the process of judicial administration. The custom of private armies, with livery and maintenance, was banned. Attainders, some posthumous, were passed against Henry VI; Queen Margaret Anjou; Edward of Westminster; Henry, the third duke of Somerset; the duke of Exeter; the earls of Devon, Wiltshire, and Northumberland; the former Chief Justice Sir John Fortesque; Lord Dacre; and Sir Andrew Trollope. The Duchy of Lancaster was returned to be held permanently by the reigning monarch, now Edward IV. And the lands of Henry Tudor, who was then four years of age, were transferred to the new king's brother, George, Duke of Clarence. Acts of Resumption were passed against many of the Lancastrian nobles. Some of the better judicial acts of Henry VI were confirmed. In particular, attainders passed in 1399 against many nobles at the time of the original Lancastrian usurpation were reversed in order to assist those people's Yorkist families.

Rebellions against Edward IV (1462–64)

After Towton, the Lancastrians still controlled most of Northumberland, especially the various castles. But by July 1462, thanks to the efforts of Warwick, most of the castles were under Yorkist control. Margaret could not get much further support from Scotland, so she sent envoys to France and obtained help from the new French king, Louis XI. Margaret was given twenty thousand francs; Pierre de Brézé was authorized to raise French troops; and Margaret agreed to hand over Calais to France within twelve months of the planned Lancastrian restoration. Margaret, Edward of Westminster, Pierre de Brézé, and two thousand French troops invaded Northumberland in September 1462. Despite terrible weather and multiple desertions, they took back the castles of Dunstanburg, Alnwick, Bamburg, and Warkworth. Then, rejoining their ships, they sailed farther north to Berwick to meet the deposed Henry VI. In severe weather, a remnant of Margaret's force was trapped on Holy Island and surrendered to the Yorkists.

In December 1462, Edward IV advanced north with a large army, but the young king was taken ill with measles and remained at Durham, so Warwick continued the campaign. He besieged Alnwick, Bamburg, and Dunstanburg Castles. Bamburg and Dunstanburg surrendered, and Henry Beaufort, the third duke of Somerset, was taken prisoner. A Scottish army under the earl of Angus tried to lift the siege of Alnwick, but they fled in bad weather, taking the Lancastrian garrison with them. The Yorkists recovered the castle in early 1463.

In May 1463, Sir Ralph Percy surrendered Bamburg and Dunstanburg to the Lancastrians. Soon after, Sir Ralph Grey of Heton surrendered Alnwick. All the good work done by Warwick was undone by these acts of treachery. Edward IV followed a conciliation policy and was properly blamed for leaving Percy and Grey in their commands, as he had hoped they would support him.

In August 1463, Edward IV arranged for a conference between England, France, and Burgundy to take place at St Omer. George Neville was sent to represent England. This resulted in a truce with France in October 1463 and with Scotland in December 1463. By using diplomacy, Edward IV was ultimately successful in depriving Lancaster of its foreign support. Under the terms of peace, Henry VI had to leave Scotland and return to England. For a time, he ruled in the four northern castles of Northumberland. But in 1464, Lancastrian forces under Henry Beaufort, the third duke of Somerset, who had newly escaped from custody, were twice defeated by Yorkist armies led by John Neville, Baron Montagu, the younger brother of Warwick – first at Hedgeley Moor on 25 April 1464, and then at Hexham on 15 May 1464. The treacherous Sir Ralph Percy was killed at Hedgeley Moor. Somerset was executed after Hexham. There were numerous other executions ordered by the ruthless earl of Warwick, which greatly reduced the number of Lancastrian leaders. The northern castles were all besieged and recovered for the House of York. John Neville was rewarded for his fine service and was made the earl of Northumberland, replacing the Percy earl killed at Towton and posthumously attainted.

With this reversal, Henry VI fled into the hinterland, where he allegedly led a happy existence as a commoner. Also in 1464, the fugitive Queen Margaret Anjou made her escape from England, but not before some famous adventures. She was mistakenly robbed by a Lancastrian partisan named Black Jack, who pleaded forgiveness on his knees when he realized what he had done to his queen. Then, Margaret was kidnapped by a Yorkist partisan named Cork of Carlyle. She was badly treated. Thanks to the faithful Pierre de Brézé, she was rescued and ultimately reached Scotland in a small boat. But she found no further support in Scotland, thanks to Edward IV's effective diplomacy. She went to Burgundy, where, again, no help was forthcoming; she went to France, where Louis XI was uncooperative; and she finally settled her court at Kœur-la-Petite in Lorraine, in a sad state of penury. She had with her Edward of Westminster, her son and heir; Henry Holland, the duke of Exeter; Dr John Morton; Edmund Beaufort, the new fourth duke of Somerset; Sir John Fortesque, the Lancastrian Chief Justice; and several others. In 1465, the fugitive Henry VI was captured at Waddington Hall. Warwick escorted the former king to the Tower of London. If Edward had not been more generous than Warwick, then Henry VI might also have been put to death. Sooner or later, the affable Edward IV would have to face the reality of a breathing rival king and multiple rebellions in his name, each amounting to treason.

After 1461, there were also other rebellions, notably in Wales and the Welsh Marches, but William Herbert, the Yorkist earl of Pembroke, suppressed them with his usual efficiency. All the castles held for Lancaster surrendered in good order, with the single exception of Harlech, which held out until 1468. When Pembroke Castle fell, the four-year-old Henry Tudor was found living there. Lord Herbert purchased Henry Tudor's wardship from King Edward IV and sent Tudor with his mother, Margaret Beaufort, to the Herbert home at Raglan Castle, to be tended by Lady Herbert. Jasper Tudor, the Lancastrian earl of Pembroke, fled to Scotland and eventually to France, but he would be back.

In London in 1462, the senior John de Vere, the twelfth earl of Oxford, and his eldest son were tried for plotting with Queen Margaret Anjou. They were brutally executed at the orders of John Tiptoft, the earl of Worcester. The younger son, also John de Vere, was allowed to become the thirteenth earl of Oxford. This latter was an example of the extraordinary generosity of Edward IV in dealing with hostile subjects. Still, in the case of young Oxford, it never paid off; the earl remained an implacable enemy of Edward IV.

The Marriage of Edward IV to Elizabeth Woodville (1464), and the Rise of the Woodville Family

In the meantime, Edward met and secretly married Elizabeth Woodville, a beautiful subject commoner who had lost her Lancastrian husband, Sir John Grey of Groby, when he was killed at the Second Battle of St Albans in 1461. By this marriage, Elizabeth had two small boys, Thomas and Richard Grey. Elizabeth's father, Richard Woodville, and brother, Anthony Woodville, were also Lancastrians who pledged loyalty to Edward after Towton. Previously, they had been abused and bullied by the Yorkist earls at Calais following their capture at Sandwich in 1460. Elizabeth's mother, Jacquetta, was the widow of the duke of Bedford. Jacquetta was the daughter of the count of Saint Pol in Burgundy, and so she claimed noble blood.

The legend is that Elizabeth met the travelling Edward IV under a large oak tree near her mother's home at Grafton Regis and pleaded for the restoration of her Grey family property at Groby. Some place the first meeting in 1461, but it was more likely 1463. Young Edward was infatuated with her and returned frequently to visit. Elizabeth resisted the king's sexual advances and even threatened to kill herself with the king's own dagger if Edward violated her. His decision to secretly marry her was undoubtedly based on passion and good conscience, and was certainly not any planned political or commercial strategy, as was the custom among medieval kings. The secret marriage occurred on 1 May 1464. There were several witnesses: the duchess of Bedford, two of her lady attendants, and a young man to sing the office. There may have been more in attendance, as exhibited in a painting of the wedding (Wavrin, 2005).

While this relationship was developing in secret, Warwick made arrangements for a French marriage treaty between Edward and Princess Bona, the sister-in-law of King Louis XI, with generous commercial advantages for England. The earl was furious when the king revealed his secret marriage with Elizabeth Woodville. Her enthronement, held at Reading Abbey in 1464 with Edward IV present, was a spectacular ceremony led by the bishops. There is a painting of this event in the Reading Museum (Board, 2012). Elizabeth's coronation, officiated by the Archbishop of Canterbury and held in 1465 at Westminster Abbey, was a splendid ceremony. Edward, according to custom, did not attend. It should be noted for later reference that in the period 1461–64, nobody considered that Edward IV was married or betrothed to anybody – and certainly not the savvy earl of Warwick, who worked so hard for a royal marriage in France, by all accounts with Edward's ready permission and cooperation. There was nothing in his lifestyle to suggest that Edward was married; in fact, it was quite the opposite, given his carefree promiscuity. The notion that Edward was married at this time would arise only twenty years later under very suspicious circumstances, after the king was dead.

Following the 1464 Woodville marriage, the new queen's talented family rapidly gained influence at Edward's court, especially Richard Woodville, the Lord Rivers, and his son Anthony, the Lord Scales. This was much to the chagrin of Warwick the Kingmaker and of Edward's younger brothers, George, Duke of Clarence, and Richard, Duke of Gloucester. Both the Woodvilles proved excellent administrators and gave Edward loyal service. Men from the upper middle class would do well under the first Yorkist king, as they would later under the Tudor rulers.

Edward approved several marriages of his Woodville relatives, which infuriated the earl of Warwick. One was the marriage of the sixty-eight-year-old Katherine Neville, the dowager duchess of Norfolk, to the twenty-year-old John Woodville, the younger brother of Queen Elizabeth Woodville. Another was the marriage of Anne Holland, the daughter of the duke of Exeter and Anne Plantagenet, the king's sister, to Queen Elizabeth Woodville's eldest son by her first marriage, Thomas Grey, later the marquis of Dorset. In the period 1464–66, there were several other Woodville marriages, as discussed later.

The Alienation of Warwick, More Rebellions against Edward IV, and the Battle of Edgecote Moor (1469)

Despite the setback over the royal marriage, Warwick continued to press for a French alliance, encouraged by French King Louis XI. But Edward, becoming more confident and assertive in his role as king, favoured an alliance with Burgundy and pushed the idea of the marriage of his sister Margaret to Charles the Bold, the son of Philip the Good, the duke of Burgundy. Such an alliance would have been more popular in England, where France was greatly mistrusted; moreover, there was a very profitable wool trade with Burgundy to be considered. In 1467, Edward dismissed

George Neville from his position as chancellor of England, presumably because of his support for his brother. When Warwick returned from an embassy in France, it became clear that an alliance with France was not likely to happen. Warwick was embarrassed and infuriated; he withdrew from the court and refused to return, expressing considerable anger against the Woodvilles, who he claimed were a bad influence on the young king.

Edward signed agreements with Burgundy and Brittany, both hostile to France, and soon agreed to the marriage of Margaret with Charles the Bold. Edward refused to sanction the marriage of his brother George, his heir presumptive, with Isabel, the daughter of Warwick, but George and Warwick disobeyed the king and continued to make plans for the union, including a papal petition to allow for the marriage of cousins. Warwick refused to appear when he was summoned to explain his dealings in France and to ratify the king's agreement with Burgundy. However, all relations were not yet ruptured; an agreement was fashioned between Lord Rivers and George Neville. In late 1468, Warwick appeared with Edward IV as Margaret made her magnificent ceremonial departure for Burgundy. Edward refused Warwick's demand for the dismissal of many of the king's advisors, especially the Woodvilles, but Edward gave Warwick yet more valuable properties, seeking rapprochement with the famous earl.

During the 1468 period, England was alive with rumours of Lancastrian conspiracies. The government spent a great deal of energy in tracking letters from France to people living in England. The threat to Edward IV was considerable and more than justified his vigorous response. Those suspected of treason included John de Vere, the thirteenth earl of Oxford, who was sent to the Tower. But he was soon released and allowed to leave for France. Another also accused of treason was Henry Courtenay, brother of Thomas, the sixth earl of Devon, who was executed after Towton. Henry Courtenay was tried, found guilty, and executed. Thomas, Lord Hungerford, who plotted with Warwick, was also executed for treason. Both Henry and Thomas were hung, drawn, and quartered at Salisbury on the same day in January 1469.

Later in 1469, a rebellion broke out in Yorkshire led by Robin of Redesdale, for reasons which were not clear at the time. It was suppressed by John Neville. Soon after, there was another rebellion in Yorkshire led by Robin of Holderness. In this case, the rebels wished to protest a new corn tax and to restore young Henry Percy as the earl of Northumberland. John Neville had little difficulty in suppressing this revolt, especially as he was the current Yorkist earl of Northumberland and stood much to lose.

In June 1469, there was yet another rebellion in Yorkshire and Lancashire, led again by Robin of Redesdale, otherwise known as Sir William Conyers. He was discovered to be a Warwick lieutenant. It was suspected, with good reason, that Warwick and Clarence were supporting these developments. The rebel army was large; it was joined by many Neville kinsmen and retainers. Edward sent instructions to Sir William Herbert, the Yorkist earl of Pembroke, and Sir Humphrey Stafford, the newly created Yorkist earl of Devon, to muster troops and join him in the Midlands at Nottingham. Edward summoned Warwick, Clarence, and George Neville to appear before him at court and explain themselves, but they disobeyed and refused to attend. Instead, they fled to Calais, where Clarence and Isabel were married by George Neville in his capacity as the Archbishop of York. The permit was apparently supplied belatedly from Rome, although others have suggested that it came from the patriarch of the Eastern Orthodox Church.

The rebel magnates, Warwick and Clarence, returned to England accompanied by the earl of Oxford. They recruited armed forces in Kent, occupied London, and went north with a large army to join with Sir William Conyers. They issued a manifesto accusing Edward of misgovernment, especially related to the powers exercised by the Woodvilles and by others not considered part of the direct royal family. The rebels protested the new taxes for which Parliament had voted and also complained of the currency devaluation which had previously occurred with the issue of a new coinage, even though Warwick had sat on the council which authorized the new issue. Warwick was now in open rebellion; he had switched to the Lancastrian side and was intent on Edward IV's overthrow. For his part, the treacherous George, Duke of Clarence, hoped that he could seize his brother's crown. The earl of Oxford, no doubt, planned to restore Henry VI.

Edward, in the Midlands at Nottingham, tried to join with the earl of Pembroke, but Pembroke and Devon had split their forces during an argument and the rebels had defeated Pembroke at the Battle of Edgecote Moor on 26 July 1469, near Banbury. Devon had arrived too late to be of any assistance, and Edward had been too far away even to make an appearance. The battle with the rebel army under Sir William Conyers was hard-fought, and Pembroke sadly missed his Welsh archers, who were with Devon. However, Pembroke was near victory when rebel reinforcements sent by Warwick arrived and the royal army found itself hopelessly outnumbered. The earl of Pembroke and his brother Sir Richard Herbert were captured and executed. Worse, soon after, Richard Woodville and his son John Woodville were also captured in the West Country, were brought to Coventry, and, without proper trial, were beheaded at the orders of Warwick. The Yorkist earl of Devon escaped from Edgecote but was hunted down and murdered in Bristol. In one efficient action, Warwick eliminated no fewer than five of his most hated enemies. This was a disaster for Edward IV. In Welsh history, Edgecote Moor is still remembered with agonized dismay.

The Imprisonment of Edward IV (1469), the First Rule of Warwick Alone (1469), the Escape of Edward IV, and the Battle of Empingham (1470)

In the meantime after Edgecote, Edward was strangely inactive, unable to cope with the astounding treachery and treason of his own cousin Warwick and of his own brother Clarence. At the terrible news of Edgecote Moor and its aftermath, and with Edward's seeming paralysis, the king's men began to desert in large numbers. The king may have dismissed Gloucester, Hastings, Anthony Woodville, and others, in the hope that they could save themselves from Warwick's vengeance. A few days later, Edward himself, with few remaining attendants, was taken prisoner on the open road by forces under George Neville, who was sent by Warwick to arrest him. The king was brought before Warwick at Coventry and was soon imprisoned in Warwick Castle. There appears to be no account of the likely angry conversation between the earl and the king at Coventry. For a brief time, Warwick ruled as dictator of England. Edward was the puppet king, doing as he was instructed. Such was the dismal state of affairs in England. The other king, Henry VI, remained imprisoned in the Tower of London. Unlike the easy-going Edward, Warwick exacted a bloody revenge on his enemies. Some French authorities have suggested that Warwick planned to declare Edward's birth illegitimate and put Clarence on the throne.

But Warwick had overreached. The magnates did not support him. There was widespread disorder in the towns, destructive quarrelling among the lords, and a Lancastrian rebellion in the north. Warwick found that without proper commissions of array, he could not raise sufficient troops to suppress it. Edward waited patiently and was soon sent to Middleham Castle. He was effectively released in September 1469. Whether Warwick intended this or Edward escaped despite Warwick is not clear; some historians suggest that his escape from Middleham was assisted by the faithful Yorkist Sir William Stanley. With the king's help in issuing legal commissions of array, Warwick was able to raise troops and suppress the northern rebellion. Sir Humphrey Neville of Brancepeth and his brother Charles, the rebel leaders, were executed at York. Edward went to Pontefract Castle, where many members of his affinity followed his summons and soon joined him. These included: the duke of Gloucester; Lord Hastings; the earls of Arundel and Essex; John Neville and his nine-year-old son, George; Lords Mountjoy, Dinham, and Howard; the young Henry Percy, the Lancastrian heir of Northumberland; and the young duke of Buckingham. Edward departed for London. On the way, others joined him, but Edward did not allow the senior George Neville or the earl of Oxford to join him, as he did not trust them. Warwick soon realized he had lost control over the king. In London, the mayor told the guards to go home for dinner. Edward entered the capital, once again in triumph, to yet another tumultuous welcome. London loved its Yorkist king.

Edward set about re-establishing his authority. He sent his brother Richard of Gloucester to Wales, where the young duke put down the rebels in short order. The king summoned Warwick and Clarence to a meeting of the council in London and pardoned them, following a policy of open conciliation with all those who had rebelled. This was a mistake, as the king soon learned.

Around this time, Edward made a pact with John Neville, as described by Mary Clive (1974). Edward promised in marriage his heir, Princess Elizabeth, to John Neville's son George Neville, who was to be made the duke of Bedford. The idea was that if Edward IV was killed, then John Neville was to ensure that young George and Elizabeth assumed the throne, not the duke of Clarence, who Edward did not trust. Edward was planning to make John Neville the marquis of Montagu and give him valuable properties.

There was then another rebellion in Lincolnshire. This began as a property feud between Sir Thomas Burgh and Richard Lord Welles, the seventh Baron Willoughby. Welles and his supporters attacked and destroyed much of Burgh's property. Edward had Lord Welles explain his actions at court. He kept Welles under arrest and proceeded north to deal with the problem. Welles's son, Sir Robert Welles, encouraged by Warwick and Clarence, who claimed that the king would savagely punish Lincolnshire, raised considerable forces to resist the king – some say as many as thirty thousand men in arms. But this figure, no doubt, was greatly exaggerated. It would appear that the rebels had various motives. Some supported Lord Richard Welles in the local conflict, some were Yorkists antagonistic towards Edward IV and supporters of Warwick and Clarence, and many were Lancastrians beholden to Henry VI. Later, it was learned that the plan was for Sir Robert Welles to join Warwick and Clarence at Leicester when their combined forces would be sufficient to attack and destroy the king. But they were too late.

Edward, finally, encouraged by his faithful supporters, took to the field and, moving with restored great speed, reached Sir Robert Welles first. Lord Richard Welles, who had admitted his earlier involvement, was executed, it is said on the battlefield before hostilities began. At the Battle of Empingham on 12 March 1470, at Losecoat Field, the rebel forces under Sir Robert Welles were utterly defeated in what amounted to a one-sided rout. The battle was so named because the rebels tore off their Warwick and Clarence livery coats as they fled the field ahead of ferocious cannonade and of Edward's far more experienced army. After the battle, a casket of letters was found that clearly implicated both Warwick and Clarence in the rebellion. Later, Sir Robert Welles was captured; he admitted that the plan was to combine with Warwick at Leicester and put Clarence on the throne. Not surprisingly, Sir Robert Welles was promptly executed for his part in the treason.

Amazingly, Edward still pursued a policy of conciliation. He demanded that Warwick and Clarence appear before him at court, but he indicated his respect for their common family ties. They requested pre-emptive pardons, which Edward could not grant them in consideration of the previous pardons. Warwick tried to obtain the support of Lord Thomas Stanley, his brother-in-law, but Stanley refused, no doubt impressed by the events at Empingham. So, Warwick and Clarence fled the country. The royalist army followed them to the south coast of England but could make no contact.

Then, Edward made yet another triumphant entry into London. He was accompanied by Gloucester, Suffolk, Essex, Hastings, Arundel, Dacre, Mountjoy, and Buckingham. The crisis appeared to be over. Edward seized Warwick's estates for the Crown. He also took this opportunity to take back the earldom of Northumberland from John Neville and restore the Percy heir, in the hope of achieving better control over the troublesome north of England. Consistent with the prior agreement, Edward attempted to compensate John Neville, who had not been disloyal, by making him the marquis of Montagu, but he did not grant sufficient property to satisfy the new marquis. So, this move, too, later proved a mistake. Montagu was dismissive of the properties given him in the West Country, calling them "a magpie's nest." These properties had belonged to the earls of Devon and were not inconsiderable, but they did not compare with Northumberland.

A list of about fifty traitors was drawn up for consideration by the royal government. Many were pardoned by the ever-affable Edward. Quite a few were sentenced to death and executed brutishly by the ruthless John Tiptoft, the earl of Worcester. Some had placed themselves beyond reach by their flight over the seas. But many eventually survived with pardons, which is evidence of the continued extraordinary generosity of King Edward IV in the face of widespread treason. In the meantime, the earl of Oxford, although he had not joined the Lincolnshire Rebellion, decided again that it was best to leave for France.

The Flight of Warwick, the Unstable Alliance between Warwick and Lancaster, the Return of Warwick, the Flight of Edward IV (1470), the Second Rule of Warwick Alone (1470), and the Readoption of Henry VI (1470–71)

The two fugitive magnates, Clarence and Warwick, ahead of the king's army, took ships at Dartmouth and headed along the south coast of England and across the English Channel. On the way, they tried to capture Warwick's flagship, the *Trinity,* in port at Southampton, but Anthony Woodville repulsed them and then pursued them at sea, inflicting significant damage on Warwick's small fleet. Warwick captured several Burgundian ships but was then attacked by naval forces under Lord John Howard and suffered further damage. At Calais, the fugitives were refused entry by Sir John Wenlock and took hostile cannon fire. Wenlock still favoured Warwick, but his soldiers thought otherwise. A pregnant Isabel Neville, who accompanied the fugitives, went into labour and delivered a stillborn daughter who was buried at sea. Warwick sailed along the coast and captured another convoy of Burgundian ships, but he was again attacked by Lord Howard. Warwick reached France, at the mouth of the River Seine, with still a considerable number of ships. He declared that he was ready to restore the Lancastrian Henry VI to the English throne.

At Amboise on the River Loire, and later at nearby Angers, Warwick negotiated with King Louis XI and Queen Margaret Anjou, who was still asserting the claim of her son Edward of Westminster. Louis XI and Margaret made a secret agreement that England would cede Calais to France if Henry VI was successfully restored. In a confrontation at Angers Cathedral, famous in English history, the haughty Warwick was forced to remain kneeling on the hard stone floor before a furious Margaret and explain why he had rebelled against his Lancastrian king and challenged the paternity of Margaret's son Edward of Westminster. As part of the agreement, Warwick's younger daughter, Anne, was betrothed to Edward of Westminster, and the two were married a few months later. The permit was apparently supplied by the grand vicar of Bayeux (Falkus, 1981). Helped by Louis XI, who finally persuaded a reluctant Margaret, Warwick prepared an invasion force on the French coast, despite a constant blockade by Edward's English and Burgundian fleet. After a long delay, and following a storm which temporarily scattered Edward's ships, Warwick, together with Jasper Tudor, the former Lancastrian earl of Pembroke; the earl of Oxford; the duke of Clarence; and Thomas Neville, the Bastard of Fauconberg, finally set sail upon the sea and invaded England with a very large army at Plymouth on 13 September 1470. They were soon joined by more Lancastrians, including John Talbot, the third earl of Shrewsbury, and the shifty Lord Thomas Stanley, who was now perhaps not so impressed with the events at Empingham.

Warwick declared that he had come to restore Henry VI. Many Lancastrians rallied to his cause. He advanced north-east to Coventry with perhaps twenty thousand men in arms. Edward had been in the north suppressing a fresh rebellion led by Henry, Baron FitzHugh and probably instigated by Warwick in support of his planned invasion. The king had difficulty in recruiting troops, perhaps because he was in a part of the country with strong Lancastrian sympathies. So, he had John Neville raise forces for him. The king had spent a long time trying to placate John Neville for the loss of the earldom of Northumberland, but to no avail. John Neville changed sides and threw in his lot with his brother Warwick. Now, Edward at Doncaster had a large opposing army to the south of him under Warwick, plus another large army to the north under Montagu. Both were closing fast. Edward knew better than to fight such a force arrayed against him. As he could not train a sufficient army in time, he fled to Burgundy, where his sister Margaret was, by then, the duchess.

Edward's flight took him through Lincolnshire, the Wash (where he was nearly drowned), and King's Lynn. Having obtained ships for his party, he departed England on 2 October 1470. Edward understood how important it was for a king to avoid capture and remain alive to fight another day, hopefully under better circumstances. Those who accompanied the king into exile included Anthony Woodville, William Hastings, Lord William Say, many knights, and, later, Richard, Duke of Gloucester. Also included was Nicholas Harpisfield, the king's clerk of the signet seal, who probably wrote *The Arrival,* an account of Edward's later return to his kingdom. After crossing the Channel, avoiding hostile ships of the Hanseatic League and having no money, Edward paid the boat captain with his expensive fur coat. In Burgundy, Edward was fortunate to be protected by his friend the governor of Holland, Louis de Gruthuuse. From Louis's magnificent house in Bruges, Edward began the difficult political negotiations necessary to gain the support of Charles, Duke of Burgundy.

In London, Henry VI was taken from the Tower by Warwick and restored as the king in the so-called Readoption of Henry VI, even though the restored king was very confused, did not understand what was happening, and probably would have preferred to remain in the peaceful surrounds of the Tower. Warwick the Kingmaker was dictator of England yet again, for the second time.

Edward has been criticized for the problems he had, considering that earlier in 1470 he had triumphed at Empingham. It was suggested that he should not have gone north to deal with Baron FitzHugh, but Edward's experience of northern rebellions was that they needed to be vigorously suppressed. Also, it would not be surprising if Warwick landed in the north anyway, where Neville family support was strong. Warwick had gained some sympathy because he was driven from the country after Empingham and deprived of all his properties. Lancastrian support was still widespread in the country. The supporters of Henry VI lacked leadership, but now Warwick had appeared. Edward had not been inactive as suggested; he had strengthened the leadership in Calais and Sandwich and other parts of the south-east shore, and he maintained powerful naval operations in the English Channel and along the French coast. The crucial problem was the desertion of John Neville, the marquis of Montagu, which had so rapidly changed the balance of power.

In the Readoption government, Warwick was lieutenant, Lord Protector, and admiral of England; George Neville, the Archbishop of York, was again chancellor; Sir John Langstrother was treasurer; and the earl of Oxford was constable of England. Parliament attainted Edward IV and his associates, reversed the attainders of the Lancastrians, repealed most Yorkist legislation, made Edward of Westminster heir to the throne – to be followed, if necessary, by Clarence and his heirs – and ordered the issue of a new coinage. A pregnant Queen Elizabeth Woodville fled into sanctuary at Westminster Abbey; gallantly, Warwick sent Lady Scropes to help the queen during childbirth. Oxford, in his role as constable, tried Tiptoft for the execution of his father, the twelfth earl of Oxford. With broad popular support, he had the wicked earl of Worcester beheaded, reportedly as requested, by three strokes of the axe representing the Holy Trinity. Although Edmund, the fourth duke of Somerset (see Appendix D), eventually returned to England, he hated Warwick and provided him with no support. Cecily, the dowager duchess of York, and her daughters, Anne, Elizabeth, and Margaret, all appealed to Clarence to return his allegiance to his brother Edward. The exiled Yorkists communicated with many of the magnates and warned them to be prepared for Edward's imminent return. Edward promised the Hanseatic League a restoration of trade relations if they would support him. Despite appearances, Warwick could not have felt very comfortable.

The Triumphant Return of King Edward IV, and the Battles of Barnet and Tewkesbury (1471)

Edward was initially not well received by Charles, the duke of Burgundy, whose aim was to defend against France and who initially thought he had no use for a deposed king of England. Edmund Beaufort, the fourth duke of Somerset, was a prominent member of the Burgundian court; he argued that Edward should be ignored. The Flemish chronicler Philippe de Commines was also influential and counselled against the Yorkist king. Historians need to be suspicious of the partisan Commines as a reliable observer of Edward IV. The Yorkist king would have done badly but for the friendship of Louis de Gruthuuse, the governor of Holland. But Warwick mistakenly pressed the reluctant English Parliament for an alliance with France, and Duke Charles soon realized that a restoration of the Yorkist king would better suit the duchy of Burgundy. When Louis XI declared all French lands in Burgundy forfeit and began hostilities on the border with France, the hand of the duke of Burgundy was forced; he began to supply Edward with secret financial and military support. This was not one of the brightest moments for the usually savvy king of France Louis XI.

In the meantime, Warwick had a difficult set of problems. His new Lancastrian allies hated him, and the Yorkists mistrusted him for his treachery, so once again he found it very difficult to establish his authority. As before, there was widespread disorder and quarrelling. Moreover, he was not sure of Queen Margaret, who showed no signs of returning to England, because she, too, did not trust him, least of all with the custody of her son. The return of a vigorous young prince like Edward of Westminster might have helped Warwick gather more Lancastrian support. There was not much patronage that Warwick could bestow, as there had been few recent major battles and not so many lords had been killed. Warwick could not take property from Yorkists to reward Lancastrians, as he needed Yorkists to at least remain quiet if they were not able to openly support him. And Clarence had realized that with Henry VI back on the throne and Edward of Westminster alive, his own chances of succeeding as king were gone. So, the alliance between Clarence and Warwick was soon to come asunder.

George Neville had Henry VI paraded in London, hoping to rally the public to support the Lancastrian cause. But the sight of the poor, dowdy King Henry slouching on his horse only made people remember the magnificent King Edward IV. Thomas Neville, the Bastard of Fauconberg, patrolled the English Channel, watching for signs of King Edward. The Lancastrian government was nervous; they all knew in their hearts that Edward would be back. John Neville watched in the north, Oxford maintained order in East Anglia, Jasper Tudor worried in Wales, and Warwick guarded the south. The newly restored earl of Northumberland, the young Henry Percy, was not trusted; it was likely that he was a closet supporter of the Yorkist king.

Edward sailed north up the English Channel with a small army, perhaps two thousand men, raised in Burgundy and transported in thirty-six ships, many donated by the now friendly Hanseatic League. He was warned that East Anglia was hostile. He battled a violent storm which scattered his fleet. On 14 March 1471, exhausted, he landed at Ravenspur on the north side of the Humber estuary, at the very same place Henry IV had landed in 1399. Nobody gave him much chance of success, especially Commines, who had a low opinion of Edward, mostly because of Edward's promiscuity and alleged laziness and debauchery! But all of the critics underestimated the extraordinary capabilities of King Edward IV.

At first, Edward thought he was alone at the Humber and was much discouraged. But Richard, Duke of Gloucester, Anthony Woodville, and others who had landed nearby joined him in a few days. The township of Hull closed its gates to Edward; history does not record if Hull ever paid a price for its failure. At the city of York, Edward was not successful in recruiting soldiers, despite the ploy that he had come only to regain his duchy of York. But this tactic was not as dishonourable as it sounds, as the duke of York was the rightful king of England. Edward remained extremely vulnerable. Even at Sandal, a Yorkist estate, he could find little support. However, Montagu at Pontefract Castle made no move against Edward IV. Waiting on the duke of Northumberland to take the lead, Montagu watched Edward pass. Northumberland, too, did nothing, as he favoured Edward. Still, he knew that his north men would not fight for the Yorkist king, as they remembered the horrors of Towton only too well.

The determined king advanced south into the Midlands towards London, where he hoped recruitment would be easier. Many now rallied to his cause. On the approach to Nottingham, there was news that Oxford and Exeter were at Newark, to the east, so Edward turned aside to threaten them. The canny earl of Oxford avoided him and evacuated Newark ahead of the king. At Nottingham, the king was joined by Sir William Stanley, Sir William Dudley, Sir William Parr, Sir Richard Harrington, and others, with a sizable number of loyal troops. The ever-faithful Hastings, with three thousand men, rejoined the king at Leicester. At this point, as he advanced south, the king had Montague behind him, Oxford and Exeter following south on his east side, and Warwick ahead of him. Edward kept the initiative and marched to Coventry, where he arrived on 29 March 1471. The earl of Warwick made a disastrous strategic mistake, as he failed to expeditiously attack the king and destroy him before he could gather sufficient forces. Instead, Warwick waited in the walled town of Coventry. Edward rode up and down before the gates, clad in full armour, on his caparisoned prancing warhorse, challenging Warwick to come out from behind the walls and fight, but the earl knew better than to confront the hostile king, who was now fully bent on a savage revenge.

Edward bypassed the earl; as Edward had no artillery, he decided to deal with Warwick later. Edward proceeded to the town of Warwick and occupied Warwick's very own castle. At this point, the turncoat Clarence begged forgiveness and joined the king with four thousand men. The three royal brothers, Edward, George, and Richard, celebrated the reunion before their respective armies. This was brilliant political theatre designed to foster support. It is suggested by David Santiuste (2010) that there were brief negotiations with messengers over reconciliation with Warwick, but nothing was achieved. The schism with Warwick was now complete, and there was no going back.

Edward reached Daventry on Palm Sunday, 7 April 1471, where he attended Mass at the parish church. As Edward prayed before a small statue of St Anne, the covering boards, in place for Lent, opened briefly with a loud crack and then closed. Edward interpreted this as a good omen. Our modern minds may be suspicious, but in 1471, the magic was widely believed. With growing confidence, Edward's army advanced south to the commercial and financial centre of England where the power resided. Yet again, on 11 April 1471, Edward entered London in triumph to find another spectacular welcome. He was reunited with his beautiful queen at Westminster Abbey and held his newborn son and heir, the future King

Edward V born in the sanctuary, for the first time. Edward was overjoyed to see his beautiful daughters, who jumped and danced around him with delight. The king sent a bewildered Henry VI back to the Tower. But it was not for long, as Edward took Henry with him when he rapidly returned north to attack the approaching Lancastrians under Warwick as they advanced south towards London.

There was no evidence of his previous passive inactivity as had occurred after Edgecote; Edward had clearly made up his mind to bring Warwick to battle. A few miles beyond Barnet, under cover of darkness, Edward moved rapidly and silently until he was very close to Warwick. His army rested for the night in battle array. The Yorkist army was the smaller, perhaps ten thousand men, compared with twenty thousand men for Lancaster. Most of Warwick's cannon fire during the night sailed harmlessly over the Yorkist army, as the Lancastrians did not realize how close Edward had approached. The Yorkists did not return fire, as that would have disclosed their advanced position.

The next day, Easter Sunday morning, 14 April 1471, Edward IV attacked with his usual ferocity, suddenly with a blast of the trumpets, at dawn and in heavy fog. Warwick was badly surprised. The two armies were not perfectly aligned. York was somewhat shifted to its right, which meant that the Lancastrian right could outflank the Yorkist left and the Yorkist right could wrap around the Lancastrian left. Edward was so intent on early attack that he did not take the time to make any adjustment. In any case, it would have been difficult in the heavy fog and would have alerted the enemy. The adventurous Lancastrian earl of Oxford broke the Yorkist left battle under Hastings and pursued the fleeing Yorkists south to Barnet. Fortunately for Edward, it was a setback not noticed by the main body of the Yorkist army, due to the poor visibility. Otherwise, it could have meant a decisive Yorkist defeat. Preliminary news did reach London that Edward was defeated (see Appendix G).

It should be mentioned here that the Yorkists always knew where Edward IV was situated, in the very front line, so there was never thought given to flight while the king lived. When Oxford returned his men to the battlefield, they were mistakenly attacked by their own Lancastrian forces under John Neville, the marquis of Montagu. In the fog, there was confusion between Oxford's emblem of "star with streams" and Edward's emblem of "sun with streams." In the meantime, Richard, Duke of Gloucester, exerted heavy pressure on the Lancastrian left under the duke of Exeter and forced his opponents back. The axis of the battle shifted from an initial east–west formation to one nearer north–south (see Appendix G). Then, Edward attacked with great violence in the centre. The Lancastrians broke and fled the field with cries of treason. John Neville was killed as the battle turned against Lancaster.

The earl of Warwick saw his brother die, knew the battle was lost, and was killed as he tried to escape on his horse. His captors stabbed him through his open visor and then stripped him naked. The king's messenger sent to request mercy for Warwick was too late. Exeter was severely wounded. He was considered dead on the battlefield, and his men abandoned him. But he survived, somehow reached sanctuary in Westminster Abbey, and was later imprisoned in the Tower. According to John Julius Norwich (1999), Henry VI, who had been deliberately placed in the front line clad in full armour, was unscathed, much to Yorkist surprise and probably much to Yorkist disappointment. Notable deaths were fewer on the Yorkist side, but they included Lords Say and Cromwell. Once again, the aggressive, daring, and always fortunate King Edward IV was triumphant. But the earl of Oxford escaped to Wales, then to Scotland, and later to France. The bodies of Warwick and Montagu were treated with respect. They were placed on view at St Paul's Church so people could be assured of their deaths, and they were soon released to the senior George Neville for burial at Bisham Abbey.

In the meantime, on the very same day as Barnet, Queen Margaret, severely delayed by bad weather, finally made her belated appearance and landed at Weymouth, in Dorset to the west, accompanied by a thousand recruits. She had with her Edward of Westminster; his new wife, Anne Neville; Sir John Langstrother; and the captain of Calais, Lord Wenlock. At nearby Cerne Abbey, Margaret was soon joined by Edmund Beaufort, the fourth duke of Somerset, who was accompanied by a more substantial force, probably about four thousand men. It should be noted that he had not assisted Warwick. With the duke was also John Courtenay, the Lancastrian seventh earl of Devon. They had not waited in London for Edward IV's arrival but had departed to meet Margaret. When Margaret heard the terrible news of Barnet, she was dismayed and wanted to return to France but was persuaded otherwise. The argument was that now they were more cohesive because the despised Warwick was dead, and they could join up with Jasper Tudor in Wales. The Lancastrians marched west to Exeter, where more recruits joined Margaret's army. From there, the Lancastrians headed north-north-east through Taunton to Bristol, where a further substantial number of soldiers were recruited and more cannons added. Margaret continued in the same direction towards Gloucester, where she hoped to cross the River Severn and reach the Pembroke lands in Wales.

Edward IV knew exactly what was needed. He also knew where the queen was headed. He stopped disbanding his army after Barnet, raised new recruits, mustered at Windsor, and, by rapid forced march, closed the distance to Margaret. Edward advanced west-north-west through Abingdon to Cirencester; he scouted hard to the south in case Margaret turned east and headed back towards London. He even briefly drew up at Sudbury Hill and waited for Margaret, so anxious was he to prevent any Lancastrian reverse towards London. At Edward's orders, sent rapidly ahead, the gates of Gloucester were closed to Margaret by the governor, Sir Richard Beauchamp. The Lancastrian forces moved upriver to find another way to cross the River Severn just where it was joined by the River Avon; but they found this deep ford impassable, presumably because of high water. Next, the Lancastrians sought to cross the River Avon at Upton, just upstream from Tewkesbury, but they could not safely reach it, so close was the Yorkist army. Edward advanced to Cheltenham, where he gave his army a much needed rest, and then advanced to Tredington. As Edward approached closely, the queen and Somerset decided to give battle at Tewkesbury, where the River Swilgate joined the River Avon just before it merged into the River Severn. They drew up in battle order, as it would have been too dangerous to attempt to reach the Upton ford with Edward hustling so close. Both armies were exhausted by the long, hot march. They rested the night in battle array. For Lancaster, Wenlock with Westminster commanded in the centre, with Somerset on the right and Devon on the left; for York, Edward commanded in the centre, Gloucester commanded on the left, and Hastings commanded the right battle (see Appendix H).

The Lancastrians held the high ground on the north side of the battlefield, which was just to the south of Tewkesbury Abbey. Edward advanced from the south. On 4 May 1471, starting, as usual, at early morning, Edward bombarded with fierce cannonade and longbow arrow-storm, inflicting considerable damage upon the Lancastrians. Then the king rapidly led his forces forward to the attack, negotiating through the hedgerows which covered the battlefield and advancing to close quarters. Lancaster had the larger army, but York had more artillery, which Edward used with telling effect. Somerset counter-attacked brilliantly by moving to his right into the trees on the west side of the field, through what is now called Lincoln Green Lane, and then emerging from the woods to attack the Yorkist left under Gloucester. Somerset gained an early advantage, but he was not supported by his centre battle under Wenlock and Westminster. Gloucester stopped Somerset and counter-attacked furiously, advancing again from the south. Edward had reserve spearmen in the same woods; they joined the attack from the west. Edward wheeled part of his centre battle left to join the attack on Somerset from the east. Somerset was attacked on three sides; his forces were routed by Edward's cavalry and then finished off by Edward's reserves. A furious Somerset killed Wenlock on the field for his failure to give the critical support that was needed, but Somerset had mismanaged the manoeuvre by emerging from the trees too early, putting him in front of Gloucester, not behind him as planned. Wenlock could not order cannonade and arrow-storm attack because Somerset's men were in the way.

Then, Edward recalled his forces, wheeled them back right to face the north, and attacked in the centre with massive violence. The Lancastrian army broke and fled the field. There was a terrible slaughter in what came to be known as the Bloody Meadow, along the left bank of the River Avon, to the west. Edward of Westminster, the Prince of Wales, who called hard for Clarence to spare him, and John Courtenay, the recently restored Lancastrian seventh earl of Devon, were both killed during the headlong flight. The fourth duke of Somerset and about twenty of his knights, including Sir John Beaufort (the duke's brother) and Sir John Langstrother (the prior of St John), tried to hide in Tewkesbury Abbey and claim sanctuary, but, despite objections from the abbot of Tewkesbury and his monks, they were dragged out of the church and placed under arrest. Two days later, they were given brief courts martial, quickly found guilty of high treason, and executed the same day on 6 May 1471, in the market square of Tewkesbury.

On the day of the battle, it is probable that other Lancastrians were killed inside the church before the Yorkist commanders could control the slaughter and the abbot could make his case. It is said that the abbey had to be cleansed of blood and gore and then reconsecrated. Edward has been criticized for all of this violence, but most of the Lancastrian leaders who were executed were habitual traitors who had been previously pardoned and could never again be trusted. Edward's argument at the abbey was that the sanctuary custom did not cover treason. Since Edward had returned from exile, he had finally understood that he could not allow these opponents to survive. Yet again, the ever-aggressive, fast-moving, brilliant King Edward IV was triumphant. At least some Lancastrians were pardoned; those were men who had received no previous pardon from Edward IV and whose only crime was their consistent loyalty to King Henry VI. This included Sir John Fortesque, who soon transferred his allegiance to the Yorkist king.

Edward left Tewkesbury and moved north-east to Coventry to deal with the usual further uprisings in the north of England. But the earl of Northumberland put down the rebels in short order, especially after they got news of the Lancastrian disaster at Tewkesbury. The earl sent word to Edward that all was under control. The northerners could count themselves fortunate that Edward did not advance further, as the king was in no mood for mercy. Young Henry Percy, the fourth duke of Northumberland, had finally come through for Edward.

Queen Margaret was captured at Little Malvern Priory a few days after the battle, it is said by Sir William Stanley's men. She was brought before Edward at Coventry, where she was allowed to subject the king to a furious tongue-lashing, the likes of which only she could deliver. It is said that Edward listened impassively until she was exhausted, and then he politely told her that since he was the victor, he would have his way. Margaret was finally demoralized by the death of her son Edward of Westminster.

Edward returned to London like a Roman consul, with the customary fanfare and a resounding welcome from the people. Commines's biased view, obvious nonsense, was that the people only welcomed the king because he would now pay his debts. The people may have had different reasons, some better than others, but they all loved their magnificent

King Edward IV. On the march into London, poor Queen Margaret was cursed by the people and stoned. She was confined in London for a time, initially in the Tower, but later in relative comfort near her friend Alice, the dowager duchess of Suffolk. Four years later, she was sent back to France for a large ransom of ten thousand crowns.

As soon as Edward returned to London after Tewkesbury, undoubtedly at the king's orders, Henry VI was put to death in the Tower on 21 May 1483, probably by the dagger but also by a crushing blow to the head, allegedly while he was at his prayers. For, while Henry lived, Edward's crown was in constant danger. The execution was probably carried out by the constable of the Tower, the elderly Baron Dudley, and his deputies. Richard, Duke of Gloucester, is often blamed, but it is not likely that he killed Henry, as the king would not have allowed his younger brother to murder an anointed king.

The violent execution was well justified by the brutal customs of medieval England. It is said that Margaret may have been allowed to see Henry upon her arrival at the Tower; no doubt, Henry would have been appalled by Margaret's tale of woe. It is to be hoped that Margaret did not see her husband's death. And so ended the life of the most unfortunate but incompetent King Henry VI. Edward was king of England, with nobody left alive to challenge him. They were all dead, with the single exception of Henry Tudor, who, following Tewkesbury and in the charge of Jasper Tudor, was smuggled out of England to a long exile in Brittany. Nobody thought much about Henry Tudor at the time while Edward IV lived. George Neville, the Lancastrian chancellor at Henry VI's Readoption, was pardoned, but he was sent briefly to the Tower for his own safekeeping.

CHAPTER 3

The Later, More Peaceful Reign of King Edward IV (1471–83)

The Rebellion of the Bastard of Fauconberg

On his triumphant return to London after Tewkesbury, Edward had to deal with a residual minor rebellion led by Thomas Neville, the bastard son of Lord Fauconberg. The rebels included soldiers from Calais and men from Kent and Essex who protested their taxes. Queen Elizabeth Woodville did not consider the rebellion a minor one. She was in the Tower, which Fauconberg bombarded from his ships on the River Thames. The rebels attacked London Bridge, Aldgate, and Bishopsgate, but they could not gain entry to the city in the face of stout resistance by the citizens. Finally, Anthony Woodville and the Lord Mayor of London Sir John Stockton drove off the rebels, and Fauconberg retreated with his ships. When the king arrived, needless to say, the rebels were brought rapidly to order. The bastard was pardoned by the ever-generous Edward, but he was soon executed for unrelated offences in the company of Richard, Duke of Gloucester. Edward proceeded into Kent, rounded up the ringleaders, and punished them, usually by large fines, but there were some executions, as well. Edward's tolerance for rebels was disappearing fast.

The Settlement of the Warwick Estates and the Bitter Rivalry between Gloucester and Clarence

Richard, Duke of Gloucester, was initially rewarded for his loyal service with many of the Warwick estates, but his plan to marry Anne Neville,

Warwick's newly widowed younger daughter, was obstructed by Clarence, who lusted after the Warwick estates. His own wife, Isabel, was also a Warwick daughter. Edward procrastinated about granting permission for the marriage to Anne. Clarence even went so far as to kidnap and hide Anne, disguising her as a chambermaid in the London house of one of his retainers. But Richard, possibly assisted by the duke of Buckingham, searched for her, recovered her, and placed her in sanctuary at St Martin's Le Grand. Gloucester married Anne Neville on 12 July 1472; a papal dispensation had been granted on 22 April 1472 (Higginbotham, 2013). As Anne was a great-great-great-granddaughter of Edward III and Richard was a great-great-great-great-grandson of Edward III, they were fourth cousins, one generation removed, and not related within the prohibited four degrees of affinity. His willingness to confirm papal permission reflected Richard's respect for papal authority in marriage matters. It is surprising that he would later declare his brother's marriage invalid without reference to the Church authorities during his disinheritance procedure against Edward IV's successor, young King Edward V. In 1472, the newlyweds moved to Middleham Castle in Yorkshire to take up Richard's appointment as lieutenant of the north; Gloucester minded the Scottish border areas, where his performance in establishing law and order proved excellent. Around the same time, Edward's third daughter, Cecily, was betrothed to the heir of James III (the king of Scotland), the future James IV.

On the matter of division of property, there were bitter disputes between Clarence and Gloucester. In the end, Gloucester had to give up many of his gains. Estates were exchanged and an agreement was finally reached with Parliament. Clarence received the earldoms of Warwick and Salisbury as compensation for Richard's great power in the north, which was an excellent result for Clarence, a most undeserving prince. Clarence's son Edward would later be the seventeenth earl of Warwick, but there was no property transfer. Much has been made of the intense rivalry between Gloucester and Clarence over this settlement. It made King Edward IV extremely uncomfortable.

The statute of 1474 completely ignored the Beauchamp countess of Warwick, who was in sanctuary at Beaulieu Abbey, still alive, and still entitled to some of her inheritance. Parliament treated her as though she was dead. Her estates were divided between Anne and Isabel, which meant that Gloucester and Clarence had near total control. Edward probably felt that the countess of Warwick deserved such treatment, considering the prolonged treachery of her husband, Warwick, then deceased. In those times, this type of treatment of a traitor's wife was not unusual. The generous duke of Gloucester had Sir James Tyrell escort his new mother-in-law to Middleham Castle, where he could look after her. It is said that Gloucester would later have other tasks for Sir James Tyrell.

But Clarence, who was incapable of loyalty, amazingly still harboured plans to overthrow Edward and seize the crown for himself. During the Readoption of Henry VI, he had been made the heir of Edward of Westminster, who was killed at Tewkesbury. Clarence seemed not to understand that the Yorkist victory had changed all that! He plotted with Louis XI, who sent the talented earl of Oxford to harass the English coast and plan an invasion. Clarence was considered a magnate who might assist Oxford; in this conspiracy, the involvement of Clarence was traced to his confederate, the senior George Neville, who in 1472 was arrested and imprisoned near Calais. But nothing was done about Clarence, the king's own brother. In 1473, Oxford was captured during a raid on St Michael's Mount in Cornwall and imprisoned at Hammes Castle, near Calais. George Neville was soon released, but the much more dangerous Oxford was held until 1483, when he escaped to join Henry Tudor in France and eventually fought very effectively for the Tudor side at the Battle of Bosworth Field in 1485 and again at the Battle of Stoke Field in 1487. But this was all in the future.

The Invasion of France and the Treaty of Picquigny

There was relative peace after 1471, but Edward harboured thoughts of revenge against Louis XI for his major role in the conspiracy with Warwick and Queen Margaret. So, Edward renewed the ancient claim of English kings to the throne of France through Queen Isabella, the mother of King Edward III, and therefore Edward's great-great-great-great-great-grandmother. Louis XI, of course, rejected the claim, as had all French kings, since France followed the Salic law, which prohibited claims through females of the line. Parliament voted Edward money because wars with France were still very popular and the recovery of lands lost under Henry VI was considered highly desirable. It is for shame what hatred does for reason. Mary Clive (1974) recounted that Edward himself was not enamoured with any French war and, in secret, assured Louis XI that he would seek peace, but only after he had landed in France to satisfy his militant supporters.

In 1475, Edward took a large and very well-equipped army and invaded France, but his ally the duke of Burgundy was not active in the field. His other ally, the duke of Brittany, negotiated a separate peace. Edward rapidly lost interest. Many believed he was losing enthusiasm even before he crossed the English Channel. There is every reason to believe that he was reluctant about the campaign. His agents negotiated the Treaty of Picquigny with the French. In return for withdrawal of his army from French soil, Edward extracted agreements from King Louis XI: to make an initial payment of seventy-five thousand crowns to Edward; to pay a large annual pension of fifty thousand crowns to Edward; to permit the betrothal of the dauphin of France with Edward's eldest daughter, Elizabeth; to provide political help in overcoming rebellious English subjects; to encourage trade between England and France; and, finally, to pay a generous ransom of ten thousand crowns for the former queen, Margaret of Anjou – all of which greatly enriched the English king's treasury. Edward considered the money to be tribute, but Louis considered it a pension.

The two rival kings met on a bridge in the middle of the River Somme, behind a lattice screen for mutual protection, and appeared to immensely enjoy each other's company, especially as Edward did well speaking French and Louis made tantalizing suggestions to the womanizing king about the French ladies at court and about a cardinal who would immediately forgive any transgressions. Although many were disappointed by the fact that there was to be no war and therefore no plunder, and while Richard, Duke of Gloucester, considered the expedition to be a waste of good money, nevertheless, Edward did very well for his kingdom by making these arrangements. Edward waited patiently for his subjects to realize that the treaty brought lower levels of taxation and further improved international trade. Despite his six magnificent victories on the battlefield (Northampton, Mortimer's Cross, Towton, Empingham, Barnet, and Tewkesbury), Edward IV always considered Picquigny to be his finest accomplishment.

Family Relations

When the king's second son, Richard of Shrewsbury, was created duke of York in May 1474, the occasion was celebrated with great feasts and a major tournament at the jousts. The marriage of the four-year-old Prince Richard and five-year-old Anne Mowbray, the heiress of the deceased fourth duke of Norfolk, occurred on 15 January 1478; the wedding was held at St Stephen's Chapel in Westminster Palace. Afterwards, there was another spectacular tournament organized by Anthony Woodville. Soon after the wedding, young Richard was confirmed in the title duke of Norfolk, but at this time he did not acquire the Norfolk estates, which remained with Anne Mowbray, the duchess of Norfolk.

There were other important social events during this period of Edward IV's reign. In 1476, the remains of Richard, the third duke of York and his son Edmund, Earl of Rutland, were disinterred from their lowly graves at Pontefract and transferred to a magnificent tomb at Fotheringhay Castle. Subjects who joined the five-day procession were each given one penny, and pregnant women were given two pennies. The festivities culminated in a banquet at which twenty thousand people were entertained, or so it is said (Clive, 1974).

The Alienation of the Duke of Clarence

The long-smouldering matter of George, Duke of Clarence, came to a head in 1477. Clarence had joined Warwick in open rebellion several times against King Edward IV and had clearly committed treason on multiple other occasions: before Edgecote in 1469; before Empingham in 1470; at the Readoption of Henry VI in 1470–71; in the period soon after Tewkesbury in 1471; and during the approach of his final arrest in 1477. Edward had repeatedly forgiven his treacherous brother, influenced, no doubt, by his blood relationship and by his own good nature. In 1476, Clarence's wife, Isabel, died in childbirth, and George decided he wanted to marry Mary, the duchess of Burgundy, widowed in 1477 and soon the new ruler of the duchy. But Edward would not agree to such a potentially hostile alignment. There were rumours that George even planned to invade England with a Burgundian army. The alienated Clarence withdrew from the court and refused to attend any further.

In 1477, Clarence accused a lady named Ankarette Twynho, a recent member of the queen's own household, of poisoning his wife, Isabel, and assisting the queen in using sorcery to hasten Isabel's death. At the instigation of Clarence, Ankarette was arrested, tried, and hanged at Warwick. Not much was done about this flagrant abuse of power. Then, Clarence publicly denounced the king. He declared that the king was not the legitimate son of his father, the third duke of York, and claimed that he himself was therefore the rightful king, never mind that his father had never denied that Edward was his son, and that Edward, not George, had twice affirmed the throne by force of arms. Clarence liked to emphasize that the Readoption Parliament had made him heir to Henry VI and Edward of Westminster, both of whom were dead. Then, Clarence attempted to incite rebellion yet again; there were disturbances in Cambridgeshire. Clarence openly accused the queen of murdering Isabel by poison and sorcery. He declared that the king's marriage was not legal on the basis that it was unlawful for the king to marry a widow. This, of course, threatened the succession to the throne, as it made the royal children illegitimate. Also in 1477, some members of the Clarence affinity, Thomas Burdett and John Stacey, were accused of plotting the king's death; they were arrested, tried, found guilty, and hanged at Tyburn. Too late, Clarence spoke at council on their behalf, suggesting their innocence and that a miscarriage of justice had occurred, which further angered the king. In mid 1477, Edward's incredible patience was finally exhausted by the constant treason. Clarence was arrested and sent to the Tower.

Mary Clive (1974) has reviewed the charges against Clarence in the indictment before Parliament. He was accused as follows: (1) Clarence paid people to say that Burdett was wrongfully executed; (2) Clarence accused the king of using black magic to poison his subjects; (3) Clarence said the king was a bastard, not a legitimate son of his father, the duke of York; (4) Clarence said the king forced people to swear allegiance to him; (5) Clarence said that he himself had been disinherited, since King Henry VI had made him heir to the throne if Edward of Westminster died without issue; and that (6) Clarence had ordered the abbot of Tewkesbury to insert a changeling boy at Warwick Castle so that young Edward, the seventeenth earl of Warwick, could be sent overseas to raise an army and invade England. Mary Clive said the indictment was "rather woolly," as it omitted multiple other, much stronger reasons for alleging treason against Clarence. But the government considered that these were sufficient for the purpose and the easiest ones to discuss in Parliament without raising other embarrassing issues, such as the multiple Lancastrian rebellions against the regime.

In early 1478, Parliament tried Clarence for high treason, with Edward providing much of the testimony. Nobody could be found to speak on the duke's behalf. The verdict was, of course, guilty, and Clarence was sentenced to death by the newly appointed seneschal of England, the young duke of Buckingham. Some historians, mysteriously, have suggested that it is not clear what led to the downfall of Clarence, but it is in fact abundantly apparent to all but the most wilful observer. Clarence's mother, the dowager duchess Cecily, asked for a private execution, not the usual barbarous public execution for treason. Ten days later, Clarence was put to death by immersion, it is said in a barrel of wine, which apparently was previously the duke's sardonic personal choice. Some historians have suggested that Cecily asked that Clarence be pardoned, but that is unlikely, as the duchess was well aware of the previous pardons Edward had issued. Also, it would have been difficult for her to forgive the accusation of adultery on her part. The king had hesitated to sign the death warrant, but the House of Commons insisted and petitioned the king. The citizens saw no justice if a magnate could go unpunished for offences sufficient for ordinary men to be hanged. Edward may have regretted the execution since Clarence was his natural brother, but the procedure was legal for the times and the victim was richly deserving.

It is said that Richard, Duke of Gloucester, blamed Queen Elizabeth Woodville for the death of Clarence; no doubt, the queen was supportive of the king's position, but how the queen could be blamed for the result is quite beyond comprehension. It is a good example of the completely unjustifiable hostility directed at Edward's queen, and it is also a continuing example of Richard's blatant hostility towards the Woodvilles. Edward made adjustments in the former Warwick estates in favour of Richard, but Richard was apparently not appeased.

It should be noted here that Clarence never made any accusation that Edward's marriage to Queen Elizabeth was bigamous. Despite his alleged association with Robert Stillington, Clarence knew nothing about any

1461 marriage contract that Edward had allegedly made. Had he known of such a contract, then, convinced of his own freedom from retribution, there can be no question that the treacherous Clarence would have spread that tale from one end of Christendom to the other. Furthermore, if the story was true, then Clarence could easily have negotiated a pardon for his silence. There can be no doubt that Clarence would have followed that course. But that specific accusation about bigamy was never made, at least for another six years until after King Edward IV was dead.

John Ashdown-Hill (2010) has claimed that Robert Stillington revealed to the duke of Clarence Edward's alleged 1461 marriage contract and that Queen Elizabeth became alarmed. For his authority, Ashdown-Hill quoted Mancini (1989). Upon examination, it is clear that Mancini wrote that Clarence thought the 1464 marriage was invalid because Elizabeth was a widow. Mancini made no mention of any alleged 1461 marriage contract, although he did claim that Edward "was legally contracted to another wife [Princess Bona] to whom the earl of Warwick had joined him." It remains true that Stillington made no serious allegation about a 1461 contract until June 1483. Queen Elizabeth was indeed alarmed in 1478, and justifiably so; it was claimed that her husband was a bastard and that her marriage to the king was invalid because she had been a widow. Elizabeth must have been one of those strange people who treasured her children and their inheritance!

Edward IV and Henry Tudor

The king made repeated attempts to get his hands on Henry Tudor, the young earl of Richmond, who had escaped with Jasper Tudor to Brittany after the Battle of Tewkesbury in 1471. Henry was the son of Margaret Beaufort, a direct descendant of John of Gaunt, the duke of Lancaster, the fourth son of King Edward III. Therefore, Henry was the lead surviving male Lancastrian claimant to the English throne (see Appendix D). The Beauforts were descended through John of Gaunt's third wife, Katherine Swynford, before they were married. But in 1396, the Pope legitimized the family, and in 1397 the Parliament declared that the family could inherit. The reader should take note of the order in which these changes were made; first, the Church acted on the matrimonial matter of legitimacy; then, the Parliament responded on the matter of inheritance. This was the usual custom and precedent in England since the thirteenth century. Those who believe that England has a constitution based on custom and precedent would say that this procedure was constitutional.

At one point, there was an agreement to send Henry Tudor to England, where Edward said he planned to marry Henry to one of his younger daughters. In fact, Henry departed for England, but the duke of Brittany changed his mind, as he was worried about Edward's intentions, and brought Henry back before he could set sail. Henry was later to invade England in 1485 and win the English throne by armed force at the Battle of Bosworth Field. And he would indeed marry one of Edward's daughters, but it would be Elizabeth, the eldest daughter, who, by 1485, was the rightful heir to the English throne. But the story is getting ahead of itself.

Trouble with Scotland

In 1480, the Scots, no doubt encouraged by the king of France, resumed their border raids on England, and Richard, Duke of Gloucester, mounted a small counter-raid. As a betrothal had been previously agreed and a dowry had been paid in instalments, Edward demanded the delivery of the future James IV for marriage to his third daughter, Cecily, but the demand was not met by the Scottish Parliament. In 1481, the English fleet under Lord Howard sailed into the Firth of Forth and destroyed a large number of Scottish ships as punishment for Scottish intransigence.

In 1482, Edward allied himself with the Scottish duke of Albany, who had quarrelled with his brother King James III, then fled to France and later reached England. Albany wished to claim the Scottish throne for himself and replace the cultured but allegedly ineffective King James III. For peace on his border, Edward thought this was a good idea. Gloucester and Albany invaded the Scottish lowlands and captured the township of Berwick, but not the citadel; they caused wide destruction as they advanced to Edinburgh. On the way, the Scottish nobles, led by the earl of Angus, rebelled against King James III at Lauder Water, imprisoned the Scottish king, and executed a number of his favourites. But the fickle Albany made a separate peace with James III and was appointed lieutenant of Scotland. Gloucester obtained only a small refund of the previously paid dowry for Princess Cecily, as well as an agreement that the English should keep Berwick. On the way home, Gloucester and Lord Stanley captured the citadel at Berwick, which confirmed the English possession. This all seemed a small reward for the withdrawal from Scotland and was hence an unsatisfactory conclusion for Edward IV. But the campaign did reach a conclusion; it stabilized the border by the recovery of Berwick, it indicated to the Scots that aggression had unpleasant consequences, and, most of all, it avoided another costly and inconclusive war.

In the summer of 1482, there was some evidence that Edward IV was in failing health (Clive, 1974), but there was no suggestion of what was the problem. This condition was the probable reason why Edward did not lead the invasion of Scotland himself that year. Instead, Edward maintained close communication with Gloucester and Albany by a complicated horse-and-rider relay system starting in London and reaching into Scotland.

Edward IV and the Duchy of Burgundy

When Charles, Duke of Burgundy, died on 5 January 1477 at the Battle of Nancy, and his daughter Mary of Burgundy, born by his second wife, succeeded to the duchy, hostilities between Burgundy and France resumed. Louis XI began military operations in the duchy of Burgundy proper and in the Free County of Burgundy, both lands situated to the south-east of Paris. As well, hostilities were resumed in several counties in the Netherlands, north of Paris, namely Artois and Picardy. Margaret, the dowager duchess of Burgundy and Edward's sister, appealed to her brother, hoping for a marriage alliance with England. The council considered a marriage of Mary to an English noble but could not find a suitable candidate, certainly not Clarence. Anthony Woodville, the second Earl Rivers, was offered, but Mary refused on the basis that Rivers was not of the royal line. Edward wished to preserve the independence of Burgundy and, at the same time, preserve his considerable French pension: a difficult conundrum for the English king. On 18 August 1477, Mary married a German prince, Maximilian, the son and heir of King Frederick III, the Holy Roman Emperor. Maximillian defended his wife's Burgundian inheritance and checked the French forces of Louis XI at Guinegate in 1479.

In 1480, Edward IV's sister Margaret paid an official three-month visit to England. The occasion was treated with appropriate splendour and hospitality. The Treaty of Picquigny had been a problem for Burgundy. Margaret tried to produce a change. She wished to arrange a marriage treaty using Edward's third surviving daughter, Princess Anne, and Prince Philip the Handsome (1478–1506), the Burgundian heir, the infant son of Duchess Mary and Maximillian. Edward wanted Burgundy to replace the French pension, which he knew would be lost. Also, he did not wish to pay a dowry for his daughter Princess Anne. A preliminary agreement was reached, with Edward providing nominal military support for Burgundy, and the trade alliance between the two countries was renewed. But Maximillian and Mary of Burgundy were not happy, so the betrothal of Anne and Philip never happened. Louis XI opened negotiations with Burgundy under threat of further military pressure; several of the Netherland provinces, Brabant and Flanders, hostile to Maximillian, joined the negotiations with Louis XI.

On 27 March 1482, Mary of Burgundy died in a horse-riding accident. The independent provinces of Brabant and Flanders, tired of the constant warfare and afraid of Maximillian, made peace with Louis XI. Under terms of the Second Treaty of Arras in December 1482, considerable territory was ceded back to France, namely the duchy of Burgundy proper and the Free County of Burgundy on the east side of the River Saône. But, more important for England, Burgundy agreed to the betrothal of Mary's infant daughter, Margaret, with the dauphin of France, later Charles VIII. The betrothal of the dauphin with King Edward's eldest daughter, Princess Elizabeth, was cancelled, and the French pension to Edward IV was to be no longer paid. This was a very unsatisfactory conclusion for the English king.

More Family Relations

In November 1481, Anne Mowbray, the bride of the king's second son, Prince Richard, died and was buried in Westminster Abbey. A few months later, in May 1482, Princess Mary, betrothed to the king of Denmark, died at Greenwich Palace and was given a splendid funeral and burial upriver at Windsor Castle. In the settlement of Norfolk, Edward IV handed the huge estate of Anne Mowbray, the duchess of Norfolk, to his son Richard, the duke of Norfolk, and had Parliament make the transfer legal. Later, there would be trouble with the heirs of Norfolk, notably Lord John Howard. However, King Edward considered that it was not unreasonable for a male to marry an heiress and later inherit her estate. Edward knew only too well how the Warwick estate had been accumulated by way of such marriages.

Events did not appear to be going well for King Edward IV, but Christmas of 1482 was celebrated in the royal court at Westminster Palace with a splendid display of wealth and national prosperity. The Croyland Chronicler (1854) recounted that the king appeared "magnificent, distinguished, elegant, and attractive," and that the royal children all appeared "sweet and beautiful." No mention was made of the corpulence which later anti-Yorkist propaganda exaggerated in the king; no doubt, the king was experiencing what we now would call middle-aged spread, which was very noticeable in those times, when people tended to be leaner. It would be doubtful if the chronicler, Bishop John Russell, who was always scrupulously honest, feared to be more accurate in his description of Edward IV. It should be noted that the Croyland Chronicler at this time was either Bishop John Russell or a very close associate of the bishop; but for future reference, the author will continue to describe the Croyland Chronicler as effectively Bishop John Russell. It should also be noted that the *Croyland Chronicle,* describing all the events of 1482 and 1483, was written in 1486, several years after the events took place. It is known that Bishop Russell spent time at Croyland Abbey in April 1486.

The End of the Reign with the Death of Edward IV

Stung by the loss of his French pension and the loss of his daughter's betrothal to the dauphin, Edward longed for revenge against Louis XI. It is said that Edward planned a fresh invasion of France for the next campaign season. The duke of Albany was to keep Scotland quiet on the northern English border while Edward was busy in France. Parliament voted the king a subsidy, but only for defence of the homeland. In the meantime, the king ordered ships to sea for the purpose of harrying French shipping in the Channel. There is little evidence that Edward began making much in the way of appropriate preparations for war with France. When Edward died suddenly on 9 April 1483, these early plans never came to fruition – and another costly, inconclusive war was avoided.

It was cold and wet at Eastertide in 1483, but Lord Hastings and the king went fishing on the River Thames at Westminster Palace, in spite of the queen's discouragement (Gregory, 2009). When they returned to the palace, they were cold and wet and exuberant after a day of fishing and drinking, a story well known in our own day and age. The kitchen prepared the fish the men had caught, and the two enjoyed the evening meal. But later that evening, the king complained of intense abdominal pain and developed a high fever. No doubt, the River Thames was contaminated in those days. By the next day, Edward was no better. He was vomiting and could retain no food; his abdominal pain was unbearable, and he was described as struggling for breath in his four-poster bed. The rumour spread throughout the court that the king was dying, but the king lingered for days. He called his council and ordered that Richard, Duke of Gloucester, be Lord Protector until the new king, Edward's son Edward V, was old enough to assume power at the age of fifteen years. The king made some changes to his old 1475 last will. Most important among these was the transfer of the responsibility of Lord Protector to his younger brother, Richard, Duke of Gloucester. The king understood how difficult it would be for the queen to act as regent, but he did not take other powers from her. Edward asked Hastings and Dorset to set aside their differences and cooperate to ensure the proper succession for the boy king; he also asked the queen and Hastings to set aside their differences. Edward IV sank slowly and died on 9 April 1483, a death which was sudden and unexpected, at the age of not quite forty-one years.

There is no agreement about the cause of death, but it was likely a disorder associated with contaminated ingestion, bloodstream infection, and acute pulmonary congestion with pneumonia – what in modern times might be called the acquired respiratory distress syndrome (ARDS). This condition results in a major inhibition of the pulmonary surface active material which is essential to maintain proper inflation of the lungs. In an age without powerful antibiotics or well-designed mechanical breathing machines, Edward had little chance for survival. Several historians said that Edward died of debauchery: excessive drinking, eating, and profligacy. But it was an age when life was short. And it is true that Edward enjoyed himself socially. But if we exclude those who did not survive infancy and those who later died in battle or by execution, the average age of Edward's sisters and daughters who all died naturally was forty-two years. Edward was not much different. The hostile Philippe de Commines claimed that he died of melancholy, upset by the loss of his French pension, but that would be entirely inconsistent with Edward's ebullient personality. It was common for fatal infections to shorten lives in the Middle Ages.

In April 1483, the king's body lay naked, except for a loincloth, at Westminster Palace, while the lords and officials in solemn state came to view him. Then, the body was embalmed and magnificently dressed for the funeral. The next morning, the body was moved to St Stephen's Chapel, also at Westminster Palace, and lay in state for eight days while the requiem masses were performed for his soul. Then, the body was placed on a funeral bier which was richly decorated. Carried by fifteen knights, the body of Edward was processioned to nearby Westminster Abbey. Ahead of the bier was Lord Chancellor, Archbishop Rotherham, accompanied by the other Lords spiritual; behind the bier was a parade of the Lords temporal, including Hastings, Stanley, and Dorset. After a sombre but beautiful ceremony in the abbey on 18 April 1483, a procession, led by Lord John Howard, conducted the royal body, which was placed on a horse-drawn carriage, to Syon Abbey, where the group rested the night. Then, they proceeded to Eton, where there were further prayers, and finally to the St George Chapel at nearby Windsor Castle. Overnight, the body was guarded by a large watch of knights and lords. On 20 April 1483, in the morning, the last funeral Mass was celebrated by Archbishop Rotherham and Bishops Russell and Dudley; the body was placed in the magnificent tomb of Edward IV, with Edward's helmet, shield, and sword. Then, the officers of the royal household threw their staves into the grave and shouted, "The king is dead. Long live the king." This referred to Edward IV's being dead and Edward V's being the new king. This was probably shouted in French, not in the common English language. Discarding of the staves indicated that the men gave up their official power.

PART TWO

The Legacy

CHAPTER 4

England without the Magnificent King Edward IV; the Road to Disaster for the House of York; and the Reign of King Edward V

The Tragic Events which Followed the Death of King Edward IV

When the king died, Edward V was a boy of twelve years of age under the tutelage of Anthony Woodville at Ludlow Castle in the Welsh Marches. On hearing the news of the king's death, which arrived in Ludlow on 14 April 1483, the royal party set out for London to complete the accession ceremonial. But there appeared to be no hurry, as Anthony Woodville had plans to celebrate St George Day on 23 April 1483 in Ludlow. He also needed time to arrange the escort. They departed Ludlow on 24 June 1483, ten days after the sad news of Edward IV's death had arrived. Edward V had been proclaimed king in London on 11 April 1483.

The former king's council in London, which met in mid April 1483, was briefly dominated by the Queen Mother and the marquis of Dorset; other members included Bishop Rotherham, Bishop Morton, Sir William Hastings, Lord Thomas Stanley, and Lord John Howard. The council, at the queen's request, had previously ordered Anthony Woodville to raise a significant force to accompany and protect the new king. It is not known how large a force was suggested, but it was perhaps sufficient to fight a pitched battle if there was an attempt to overthrow the boy king. Five thousand men would be a near estimate. The council also ordered Sir Edward Woodville to take the English fleet to sea and deal with French raiding parties under the French baron Lord Cordes. They had been harassing English shipping for several weeks since Edward IV died. This order by the council may have been an overreaction, but the times were uncertain and the threat was real. Sir Edward and the fleet left port on 29 April 1483. It has been suggested that the French attacks were in response to English attacks on French shipping, which Edward IV had ordered during the last week of his life. The council, which met during April 1483, soon after Edward IV's death, was not enamoured with the fact that Richard, Duke of Gloucester, was Lord Protector. They, rather, favoured his being chairman of the council so that some limits on his power could be imposed. This would mean something more akin to a regency. They voted in the majority for this latter proposal, although a significant number of members disagreed.

The date for the coronation was set for 4 May 1483, a time far too early for adequate preparations to be made. But the council was entitled to make some decisions. Dorset has been criticized for suggesting that the council could not wait for Gloucester to arrive in London. Perhaps Dorset revealed modest antipathy, but he had a point, as Gloucester was still far away in the north and some decisions needed to be made. The council ordered that the judges of the King's Bench and the Court of Common Pleas be reappointed in order to maintain the judicial system. They proceeded with the appointment of county commissioners to administer the collection of a new tax on foreign merchants, legislation for which had recently been approved by Parliament. They ordered that a small force of troops be sent to Calais to make sure the fortress remained quiet and was not used for an invasion of England, as had happened in the past when Warwick was in charge.

It was alleged by Dominic Mancini (1989) that the Woodvilles stole the royal treasury from the Tower, a very serious charge. The money was allegedly divided between the queen, Dorset, and Sir Edward Woodville. As discussed by Susan Higginbotham (2011A), Mancini was describing hearsay, a rumour, not an eyewitness account. Neither the *Croyland Chronicle* nor the *Great Chronicle of London* made mention of any such theft. There is absolutely no evidence that the Queen Mother took any treasure with her when she later entered sanctuary; nor is there evidence that Dorset, the deputy constable of the Tower, took any part for his personal benefit. But Sir Edward Woodville probably took a small portion from an English ship in port, most likely to pay his sailors, and apparently did take appropriate measures for a safe accounting.

Some have claimed that Edward IV removed the queen from any power in the added codicils of his last will, but the queen's presence and active participation at the council meetings of April 1483 suggest that this was not so. It has been pointed out that everything that the council had done since Edward IV died could lawfully be cancelled by the Lord Protector (Kendall, 2002). To follow precedent, the council should have resigned at the death of Edward IV and been replaced by new appointments. But the council decided, reasonably, to continue until such new appointments were made by the duke of Gloucester.

Following the early and brief Woodville domination, other members of the council asserted themselves, chiefly Lord Hastings. They persuaded the Queen Mother that a very large force to accompany the new king was too aggressive and might incite retaliation. The Queen Mother Elizabeth immediately gave way and sent a countermanding order to Anthony Woodville; he was to raise only a modest force to accompany the new king, no more than two thousand men, as agreed with Hastings. The council was frightened that civil war would resume. The Croyland Chronicler noted how anxious the Queen Mother was that all should be harmonious. In retrospect, it seems that the Queen Mother's desire for a larger force might have been correct, as lack of a larger force may have resulted in the sad events which were to follow. The Queen Mother knew the duke of Gloucester better than most, but she met solid resistance from the lords, who did not trust her, and quickly consented to the more cautious approach.

Soon after the death of Edward IV, Lord Hastings and the duke of Buckingham had sent messengers to Richard, Duke of Gloucester, in Yorkshire. They almost certainly informed him that Edward IV intended for him to be the Lord Protector. It would be surprising if they omitted such vital information. It is estimated that the communications arrived at Middleham Castle by 14 or 15 April 1483. It has been suggested, wrongly, that there was a deliberate delay in notifying Richard of Edward IV's death. This was about the same time as the news arrived in Ludlow. The intended implication that any delay was the fault of the Queen Mother is not reasonable, as it was not her responsibility – and she was probably aware that Hastings had sent notification.

After Hastings' message arrived, Richard sent his messenger to Anthony Woodville, suggesting that Gloucester and Hastings meet at Northampton on the way to London, to which proposal Anthony readily agreed. After receiving Buckingham's message in which he promised loyal support, Richard sent his messenger to Buckingham, inviting him also to meet with the new king's party at Northampton.

Richard set out for London on 24 April 1483 to assume his appointment, accompanied by armed retainers, probably about three hundred men. Richard paused at York to pay homage to the new king and to swear his allegiance. He sent a very sympathetic letter to Elizabeth, assuring her of his loyalty, but she was probably sceptical. Richard, Duke of Gloucester, and Henry, Duke of Buckingham, the latter with an additional three hundred retainers, planned to meet the royal party at Northampton on 30 April 1483. This date may have been Anthony Woodville's suggestion. The king's party could not be accommodated in Northampton on 29 April 1483, so they proceeded fifteen miles to Stony Stratford. The king sent Anthony Woodville back to Northampton to meet the dukes, as arranged. Gloucester and Buckingham assumed custody of King Edward V at Stony Stratford on 30 April 1483, despite the boy king's quite vigorous protests and defence of his family and escort. When the new king defended the Queen Mother, Buckingham told him bluntly that women had no role in the government. Such unenlightened views were common in those times, but they were not consistent with the new king's liberal education.

On the night before, on 29 April 1483, over dinner in Northampton, Anthony Woodville had explained to Richard the council view that he should be a chairman of the council or the regent rather than Lord Protector. Richard kept his silence, for he knew from Hastings that the dead king's intention was for him to be the Lord Protector, a more powerful position. Despite his seeming cordiality in Northampton, on the morning of 30 April 1483, before proceeding to Stony Stratford, Gloucester arrested Anthony Woodville. At Stony Stratford, Richard Grey and Thomas Vaughan were also arrested, much to their surprise, and the new king's military escort was dismissed. The soldiers apparently departed without protest or complaint, even though they greatly outnumbered

Richard's men and could have effectively resisted if they were ordered thus. It appears plain they were not so ordered.

It is known that Gloucester disliked the Woodvilles and had long resented the power they had accumulated during his brother's reign. In particular, he feared the influence they exerted over King Edward V. Gloucester had always regarded them disdainfully as low-born interlopers. It would appear that Richard believed that Woodville, Grey, and Vaughan were conspiring together to ambush and murder him, presumably on the road to London after leaving Stony Stratford. If that was indeed the case, then the plan was destroyed by their arrest. After his arrival in London, Richard accused the Woodvilles before the council without a shred of evidence to back his claim. He produced a cartful of weapons, which everyone knew had been previously laid up for the defence of London. By his friendly and cooperative behaviour at Northampton, it is very clear that Anthony Woodville had no such intention to act against Richard, Duke of Gloucester. Anthony, like many good men, was naively taken completely by surprise at the time of his arrest. Richard's strange explanation for the arrests, given to the Lord Mayor of London, was that he had rescued Edward V from the hands of traitors, namely Anthony Woodville and his party. Somehow, the move from Northampton to Stony Stratford was seen as an evasive hostile act, in which case it is difficult to understand why Anthony Woodville returned to Northampton to meet the dukes and spend the night. Horace Walpole (2013), writing much later in 1767, claimed that the Queen Mother's order to bring Edward V with a large body of troops was "the first overt [hostile] act of the reign" and was bound to cause resentment. He thought this meant that she planned "to exclude the Dukes and to govern in concert with her own family." Although this reflected Walpole's unjustified scornful opinion of Elizabeth, it is quite likely that it is what Gloucester and Buckingham may have believed, too.

It should be obvious that the Woodville affinity did hope to retain much of its power. The best way to achieve that was to have an early coronation so the office of Lord Protector could be abolished and replaced with a regent and a chancellor, possibly, but not necessarily, men of their own faction. According to Giles St Aubyn (1983), precedent had established that protectorates ended immediately when the king was crowned. Hence, the Woodvilles aimed for an early coronation on 4 May 1483. Anthony

Woodville made a big mistake by taking so much time to reach London, but he was unaware that there would be a problem. It is clear that those who attended the new king offered no resistance to Richard when he assumed control at Stony Stratford.

The Woodvilles in London had not expected the king to meet with Gloucester before his arrival in the capital. Anthony Woodville had apparently not informed them. Those in London would have been somewhat agitated by the turn of events. Some historians have described the events at Stony Stratford as a coup d'état by the duke of Gloucester, but others have concluded that this position was an exaggeration, as the duke had been named as the Lord Protector by Edward IV. At the news, which arrived in London just before midnight on 30 April 1483, there was panic among the populace of London. Armed citizens appeared in the streets, but only some were in support of the Queen Mother. Most went home after Lord Hastings and others issued reassurances that the Lord Protector would be respectful of the new king. At a council meeting at St Paul's on 1 May 1483, there was discussion about taking up armed resistance against Gloucester, but it was decided that such a thing would be counterproductive (Mancini, 1989). After initial attempts to gain support, it became clear to the Queen Mother that there was little she could do about the situation. Hastings was so worried that he began to regret his initial support for the duke of Gloucester.

On or about 2 May 1483, the queen fled into the sanctuary at Westminster Abbey. What she feared had happened: Richard, Duke of Gloucester, had control over the new king. She took with her Thomas Grey, the marquis of Dorset; her younger son, Prince Richard of Shrewsbury; Lionel and Richard Woodville; and all the new king's sisters: Elizabeth, Mary, Cecily, Anne, Katherine, and three-year-old Bridget. She took with her many of her possessions, such as furniture. This is seen as avaricious by some authors who ignore the size of the queen's family and her motherly desire to see that they remained comfortable. The decision also reflected that she planned a prolonged stay in the sanctuary. The queen's instincts ultimately turned out to be correct; no doubt, she suspected Richard's intention in relation to the crown. If it should follow that Edward V was not to survive, then she understood that she needed to protect young Prince Richard, the conditional new heir to the throne, from falling into the hands of the duke of Gloucester. But the lords of the kingdom knew better, as we shall see; they either trusted Richard or were afraid of him. The Queen Mother's early flight into sanctuary is good evidence that she never planned to exclude the two powerful dukes from the government. She knew that she could not effectively oppose them. The idea that she planned to try excluding them, expressed by some historians, reflects that they wrongly considered her to be a foolish woman. Buckingham had already expressed his negative opinion of women in government, much to the aggravation of the new king.

Richard took time to show young Edward to the people, so his progress was deliberately slow. He arrived in London on 4 May 1483, the day of the intended coronation, plans for which, unsurprisingly, had already been abandoned. Gloucester installed the new king, first at the Bishop's Palace, but soon, on 19 May 1483, at the Tower Palace, which was the traditional starting point for the coronation procession. Soon after his arrival in London, Gloucester again had all the lords swear allegiance to the new king.

The council could be divided into three groups: first, the Queen Mother's party with the Woodvilles and some of the prelates, in particular Rotherham; second, the king's party led by Hastings and including Stanley and Morton; and third, the Gloucester party, which included Buckingham and Lord Howard. By the first days of May, the Queen Mother's party had more or less disappeared into prison or sanctuary or had fled into exile. The king's party wanted Edward V to be crowned but was somewhat hostile to the Queen Mother and ambivalent about Gloucester. The council did not want the Woodvilles to dominate any new government, but many members also had reservations about Richard, Duke of Gloucester, as Lord Protector.

At the council meeting on 7 May 1463 at Baynard Castle, which was attended by Richard, Duke of Gloucester, with the prelates and the magnates, and no Woodvilles present, all power was taken from the Queen Mother. Archbishop Bourchier took possession of the Great Seal and the privy and signet seals, presumably in the name of King Edward V. The treasure of Edward IV, stored in the Tower, was seized in the name of the new government. Edward's last will with added codicils did not strip Elizabeth of her power as Queen Mother and executrix of his last will, nor did it take the king's treasure away from the queen's supervision. Otherwise, the council would not have found it necessary to strip Elizabeth of her power and to assign the king's treasure to the government. These developments were a direct repudiation of Edward IV's last will. This was not necessarily unlawful, as the late king may not control events after he is dead, but it showed a concerning lack of respect for the wishes of King Edward IV and for time-honoured precedent.

Also, it raises the question of what exactly was the king's treasure. It could have been his own private wealth, the result of his own personal enterprise, or it could have been resources belonging to the State, the result of general taxation. Edward followed a policy of sometimes mixing the two, private and public funds, in order to keep general taxation low. In any case, the council made it belong to the government, as was the council's privilege. Some have claimed that the treasure did not amount to much, but it is also suggested that Edward left his kingdom with a considerable surplus and a balanced budget. Perhaps the so-called treasure in the Tower was simply Edward's massive private wealth; the State money was in the royal chamber at Westminster Palace, where it is known that Edward IV usually banked it in order to closely control its expenditure.

The Croyland Chronicler wrote in 1486 that most of the treasure in the Tower was taken by the Lord Protector's government and ultimately by Richard, Duke of Gloucester, personally. The Chronicler stated, "He [Richard] had taken possession of all those [treasures] which the most glorious King Edward, his deceased brother, had, by dint of the greatest care and scrupulousness, amassed … and had entrusted to the disposal of his executors … in his Last Will." So, for those many critics who thought that the money had been stolen by the Woodvilles, Croyland thought otherwise. The civil government took it first, and then Gloucester seized it when he later decided upon the usurpation. King Richard III used the treasure for the purpose of bolstering his political position. Croyland had no doubt that Richard largely wasted the money by spending extravagantly, attempting to buy popular affection and political support. According to Croyland, King Edward IV had intended fully half of his treasure to be given to the poor, and the rest was to pay back his debts at a considerable premium. Edward gave these instructions in his last will and appointed his queen as executrix. This all might confirm that the treasure in the

Tower was Edward IV's personal wealth, accumulated by his own business enterprise.

At the council meeting of 10 May 1483, there were again no Woodvilles present. Richard's appointment as the Lord Protector was confirmed, and Bishop John Russell was made chancellor of England in the place of Rotherham, who had shown partisan favour to the Queen Mother. The coronation of Edward V was planned for 22 June 1483. But the council refused to allow the execution of Anthony Woodville and his comrades, indicating that a trial was necessary to examine the evidence.

The council did not agree with Richard that the Woodvilles had committed treason by escorting Edward V from Ludlow, nor did it agree that there was any evidence that the Woodville party had plotted the ambush and death of Richard on the road to London. These accusations by Gloucester are difficult to understand, but they obviously reflected great personal antagonism, much of it unjustified. Maybe, for some reason, Richard thought it was his privilege to escort King Edward V from Ludlow, not the privilege of Anthony Woodville. Richard had expected to meet the king at Northampton, not at nearby Stony Stratford, closer to London. Maybe he did not accept Anthony Woodville's explanation that they had moved on to Stony Stratford because Northampton could not provide sufficient accommodation for the sizeable royal escort, or maybe Richard thought they were trying to escape his lawful supervision. It is sometimes stated that when Gloucester arrived at Stony Stratford, the king was mounted and preparing to leave for London. But this was a decision the king could legitimately make for himself.

At this same council meeting of 10 May, Richard's request that he continue as the Lord Protector after the coronation was also refused on the basis that this matter was up to the Parliament. Although plans for a new Parliament were made, and although writs were issued in the name of King Edward V on 13 May 1483, these plans were eventually cancelled as Richard's own plans progressed. Under the council plan, Parliament was to meet on 25 June 1483, three days after the expected coronation on 22 June 1483; if it had happened, then it would have been King Edward V's first and only Parliament.

On 14 May 1483, Richard ordered Sir Edward Brampton and other captains to sea and for the English fleet to return to port. Most ships complied, but Sir Edward Woodville, perhaps with a very small part of the private treasure of Edward IV with which to pay his men, sailed on to join Henry Tudor in Brittany. It was obvious by now that the Woodvilles expected Richard to seize absolute power in the very near future. Dominic Mancini (1989) appeared to believe that Gloucester had determined to seize the crown soon after he had control of Edward V at Stony Stratford on 30 April 1483. Mancini may not have been precise, but he was only describing what he learned by way of hearsay.

There was concern, mostly among the prelates, that the Queen Mother remained in the sanctuary; it was difficult to envisage a coronation for King Edward V without the Queen Mother and her family in attendance. A committee was sent to reassure her and persuade her to leave, but she remained adamant that she would stay in the sanctuary. The lords and the prelates thought they could control Gloucester, but Elizabeth knew better. She understood that she needed to keep Prince Richard with her and remain in the sanctuary. By this time, Gloucester was firmly in control and the Woodvilles were defeated; Anthony Woodville was in prison, the Queen Mother Elizabeth and her son Dorset were with other Woodvilles in sanctuary, and Sir Edward Woodville was at sea, fleeing to Brittany. If the Woodvilles could have ever been considered to be among the so-called overmighty magnates, it is noteworthy that they had collapsed in the space of three weeks. Their power was entirely dependent on the presence of a living King Edward IV, whereas the power of Gloucester was independent and much more effective. There were probably harsh words between the Queen Mother and the council representatives; they refused to return to the sanctuary and try a second time to persuade her to leave. It is not difficult to imagine that Elizabeth told them all they were being duped. But the councillors would not have liked the alternative: a hostile confrontation with the Lord Protector.

However, Gloucester must have had considerable concerns about his own position. In three years' time, the king would be old enough to assume power in his own right, and in the meantime, Gloucester had greatly alienated the king. He had arrested the king's governor, Anthony Woodville; he had postponed the early coronation planned for 4 May 1483; and he had detained the king in the Tower against his royal will. It is said that conversations between the Lord Protector and King Edward

V were tense and unfriendly (Kendall, 2002). Should the Woodvilles ever return to power, Gloucester considered that he would be very much out of favour and in danger for his life. Richard had always believed, wrongly, that the Woodvilles were responsible for the execution of his brother Clarence. Nevertheless, it is true that as late as 5 June 1483, Gloucester continued with plans for the coronation on 22 June 1483; he issued summons to forty squires who were to be knighted into the Order of the Bath for the ceremonial occasion. This may mean that he intended to continue in his role as Lord Protector, but it may also mean that he was disguising his true plans.

Prelude to the Seizure of the Crown by Richard, Duke of Gloucester – the Marriage Contract Story

Soon after the early council meetings in April and May, in early June 1483, Richard the Lord Protector made the final decision to depose the boy King Edward V and assume the throne himself. It is believed that this decision was based on the proposition that the marriage of King Edward IV and Elizabeth Woodville was invalid, due to the alleged existence of a prior marriage contract binding Edward IV with a certain English lady. Although not clear to observers in early June 1483, it was suggested later in June 1483 that this person was Lady Eleanor Butler, the widowed daughter of John Talbot, the first earl of Shrewsbury. It was assumed that this marriage contract was made in the year 1461, soon after Edward IV became king. Although there was no precise date suggested, this would have made Edward's 1464 marriage to Elizabeth Woodville bigamous and therefore invalid – and it would have made all the children of this marriage illegitimate, including young Edward V, who was therefore not entitled to be king. According to fifteenth-century canon law, a marriage contract was a binding agreement to marry and carried the same significance as a formal marriage. Based on an alleged valid marriage contract, it could be suggested that Edward IV was first married in the year 1461.

As far as it is possible to tell, no legitimate documentation or other substantiation for this alleged marriage contract, direct or indirect, was available in early June 1483 when the decision was apparently made by the council. And it is noteworthy that no supportive evidence has since appeared in the long history of England. Not only was there no precise date on which the alleged contract was made, but also there was no suggested place at which it was agreed. At the time in 1483, the two parties to the alleged contract were both deceased. Neither had ever acknowledged the alleged marriage in public during their lifetimes, so far as is known. As mentioned, there is no good evidence that Lady Eleanor Butler was named in early June 1483. Either Stillington did not name anybody, which seems unlikely, or Lady Eleanor's name was not reported in the minutes – or it was not leaked by anybody who attended the meeting. As there was no conclusive proof for the alleged 1461 marriage contract, that should have been the end of the matter. But it was not. It suited Richard's decision to depose the young king and assume the throne.

In the literature, this marriage contract is often referred to as a pre-contract, meaning a marriage contract made before a second, bigamous marriage. The author has chosen to refer to it as a marriage contract or simply as a contract, and to sometimes specify the year it was allegedly made or the alleged bride's name. This alleged contract agreement was considered in canon law to be just as binding as a formal marriage.

The Statements by Philippe de Commines

The historical notion that Gloucester and his council, in early June 1483, believed that the marriage contract was made with Lady Eleanor Butler was claimed to be derived from the report of the chronicler Philippe de Commines (1447–1511), writing ten years later in 1493. But about this there must remain considerable doubt. According to Commines, the marriage contract story was introduced by Robert Stillington, the bishop of Bath and Wells; actually, Commines did not name Stillington but described him as the bishop of Bath, who is known to have been Robert Stillington. Commines's account of the bishop's allegation is quoted as follows:

> This Bishop [of Bath] affirmed, that King Edward, being in love with a lady which [who] he named [in fact, no name was stated in the text], and otherwise unable to have his desires of her, had promised her marriage, and caused him [Stillington] to contract them [Edward and the lady]; upon which he [Edward] enjoyed her, though his promise was only to delude her (Commines, 1817).

It should be noted that this description was written in 1493 after all the events of 1483 had occurred. The part played by Lady Eleanor had allegedly been suggested and possibly confirmed.

Elsewhere, in a translation from the French made by Michael Jones (1972), the above quotation is given as follows:

> This bishop [of Bath] revealed to the Duke of Gloucester that King Edward, being very enamoured of a certain English lady [again, not named in the text], promised to marry her, provided that he could sleep with her first, and she consented. The Bishop said that he had married them when only he and they were present. He [the bishop] was a courtier so he did not disclose this fact [the marriage] but helped to keep the lady quiet and things remained like this for a while (Commines, 1972).

Again, it should be noted that Commines was writing in 1493, ten years after all the events of 1483.

For those who are sceptical, these statements seem to establish that it was the bishop of Bath who made the allegation about an earlier marriage contract. But that is about all. Lady Eleanor Butler does not seem to be definitely named in early June 1483, when the council decision to seriously consider deposing Edward V was made. And, there is no date or place given for the marriage contract. This means that the alleged date for the marriage contract (1461) was an assumption; this does not necessarily mean the assumption was wrong, but it suggests considerable uncertainty for something as important as a contract. The time when the bishop of Bath was speaking before the council does not seem clear, either, but it is generally assumed to have been in early June 1483, about the time when Gloucester made up his mind about assuming the throne.

The alleged marriage contract was kept secret, which proved to be a problem. The stated time period for which the secret about the alleged marriage contract was kept was described as "for a while," but it turned out to be nearly twenty-two years (1461–83), enough time for both parties to die.

It is not clear where Commines obtained his information, but almost certainly it came from Stillington, maybe indirectly, since Commines was writing in 1493 and had access to all the events, rumours, and conclusions of 1483 and 1484. But in a notation, Sir Clements Markham (1906) claimed that the bishop "told Commines" that afterwards Stillington had married Edward and Lady Eleanor. If that is the case, then it suggests there was a conversation, or an exchange of messages, between the two men. The date on which this communication occurred is not known, but if it was 1461, then Commines, born in 1447, was a young man, only fourteen years old, which suggests that the exchange more likely occurred in 1483. None of the English chroniclers seemed to be in possession of such information in early June 1483. It is not clear why the bishop would have given the information to a Flemish chronicler and not, apparently, to any English chronicler. It has been suggested that, possibly, Commines made a fact-finding visit to England in 1483, when he received his information from Bishop Stillington ("Richard III," 2013), but it is difficult to confirm such a visit to England. Presumably, for fear of contradiction, Commines did not put any name on paper. It is likely that Commines, writing in 1493, worried that Stillington might not have been truthful; Commines stated that if the story were true, then "this malicious prelate [had] smothered this revenge in his heart [for] near twenty years."

The Council Meetings of Early June 1483

According to Sir Clements Markham (1906), the contract story was presented to the council on 8 June 1483 by Robert Stillington, the bishop of Bath and Wells, an expert in canon law, but a prelate possibly hostile to Edward IV. Stillington declared that King Edward IV had made a marriage contract with a woman, assumed by Sir Clements Markham to be Lady Eleanor Butler, in exchange for sexual favours. Sir Clements did not know that it was Lady Eleanor in early June 1483, as there was no such documented report or any other substantiation available at that time. Obviously, Sir Clements knew what was established in later June 1483, so he assumed that it was Lady Eleanor in early June. It is obviously distasteful that such a poorly documented contract was soon to be used for the purpose of deposing a lawful king of England.

Stillington said that he was present when Edward made the marriage contract promise, and he also said that King Edward then slept with the lady. Either soon after this or at an unspecified interval later, Stillington married Edward and the lady when nobody else was present. So, for the alleged marriage contract, Stillington was apparently the solitary witness; and for the alleged formal private marriage, Stillington was apparently priest, without any witness at all. Commines wrote that Stillington kept the matter secret and persuaded the lady to do the same.

The absence of a witness for the formal private marriage is exceedingly difficult to understand, as Stillington would have certainly known that several witnesses were required for a formal marriage to be valid, especially one involving the king of England. Some authors continue to believe that an ordained priest would marry a king of England in secret, in the absence even of a single witness. But many authors do not believe any such thing and consider the formal marriage part of the story to be entirely false, a concocted invention (Okerlund, 2005). Many of these sceptics might reasonably also suggest exactly the same of the alleged marriage contract part of the story.

As the formal marriage story was not viable, even in the eyes of the council, the important agreement in history became the alleged marriage contract story, for which Stillington was apparently the sole witness. It is reasonable to assume, as that is how the council also would have interpreted the allegations. It should be noted that there was no second or other witness to confirm the story of the contract. The king never told anybody else he was married, nor did Edward treat Lady Eleanor in a way which suggested they were married. As we have seen, the savvy earl of Warwick, searching for a French bride in 1464, obviously did not believe that King Edward was married at that time. Nor did anybody else.

Again according to Sir Clements Markham (1906), Stillington, on 9 June 1483, presented to the council "instruments, authentic doctors, proctors and notaries of the law with depositions of diverse witnesses" to prove his case. It appears that Bishop Stillington must have thought that such documents were necessary to establish a valid marriage contract made in 1461. He must have realized that his solitary assertion of a marriage contract would not be sufficient. Or, it is possible that the council might have suggested to him that better supportive evidence was required or that, perhaps, a second witness to the contract would be reassuring. For the sake of simplicity, it seems reasonable to make a huge assumption and guess that one or several persons signed sworn depositions before attorneys to the effect that they considered Edward and Lady Eleanor to be married prior to 1464. However, there has never been the slightest suggestion of a second eyewitness to the alleged 1461 marriage contract, other than Bishop Stillington. It would be remarkable if a marriage contract were considered valid if supported by only a single witness. All manner of corruption would be possible if that were true, especially in matters of inheritance.

For his authority concerning the above-mentioned proofs, Sir Clements Markham quoted Bishop Morton's providing to Richard Grafton, many years later, an account of a conversation that Bishop Morton had with the duke of Buckingham, as described in *Edward Hall's Chronicle* (Ellis, Grafton, and Hall, 1809). The statement about the proofs was made by Buckingham, who also stated that, although he believed the proofs at first, he later realized that the depositions were fakes. Buckingham is quoted as follows: "He [Gloucester] then brought in [to the council meeting] instruments, authentic doctors, proctors and notaries of the law, with depositions of diverse witnesses, testifying King Edward's children to be bastards, which depositions then I thought to be as true, as now I know them to be fayned [false], and testified by persons with rewards untruly subornate [suborned]."

If Buckingham himself said the documents were false, then this testimony can hardly be considered reliable. But it should be noted that Buckingham changed his opinion much later, sometime after June 1483, so the council in early June 1483 might well have accepted the documents. The nature of the documentary evidence has never been revealed, which makes it very difficult to believe that it was legitimate. There is no mention that Stillington was cross-examined by members of the council about his original assertion of a 1461 marriage contract or about the source of the alleged supportive documentary evidence, although such cross-examination cannot be excluded.

These sensational events, possibly before the council meeting in early June 1483, were not reported by any contemporary English chronicler. There were apparently no leaks concerning this astonishing testimony by those at the council meeting. The historical record is dependent on the ten-year-old 1493 account given by Commines as described, as well as the above-mentioned conversation much later described in *Edward Hall's Chronicle* (1809). It is commonly believed that Lady Eleanor Butler was named by Bishop Stillington in early June, but that does not seem at all

80

clear from Commines's written account. And if he was writing in 1493, then he would have known that the lady of the alleged contract was indeed Lady Eleanor Butler, as was better established later, in June 1483.

The Croyland Chronicler, in his 1486 account, did name Lady Eleanor Butler, but his account described the events of later June 1483 and also 1484, when more information was available and, conceivably, the potentially false story had been better refined. At the time when the council made its decision to invalidate the marriage of Edward and Elizabeth, in early June 1483, it is not clear who was specifically identified. We must simply assume that the council thought it was the deceased Lady Eleanor Butler. Later in June, on 22 June 1483, and again on 24 June 1483, two close confederates of Gloucester stated in public speeches that it was Elizabeth Lucy who was contracted to the king before the 1464 Woodville marriage (More, 2005). A day later, on 25 June 1483, in a speech at Westminster Hall, the duke of Buckingham said it was Lady Eleanor Butler who was contracted (*Croyland Chronicle,* 1854). Dame Elizabeth Lucy, one of Edward's best-known concubines, was still alive in 1483. So, by late June 1483, it is possible that the bishop of Bath and Richard, Duke of Gloucester, sensing a problem with Elizabeth Lucy, decided that the deceased Lady Eleanor Butler was a better choice of invented bride for the invented 1461 contract. Elizabeth Lucy was much closer to the king in his affections, but it may have become apparent to Gloucester that Elizabeth Lucy had denied any such contract in 1464, prior to the king's Woodville marriage. In fact, it seems reasonable to speculate that Cecily, the dowager duchess of York, may have told Gloucester so, since it was she who questioned Elizabeth Lucy in 1464 before the Woodville marriage (More, 2005).

The minutes of the above council meetings of 8 and 9 June were unfortunately lost or possibly destroyed, but a letter covering the council meeting on 9 June 1483 had been published, written by Simon Stallworthe (Kingsbridge, 2006), a secretary for Bishop John Russell. It indicates that the council meeting of 9 June 1483 discussed plans for the forthcoming coronation of Edward V on 22 June 1483, as would be expected; but there was no mention of the supposed astonishing testimony given by Bishop Stillington the previous day on 8 June 1483, let alone the alleged documentary proofs presented on 9 June 1483. Some have suggested that the information was so sensational that Stallworthe would have refrained from mentioning it to his friend Sir William Stonor, to whom the letter was written. But many critics are unable to believe that proposition. It seems reasonable to assume that Sir Clements Markham set the dates for the Stillington testimony before council, according to the Stallworthe letter to Sir William Stonor, but no direct association can be shown between the dates and the contract story. Stallworthe only said that the council discussed plans about the coronation.

For those who have remained doubtful of this whole story, the absence of a precise date and a precise place for the 1461 marriage contract, the uncertainty about whether or not Lady Eleanor Butler was named at the council meeting in early June 1483, and the inability to discover the nature of any supportive documentary evidence, including that of a second witness for the contract, have aroused very considerable suspicion – in fact, total disbelief – in many. Unfortunately, the problem for the boy King Edward V was that, even with the above-mentioned serious deficiencies, the story was considered believable, based on Edward IV's notorious promiscuity. It is noteworthy, indeed disgraceful, that none of the prelates on the council came to the defence of the lawful boy king. If the bishops had joined together and threatened Richard with excommunication, as was certainly justified, then the course of English history might well have been different. Perhaps the bishops were unwilling to challenge the testimony of another bishop.

Nevertheless, from about 10 June 1483, no doubt encouraged by Gloucester, the council proceeded to act on the notion that Edward IV's marriage to Elizabeth Woodville was invalid, based on the above-discussed unsubstantiated story, whatever its validity. Therefore, Edward V was not a rightful king. This change by the council would be consistent with the dates suggested by Sir Clements Markham, but the information is far from precise. However, if Stillington did not relate such a story before the council, as seems quite likely to be the case, then it would be reasonable to believe that Richard introduced the story himself at around this same time, based on his private conversations with Stillington, and that the duke of Buckingham came to be in agreement, at least initially, before later changing his mind. So, Richard consolidated his plans to assume the throne.

Setting aside the numerous reasons not to believe the presented contract story, it is seriously doubtful that the council had the authority to effectively invalidate the marriage of the deceased King Edward IV. Even in our own time, let alone in the Middle Ages, only the Church could set aside a marriage performed by a Catholic priest. This would have been especially so in the case of a king of England, even more so in the case of a dead king of England. The testimony had not been heard by an ecclesiastical law court, and Richard and his legal advisors almost certainly knew that the supportive evidence, such as it was, would never stand up in such a hearing. If an ecclesiastical law court had heard the case, then at least some reasonable supportive evidence would have been required. No such evidence was ever found or proven ever to have existed.

There is a closely related reason why the problem was not reviewed by an ecclesiastical law court. The court would not have accepted Stillington's solitary assertion about a marriage contract, as the canon law would have required a second witness before accepting the alleged 1461 contract as an established fact (Helmholz, 1974). What is more, the entire onus would have been on Gloucester to prove his case; otherwise, the default conclusion of the court would certainly have favoured the well-established, nineteen-year-old, valid marriage of King Edward IV and Queen Elizabeth Woodville. So, the Lord Protector and his confederates never went down that path. They understood they would lose in an ecclesiastical law court. Perhaps this was explained to Gloucester by one or more of the bishops. But for this postulated conversation, there was never any evidence.

Based on the lack of an ecclesiastical law court's ruling upon the matter, it is reasonable to conclude that the Stillington allegation about a marriage contract was entirely unsubstantiated. Nevertheless, there is no evidence that the frightened bishops on the council defended the legitimacy of the new king. Such was their fear of minority government and their quite reasonable and growing fear of the duke of Gloucester and his magnate supporters. The Woodville faction would not have been pleased with the news of this audacious conclusion by the council; but after these council meetings in early June 1483, probably 10 June 1483, the administrative decisions were no longer released under the privy seal of the uncrowned King Edward V.

In the meantime, to further his cause, Gloucester divided the council into committees and held meetings at different locations, such as Westminster Palace, the Tower of London, Baynard Castle, Crosby Hall, and other, individual homes. In this way, he could hide his intentions from those who he knew opposed him and search out those likely to support his plans to depose Edward V and assume the throne himself.

Richard, Duke of Gloucester, Moves Ahead with His Plans for the Usurpation

On 10 June 1483, Gloucester sent letters to the city of York asking that northern troops be sent to London to give him support, because the Queen Mother Elizabeth was plotting to murder him and his supporters. This was the same Elizabeth who was almost helpless in sanctuary at the abbey. The fact that Richard needed to send for northern troops is good evidence for the unpopularity of his position in London. As Richard was considered a northerner, some authors like to suggest that the potential conflict at this time was a north-versus-south problem, a sort of English version of the American Civil War (Drewett and Redhead, 1984). It is an interesting exaggeration.

At this stage, with a decision to seize the crown made, the supporters of Gloucester included Lord John Howard, anxious to procure his inheritance, namely the duchy of Norfolk, which Edward IV had denied him; Henry Stafford, the second duke of Buckingham, anxious to further increase his inheritance with the Hereford estate, which Edward had denied him; Viscount Francis Lovell, a long-time friend of Richard, anxious for promotion within the new government; Bishop Robert Stillington, a former chancellor of England, still hoping for the restoration of his previous political influence; John de la Pole, Richard's nephew, the earl of Lincoln, perhaps calculating that his own path to the throne might be accelerated if young Edward V was deposed; and Thomas Langton, a cleric, later appointed to be the bishop of St David's.

The boy king's supporters included William Hastings, the lord chamberlain; John Morton, the bishop of Ely; Thomas, Lord Stanley, the steward of the royal household; Thomas Rotherham, the Archbishop of York; Thomas Bourchier, the elderly Archbishop of Canterbury; and, of course, what was left of the obliterated Woodville faction. Reluctantly, they supported Richard as Lord Protector, but definitely not Richard,

Duke of Gloucester, as king. Unfortunately for young King Edward V, both Hastings and Stanley were rather ambivalent with their support, and not one of the bishops was prepared to tell Richard that his proposal was illegal (and unconstitutional) in the absence of an ecclesiastical law court decision. And they all knew that the Lord Protector's proposal, being a matter of inheritance, would later require an act of Parliament.

The Murder of Sir William Hastings on 13 June 1483, and the Hastings Conspiracy

At a meeting of the partial council at the Tower on 13 June 1483, Lord Hastings, who disagreed with the planned usurpation, was accused of conspiracy and treason. He was seized by Richard's soldiers, taken outside in the Tower garden, and executed without delay and without trial. Morton and Rotherham were briefly imprisoned in the Tower. Stanley, who needed medical attention for a cut on his head obtained when he tried to escape the commotion, was placed under house arrest at his London residence. It would appear that soon after, he, too, was sent to the Tower. Morton was sent to Wales to be held in the custody of the duke of Buckingham, and Rotherham was placed under the close supervision of Sir James Tyrell. Gloucester felt that he needed to be careful in how he treated the prelates who opposed him. Jane Shore, the mistress of Hastings who may have carried messages to the Queen Mother in the sanctuary, was made to do penance in the streets of London before being imprisoned at Ludgate. She, an attractive woman walking half dressed, aroused enormous sympathy among the people. The council was astonished and suitably intimidated by these outrageous acts.

Not believing that the Church would protect them any longer, Thomas Grey, the marquis of Dorset, and Lionel Woodville, the bishop of Salisbury, left the sanctuary at Westminster and fled into hiding elsewhere. The government hunted for Dorset with bloodhounds, but without success. Some other authorities, including Sir Clements Markham (1906) and Bertram Fields (1998), believed that Hastings was first imprisoned, then properly tried, and then executed on 20 June 1483, a week later. This would be a scenario more favourable to the reputation of Richard, Duke of Gloucester, but only slightly so. In any event, it is unlikely to have been accomplished in a week. Further, there were many witnesses, and the account of Bishop Morton has always been accepted.

Before all this happened, it is probably true that Hastings supported King Edward V, did have conversations with the boy king at the Tower, and did have communications with the Queen Mother in the sanctuary, some possibly through Jane Shore. But he was still trying to make up his mind about the proper disposition of authority in England. His actions were not treasonous because Edward V, not Richard, was king at that point in time. This was so according to the Act of Treasons passed in 1351 during the reign of Edward III. It is believed that Hastings discussed his concerns at a private meeting with Rotherham, Morton, and Stanley, when a plan to release Edward V from the Tower and frustrate Gloucester's plan was considered. But it was decided that such a plan was too dangerous, as it would be an affront to Gloucester, and so it was abandoned. Richard was probably informed of this meeting by Sir William Catesby and reacted decisively against those involved, as we have seen. This was one of the Lord Protector's great strengths – his ability to act decisively. The Croyland Chronicler (1854) was outspoken in his condemnation. In reference to the removal of Hastings, Morton, and Rotherham, the chronicler wrote in 1486: "The three strongest supporters of the new king [Edward V], being thus removed without judgment or justice, and all the rest of his faithful subjects fearing the like treatment, the two dukes [Gloucester and Buckingham] did thenceforth just as they pleased."

But Paul Murray Kendall (2002) described a more organized conspiracy involving Hastings, Morton, Stanley, and Rotherham. He wrote that there was more than just a single meeting and that there was a definite positive plan of action. These men had been at the centre of Edward IV's government, but they were now being pushed aside by Gloucester, Buckingham, and Howard. Kendall called them the "quadrumvirate of the dispossessed." They conferred with the king in the Tower and with the Woodvilles in the sanctuary, often using Jane Shore, Hastings' mistress, as an intermediary with the Queen Mother. It was alleged that they planned a strike against Gloucester, probably an assassination, followed by the release of the king from the Tower. Buckingham warned Richard of the danger; the Lord Protector knew that his life was threatened. As with most conspiracies, it is difficult to know the evidence. But it explains why Richard called for northern troops in his letter of 10 June 1483 and why he reacted with such ruthlessness against Hastings on 13 June 1483. On balance, it must be admitted that the Kendall proposal for the so-called Hastings Conspiracy seems likely.

The Removal of Prince Richard from the Sanctuary on 16 June 1483, with His Transfer to the Tower

On 16 June 1483, the Queen Mother Elizabeth was persuaded by Thomas Bourchier, the Archbishop of Canterbury, accompanied by several lords of the council, including Buckingham and Howard, and by the presence of more armed soldiers surrounding the abbey sanctuary, to allow Richard of Shrewsbury, her second son, to leave the sanctuary and join Edward V at the Tower Palace. No doubt, Elizabeth was told that the coronation of Edward V was being planned and that Prince Richard needed to be prepared. The Queen Mother would probably never have agreed to the transfer of her younger son if the executions of Anthony Woodville, Richard Grey, and Thomas Vaughan had already occurred at Pontefract. As described by Arlene Okerlund (2005), quoting Sir Thomas More (2005), the multiple arguments for the transfer of the prince were only partly convincing. It seems notable that the council feared that Elizabeth was inciting the hatred of the people against the nobles of the council; they feared that Elizabeth might send Prince Richard safely out of the country; and they implied that the young prince did not need sanctuary since he had committed no offence. But the small boy had committed an offence by his very birth; he was the heir to a throne threatened by usurpation and regicide, and he could be declared king in his own right if his older brother, King Edward V, should die. It is notable that popular resentment against the government was mentioned and used as an argument in favour of taking custody of young Prince Richard.

The Queen Mother, a single woman resistant, made multiple brilliant arguments for her position against the power of the gathered Lords spiritual and temporal of England. She declared that there were three laws which allowed her to keep her son: (1) English law that the mother was the guardian of her children; (2) nature's law that the mother should keep the issue of her body; and (3) God's law that provided sanctuary for her son when threatened with possible harm (Vergil, 1844). The archbishop knew only too well that harm to the heir might result; he knew that he was defeated, so he solemnly pledged his own body and soul for the surety of the prince (Okerlund, 2005). At that point, Elizabeth could no longer refuse. But the archbishop would later not be able to keep his solemn promise.

Against all her true and just instincts, Elizabeth conceded to Archbishop Bourchier, a trusted friend of herself and her beloved husband. It was a huge mistake, but the pressure was enormous and it appeared that, with the gathered force outside, she had little choice. There followed a sad and pathetic parting, a mother from her ten-year-old son, much to the shame of the royal government. Young Richard was sent to the Tower Palace to join his older brother, King Edward V. Neither boy ever left the Tower alive; suggestions that later they lived at Sheriff Hutton Castle in Yorkshire, or that young Richard later escaped to Flanders, remain without any serious foundation despite the best efforts of some historians.

Around the same time that Prince Richard was transferred from the sanctuary to the Tower Palace, Gloucester arranged for the eight-year-old Edward, the seventeenth earl of Warwick, and also the heir of Clarence, to be sent to the household of his wife, Anne, the duchess of Gloucester, at Crosby Hall in London; there, the boy could be better controlled and supervised. Not long after, in September 1483, young Warwick was sent to Sheriff Hutton Castle in Yorkshire for still-closer supervision. The seventeenth earl of Warwick was a lawful male heir to the throne, next in line following Richard of Shrewsbury and ahead of Richard, Duke of Gloucester. Soon after these events, on 17 June 1483, the two princes in the Tower were deprived of nearly all their attendants and sent deep into the internal chambers of the Tower for a much more severe form of detention. King Edward V was less often seen by observers; the king and Prince Richard were then in the Tower prison, no longer in the Tower Palace.

As his confidence in the situation grew, Richard, Duke of Gloucester, began to behave with increasing royal munificence, parading through London in royal purple robes and entertaining lavishly at Crosby Hall, attempting to build political support for himself. When Dominic Mancini was safely home in Europe, he wrote of these events: "When he [Richard] exhibited himself through the streets of the city[,] he was scarcely watched by anybody, rather did they curse him with a fate worse than his crimes, since no one now doubted at what he was aiming" (Mancini, 1989). Some defenders of Richard assert that Richard was not unpopular at this time.

Mancini, an Italian cleric, may not have been a good witness for some of the political activity, but he was a reliable observer of the English people. At this point, Richard's crimes were as follows: seizure of the king's person against his royal will, strict detention of both princes in the Tower prison, the illegal arrest of Anthony Woodville and his comrades, the execution of Lord Hastings without trial, and the close detention of Morton, Stanley, and Rotherham.

The Cancellation of the Meeting of Parliament and of the Coronation of King Edward V

Also, on or about 17 June 1483, the planned meeting of Parliament was cancelled. For those who supported Edward V, this was a very serious problem, as a properly constituted Parliament, particularly one with a full House of Commons present, might well have interrogated Bishop Stillington and defended the boy king. Such a body might have suggested that the validity of Edward IV's 1464 marriage be decided by a church court, in keeping with the usual custom. It might have also encouraged the bishops on the council to be more forthcoming. There may be some doubt about this cancellation, as it is infrequently mentioned, but it is an historical fact that King Edward V had no Parliament during his short reign of seventy-seven days, and that King Richard III had only a single Parliament that met in January 1484, not in June 1483, before he was king ("List of Parliaments of England," 2014). Sir Clements Markham (1906) claimed that the cancellation was not issued with the consent of Gloucester but by his remaining opponents on the council. Markham described the document as a supersedeas, an order superseding the previous orders. Mancini said that the order arrived at York on 21 June 1483, indicating a passage of four days from London. Other historians have been plain; Richard ordered the cancellation (Smith, 1894). Bishop John Russell, the chancellor of England, had prepared a speech with which he planned to open Parliament representing the king, but his speech was never given, although copies remain in existence. Russell recommended that Gloucester should remain Lord Protector beyond the coronation, until Edward V came of an age sufficient to take over and rule for himself. That was what Gloucester more or less had originally intended, but it was not consistent with Gloucester's more recent plans to make himself king. It is a shame that a proper Parliament never met in 1483; the course of English history might have been different. English law was not precise about the age of majority, perhaps taking into account individual variation. Henry VI ruled as king at the age of sixteen years; Edward IV had nominated fourteen years when young Edward no longer needed supervision as the Prince of Wales (St Aubyn, 1983); and age fifteen years might have been a good suggestion for a well-trained prince like Edward V.

Soon after the cancellation of Parliament, maybe on 18 June 1483, the coronation of Edward V, which had been set for 22 June 1483, was postponed indefinitely. The English people were not pleased with these developments. It was clear to many that Gloucester had made up his mind about seizing the throne. At this time, too, Gloucester sent orders to Pontefract for Anthony Woodville, Richard Grey, and Thomas Vaughan to be executed. This had specifically not been authorized by the council, although defenders of Richard III have claimed that the council did later authorize the executions (Drewett and Redhead, 1984). In the absence of a proper trial procedure, this seems most unlikely.

Richard must have felt increasing confidence as he now had all important claimants to the throne under his control. Killing young Edward V alone would not suffice, as young Richard, Duke of York, would be proclaimed king in that event. Killing both of Elizabeth Woodville's boys might not suffice, either, as the seventeenth earl of Warwick, the heir of Clarence, might be proclaimed king. But Gloucester controlled young Warwick, too. They all had a better claim to the crown than did the Lord Protector, the youngest of the sons of Richard, the third duke of York, who died in 1460. But Richard, Duke of Gloucester, by then had made adequate preparations. He had still not made up his mind about the disposition of the princes, but he must have been aware that previous deposed kings of England had all been murdered, namely Richard II, Edward II, and Henry VI. And he may have also known about Prince Arthur, heir to King Richard I, who was murdered in 1203, allegedly by King John.

CHAPTER 5

The Beginning of the End of the Short Reign of King Edward V

The Speech by Dr Shaw at St Paul's Church

On Sunday 22 June 1483, Dr Ralph Shaw, a distinguished Cambridge-educated theologian, the half-brother of the Lord Mayor of London, accompanied by Gloucester and Buckingham, gave an open-air sermon in front of St Paul's Church. It is said that the theme of Shaw's sermon was taken from the Book of Wisdom in the Apocrypha (chapter four, verse three), quoted as follows: "But the prolific brood of the ungodly will be of no use, and none of their illegitimate seedlings will strike a deep root or take a firm hold" (Coogan, 2010).

In the sermon, it was claimed that both King Edward IV and George, Duke of Clarence, were not the legitimate sons of Richard, the third duke of York, who died in 1460. This appeared to be based on the notion that both Edward and George were tall and physically well built, whereas Richard was short and slightly built like the third duke of York. Also, Richard's facial features more closely resembled those of his father. To quote Sir Thomas More (2005):

> Neither King Edward himself nor the Duke of Clarence, among those that were secret [placed] in the household [of the duke of York], were reckoned very surely for [to be] the children of the noble Duke, as those that by their favours more resembled other known men than him [the duke of York], from

91

whose virtuous conditions he said that King Edward was far off [did not closely resemble].

This implies that both Edward and George were not legitimate children of their father and that Edward IV's heirs, Princes Edward and Richard, and Clarence's heir, the seventeenth earl of Warwick, could not inherit the throne. This made Richard, Duke of Gloucester, the only rightful king, unless the earl of Lincoln, the son of Elizabeth, Richard's older sister, was also considered. It appeared to be a very effective argument since it destroyed nearly all of the serious targets with a single blow. It was probably the argument which Richard, Duke of Gloucester, favoured for its simplicity and efficiency; furthermore, Richard had long doubted the legitimate birth of Edward IV, in agreement with his cousin, the deceased sixteenth earl of Warwick, and others. This was, however, a common accusation in the Middle Ages. For instance, the famous John of Gaunt was often accused of not being a legitimate son of King Edward III. The accusation was even more common for people not born in England. Edward IV was born in Normandy, and John of Gaunt was born in Flanders at Ghent (Gaunt). But there appeared to be an important problem with the argument, one sufficient enough to invalidate it; the dowager duchess of York, in London for the coronation of her grandson Edward V, made loud public objection regarding the serious insult to herself concerning the alleged serial adultery. In other words, she denied the assertion. And, for the record, it should be noted that the first specific public assertion made by a confederate of the duke of Gloucester in this matter was an openly contradicted lie.

Perhaps anticipating the difficulty with Cecily, elsewhere in his sermon, according to Sir Thomas More, Dr Shaw also claimed that Edward IV's 1464 marriage was invalid on the basis of the 1461 marriage contract story, but he seemed to think that the bride in the marriage contract was Dame Elizabeth Lucy, one of the better-known concubines of Edward IV. To quote Sir Thomas More (2005): "He [Dr Shaw] declared then that King Edward was never lawfully married to the queen, but was, before God, husband to Dame Elizabeth Lucy, and so his children bastards."

Why the protagonists of the Lord Protector resorted to the first story – that both Edward IV and Clarence were illegitimate and that their mother had committed serial adultery – is not immediately clear. After all, it is believed that the council meetings of early June 1483 had been concerned with the marriage contract story. There must have developed serious concerns about that contract story. One problem with the 1461 contract story was that it only affected Edward V and Richard of Shrewsbury; it did not affect the son of Clarence, the seventeenth earl of Warwick, whose claim was still better than that of Richard, Duke of Gloucester.

It is noteworthy that Lady Eleanor Butler was not mentioned at this time, only later, as we shall see; at least that is the conclusion drawn in the account of Sir Thomas More (2005) and others. It is tempting to believe that in the preparatory discussions before this sermon, with Richard and his confederates, that it was Elizabeth Lucy who was described as the alleged 1461 bride of Edward IV, not Lady Eleanor Butler, as might have been suggested by Bishop Stillington. It should be noted that some accounts (Weir, 1999; St Aubyn, 1983) suggest that Dr Shaw on 22 June 1483 did not mention a problem with Edward IV's marriage, but he confined himself to the matter of the alleged adultery of Edward's mother, the dowager duchess of York. Strangely, that might suggest that the Stillington testimony of early June 1483 was completely ignored, at least temporarily.

It was no surprise that the sermon of 22 June 1483 was not well received by the people, as there was no applause. According to Sir Thomas More, the people "stood as though they had been turned into stone, for wonder of this shameful sermon." Many left in tears. Most people departed mystified. The reception for Dr Shaw's sermon was so bad that the theologian soon regretted his claims and was mortified by his mistake; he disappeared from public view and died less than a year later, many said from shame. The defenders of Richard III would prefer not to hear about the public's reaction to Dr Shaw.

On the same Sunday, similar sermons were given by other prelates in London, with similar misconceptions and similarly unhappy results. According to Mancini (1489), most of these other sermons were concerned with the illegitimacy of Edward IV himself and his mother's alleged adultery. Because the reception was so bad and the dowager duchess of York was so outraged, the notion that Edward IV himself was illegitimate was quietly dropped, in favour of the 1461 marriage contract argument. Alison Weir (1999) wrote that Richard's supporters would later use the argument that Edward himself was illegitimate to help establish Richard's title to the crown. And soon they would need to take into account the seventeenth earl of Warwick, whose superior claim to the throne was unimpaired by the 1461 marriage contract story. They would need to introduce the claim that Clarence could not inherit because of his 1478 attainder and execution, and hence his son young Warwick could not inherit, either.

The Speech by the Duke of Buckingham at the London Guildhall

Two days after Dr Shaw's speech, on Tuesday 24 June 1483, Buckingham gave an eloquent address at the London Guildhall before the Lord Mayor of London, the gathered aldermen, and other important citizens, in which he claimed that the marriage of Edward IV and Queen Elizabeth Woodville was invalid for the following reasons, in order: (1) it was secret with no published banns; (2) the church was unconsecrated; (3) the consent of the lords was not obtained; (4) the Woodvilles used sorcery to persuade the king; and (5) there was an earlier marriage contract which made the marriage to Elizabeth Woodville bigamous and, thus, invalid. In fact, according to Arlene Okerlund (2005), quoting Sir Thomas More, Buckingham did not mention Lady Eleanor Butler but claimed that the marriage contract was with Dame Elizabeth Lucy. According to Arlene Okerlund, again quoting Sir Thomas More, Buckingham claimed: "The children of King Edward IV were not legally begotten, forasmuch as the king, leaving his wife Dame Elizabeth Lucy, was never lawfully married unto their mother."

Accepting Sir Thomas More's account, it seems that neither Shaw nor Buckingham could keep his concocted story straight. They both thought that Elizabeth Lucy was Edward's bride at the 1461 contract. But eventually, on the next day, Buckingham would finally get it right – or as Gloucester and his confederates had most recently decided!

In fact, none of the above-mentioned factors described by Buckingham would have invalidated a marriage, with the exception of a 1461 marriage contract, provided it was *not* with Dame Elizabeth Lucy, who was known to have issued, earlier in 1464, a denial of any such contract. And, again, it is reasonable to ask why the marriage contract was only mentioned last by Buckingham, after the other extremely lame reasons. Other reports suggest a different order for the reasons, but all consistently place the 1461 marriage contract story last.

Of course, Edward and Elizabeth did have witnesses for their marriage; Jacquetta Woodville had seen to that in 1464. The dowager duchess of Bedford apparently knew as much about the canon law as the embittered Bishop Stillington did. Perhaps in partial defence of Dr Shaw, a well-educated theologian, it should be noted that he did not mention secrecy, lack of a proper church, lack of official assent, or sorcery as reasons to consider Edward IV's 1464 Woodville marriage invalid. He knew that none of those factors invalidated a marriage. Dr Shaw noted only the 1461 alleged marriage contract, but he had the name of the alleged bride wrong, very possibly because that is what he had been told to say.

At the guildhall, the people of London listened, but they did not cheer. A few of Gloucester's supporters in the audience voiced their agreement, but the response was almost exclusively one of stunned silence or low-murmured complaint. Buckingham said softly to the Lord Mayor, "What means this that these people be so still?"

To this, the Lord Mayor replied, "Sir, percase [perhaps] they perceive you not well." Buckingham repeated his arguments, hoping that they would be better understood. The city magistrate recorder, Sir Thomas FitzWilliam, also reviewed the story for the people. But it made no difference. The people remained silent; they had "never heard such an evil [false] tale so well told."

The duke said to the Lord Mayor, "This is a marvellous obstinate silence." When the meeting was over and the lords departed, they were very sorrowful. According to Sir Thomas More, "They were fain [obliged] at his back [as they left] to turn their face to the wall [attempting to conceal], while the dolour [sorrow] of their heart brast [burst] out at their eyes [i.e. they wept]."

A brilliant public married life such as that of Edward and Elizabeth, with all its beautiful royal children, with all its splendour and religious ceremonies, with all the baptisms, weddings, and funerals, and with all its grand occasions, simply could not be set aside and declared invalid. It made no sense to the English people. But the bad reception did not stop Richard, Duke of Gloucester; he was fully committed to his malignant course. And again, the defenders of the last Yorkist king do not want to hear about the equivocal public reaction to the duke of Buckingham's speech.

The 1461 contract story also made illegitimate young Prince Richard in the Tower and all of Edward IV's young daughters, to all of whom Gloucester was closely related as their uncle. It is not possible to exaggerate the utter shamefulness of this story. If Richard was a good and decent man, and there is much evidence presented by his defenders that this was indeed the case, then the contract story must have aroused within his conscience barely tolerable feelings of regret and guilt. Those feelings were repeatedly mentioned by Paul Murray Kendall (2002) in his biography of Richard III. It was a huge conundrum for Gloucester: with one story, he alienated his mother, but with the other story, he alienated his nephews, his nieces, and all the common people who treasured their children.

Some authors more sympathetic to Gloucester have accused Sir Thomas More of deliberately confusing the issue of Dame Elizabeth Lucy. For his authority, Sir Thomas More depended on many people: his father, Sir John More, a London judge; his son-in-law, John Roper, later the Attorney General for Henry VIII; Bishop John Morton; Dr John Argentine; and other of the interviewed witnesses who may have attended these London events in 1483 or heard about them soon after. Perhaps it is possible that their memory was faulty, but memories of such astounding events often remain remarkably clear for a very long time. Maybe there was not much disagreement among them.

There was another problem with the marriage contract story as told that day. It was pointed out by Sir Clements Markham (1906) that if Edward IV and Dame Elizabeth Lucy were legally married, then their children – Arthur, Lord L'Isle; Elizabeth, the lady Lumley; and even young Grace Plantagenet – were legitimate heirs to the throne ahead of the duke of Gloucester. However, Dame Elizabeth Lucy, who was alive in 1483, was known to have specifically denied in 1464, before Edward married Elizabeth Woodville, any such contract (More, 2005). In *Edward Hall's Chronicle* (Ellis, Grafton, and Hall, 1809), it is stated that Edward's mother, the dowager duchess of York, was concerned about the possibility of a marriage contract before Edward married Elizabeth Woodville in 1464. The dowager duchess was concerned not only about Elizabeth Lucy, but also about "diverse other lettes [ladies]." There were prolonged discussions with the king in which other possibilities were considered: "All which doubts were resolved, and all things made clere [clear], and all cauillacions [cavillations, objections] auoyded [avoided, clarified]. And so privately he married her at Grafton, where he first fantasized her visage [met her]."

Allegedly, in these discussions, the king denied that he was married to anybody. This would also cast considerable doubt on other ladies who might be considered as subjects for a marriage contract. Of course, these doubts would also have included Lady Eleanor Butler.

But there were more important problems for Richard, Duke of Gloucester. Most of the common people of England and many of the peers did not believe the concocted marriage contract story. Their resentment would fester and grow. The path was set for the destruction of Richard, Duke of Gloucester, and for the fall of the famous Royal House of York.

The Testimony of Dominic Mancini, Discovered in France in 1933

Here comes yet another version of this sad story. Mancini (1969) claimed that Edward IV, at the intervention of the earl of Warwick, was married by proxy to Princess Bona of Savoy. In the historical notes of his book, Mancini's editor, C. A. J. Armstrong, said that Mancini had accepted a report that Warwick had betrothed and married Edward IV to another woman. As it was well known that Warwick was negotiating such a union in France, it was assumed that Edward had married Princess Bona by proxy in early 1464. But if this had been true, then Warwick would have said so when the Woodville marriage was announced. It is plain that he did not. This suggestion can be easily and confidently rejected. But, more important, it must have been considered at one point in the discussions among Richard's confederates.

Mancini (1989) may be quoted as follows:

> He [Richard] secretly dispatched the Duke of Buckingham to the lords with orders to submit to their decision the disposal of the throne. He [Richard] argued that it would be unjust to crown this lad [Edward V], who was illegitimate, because his father, King Edward IV, on marrying Elizabeth [Woodville], was legally contracted to another wife to whom the Earl of Warwick had joined him. Indeed on Edward's authority the Earl had espoused the other lady by proxy.

It is reasonably clear at which meeting this was considered. Mancini does not mention anywhere Buckingham's speech at the guildhall, which was attended by the Lord Mayor and the aldermen on 24 June 1483. The Mancini quotation most likely refers to the meeting of the Great Council at Westminster on 25 June 1483 (see next page). If Mancini's quotation of Richard is to be accepted, then it suggests that even Richard was not sure about the 1461 contract with Lady Eleanor Butler. Richard seemed to think that possibly young King Edward V was not legitimate because Edward IV was married by proxy to Princess Bona, with Warwick standing in for the king. The multiple suggestions for Edward IV's alleged bride (Lady Eleanor Butler, Dame Elizabeth Lucy, Princess Bona) and the accusations of adultery against Cecily, the dowager duchess of York, indicate the confusion and incoherence in the policy followed by Richard and his confederates – and the strong likelihood that it was all a poorly planned set of lies. There was no proof for any of it.

The Execution of Anthony Woodville and His Companions at Pontefract on 25 June 1483

A day after the guildhall speech, on 25 June 1483, the executions of Anthony Woodville, Richard Grey, and Thomas Vaughan, at Pontefract Castle in Yorkshire, were performed. There was at most a perfunctory hearing before the fourth earl of Northumberland and Sir Richard Ratcliffe, at which none of the prisoners was allowed to speak in his own defence. The eloquent Anthony Woodville would have made short work of the scanty evidence for a plot to kill the Lord Protector on the road to London. As he understood the hatred that Richard apparently held for him, Anthony knew that the outcome of the proceedings was already decided. Anthony had made his last will on 23 June 1483; he appointed as executors the bishops of Lincoln (John Russell) and Worcester (John Alcock), the two chief judges of the King's Bench and the Court of Common Pleas, and six others. Being a most forgiving man, Anthony also politely asked that his executors follow his simple instructions at the pleasure of the duke of Gloucester, who, contrary to what is sometimes claimed, was not named as an executor of Anthony's last will.

The Meeting of the Great Council at Westminster Hall on 25 June 1483 and the Shameful Deposition of the Twelve-Year-Old King Edward V. The Path Is Continued for the Fall of the House of York

On the same day as the Woodville executions, Wednesday 25 June 1483, the duke of Buckingham repeated his speech at Westminster Hall before a gathering of the bishops, the great magnates, the lords, the gentry, and others, this time with the desired effect. If lies are repeated often enough, they come to be accepted. Buckingham opened with a malicious and largely false attack on the government of King Edward IV. Buckingham then moved on to the main argument: Edward IV's marriage to Queen Elizabeth Woodville was invalid for four reasons: (1) there was no official assent from the lords; (2) it was made by means of sorcery; (3) it was made in secrecy without banns; and (4) the king was already contracted and married to Lady Eleanor Butler. The other argument that Edward IV's birth was not legitimate may have been mentioned. It would definitely reappear in the 1484 Titulus Regius (see Chapter 8), which was widely believed to be based on this speech of 25 June 1483.

The first three reasons were not sufficient to invalidate a marriage (see discussion of canon law in Chapter 11), but the alleged contract was a potential problem if it was true. The Croyland Chronicler (1854), referring to the meeting at Westminster Hall, wrote in 1486: "It was set forth, by way of prayer, in an address in a certain Roll of Parchment, that the sons of King Edward were bastards, on the ground that he had contracted a marriage with one Lady Eleanor Butler, before his marriage to Queen Elizabeth."

It appears confirmed that Buckingham used the name of Lady Eleanor Butler on 25 June 1483; the duke finally got the story right, or, more likely, said what he was instructed to say. It is possible that Gloucester asked that Princess Bona also be considered (Mancini, 1989), as suggested above, but Buckingham would have known about Warwick's failure to report any such proxy marriage and therefore did not mention it. If Mancini (1489) is to be believed, then it is more evidence that Richard, Duke of Gloucester, remained unsure about who exactly was the bride in the alleged 1461 marriage contract. As well, he was equally unsure about the very existence of the 1461 contract, given that the postulated proxy marriage to Bona, if true, would have occurred in early 1464, well after the alleged 1461 contract.

Then, Buckingham stated that the children of King Edward IV were "unable to claim anything by inheritance, by the law and custom of England." Next, Buckingham claimed that the seventeenth earl of Warwick could not inherit because of the attainder and execution of the duke of Clarence, his father, in 1478; that attainder had never been reversed. According to Buckingham, it followed that the true heir to the throne was Richard, Duke of Gloucester, the Lord Protector. He was male, legitimate, not dead, and fourth in line following the male heirs of Edward IV and George, Duke of Clarence, namely Edward V, young Richard, and young Warwick, all of whom were now disqualified. As the children of Elizabeth, the duchess of Suffolk, Richard's older sister, were not mentioned, it apparently remained the orthodox custom to exclude inheritance through females, despite the 1460 Act of Accord, which had clearly validated such a mode of inheritance (see Appendix C). Buckingham was not to know that within seventy-five years, there would be two queens regnant of England, Queen Mary I and Queen Elizabeth I.

There does not appear to be a separate account of Buckingham's speech in existence, but it is generally stated that the account given later in the 1484 Titulus Regius followed more or less exactly what the duke said at Westminster that day. There seems no harm in accepting such a suggestion. That means that Lady Eleanor Butler was the alleged bride in question. But it should be noted that in 1483, both Dame Elizabeth Lucy and Princess Bona were alive, and Lady Eleanor was very much dead. The confederates of Gloucester had settled on somebody who could not issue a denial, as had Cecily, the dowager duchess of York, when the adultery story was presented by Dr Shaw. And that may be the same reason why Bishop Stillington used the deceased Lady Eleanor Butler for his concocted tale.

The matter of the bride in the alleged 1461 marriage contract can be summarized briefly as follows: at the council meetings of 8–9 June, it was very possibly Lady Eleanor Butler, but it was not clear at the time and was possibly based on information which only became apparent a few weeks later; at Dr Shaw on 22 June, it was Elizabeth Lucy; at Buckingham on 24 June, it was also Elizabeth Lucy; at the Great Council on 25 June, it was maybe Princess Bona, but much more likely it was Lady Eleanor Butler; and in the Titulus Regius of 1484, it was undoubtedly Lady Eleanor. This all suggests how uncertain the confederates of Richard, Duke of

Gloucester, were. But in the end, they settled on the one who was dead. It strongly suggests that they were never sure.

By the time of the meeting at Westminster on 25 June 1483, northern troops were arriving in London in large numbers, as earlier requested by Gloucester on 10 June 1483, and the populace of London was deeply frightened. It is estimated that five thousand troops were gathered, but maybe not all within the walls of London. And maybe the Londoners' fear was increased by the knowledge that more soldiers were on the way from the north.

The magnates and the lords were in London for the coronation of Edward V, which had earlier been set for 22 June 1483. People had remained in London to hear what the government had to say about the recent astonishing events. The gathering on 25 June 1483 could be called a Great Council of the Realm. The meeting was certainly not a Parliament, as many have suggested. There were no viable writs issued in the name of King Edward V, as the meeting of Parliament had been cancelled on 17 June 1483 with the issue of countermanding writs; there was no king at liberty to open the Parliament with a speech, and Richard, Duke of Gloucester, had refused to play the role; and Chancellor Russell did not give the speech he had prepared in King Edward V's name for the opening of Parliament. There was no act or proceeding placed in the Parliamentary Record at that time. If it was a Parliament, then it would be listed under King Edward V. No such Parliament appears in the historical record ("List of Parliaments of England," 2014).

The only Parliament of Richard's reign occurred in late January 1484, at which time an act of Parliament was certainly placed in the Parliamentary Record. Bertram Fields (1998) called the gathering on 25 June 1483 "the Assembly of the Three Estates," meaning the prelates, the lords, and the commons. This was the view of the famous lawyer, and it avoided use of the term *Parliament,* although that was the impression that he and others undoubtedly wished to convey. Some have suggested that in the absence of the king, the assembly might be called a Convention Parliament, as in April 1660 for the Restoration, or as in January 1689 for the English (Glorious) Revolution, but history has not judged this 1483 assembly as such. Only about half the members were present; there were relatively few representatives of the House of Commons; and the numbers were made up with unelected London citizens who were not lawfully appointed.

It has been asserted by Sir Clements Markham (1906) that Bishop Stillington again presented the supportive documentary evidence for the 1461 marriage contract at this meeting on 25 June 1483; this was the same evidence which allegedly had been presented to the council on 9 June 1483. Markham wrote as follows: "The proofs of the previous contract of Edward IV with Lady Eleanor Butler were laid before this assembly by Bishop Stillington and his witnesses." Possibly, this allegation makes a great deal of sense, as, surely, some who attended the Great Council would have liked to see the evidence for Stillington's solitary assertion of a 1461 marriage contract. But in other descriptions of this Westminster meeting, there is no mention that Stillington made any such presentation; his proofs and depositions were not mentioned by the Croyland Chronicler (1854,) who must have been present at the assembly. The Croyland Chronicler said that he was appalled by "such seditious and disgraceful proceedings." It is difficult to understand how Stillington could have produced the witnesses mentioned by Sir Clements Markham, at least witnesses for the 1461 formal marriage, because the bishop had claimed that the 1461 marriage was private and secret, with no witnesses. It seems doubtful that Stillington, in good faith, could have devised any supportive documentary evidence for the 1461 marriage contract, as there were no witnesses other than himself. More likely, somebody else devised the presented documents.

Bertram Fields (1998) has described a sinister source for the so-called depositions. As we have seen already, in *Edward Hall's Chronicle* there is quoted a long conversation between Buckingham and Bishop Morton, in which it was asserted that the "doctors, proctors and depositions" were "brought in" by Richard, Duke of Gloucester. This makes a great deal more sense, especially if one can accept that Richard was capable of such dishonesty. If this alleged conversation reflected something near the truth, then it probably occurred when Buckingham and Morton were together at Brecknock Castle in Wales, in August 1483, and had the long conversations reported in *Edward Hall's Chronicle* (Ellis, Grafton, and Hall, 1809). It was not Morton who made the statements, but Buckingham. The duke also said that later he decided the instruments were false. The statements by Buckingham were later related to Richard Grafton, one of the authors of *Edward Hall's Chronicle,* almost certainly by Bishop Morton. It seems appropriate for good measure to present Buckingham's statement in

Edward Hall's Chronicle as follows: "He [Richard] then brought in [to the Great Council] instruments, authentic doctors, proctors, and notaries of the law, with depositions of diverse witnesses, testifying Edward's children to be bastards, which depositions then I thought to be as true as now I know them to be fayned [false], and testified by persons with rewards untruly subornate [suborned]." It seems very clear. But again, it should be noted that Buckingham changed his mind only later, sometime after the meeting of the Great Council on 25 June 1483.

It is a major problem in the historical record that there appears no description of the nature of the supportive documentary evidence for the 1461 alleged marriage contract that was presented before the assembly of 25 June 1483 at Westminster Hall. Nevertheless, remarkably, the assembly agreed that Edward V should be deposed and that Richard, Duke of Gloucester, should be king. According to Helen Maurer (2000), there was a petition drawn up, a parchment roll addressed to Gloucester, which some members of the assembly signed on 25 June 1483. When safely home in Europe, and referring to the Westminster assembly, Dominic Mancini wrote that the assembled lords "consulted their own safety, warned by the example of Hastings, and perceiving the alliance of the two dukes, whose power, supported by a multitude of troops, would be difficult and hazardous to resist; and therefore they determined to declare Richard their king and ask him to undertake the burden of office" (Mancini, 1989).

Mary Clive (1974) summed up her opinion with simple beauty, as follows:

> A man could not disinherit his nephews merely by announcing that his brother's marriage was not valid; there had to be proofs and witnesses. Edward's marriage to Elizabeth had always been considered valid, and it would remain valid until it was examined by an ecclesiastical court, found wanting, and annulled by the Church authorities. No [other] witnesses [the meaning is plural] for Edward's other [1461 alleged] marriage ever came forward, no one suggested any details, any date, any place; and the crowd could see that if Gloucester had a leg to stand on he would have got lawyers to make out a case, and Edward's children would have been disinherited in form.

By this, she meant that an ecclesiastical law court decision was necessary.

As stated by Charles Ross (1999): "If the marriage [Edward IV's] was invalid, this was a matter for the ecclesiastical courts, not for Parliament, which had no jurisdiction over matters of morals [marriage and legitimacy]."

Tellingly, there was no second witness to support Stillington's solitary assertion. In canon law, neither the alleged 1461 contract (with one witness) nor the alleged formal marriage which followed (with no witness) was a proven fact. R. H. Helmholz (1974), stating a general rule, may be quoted as follows: "In Canon Law the testimony of one witness was insufficient evidence of any fact."

In the end, Edward V, the lawful king of England, was disinherited by a 1461 marriage contract which was unwritten, undetailed, unplaced, undated, unsigned, and unsupported. Amazingly, some authors still believe it valid; most others believe that Stillington simply invented it. Later, we shall examine the 1484 parliamentary statute supporting the Stillington statement, and we shall find again that no claim was made that legitimate documentary proof for the contract existed. The authors of the 1484 Titulus Regius simply stated that the allegation was true. Such an unsubstantiated charge could be made against anyone: lord, bishop, commoner, or, in this case, England's great Warrior King, Edward IV, just two months silent in his grave. Nobody, not Richard, not Buckingham, not Howard, would have dared to make such a despicable accusation if Edward IV had been alive. But they did dare to bully the imprisoned boy king, aged a mere twelve years. It was disgraceful; naked ambition had supplanted all common sense.

When it became necessary, alleged documentary evidence for the 1461 marriage contract was somehow produced by invention. It makes sense that at some point, after Buckingham had spoken, some evidence might have been presented to the Great Council; but on that point, there is simply no confirmation. It remains true that the details were unknown before June 1483, the details were not reported in June 1483, and the details have remained unknown for the five hundred years since. If they ever existed, then the details remain to this day a well-preserved secret. That in itself would be truly amazing, considering how many people attended that meeting of 25 June 1483. It is surprising how well the astonishing secret was kept and how nothing was ever leaked. Surely, the details of such an extraordinary event would have found their way to the light of day. As far as we know, the ordinary requirements for any legal document, even those in the Middle Ages, were simply not met. There was nothing to suggest that the documents were legitimate; if the depositions existed, then there was much to suggest they must have been suborned, just like the duke of Buckingham said.

Consideration of Possible Evidence to Support the Solitary Assertion of a 1461 Marriage Contract

It is difficult to know exactly what might have been the nature of this alleged documentary evidence for the 1461 marriage contract. Some of the possibilities are enumerated as follows:

1. It could have been a contract document signed by Edward and Eleanor, but that is not likely; Stillington surely would have said so and the case against King Edward V would have been proven.
2. It could have been an affidavit signed by an additional person who witnessed the contract, but that, too, is not likely for the same reason; Stillington would have said so.
3. It could have been a document from somebody, perhaps Eleanor herself or a member of Eleanor's own family, who was prepared to say that Edward and Eleanor had lived together as man and wife in the same household. If so, then that person was not stating the truth. There is no evidence that Edward and Eleanor ever lived together in the same household (Ashdown-Hill, 2010).
4. It could have been evidence that a child – an heir and a possible claimant to the throne – of the union was produced. There is no such reasonable evidence to support this suggestion (Ashdown-Hill, 2010).
5. There could have been some public acknowledgement, such as an ecclesiastical law court proceeding, to establish validity of the union, or there could have been a civil law court proceeding for some other matter which involved both parties in common suit. There is little reason to think that this is true.

6. Maybe Edward and Eleanor consulted together with a doctor, a lawyer, or a priest about some very personal matter, and later the doctor, lawyer, or priest was prepared to sign a deposition to that effect. Such persons remain unknown.

There would be other possibilities, but no detailed statements were ever given, either before the council in early June 1483 or before the Great Council later in June 1483. None of those suggestions had any collateral evidence to support them – none that has ever been discovered.

Five hundred years later, we still do not know the nature of this evidence. Even more surprising, there seems to be no evidence that Stillington himself ever personally claimed to have any supportive physical evidence for his allegations. Surely, an ordained priest who performed a marriage contract for the king of England would have taken care to have some form of evidentiary proof in his possession, even if it was his intention to keep the whole matter secret. He must have been aware that the king's subjects would eventually require assurance on the matter. Surely, the Lord Privy Seal would have made certain that he preserved some form of independent proof, aside from his own lonesome word. It should not have been necessary for Gloucester, or anybody else, for that matter, least of all Richard, to invent the documents and perjure himself. Many observers have therefore remained deeply suspicious of the bishop's statement, and especially of the alleged supportive evidence.

It is dismaying that some well-qualified authors continue to deny that proof was needed. Apparently, to them, an unsubstantiated accusation was enough. In discussing the claim of Henry VII to the English throne, the fine attorney Bertram Fields (1998) analyzed the marriage of Henry's paternal grandfather. Owen Tudor had two sons with Catherine of Valois, namely Edmund and Jasper Tudor. Despite Owen's claim that he and Catherine were secretly married before Edmund was born, Bertram Fields said, "There was no proof of this beyond Owen's word." So, Bertram Fields suggested that Henry Tudor's father, Edmund, Earl of Richmond, may have been illegitimate. The author demanded proof of Owen Tudor's marriage before he would accept legitimacy, but he happily accepted Stillington's equally unsubstantiated assertion about Edward IV's alleged marriage contract in 1461.

There is no evidence that Stillington was ever properly questioned by lawyers or bishops about his allegations, and there is certainly no record of such in the rolls of any Parliament. And if evidence was presented at the Great Council meeting at Westminster, then history is still waiting for the signs of validity in those alleged deposition documents. No clarification appears in the record. Sir Clements Markham suggested that Stillington had "witnesses" at the Great Council assembly; this might suggest people who made personal appearances before the assembly of 25 June 1483. But nobody knows who they were, what their names were, where they lived, or even if they existed.

Taking all this into consideration, this is why the whole matter should have been considered by an ecclesiastical law court. Then, Stillington could have been properly interrogated about his original assertion. After that, he could have been questioned about the source and the nature of any supportive documents. The court could have reached a conclusion and made a clear official declaration: the assertion of a 1461 marriage contract was substantiated by legitimate evidence or it was not substantiated. Even if the law court had refused to describe the evidence for public consumption, the decision of the court would have been lawful. The court had seen the evidence and had found it either acceptable or unacceptable, according to the canon law.

The proper procedure in 1483 should have been that, first, the Church made a decision about the validity of Edward IV's 1464 marriage, including the 1461 contract, and second, that a proper Parliament made a decision about the inheritance of Edward V. This procedure was illustrated in the last decade of the fourteenth century in the matter of the famous Beaufort family (see Appendix D). Initially illegitimate, after John of Gaunt married their mother, Katherine Swynford, on 13 January 1396, the Beaufort children were first legitimized by Pope Boniface IX on 1 September 1396 and then subsequently allowed to inherit by an act of Parliament on 9 February 1397. This was the custom and precedent in Christendom under the medieval Church; it was accepted in England as it was elsewhere in Europe (O'Regan, 1976). The findings of the ecclesiastical law court could then have been considered by the Parliament, and a decision could have been made about Edward V's right to inherit the throne. Instead of the proper procedure, there was a meeting of a Great Council on 25 June

1483. This Great Council declared Edward's 1464 marriage invalid and then disinherited Edward V; this was not consistent with custom and precedent and was not lawful. As the unwritten constitution of England is always claimed to be based on custom, precedent, and legislation, it can be stated that the decision was unconstitutional. This author's conclusion, along with that of many others, is that the mysterious depositions, if they existed, were fabrications. It is easy to predict that they would not appear in the 1484 Titulus Regius, as we shall see later.

Again, on the matter of a hearing before an ecclesiastical law court to consider the status of Edward IV's marriage to Queen Elizabeth Woodville, it is noteworthy that fifty years later, when he decided to set aside his marriage to Queen Katherine of Aragon, King Henry VIII had to rely entirely on the Church for his authority, not on his council, not on his Great Council, and, initially, not even on his Parliament. In fact, he had to make momentous changes in the Church of England before he could move ahead and achieve his objective. This matter is discussed later in great detail in the section on Henry VIII, who was a grandson of Edward IV. In relation to matrimonial matters, such was the custom and law of England in 1483. Richard III was allowed to trample on the law, but Henry VIII had to make revolutionary changes.

No doubt in fear of another boy king and a prolonged protectorate or regency, those at the Great Council meeting of 25 June 1483 responded to the urging of Henry Stafford, the second duke of Buckingham, and agreed that King Edward V should be deposed and that Richard, Duke of Gloucester, should be king. In view of past history of the disastrous reign of Henry VI, this decision can be understood, but it was not lawful. The Great Council bullied the imprisoned and unrepresented twelve-year-old King Edward V. The English people, their descendants included, should hang their heads in shame that they allowed such a thing to happen. A Great Council, if it can be called that, did not have the power to nullify a marriage or the power to depose a lawful king. The former power resided with the Church, and the latter power resided with a properly constituted Parliament. Many authors appear to claim that the meeting was a Parliament. It is not clear if this is a deliberate mistake or a lack of understanding of what constitutes a proper Parliament. Or, calling the meeting a Parliament may be the only way to make the shocking decision appear palatable. The Great Council meeting was held in Westminster Hall, where Parliament normally met; perhaps this caused the confusion or served as the justification. It is a simple fact: there was no Parliament during the reign of King Edward V ("List of Parliaments of England," 2014). Setting this problem aside, the Great Council decision was not founded on a judgement handed down by a proper ecclesiastical law court.

The Meeting at Baynard; the Parchment Roll; Edward V Deposed; Gloucester Accepts the Throne

On 26 June 1483, Buckingham and the lords gathered at Baynard Castle where Richard had positioned himself, and, using the parchment roll prepared and signed on the previous day, petitioned Richard to accept the throne. According to Mancini (1989), "There the whole business was transacted; the oaths of allegiance given." Edward V was deposed and Richard was made king. Afterwards, Buckingham and the other lords went to Westminster Hall, where the new king sat on the throne and the lords paid homage to King Richard III.

The Differing Accounts of Contemporary and Near-Contemporary Authors

If a riot occurs in a public square and ten witnesses are questioned, then there will be ten different accounts. Still, there was a riot. For the present account, the author has followed the chronology given by Alison Weir (1999), which is largely supported by other accounts. But it is subject to minor variation, as seen in the following accounts in which there are obvious differences. The meeting at Westminster Hall on 25 June 1483 seems not well described, yet it is widely accepted as having occurred.

The Abbreviated Account of Polydore Vergil

The historian described Dr Shaw's speaking at St Paul's Church, saying that Edward's lack of resemblance to his father proved that neither he nor his son Edward was legitimate. The people did not believe this accusation. Many later made loud objection, and Dr Shaw acknowledged his error and died of shame soon after. This account does not mention a marriage contract or Lady Eleanor Butler, Dame Elizabeth Lucy, or Princess Bona, but it does state that Buckingham, speaking at the guildhall, possibly on 24 June 1483, delivered "in long process Duke Richard's mind [opinion]" that Edward IV, being not legitimate at birth, had defrauded Richard, Duke of Gloucester, of his rightful inheritance. According to Vergil, after this speech by Buckingham, Richard rode to Westminster Hall and sat in the "royal seat," telling the magistrates that henceforth they should do all things in his name, and telling the nobles that they should appoint a day to assemble and pay him homage, which was probably the occasion of 26 June 1483. It would appear that Vergil made no mention of the meeting at Westminster on 25 June 1483.

Of the coronation of Richard III in early July 1483, Vergil wrote, "Richard, without the assent of the commonality, by might and will of certain noblemen of his faction, enjoyed the realm, contrary to the law of God and man." This latter statement is consistent with his omission of the Great Council meeting of 25 June 1483, at which assent was indeed given by the assembled lords. When the news of Richard III spread, the people were not supportive; the Yorkists said he was bringing his House of York into ruin, and the Lancastrians said his rule would be so oppressive that soon they would call Henry Tudor to be king. It should be noted that Vergil was the official historian of Henry VII; the account was first published in 1534 during the reign of Henry VIII.

The Abbreviated Account of Dominic Mancini

The speech by Dr Shaw was described. The theologian said that Edward did not resemble his father, so Edward was not legitimate at his birth, and so neither was his son Edward V legitimate. Young Warwick could not be king because of the attainder of his father, Clarence. There was no mention of any marriage contract by Dr Shaw. And there was no mention of the Buckingham speech at the guildhall. Richard sent the lords to hear Buckingham and make a decision about the disposal of the throne; this must have been the Westminster Hall meeting of 25 June 1483. Mancini gave no details of Buckingham's speech that day, so there was no mention of Lady Eleanor Butler in his account. When he sent Buckingham to this meeting, Richard gave his opinion: "It would be unjust to crown this lad [Edward V], who was illegitimate, because Edward IV, on marrying Elizabeth[,] was legally contracted to another wife to whom the Earl of Warwick had joined him." This meant Princess Bona of Savoy, since Warwick had been trying to make these arrangements for some time.

But if this was so, then Richard Neville, the sixteenth earl of Warwick, would have said so in 1464 when Edward announced his marriage to Elizabeth, about which Warwick was so angry. Mancini's editor, C. A. J. Armstrong, said that the proxy marriage suggestion was good evidence of the improvised nature of Richard's usurpation strategy. It was not stated, but what the editor meant was that somebody was not truthful. On 26 June, the lords assembled at Baynard Castle and Buckingham petitioned Richard to accept the throne. Richard accepted. Mancini stated, "There the whole business was transacted, the oaths of allegiance given, and other indispensable acts performed." There was no mention that Richard went to Westminster Hall later that same day. Mancini's account was discovered in the municipal records of Lille, France, in 1934 and subsequently first published in 1936.

The Abbreviated Account of the Croyland Chronicle

The chronicler stated that "the said Protector Richard assumed the government of the kingdom, with the title of king, on the 20th day of the month of June; and on the same day obtruded himself into the marble chair." This sounds like the occasion of 26 June 1483 at the Great Hall of Westminster, where Richard sat on the throne. Next, this is stated:

> The colour [reason] for this act of usurpation, and his thus taking possession of the throne, was the following: it was set forth, by way of prayer, in an address, in a certain Roll of Parchment, that the sons of King Edward were bastards, on the ground that he had contracted a marriage with one Lady Eleanor Butler, before his marriage to Queen Elizabeth; added to which, the blood of his brother, George Duke of Clarence, had been attainted; so that, at the present time, no certain and uncorrupted lineal blood could be found of Richard Duke of York [who died in 1460], except in the person of the said Richard Duke of Gloucester [Lord Protector at that time]. For which reason, he was entreated, at the end of the said Roll, on [the] part of the lords and commons of the realm, to assume his lawful rights.

Again, this most likely reflected the occasion of 26 June 1483 when a petition, in the form of a parchment roll, was presented to Richard, asking that he accept the throne. The date 20 June 1483 must be a mistake; perhaps in the original, the zero may have been a six. The chronicler expressed his view of this event as "such seditious and disgraceful proceedings."

There was no mention of Dr Shaw on 22 June 1483, or of Buckingham at the guildhall on 24 June 1483. The Great Council meeting of 25 June 1483 seems not to be mentioned; but it might be assumed that it was there that the arguments were set forth, that the roll of parchment was prepared, and that some of the lords signed it.

It should be remembered that the pertinent part of the chronicle was written in April 1486 and included a copy of the 1484 Titulus Regius. After repeal and destruction of this 1484 statute in 1485, only this single copy in the *Croyland Chronicle* survived. It was discovered and published by Sir George Buck in 1619.

The Abbreviated Account of Sir Thomas More

Despite its deficiencies, this account provides much information. It is provided by one of England's finest lawyers, one of the greatest scholars of the age, after his prolonged and determined effort to find out the truth from witnesses who likely knew the details. Sir Thomas More was quite capable of discerning lies and bias, both in himself and in others. Because the truth may be unpleasant for some is no reason to discard More's version as fiction, but many have been critical of his account. It is so detailed that there must be truth in his story; it is consistent with the other less detailed accounts, such as they are. It was so harmful to the reputation of Richard III that Sir Thomas More may have had his regrets, which might explain why it remained unpublished at his death and why he may not have checked it for minor errors as thoroughly as he should have.

The speeches by Dr Shaw on 22 June, by Buckingham on 24 June, and by Buckingham on 25 June and 26 June are all mentioned. Dr Shaw said that Edward's birth was not legitimate because Edward did not look like his father; and for the same reason, Clarence was not legitimate, either. The dowager duchess of York made loud objection against the insult to herself concerning adultery. Dr Shaw may also have said that Edward's marriage was invalid because there was an earlier marriage contract, but it was with Dame Elizabeth Lucy.

Buckingham also said that Edward's marriage was invalid because of a prior contract with Dame Elizabeth Lucy; he made no mention of

Edward's birth being illegitimate, but he hinted that he did not wish to offend Edward's mother any further. The people did not believe these accusations.

On 25 June 1483, there was a meeting at Baynard Castle, not, apparently, at Westminster Hall. It was attended by many lords and commoners. There is not much detail about what Buckingham said, but the duke persuaded Richard to accept the throne. There is no mention of Edward IV's birth, no mention of Lady Eleanor Butler, and no mention of a petition.

The next day, 26 June 1483, Richard and a large following went to Westminster Hall. Richard declared that he accepted the crown and sat on the throne.

The Very Abbreviated Account in the Titulus Regius (Probably Written by Bishop Stillington)

The statute said that the reign of Edward IV was a disaster for everybody. It said that Edward V was not legitimate because Edward IV's marriage was invalid because of a prior marriage contract with Lady Eleanor Butler. No proof for the prior (1461) contract was attached or offered at a later date. It was stated that Richard III was "the undoubted son" of his father, with the implication that Edward IV was not. Young Warwick could not inherit because of the attainder of his father, Clarence. The petition, the roll of parchment, was mentioned. The statute claimed that Richard III was the rightful king and also described his alleged title.

CHAPTER 6

The Reign of Richard III

Richard, Duke of Gloucester, Accepts the Crown

After the doubtful Westminster Hall decision of 25 June 1483, on the next day, 26 June 1483, at Baynard Castle, with a "Petition to Richard Duke of Gloucester" in his hand and a deputation of lords present to support him, Buckingham asked Gloucester to take the throne, an invitation which Richard accepted after a brief show of reluctance. The petition has been lost and cannot be directly examined, but a description of its contents was copied into the *Croyland Chronicle* written in 1486. A single copy of the publication was discovered much later by Sir George Buck during the reign of King James I and was published soon after. The petition was described as a parchment roll, and Lady Eleanor Butler was definitely named as the subject of Edward's earlier alleged marriage contract (Ashdown-Hill, 2010). As well, the Croyland Chronicler said that the claim was made that the heir of Clarence was excluded on the basis of the duke's attainder in 1478. This argument had to be introduced to exclude young Warwick from inheriting the throne after the Dr Shaw sermon had failed so badly. It is too bad that we do not have the names of those who signed the petition. *They did not know it at the time, but they signed the death warrant for the Royal House of York.*

The people of London heard the news, but they did not cheer; they did not believe that the beautiful children of their beloved King Edward were all bastards. After all, the Church had performed the coronation of the queen in 1465, so she must have been legally married to the king.

Then, on the same day, 26 June 1483, Richard processioned to Westminster Hall, sat on the throne (the marble chair of the Chief Justice), and, before the Court of the King's Bench, took the oath of the king of England. Soon after, on 28 June 1483, the new king rewarded Lord Howard with the duchy of Norfolk, and his son Thomas Howard with the earldom of Surrey. The new king rewarded Lord Berkeley with the earldom of Nottingham; he again promised the Hereford inheritance to Buckingham; and he made further awards to other supporters, like the fourth earl of Northumberland. Although the Norfolk estates belonged to young Prince Richard, confirmed by an act of Parliament, there is no good evidence that the prince was dead at this time or that Parliament had ever reversed its award to young Richard. This anomaly was explained with a new theory: whatever young Richard's status, as soon as Richard was king, whether or not the boy was alive, by law, young Richard was "legally dead." Such are the contortions of our attorneys! It is reminiscent of Parliament's treatment of Warwick's wife, Anne.

It was not until 23 January 1484 that a properly constituted Parliament met and passed the Acts of Settlement, including the Titulus Regius, a statute which in effect ruled that Edward V and his siblings were illegitimate; that Edward V was lawfully deposed; that the heir of Clarence, namely the eight-year-old seventeenth earl of Warwick, could not inherit the throne because of the attainder and execution of his father, the duke of Clarence; and that Richard, Duke of Gloucester, was the rightful king of England (Smith, 1894). It is finally clear that in this document, the 1484 Titulus Regius, Lady Eleanor Butler was appropriately named as allegedly married to Edward IV; and if that truly was the case, then Gloucester's argument in favour of deposing Edward V was finally and appropriately, for the first time, set forth. But in the statute, there was a grave admission: those who gathered and devised the petition (on 25 June 1483) were not a lawfully formed Parliament, but the object of the lawful 1484 Parliament was to confirm all that was devised by the meeting of 1483. So, it is easy to conclude, as we have already, that King Edward V was not deposed by a lawful Parliament until seven months after the fact.

According to George Barnett Smith (1894), "The proceedings of the June Council [the Great Council of 25 June 1483] were transformed into law, [the] Parliament [of 23 January 1484] giving the force of a statute to many statements which were certainly the reverse of the truth." The legality of this decision by the 1484 Parliament has been constantly questioned. In the next reign, the statute was totally overthrown and removed from the rolls of Parliament, as shall be described. Based on the proceedings of the 1484 Parliament and its very own opinion expressed, there can be no question that on 25 June 1483, the deposition of Edward V was unlawful. It took another seven months before Parliament belatedly tried to make the proceedings lawful (in January 1484). But in twenty-two more months, in November 1485, Parliament reversed itself and made the proceedings of 25 June 1483 again not lawful. Only the Church could invalidate the 1464 royal marriage of Edward IV and Elizabeth and allow the subsequent deposition by a properly constituted Parliament to be lawful. But even so, without doubt, Parliament could rule on the subject of inheritance, even if retrospectively, seven months after the usurpation and again twenty-two months later. This controversy and similar problems are among the reasons why, in modern times, England has a High Court, the United States has a Supreme Court, and other countries have similar overarching courts; governments do not always do things which are legal or constitutional and in accordance with accepted historical custom and precedent.

The Coronation of Richard III

Richard III was crowned as the new king with great pomp and circumstance on 6 July 1483, an act that was in total rejection of the implicit wishes, expressed in his last will before witnesses, of the late King Edward IV. Sir Clements Markham (1906) pointed out that the ceremony was well attended by the nobles of England. This could have been because the coronation was popular, but it could equally have been because the monarchy was feared and respected, and the threat of minority rule and open warfare was removed.

There were some notable absentees, however: the former Queen Mother, Elizabeth Woodville; Katherine, the duchess of Buckingham; Cecily, the dowager duchess of York, the new king's very own mother; and the princes in the Tower. Archbishop Bourchier crowned the king, if unwillingly (Mancini, 1989), but did not attend the coronation banquet, his place at the table having been taken by the bishop of Durham. The archbishop probably remembered his solemn promise to Queen Mother

Elizabeth when she handed over her son Richard of Shrewsbury, following her eloquent defence. Young Richard was still alive, but the archbishop suspected that the lad was doomed. Elizabeth was in the sanctuary and no doubt heard the fanfare at the nearby Westminster Abbey. Katherine, being a Woodville, may have been forbidden to attend by her husband, the duke of Buckingham, who must have been aware of her hostility towards Richard III. The duke would soon learn that his wife, a mere woman, had understood the truth about Richard III: the great good man had made a serious mistake. The dowager duchess of York was still vigorous; she did not die for another ten years and could have attended, if she had so desired. She was in London intending to be at the coronation of her grandson Edward V; but she knew that Richard III's coronation was all wrong. The legal monarch was her child or that same child's heir, in the proper order of birth, which made Richard III near last in her family. Of course, Edward V and his brother young Richard had solid reasons for not attending the coronation of Richard III, as they were locked up in the Tower. It should be noted here that Cecily did not attend the coronation of Queen Elizabeth Woodville, either; it can be presumed that she remained equally upset about both coronations.

Some have claimed that the deposed Edward V actually walked in the coronation procession of Richard III. He must have been heavily disguised, for this notion is palpable nonsense. The palace wardrobe may have prepared his gown, probably without the king's permission, but Richard III never planned to risk exposing King Edward V to public view.

In the upper echelons of the Yorkist hierarchy, three gentlewomen – the former Queen Mother; the duchess Katherine; and the dowager duchess Cecily, the king's very own mother – clearly understood what was happening. The male magnates of the realm simply did not understand, at least not yet. Sir Winston Churchill (1995), writing five hundred years later in the twentieth century and referring to the coronation of Richard III, stated: "From this very moment there began that marked distrust and hostility of all classes to Richard III, which all his arts and competence could not allay." George Barnett Smith (1894) said that Richard was initially popular, but after his accession was deeply mistrusted. Sir Francis Bacon (1889), writing in the reign of King James I, stated as follows: "After that [the coronation] was Richard, the third of that name, King in fact only, but tyrant both in title and regiment, and so commonly termed and reputed in all times since." By his use of the word *tyrant,* Bacon may have meant "despotic ruler," but more likely he meant "usurper" and all that the word implies, with violence and illegality.

Plots and Rebellion against Richard III; Anticipation of the Death of King Edward V and His Brother Prince Richard, the Duke of York

With the coronation of Richard III, the people of England began to realize what had happened. Previously, they had heard only about rumours and possibilities, but with the coronation, serious doubts intensified. At the time he left London, a week after the coronation of Richard III, Dominic Mancini (1989) said there were already suspicions that the princes were dead, but he did not know for certain. Perhaps in mid July 1483, an attempt to free the princes was prevented by the Tower guard (Gregory, 2010); but this event is poorly described, although it may have been facilitated by the creation of diversionary fires in London. A man named Robert Russe and others were tried and executed (Higginbotham, 2013). There was also a so-called Sanctuary Plot, in which it was planned to send the royal princesses to Europe so suitable royal husbands could be found. An appropriate husband could then invade England and reclaim the crown in the name of his Yorkist wife. This plot was hatched at Westminster Abbey. Elizabeth, in the sanctuary with all her daughters, was almost certainly involved. The guard around the abbey sanctuary was reinforced to prevent the escape of any of Elizabeth's daughters. In August 1483, Richard III appointed commissioners to investigate who might be involved, but most of the conspirators had fled over the sea, had gone into hiding, or were in the sanctuary. And Elizabeth could not yet be touched, at least while the council was full of bishops and her sanctuary was respected. It is reasonable to believe that the bishops might have threatened Richard with excommunication if he touched Elizabeth in the sanctuary.

It should be noted that the Sanctuary Plotters in late July 1483 made the assumption that the princes in the Tower were dead, which may not have been yet true; but it was a solid assumption that looked like it might soon be true. It can be assumed that these early plots against his crown caused Richard to realize that he would soon need to settle the matter of the princes. In post-Conquest English history, three kings had been deposed, following which, Edward II, Richard II, and Henry VI had all been murdered. There was heavy precedent, so it was a fair assumption that King Edward V would soon be murdered, too. That is what the English people believed. That was the source of all the rumours.

In the weeks that followed the news of these desperate plots, in July and August 1483, it became common belief that the princes in the Tower were dead, presumably murdered. The new king was widely blamed for this horrendous act. England was flooded with tales of the murders, most of them probably inaccurate at that time. It may be that with the plots, people simply concluded that Richard would have to put the princes to death just to protect himself, but there was no conclusive evidence. The modern argument is that the princes were still alive through most of August 1483. Some have suggested that Richard himself, sensing his unpopularity, may have started the rumours, hoping that people would be more accepting of his own government if the princes were dead. If it should be true, then it only deepened the fierce resentment of the English people against the king.

Whether or not the new king murdered the princes, most of the people of England, commoner and peer, believed that he was responsible not only for the princes' safety, as Richard was Lord Protector, but also for their deaths. This would prove to be a huge political liability, so enormous that it would prove utterly impossible for even the talented Richard III to overcome. As written by David Baldwin (2002), with superb understatement, "Richard's fundamental problem was that he had taken the crown in a manner which was unacceptable to the majority of his subjects."

According to the Croyland Chronicler, probably Bishop John Russell, the chancellor of England, the princes were not seen by witnesses again after the end of August 1483, although the Croyland Chronicler did infer that he thought the princes might still be alive in the first days of September 1483. However, Sir Thomas More, writing years later but with contemporary evidence from his father, his father-in-law, Bishop Morton, and several others, suggested that they disappeared from view sometime shortly after mid August 1483. There was so much security and secrecy at the Tower that it was hard to be any more precise. As the princes were viewed so infrequently, this statement by Sir Thomas More may still mean that the princes did not die until a later date, maybe late August 1483 or, possibly, shortly after that.

Even at this early stage, even when the princes were probably alive, some people suspected that Sir James Tyrell, the master of the king's horse, was responsible for their deaths. Sir James was a loyal servant of Richard III; he was an obvious choice if the king needed a special task to be performed. Most important, these suggestions about murder were present soon after the coronation of Richard III (Mancini, 1989); they did not just appear later, after Richard III was dead, or during Tudor times, as claimed by persistent defenders of Richard III. It was not a case of history being rewritten by the Tudor victors, those who had seized all power and wished to denigrate the previous regime.

Why the Duke of Buckingham Changed His Mind about Richard III

In the meantime, the doubly treacherous Buckingham secretly withdrew his support from Richard III, allegedly over the missing Edward V and his brother. This change occurred during August and September 1483, while he was at Brecknock Castle in Wales, in the company of Bishop Morton, his prisoner. The reasons are not known for certain, but there are several possibilities.

Buckingham may have been outraged by the illegal execution of Hastings on 13 June 1483, but that is not likely to have been his only reason. Buckingham was descended from Thomas of Woodstock, the youngest son of King Edward III (see Appendix F); Buckingham's Stafford family members were staunch Lancastrians, so he may have intended to claim the crown for himself. Between him and the crown stood very few likely candidates: the increasingly unpopular Richard III; the sickly Prince of Wales, Edward of Middleham; the partially disabled son of the attainted Clarence, the eight-year-old seventeenth earl of Warwick; and the two princes in the Tower, who might already be dead or soon would be. Buckingham did not think that Edward IV's daughters could claim the throne, for, apparently, he did not understand the meaning of the 1460 Act of Accord. Buckingham had played a major role in the usurpation, but as soon as Richard was crowned, some said that Buckingham became extremely jealous and started to covet the crown for himself.

Another possible reason for Buckingham's alienation was a disputed inheritance from Mary de Bohun, the youngest daughter of Humphrey de Bohun, the late seventh earl of Hereford. Mary was the sister of Buckingham's great-great-grandmother, Eleanor de Bohun, the wife of Thomas of Woodstock, the youngest son of King Edward III. Buckingham had already inherited Eleanor's share of the Hereford estate. Mary de Bohun had married Henry IV, and her share of the Hereford estate had passed through Henry V to Henry VI. When he became king, Edward IV had appropriated this estate for the Crown. Richard III had promised to give Buckingham this enormous inheritance, but he was slow to make the decision. In the end, on 13 July 1483, he made only a provisional assignment of the inheritance to Buckingham, dependent on the views of the Parliament. This possible reason seems unlikely, as the process had clearly been initiated and only patience was needed for its satisfactory conclusion.

Another possible reason for Buckingham's change of heart is that the king told Buckingham in late July 1483, at the town of Gloucester, that he had recently ordered that the princes be put to death in the Tower. If Buckingham was not expecting these deaths, then he might have been outraged. But it is frequently speculated that Buckingham had earlier advised Richard to put the princes to death. So, if this should be true, then it is less likely that this was the reason for his change of heart. This speculation is based on rumours circulating at the time when Buckingham had given such advice to the king; and it is supported by documents in the College of Arms in London and in the Ashmole Collection at Oxford University. If this speculation should be the case, then, in late July 1483 at Gloucester, the duke of Buckingham may have been well pleased that the king had taken his advice, so there would have been no major disagreement between them and no serious parting of the ways.

Last, it may be that Richard, asserted by some to be a great good man but likely still tormented by his conscience, admitted to Buckingham in their late July conversation at Gloucester that the 1461 marriage contract story was false, a suggestion made recently by Susan Higginbotham (2010). As confirmation, Bishop John Morton may well have made a similar claim with a convincing argument soon after the duke of Buckingham arrived home at Brecknock Castle in early August 1483. This may be the time of the conversation between Buckingham and Morton quoted in *Edward Hall's Chronicle*. It is notable that Buckingham said that he had come to believe that the supportive documentary evidence for the 1461 marriage contract story was false (Ellis, Grafton, and Hall, 1809). If all this is taken to be true, then it is not difficult to understand how angry the duke of Buckingham would have been, in late July 1483 at the town of Gloucester, when he realized that he had been badly deceived. It becomes easy to understand why he soon rebelled against Richard III.

The Decision to Put to Death the Princes in the Tower

As described by Alison Weir (1999), Richard went on a royal progress starting from London on 22 July 1483 to show himself to the people, hoping they would accept him as their king. According to the account of Sir Thomas More (2005), when the king, after passing through Oxford, arrived at the town of Gloucester, he sent John Greene to Sir Robert Brackenbury, the newly appointed constable of the Tower, with instructions to put the princes to death. There may have been a letter, but to avoid incriminating himself, the king probably relied on verbal instructions from John Greene. Brackenbury refused the request, unconvinced of the legality of the order and horrified at the thought of what would happen to him when he died. Like many Europeans in the fifteenth century, he was terrified of the flames of hell. If there had been a letter in the king's hand, then it is possible that Brackenbury might have been more accepting of the order – and there may have been an order to destroy the warrant once it was read.

At first, Buckingham did not join the king on the royal progress. He caught up with him in the town of Gloucester at the end of July. Then, there was a disagreement between the two men, some say a furious argument, and, on 2 August 1483, Buckingham left the town of Gloucester for his home at Brecknock Castle in Wales, never to see Richard III again. It is possible that they argued about the Hereford inheritance or about what to do with the princes in the Tower. Richard may even have told Buckingham of his execution order carried by John Greene to the Tower. Very likely, Richard, consumed by guilt and perhaps challenged by Buckingham, admitted that the contract story was false, as we have already discussed. Buckingham excused himself from attending the remainder of the royal progress. Since he was the newly appointed constable of England, this was a very strange thing to happen, as it was his responsibility to accompany and protect King Richard III. But at this point, early August 1483, Buckingham, knowing of the royal order given and knowing the absolute power of the king, may have believed that the princes had already been put to death, but this was probably not yet true.

After Buckingham had left for Wales and when the royal progress reached Warwick, John Greene returned from London with the news of Brackenbury's refusal to kill the princes. It is known that Richard was very disturbed and complained bitterly about the unreliability of his servants, but we do not know for certain which servants he had in mind: Greene, Brackenbury, Buckingham, or somebody else. Nor do we know for certain about what the king was complaining, but we can make a very good guess. At the suggestion of an unnamed person identified as a page, Richard engaged the services of another one of his most loyal retainers, Sir James Tyrell, the master of the king's horse, later the master of the king's henchmen. Together, the two men decided on a new secret plan (More, 2005). The king continued on his progress and reached Pontefract Castle, near York, on 27 August 1483.

The Death of the Princes in the Tower

On or about 30 August 1483, Sir James Tyrell left York and rode to London to collect wardrobe materials for the investiture of Edward of Middleham as the Prince of Wales, which was planned for 8 September 1483. According to Alison Weir (1999), Tyrell's location in London four days later is known from the record of the Palace Wardrobe Accounts (Kendall, 2002). The knight carried a letter from the king instructing Sir Robert Brackenbury to give Sir James Tyrell the Tower keys for one night; nothing else was stated, so plausible deniability for Sir Robert Brackenbury was preserved. While the knight was in London, it is alleged by Sir Thomas More (2005) that Sir James Tyrell had the sleeping princes smothered by John Dighton and Miles Forrest and then buried in the Tower. Alison Weir (1999) claimed that this heinous crime was committed on 3 September 1483. She appears to believe that the Croyland Chronicler may have been mistaken in his belief that the princes were there in the first week of September; perhaps he did not actually see the princes then but simply believed, erroneously, that they were still there. Alison Weir's estimate for the murder date was derived by calculating that four days were needed to ride from York to London, and four days to be back in York by 8 September 1483 for the planned investiture.

The next day, Sir Robert Brackenbury would have found the princes missing, but, being from the North Country and fiercely loyal to Richard, he said nothing, except maybe to his daughter Elizabeth, and carried the secret to his grave. He died fighting for his king at Bosworth Field in 1485. Brackenbury knew that the king would have to eliminate the princes, but he did not wish to be the instrument. Dr John Argentine, who often attended Edward V for medical reasons, would have noted the missing princes, but how long after their deaths is not clear. When young Edward of Middleham was invested as Richard's Prince of Wales on 8 September 1483, it may have signified that Edward V, Edward IV's Prince of Wales, was already dead. In fact, when Edward V was deposed on 25 June 1483, the title Prince of Wales was merged back into the Crown, so it was Richard's to do with as he wished. But Richard constantly worried that the deposition might not have been legal, and so the estates associated with the title remained with Edward V until Parliament had time to act. It would not do to have two persons claiming to hold the estates of the Prince of Wales. It is tempting to believe that Richard made arrangements for the investiture in early August, believing that, by then, Edward V would be already dead, as he had ordered in late July.

After the murders, it is stated in *Edward Hall's Chronicle* that Richard was never the same man again. According to his attendants, who the authors may have interviewed, Richard lay awake for hours, slept restlessly, had bad dreams, and frequently leapt from his bed with sudden panics and ran about his chamber (Ellis, Grafton, and Hall, 1809). The king lived in fear that somebody would seek revenge for the abominable deed; accordingly, the king always kept his dagger close. The signs suggest that Richard lived with unbearable guilt. That would not be surprising if Richard was as honest and upstanding as his supporters claim, something for which there is good evidence (Kendall, 2002).

At some point in time, it is not known precisely when, but possibly in mid September 1483, somebody in the government went to the Westminster Abbey sanctuary and informed Dowager Queen Elizabeth that the princes were missing and certainly dead. It was probably Dr Lewis of Caerleon, the physician shared by Elizabeth Woodville and Margaret Beaufort, the mother of Henry Tudor. Or it was Dr John Argentine himself. It must have been somebody who the dowager queen would have trusted as being well informed. Elizabeth probably already knew it, but she lived with a faithful mother's forlorn hope. According to Polydore Vergil (1844), as quoted by Arlene Okerlund (2005), upon hearing the terrible news, Elizabeth was hysterical. She fell to the floor in a swoon and lay motionless. When she arose, she beat her breast, pulled her hair, screamed and shrieked, cried out in agony, and wept inconsolably. Her anger, at first, was directed at herself because she had allowed her younger son to leave the sanctuary; she understood that if she had kept her younger son, then Gloucester's plan would not have worked, as her younger son Richard could have been proclaimed king. But Elizabeth was human and sorely stressed. In the end, she threw herself on her knees and prayed loudly to God for revenge on King Richard. This account appears too plausible to be considered untrue. Later, as Richard III's reign fell into ruin, many people believed that Elizabeth's prayer that day was answered.

The Margaret Beaufort Conspiracy (c. Late August, Most of September, and Early October 1483; After Initial Failure, It Continued through 1484 and 1485)

After he changed his mind about Richard III, Buckingham at first considered overthrowing Richard III and assuming the throne himself. But then he considered how much opposition he would face from all sides: from the Woodvilles, from the Yorkists, and from those supporting Henry Tudor. Knowing of Margaret Beaufort's ambition for her son, Buckingham decided that Henry Tudor would be the most suitable candidate to overthrow Richard III. When recounting these thoughts to Bishop Morton, his prisoner at Brecknock Castle, Buckingham conceived the idea that Henry Tudor should overthrow Richard, seize the throne, marry Princess Elizabeth of York, combine the white and red roses, and end the dynastic struggle between York and Lancaster. It is not clear who originated this plan, but it developed between the two of them, perhaps with Morton leading his subject.

Morton at Brecknock sent for Reginald Bray, who was in Lancashire with Lady Margaret. Morton sent Bray back to Margaret with the plan and asked her to contact the Queen Mother in the sanctuary. Margaret hurried to London and, in strictest confidence, sent Dr Lewis of Caerleon, her physician, to Elizabeth and her eldest daughter, who both approved the plan. Lady Margaret then sent her priest Christopher Urswick to Brittany to inform Henry Tudor, who must have been well pleased. Margaret Beaufort and Elizabeth Woodville busied themselves with contacting their supporters and organizing them to be ready in mid October for the uprising (Routh, 1924). The Woodvilles had been planning a rebellion, but now they were joined by the duke of Buckingham, Margaret Beaufort, and Henry Tudor. They would have been much encouraged.

The Buckingham Rebellion of October 1483

The Buckingham Rebellion began as a conspiracy among Yorkist supporters to put Edward V back on the throne. The most prominent participants were probably as follows: Bishop John Morton; Richard Woodville, the third Earl Rivers; Lionel Woodville, the bishop of Salisbury; Thomas Grey, the marquis of Dorset; Thomas Rotherham, the Archbishop of York; Peter Courtenay, the bishop of Exeter, and his cousins Edward and Walter Courtenay; Thomas St Leger, a brother-in-law of Edward IV; the former queen, Elizabeth, still in sanctuary; and a large number of mid- to upper-level government supporters of Edward IV, for example Sir Giles Daubeney, Sir Richard Guildford, Sir Thomas Ramney, Sir John Cheney, and others. As we have seen, later they were joined by Buckingham, and about the same time by Margaret Beaufort, the mother of Henry Tudor. When Buckingham joined the conspiracy, he probably recounted his conviction that the princes were already dead, based on his late July conversation with Richard III. Depending on when exactly he joined the conspiracy, this may or may not have been true. This rebellion was heavily supported by people in the southern and western counties of England, where resentment against Richard was greatest; what meagre support the king did have came from people in the northern counties. People from the isolated north were greatly feared in the allegedly more sophisticated south.

As it became more certain that the princes were dead, as they had not been seen for several weeks, a new plan had to be developed. Lady

Margaret Beaufort, working from the London house of her third husband, Thomas, Lord Stanley (Gregory, 2010), contacted Elizabeth Woodville in sanctuary at Westminster Abbey, using their common physician, Dr Lewis, as the messenger. An agreement was made that Henry Tudor should be king, provided he could overthrow Richard III and then marry Princess Elizabeth, the eldest daughter of Edward IV, the new Yorkist heir. This meant that Elizabeth Woodville, who had recently been told the fate of the princes, had accepted that her sons were dead; otherwise, she would not have agreed that her daughter Elizabeth was the Yorkist heir. It also meant that they were overlooking the underage Warwick held tightly at Sheriff Hutton Castle in Yorkshire; and it also meant that they were ignoring John de la Pole, the earl of Lincoln.

Margaret Beaufort began raising cash to send to Henry Tudor so he could make plans for the invasion of England. Christopher Urswick, Margaret's priest, went to Brittany to advise Henry Tudor of Buckingham's support, with encouragement to invade England, overthrow Richard III, assume the crown, and marry Princess Elizabeth. With the strong likelihood that Edward V and Prince Richard were dead, Buckingham sent messengers to Henry Tudor on 24 September 1483, advising that the intended date for the rebellion was 18 October 1483 and that Henry should land in Wales, where support for the Tudor family was strong. This plan was quite well developed by that time. The modified plot was basically to restore the House of Lancaster through the female Beaufort heir, Margaret Beaufort (see Appendix D), since the usurpation by Richard III was so distasteful and the best male Yorkist heirs were considered certainly dead. It should be noted that Margaret Beaufort must have withdrawn her own claim to the crown in favour of her son. For those who question that the dowager queen would have supported this conspiracy, it should be recalled that she and her Grey family were originally Lancastrian until she married Edward IV. It can also be reasonably asserted that she had become deeply disenchanted with the destructive behaviour of successive Yorkist leaders, such as Warwick, Clarence, and, lately, Gloucester.

Richard III had spies everywhere and was aware of the plot; his forces were in the field. He had his deputies watch Brecknock Castle and destroy the River Severn crossings at Gloucester in order to obstruct Buckingham. Lord John Howard blocked the rebel advance on London. But in the end, the conspiracy was thwarted by extreme and unusual stormy weather which inundated the south of England. The massive storm dispersed Buckingham's rebel Welsh forces at the flooded River Severn, scattered multiple risings in many townships of southern England – Kent, Surrey, Berkshire, Wiltshire, and Devon – and forced Henry Tudor's fleet in the English Channel to return to Brittany. This storm, for many years, was referred to as "the duke of Buckingham's great water." Buckingham fled to Wem and stayed at the home of his tenant, Ralph Bannister, who turned him over to the sheriff of Shrewsbury for the monetary reward that was publicly offered. In the custody of Sir James Tyrell, Buckingham pleaded for an audience with the king, but Richard angrily refused. After it was all over, Richard III acted decisively and had Buckingham executed for treason on 2 November 1483 at Salisbury. Richard and the royal army advanced west as far as Exeter, but the rebels, including Peter Courtenay, the bishop of Exeter, and his cousins Edward and Walter Courtenay, had fled over the sea to join Henry Tudor in Brittany.

There followed a long list of attainders, indictments, and exiles. Some people were executed ("Richard's Rebels," 2008). Bishop Morton hid in the Fens of East Anglia, made his escape through King's Lynn, and settled in Antwerp to await events. Lord Thomas Stanley, who had not been involved despite his very independent wife, had to keep Lady Margaret under house arrest in one of his northern castles; she was fortunate to avoid harsher punishment for her treason. But the cunning lady was able to continue her conspiracy through the services of her priest and confessor, Christopher Urswick, who carried further messages to Henry Tudor in Brittany. It is assumed that Richard III treated Margaret so well because he needed to retain Lord Thomas Stanley as a loyal supporter.

Events Following the Buckingham Rebellion

Angry with the duke of Brittany for his support of Henry Tudor and his part in the Buckingham Rebellion, Richard launched hostile naval operations against Breton shipping in the English Channel, which soon involved French and Scottish shipping, as well. This had the effect of making new friends for Henry Tudor. His army at Bosworth Field would be composed of French, Breton, and Scottish soldiers, as well as English and Welsh troops. Brittany, fearful of France, asked for military assistance, but Richard III, still irritated, did not respond. For the time being, Henry Tudor stayed safe in Brittany.

With England flooded by rumour and innuendo, the credibility of the king continued on an accelerating downward path. After the rebellion, Richard replaced many officials in the south with his own men from the north of England who he could better trust. This caused even more fierce resentment in London and southern England, where northerners were greatly distrusted.

About this time, too, Richard appointed the youthful earl of Lincoln as president of the Council of the North to help in keeping the king's peace; this had the effect of alienating Henry Percy, the fourth earl of Northumberland, who did not feel that he needed any assistance from the young prince, who had no experience of the northern counties. This appointment proved to be a major mistake on Richard's part.

Consistent with the arrangements made in the Margaret Beaufort Plot, Henry Tudor, at Rennes Cathedral in Brittany, did announce on Christmas Day 1483 that he was betrothed to marry Elizabeth Plantagenet of York, which, he knew, would greatly strengthen his claim to the English throne. This implied that he knew from his intelligence sources that the princes in the Tower, the best male Yorkist heirs, were dead and that he would soon again attempt to invade England and overthrow Richard III. It made no sense for him to invade England if the princes were still alive and able to claim the throne. The exiles paid Henry Tudor homage and declared him to be the rightful king of England. It is obviously doubtful that Henry Tudor would have made this promise without the support of Princess Elizabeth's mother, Elizabeth Woodville. The detailed evidence for such back-and-forth communication, obvious treason, remains a well-hidden secret to this day. Prior to the Buckingham Rebellion and the Rennes announcement, Henry Tudor had never been considered a viable claimant to the English throne, but with his declaration, he had to be taken seriously. Richard's usurpation had made it so.

Richard tried to have Henry Tudor extradited from Brittany. When it looked as if Richard's efforts might succeed, and when Bishop John Morton warned his supporters in Brittany, Henry Tudor fled, in June 1484, to the protection of King Charles VIII and his regent, Anne of Beaujeu, in France. The French king was only too pleased to offer Henry assistance, as he regarded Richard III as a potentially hostile king, especially in view of the recent English naval attacks.

Richard III's Only Parliament, which Occurred in January 1484

On 23 January 1484, Richard's first and only Parliament finally gathered. There were fifteen statutes passed, including that known as the Titulus Regius, which settled the title of King Richard III. This statute ratified the conclusions of the Great Council meeting of 25 June 1483, declared the valid marriage of King Edward IV to be invalid, and confirmed the usurper Richard III as the rightful king. The statute followed closely the arguments set forth by Buckingham on 25 June 1483, as well as those in the "Petition to Richard Duke of Gloucester" presented on 26 June 1483. The Parliament did not have much choice, for Richard had already been on the throne for over six months. The statute will be considered in full in the discussion of the legacy of King Edward IV (see Chapter 8).

Included in the Acts of Settlement were ninety-five attainders, an unusually large number. The considerable property of Margaret Beaufort was declared forfeited; the properties and grants previously awarded to Queen Elizabeth Woodville were resumed by the Crown; the Benevolences, so favoured by Edward IV and so unpopular with some of the wealthy, were declared illegal; and the custom of livery and maintenance was again declared unauthorized. The Croyland Chronicler (1854) expressed his opinion of all the resumptions:

> What immense estates and patrimonies were collected into this king's treasury in consequence of this measure, all of which he distributed among his northern adherents, who he planted in every spot throughout his dominions, to the disgrace and loudly expressed sorrow of all the people in the south, who daily longed more and more for the hoped for return of their ancient rulers, rather than the present tyranny of these people.

If Richard needed friends, he was not making any.

England's first statute of limitations was enacted, and the customs were awarded to the king for life. Another reform was that bail could be granted by a single judge; a full bench was no longer needed. Other changes included the introduction of a legal aid system for the poor, liberalized changes in qualification for jury selection, and reform of land tenure laws. There were several statutes concerning trade and commerce. These excellent laws, much admired by those sympathetic to Richard III and by many others, too, did not make the magnates any happier, as they were the ones giving up some of their privileges. The commoners, despite new rights, remained sullen and suspicious of the king for his treatment of the sons of King Edward IV.

According to the *Croyland Chronicle* (1854), probably in February 1484, Richard III had all his nobles swear an oath of loyalty to his son Edward of Middleham, the Prince of Wales, at the Palace of Westminster. Some have suggested that Richard III sensed danger, but such a procedure was common at the time among all kings.

The Reign of Richard III and His Futile Struggle for Acceptance
Later during his short reign, Richard established the Council of the North, now the modern Northern Department, which was responsible for the development of the northern counties. He established the court of requests to aid the poor, an extension of Edward IV's commission, and he founded the College of Arms in London. Some authors, perhaps unfairly, claim that Richard's fine legislative activity was a desperate effort to establish political support, and therefore they continue to give him little credit for his legislative vision. But if the reforms gained him support, then Richard was grateful for whatever he could gather.

Richard III worked very hard to improve his personal support; he turned out to be a very good king in many ways. He was very generous with his distribution of financial assistance to many people. This included the gift of offices, wardships, grants, pensions, and abatements. But he was not particularly generous with his creation of earldoms and baronies, as had been the case in previous reigns.

Despite his generosity, he could never overcome his one enormous political liability: that the princes in the Tower were his foremost responsibility and he completely failed to protect them. Sir Thomas More (2005) wrote that, despite his best efforts, Richard gained only "unsteadfast friends."

In his annual city calendar ending 30 September 1483, Richard Ricart, the recorder of Bristol, stated: "In this year the two sons of King Edward were put to silence in the Tower of London." In the *Chronicles of London*, in reference to Richard III, it was written that: "he also put to death the two children of King Edward, for which cause he [Richard] lost the hearts of the people" (Okerlund, 2005). The *Great Chronicle* reported in 1484 that: "after Easter, much whispering was among the people that the King had put the children of King Edward to death." Arlene Okerlund (2005) wrote that: "by 1485, public anger at Richard III was so great that the *Great Chronicle* returned to a general discussion of how the princes had died in the Tower." Sir Winston Churchill (1995) wrote: *"No fact stands forth more unchallengeable, than that the overwhelming majority of the nation was convinced that Richard had used his power as Protector to usurp the crown and that the princes had disappeared in the Tower. It will take many ingenious books to raise this issue to the dignity of an historical controversy"* – by which he meant that there was little disagreement, and not much controversy, about the guilt of Richard III among the people. In the *Great Chronicle of London*, it was stated that: *"the more in number grudged so sore against the king for the death of the innocents [the princes] that as gladly would they have been French, as to be under his subjection"* (Okerlund, 2005). The claim was that the English people preferred to be governed by the French, their ancient enemies, rather than continue under the rule of Richard III.

In fact, it was almost universally assumed that Richard himself had ordered the murders. This was so not only in England, but also on the Continent, among government leaders and among the political chattering classes. The chancellor of France, William de Rochefort, stated plainly before the Estates General in January 1484 that Richard III had murdered the princes in the Tower. Some consider that Rochefort was informed by Dr John Argentine, who had visited him in France; others have suggested that Dominic Mancini had given his opinion to Rochefort.

It is interesting to quote Commines in describing the views of that master Spider King, Louis XI of France:

> Not long after [Edward IV's death], he [Louis XI] received letters from the Duke of Gloucester, who was made king, styled himself Richard III, and had barbarously murdered his two nephews. This King Richard desired to live in the same friendship as his brother [Edward IV] had done, and I believe would have had his pension continued; but our King looked

upon him as an inhuman and cruel person, and would neither answer his letters nor give audience to his ambassador.

In the Foreword of Sir Thomas More's book (2005), Sister Wendy Becket describes what Sir Thomas More thought of Richard III: "He was a prime example of a man who manipulated, ignored conscience, twisted the laws of God and [m]an, and in the end found himself the pitiable and haunted figure that Sir Thomas More describes." If the twisted laws were those of inheritance, then this sounds like a very reasonable assessment.

However, these conclusions may have been unfair, for Richard III, in some respects, was a great good man. There is much evidence to support that case (Potter, 1983). But such good lords may also make horrendous mistakes and then commit further crimes in order to conceal the secondary problems. And although Richard must accept final responsibility, there is evidence that, not surprisingly, he was advised by others to put the princes to death. In a London *Commonplace Book,* covering the twelve-month mayoral period ending 29 October 1483, it is stated with authority that: "*this year, King Edward V, late called Prince of Wales, and Richard Duke of York, his brother, King Edward IV's sons, were put to death in the Tower of London by the vise [advice] of the Duke of Buckingham*" (Green, 1981). A *Commonplace Book* is much like a yearbook – a collection of statements, quotes, reports, and treatises – although the arrangement is much less formal than in a yearbook. The document was discovered in the College of Arms in 1980 and is referred to as the MS 2M6; it appears to be a collection of reports by multiple members of a merchant guild in London. In the Bodleian Library at Oxford University, in the Ashmole Collection of documents, another document, the MS 1448, states anonymously, in reference to the princes in the Tower, that: fearing that his nephews might handicap his reign, "*Richard, first taking counsel with the Duke of Buckingham, removed them from the light of this world, by some means or other, vilely and murderously.*"

Some authors believe that since "Parliament" made the princes illegitimate, Richard had nothing to fear from them and hence had no need to murder them. But Richard knew there was a problem, a big problem. Such decisions about marriage and legitimacy were up to the Church authorities, not up to the civil power. And the English people, familiar with broken marriages, knew that this was true. With hostile opinions spreading widely, it was no wonder that Richard's struggle to earn respect was futile. He tried hard, but the burden was too heavy for him to bear.

Queen Elizabeth Woodville Finally Leaves the Sanctuary in March 1484

It was a thorn in Richard's side and a constant irritant that the former queen, then styled Dame Elizabeth Grey, remained in sanctuary. But on 1 March 1484, following prolonged negotiations in February, Elizabeth Woodville finally agreed to leave sanctuary, after the king had publicly promised to protect her *and her daughters.* Despite her vulnerability, Elizabeth had driven a hard bargain. It is highly significant and should be noted that *there was no promise to protect her sons in the Tower,* which means, of course, that they were long dead. Richard offered, and Elizabeth accepted, an annual pension of seven hundred marks. According to Polydore Vergil (1844), the men sent to negotiate with Elizabeth had mentioned that the princes were dead, and this had greatly upset the former queen.

Before a gathering of magnates and bishops at Westminster, the king swore an oath to protect the lives and the welfare of Elizabeth's "illegitimate" royal daughters, the king's very own nieces, if they would leave the sanctuary. It would be hard to imagine that Elizabeth did not ask that her boys be protected also, but she knew what had happened. Richard made no such offer for them, and that confirmed Elizabeth's convictions. It did Richard's reputation no good when he made such an humiliating declaration; it only added to the political damage. Since the king's statement was public, many people would also have noticed that Elizabeth's sons in the Tower were not included in the guarantees. But Richard understood that the eldest daughter of Edward IV, Princess Elizabeth, was considered by many to be the rightful monarch. If he could arrange her marriage, any marriage, then it would ruin the plans of Henry Tudor. It would be even better if he could get his hands on Henry Tudor.

If they had met in private before the agreement, or if messages were carried back and forth, as seems more likely, it is hard to know what Richard would have said to Elizabeth. The king's defenders, underestimating Edward IV's fine queen, often claim that her acquiescence meant that she did not think Richard was guilty of the murders in the Tower. But that takes no account of Elizabeth's vulnerable position and assumes that she was easily deceived, which she was not, especially in matters which concerned her brother-in-law. Richard must have admitted the boys were dead; to have said otherwise would have been unbelievable, since he was not offering to protect them, only his nieces. But the king would have denied that he had anything to do with the death of the princes; and most likely he would have blamed the duke of Buckingham, who by then was safely dead and could not issue any denial. The dowager queen was almost certainly sceptical of Richard, as always, but she had no way to contradict the king – and she desperately needed release from her discomfort in the sanctuary. So, she accepted the offer but continued in her secret conspiracy with Margaret Beaufort against the king. As an aside, it appears probable that Richard also offered a conditional pardon to the marquis of Dorset (Ashdown-Hill, 2011); this explains why Elizabeth Woodville much later, actually in mid 1485, tried to persuade Dorset to return from his self-imposed exile. The likelihood that she had forgiven Richard, as claimed by his defenders, is small; he had physically destroyed both her brother Anthony and three of the children of her body. The reader should ask any devoted mother who to believe.

Richard may have considered marrying Princess Elizabeth to his own son Edward of Middleham; that would have been a clever manoeuvre, as young Edward would be unlikely to rebel and claim his bride's crown against his own father. But Elizabeth and Edward were first cousins, their relationship well within the prohibited four degrees of affinity, which was a severe impediment to their union. And besides, the sickly Edward soon died. Commines alleged that the king even considered the illegitimate son of Bishop Stillington. But that would have been outrageous, and no Woodville would have agreed to it. As it was, not much happened. Stillington's son died a prisoner in France. Meanwhile, the former queen retired to a country house, possibly, but not certainly, near Hertford Castle close to London, under the supervision of Sir John Nesfield, who was responsible for paying the quarterly instalments of her annuity. Others have suggested that she lived in Wiltshire, farther away from London. Some authors claim that Elizabeth was boarded in a back room at Westminster Palace, but the proud dowager queen, busy with her conspiracy, would never have agreed to that. She may have had her daughters with her at times, but the royal princesses were also allowed to spend considerable time at the royal court, where more problems soon arose for King Richard III.

The Final Crisis for King Richard III: His Accelerated Loss of Credibility and the Death of Edward of Middleham

Richard's son and heir, Edward of Middleham, the Prince of Wales, always in poor health, died on 9 April 1484, on the same day of the year as his uncle, King Edward IV, had died. King Richard and Queen Anne were in agony at Nottingham Castle. It was possibly tuberculosis contracted from his mother which caused the death of the young prince. As time passed, it was clear that Queen Anne would have no more children, so Richard said that he would no longer have marital relations with her. Such was his desire to open the way for a new wife and a new heir. Richard said he avoided his wife at his doctor's orders, as she probably had tuberculosis, which was likely true. The king complained openly and bitterly about her inability to have more children, never mind the humiliation this heaped upon his faithful, dying queen.

In July 1484, a man named William Collingbourne published his famous seditious ditty, "The Cat, the Rat, and Lovell, Our Dog, Rule All England under the Hog" (the king's emblem was the wild boar). The ditty was posted on the door of St Paul's Church. To the modern mind, this sounds entertaining, but in the Middle Ages, this was a very serious matter, bordering on treason. Needless to say, the king was not amused. Some claim that Collingbourne was a Lancastrian who was encouraging Henry Tudor to invade England. For his trouble, Collingbourne was hung and drawn and quartered. But most people thought that the punishment was for the sardonic ditty. There was not much time left for the tyrannical King Richard III.

The naval war, which had started just before Edward IV died, began with English attacks on French shipping, but soon it involved retaliation with French attacks on English shipping. Then, after the October Rebellion, it involved accelerated English attacks on both French and Breton shipping as well. Later, it spread to Scottish shipping. This continued into 1484 and proved an expensive campaign for Richard. The English requested that the Bretons keep Sir Edward Woodville under close supervision; they had always requested close supervision for Henry Tudor. The French, fearful of England, demanded that Brittany hand over Henry Tudor, perhaps thinking they could use him for leverage.

Richard III, now fearful of Henry Tudor after the Rennes announcement, needed to reach an accord with the Bretons. During the early summer of 1484, the naval war with Brittany had continued. In June 1484, an agreement was made: the truce was to last from July 1484 to April 1485; Richard promised to provide a thousand archers to help Brittany defend its borders against France; and Brittany promised to hold Henry Tudor in closer custody and to consider possibly even sending him to England. Richard almost succeeded in extraditing Henry Tudor from Brittany, following negotiations between Pierre Landais, the Breton treasurer, and Sir James Tyrell. However, not much happened with this truce, for, warned by Bishop Morton, Henry Tudor escaped to France in September 1484 and the duke of Brittany allowed the English exiles to follow Henry Tudor, no doubt glad to be rid of them. The archers promised by Richard were never sent to Brittany. The suspicion was that Morton obtained his accurate information from Lord Stanley and that the information was passed through Margaret Beaufort. The situation had changed, for the wealthy king of France was much more capable of supporting Henry Tudor than the relatively poor duke of Brittany.

Earlier, in February 1484, Richard had started planning to invade Scotland with attacks by land and sea. He was nearly ready by May 1484. The Scots appealed to France for renewal of the Auld Alliance. In July, the English suffered a disastrous naval loss to a combined Franco-Scottish squadron, and two English captains, including Sir John Nesfield, were captured and had to be ransomed. The Scots had sent repeated missions asking for peace, but Richard showed no interest. In mid 1484, Richard gave his permission for an attack on Scotland led by Scottish exiles; on 22 July 1484, the duke of Albany and the earl of Douglas, at the head of a force of English cavalry, were defeated by royalist forces at the Battle of Lochmaben. Douglas was captured, and Albany fled to France.

In September 1484, Richard III finally responded to James III and made a peace treaty with Scotland. The hostilities of 1481 and 1482 had remained unsettled, the naval conflicts of 1483 and 1484 had continued, and the Lochmaben attack had proved futile. It was in the interests of

Richard and England alike to settle matters. Under threat from Henry Tudor, England would have a problem if Scotland joined Henry Tudor against King Richard. James III sent his commissioners, and the agreement was signed at Nottingham Castle in September 1484. It should be noted, however, that relations between Richard III and James III did not improve. The truce did not stop James from later supporting Henry Tudor with Scottish troops at Bosworth Field in 1485 (Miller, 2003). It can be easily summarized that Richard's foreign policies were far from successful.

Late in 1484, the earl of Oxford escaped from Hammes Castle in Calais and took with him the commander, Sir James Blount, and a good many English soldiers. They joined Henry Tudor in France. Young Blount's wife then defended Hammes for several weeks; the only way the king could take back the Castle of Hammes was to guarantee the lady's and her soldiers' safe passage to France in early 1485. It was a frustrating humiliation for King Richard III.

Richard courted the voluptuous Princess Elizabeth, newly arrived at court from sanctuary, and soon gave serious consideration to marriage with her. Princess Elizabeth, eighteen years old, an ambitious young woman, was no doubt impressed by the serious attentions of the powerful king. According to the historian Sir George Buck, writing in the early seventeenth century, the princess indicated in letters to the duke of Norfolk that she was very much in favour of her union with Richard III and that Elizabeth Woodville made no objections. The critics of Elizabeth Woodville delight in suggesting that the former queen saw an alternative way to restore the fortunes of her Woodville family. Nobody could accuse Elizabeth Woodville of lacking resourcefulness, but she knew that there were huge objections to such a marriage, namely the close affinity of an uncle with his niece, well within the four degrees of affinity. And besides, she was busy with other plans, trying to increase support for Henry Tudor. Nevertheless, the idea is plausible. It would have been a brilliant move by Richard III if he could have achieved this union, as it would have greatly weakened the strategy of Henry Tudor. Some have suggested that the Pope could have been persuaded to grant permission, in which case Richard would have become the rightful king of England by marriage, in right of his new wife, and no longer considered the Usurper King. It should be noted that when Henry Tudor heard of these events at the English court, there must have been some consideration that his betrothal with Princess Elizabeth was voided. It was claimed that the Tudor government later punished the dowager queen, but Henry knew that she was working hard with her late husband's friends to improve Henry's political support in England.

By late 1484, the king, short of money, resumed the use of Benevolences, contravening his own law. In December 1484, Richard III issued a public proclamation in which he branded Peter Courtenay, the bishop of Exeter; Thomas, Marquis of Dorset; Henry and Jasper Tudor; John, Earl of Oxford; and Sir Edward Woodville as "traitors, murderers, adulterers and extortioners," which was quite an exaggeration. It would appear that Elizabeth had not yet asked Dorset to return to England. The king declared that Henry Tudor had no right or title in the Realm of England. Richard warned that the rebels would subvert the laws of England, confiscate the lawful property of Englishmen, and abandon the ancient claim of England to territories in France.

Also in December 1484, Richard issued a pardon to Bishop John Morton, but the bishop turned it down; he did not believe that Richard had long to serve as king of England. He could not have based his opinion on the superior forces of Henry Tudor; more likely, he based it on the unpopularity of Richard III, which he easily discerned. In March 1485, Richard also offered pardon to Richard Woodville, the third Earl Rivers, but he, too, turned it down. It was difficult to pry Henry Tudor's supporters away.

The Death of Queen Anne; Richard III's Thoughts of Remarriage; and the Rejection of Lady Elizabeth of York

A mournful and humiliated Queen Anne died on 16 March 1485. On the day of her death, from what was likely pulmonary tuberculosis, there was an eclipse of the sun, which briefly darkened the land. It was heavily rumoured that Richard had hastened her death by poisoning. Although this was likely not true, it reflected the superstition of the age and the virulent anger of the English people against the king. With no obvious heir and with Richard in desperate need of a fertile wife, the royal succession was severely compromised.

Richard's plan to marry his niece Elizabeth Plantagenet was never considered viable by the council. As it required papal dispensation for an uncle to marry his niece, it would mean reversing the Titulus Regius to legitimize Elizabeth and thus admit the falsehood of the 1461 marriage contract story. Also, it would mean an accommodation with the hated Woodville family, which would have been way too much for Richard's confederates. The king was told by his most trusted advisors, Sir William Catesby and Sir Richard Ratcliffe, that he had no support for this marriage, particularly in the north of England where Queen Anne's Neville family was revered and where the king's residual support was centred. No doubt, Catesby and Ratcliffe greatly feared the possible return of their Woodville political opponents. According to the *Croyland Chronicle* (1854), Catesby and Ratcliffe assembled twelve doctors of divinity who assured the king that the Pope would not allow such a marriage between an uncle and his niece. That Catesby had to go to such lengths confirms how seriously Richard considered this marriage. It is too bad that Catesby did not show a similar respect for the valid authority of the Church in matrimonial matters when Richard, in 1483, needed to invalidate the 1464 marriage of King Edward IV. Perhaps the twelve doctors of divinity could have told Catesby the lawful way to proceed, consistent with long custom and precedent.

Some critics have denied that Richard was attracted to Princess Elizabeth, but, again, we must consider the reliable Croyland Chronicler (1854), who described the behaviour of Richard and Elizabeth together at Christmas 1484 as exceedingly close, especially considering that Queen Anne was still alive. Croyland made the following observations: there was "far too much attention given to dancing and gaiety, and vain changes of apparel"; this behaviour "caused the people to murmur [gossip] and the nobles and prelates to wonder thereat"; and it was "said by many that the king, anticipating the death or divorce of the queen, was bent on contracting a marriage with the said Elizabeth."

After the death of Queen Anne, the rumour and innuendo ran so hot that on 30 March 1485, Richard had to make a public announcement at the priory of the Knights of St John at Clerkenwell in London, saying that he greatly regretted the death of the queen and that he did not intend to marry Princess Elizabeth, who he planned to send away from the court to Sheriff Hutton Castle in Yorkshire. The king had to assure his subjects that he truly loved his queen. It was another humiliating fiasco for the last Yorkist king. With his treatment of the queen and his incestuous relationship with his niece, Richard III's political support, always poor, eroded still further.

Richard began again looking for a husband for Elizabeth, as he had promised her mother. He had in mind first the earl of Desmond in Ireland and, later, Manuel, the duke of Beja, in Portugal. More important, the king looked for a new wife and a new queen for himself; he opened negotiations with Portugal for the hand of Princess Joanna (1452–1490). She was the daughter of King Alfonso V, the granddaughter of King Edward I of Portugal, and the great-granddaughter of King John I, who had married Philippa, a daughter of John of Gaunt and his first wife, Blanche of Lancaster. Philippa is shown in the Lancastrian family tree (see Appendix B). The negotiations included the possibility of a double wedding, Richard and Elizabeth together with the Portuguese royals! It appears that Joanna, a deeply religious woman, had a prophetic dream that Richard III would be killed in battle, and therefore she said that she would marry Richard III if he was still alive. She was said to be convinced that she would not have to honour her promise; no doubt, she also feared the grave political risk. Joanna was thirty-three years old at the time, and she died five years later. It is doubtful that this proposed marriage would have solved King Richard III's great problem. The impatient earl of Lincoln, son of Elizabeth, the older sister of Richard III, must have been convinced that he could yet be king.

Another possible bride for Richard was the fourteen-year-old Isabel of Castile; she was the great-granddaughter of Catherine, a daughter of John of Gaunt by his second wife, Constance of Castile. But her claim was considered junior to that of Joanna. Nevertheless, a younger wife would have provided more hope of an heir for Richard. In either case, these possible marriages would have satisfied Richard's desire to combine the Houses of Lancaster and York and so end the long dynastic conflict.

The Events of Mid 1485 and the Approach of Doom

In the meantime, Princess Elizabeth York was not happy about her rejection at Clerkenwell; she joined with Lord Thomas Stanley, her Woodville mother, and Margaret Beaufort in giving further encouragement for Henry Tudor to invade England. Princess Elizabeth sent Henry Tudor a letter and a ring, explaining that she was still interested in becoming his wife. The ballad "The Song of the Lady Bessy" reflects Lady Elizabeth's support for Henry Tudor and her newfound antagonism towards Richard III. It is plausible that this developed mostly after Clerkenwell. The ballad, written by Humphrey Brereton (1829), a servant of Lord Thomas Stanley, describes how Elizabeth conspired with the Stanleys and had Brereton take her letter and ring with a shipment of gold to Henry Tudor in France. Brereton was said to sail secretly out of Liverpool, a little-used port in Lancashire, the home of Lord Stanley. Whether this tale is true cannot be established, but it seems plausible, considering the precarious political situation.

On 11 March 1485, Richard III had appointed his sixteen-year-old illegitimate son, known in history as John of Gloucester, to be the captain of Calais. The king referred to John as "our dear bastard son." Never mind what happened to his dear "bastard" nephews, Edward and Richard. The magnates were appalled by the royal hypocrisy, and the commons heard the rumours. Never mind the youth and inexperience of such a young man as John of Gloucester.

In June 1485, a similar proclamation to that in December 1484 was issued, but it omitted the name of Dorset, who Richard may have pardoned (Hammond, 2010). Henry Tudor must have noticed this omission. Soon after, probably in July 1485, in response to his mother's belated plea, Dorset made an unsuccessful attempt to return to England, but he was arrested by Henry Tudor's men before he could leave France. As Dorset knew Henry Tudor's plans, Richard was thereby deprived of valuable intelligence.

On 24 July 1485, Richard III dismissed Bishop John Russell, the chancellor of England. As Russell had no doubt that Richard had usurped the throne, the relationship between the two men must have been increasingly strained. To dismiss a man of such high reputation was probably also a mistake and contributed to the king's failing credibility.

Also in July 1485, Lord Thomas Stanley, with the king's permission, left court to visit his estates in Lancashire, or so he said. Richard was suspicious, so he held the magnate's son, George Stanley, Lord Strange, as hostage for Lord Thomas Stanley's good behaviour and support. This was a rather unusual thing to do and much against the standard rules of knighthood, but Richard's desperation can be understood. After Lord

Strange told Richard that Sir William Stanley supported Henry Tudor, the king, always suspicious, made an official declaration that Sir William Stanley, the brother of Thomas Stanley, was a traitor. But the king made no move against the knight, which proved to be another mistake. These ill-considered decisions meant that both Stanleys came to believe that they might do better if Richard did not survive when Henry Tudor invaded. Later, at Bosworth, in response to threats against Lord Strange, the cold and crafty Lord Thomas Stanley simply said that he had other sons. He had two more.

As the crisis approached, Richard III became nervous and agitated and suffered from insomnia. He was sometimes mentally confused. The pressure on him must have been enormous. He took a few days off to go hunting in Sherwood Forest. But when the news of the Tudor landing in Wales came, Richard, staying at Nottingham Castle, said confidently that he welcomed the chance to settle the score, once and for all time. Richard set about raising an army for the defence of his kingdom. It might be surmised that this was not a serious problem for the king of England, but Richard had to use considerable persuasion. Numerous letters were sent commanding all who owned property in England to attend him on the battlefield; refusal by anybody would result in the loss of possession, inheritance, or even life. Nevertheless, Charles Ross (1999) reviewed the number of the earls in England who attended the king at Bosworth and found it to be quite satisfactory, considering that some were very young and some were very old. But of the four great magnates who had earlier supported Richard III, only Howard of Norfolk remained true; Buckingham was already executed for treason, Northumberland attended at Bosworth but would not join the fight, and Stanley attended but sent his men late to support Henry Tudor. It is said that whereas the City of York sent three hundred well-armed men in June 1483 for the usurpation, this time, in 1485, they sent only eighty men – and they did not arrive in time to help the king. This may have been part of the alienation of the duke of Northumberland, who may have been slow to call out the men of York. But if it is true that King Richard found it difficult to gain assistance, then the same could also be said of Henry Tudor, who was not widely supported either, at least not with arms at Bosworth. The English aristocracy was tired of the warfare and was not easily persuaded to join with either side.

In retrospect, it became obvious that Richard's foreign policy was a dismal failure. Despite his best efforts, in the end his neighbours around the English Channel all decided against him. When Edward IV ruled, the French dared not risk an invasion of England; the memory of Edward at Picquigny in 1475 was too much to bear. While Edward lived, the duke of Brittany kept Henry Tudor under tight control, but once Edward was gone, Henry Tudor had much more freedom in Brittany – and even more after he fled to France. And despite the September 1484 treaty with Scotland, the Scots still managed to appear at Bosworth Field to support the Tudor invasion of England. Stronger, more-peaceful diplomatic missions may well have prevented all this and allowed Richard to rule England in peace.

Henry Tudor Invades England; the Battle of Bosworth Field in August 1485; the Fall of the House of York; the Death of Richard III

From his position in France, Henry Tudor raised his invasion force. He had perhaps five hundred English exiles with him. There were additional English soldiers from Hammes, supplied when the earl of Oxford and Sir James Blount had escaped to join the exiles. There were additional soldiers who accompanied the wife of Sir James Blount, and about a thousand Scots sent by King James III (Miller, 2003). There were eighteen hundred French soldiers supplied through Lord Cordes by King Charles VIII. So, in all, Henry Tudor had an army of nearly four thousand men when he left France (Ross, 1999). On 1 August 1485, his force sailed down the River Seine and put to the open sea, bound for England. They avoided Richard's fleet in the English Channel. With a Tudor wind, on 7 August 1485, Henry Tudor landed near Milford Haven in Wales. He kissed the ground and said his thanksgiving, and he advanced to Cardigan and then to Shrewsbury to recruit more Welsh and English forces. Neither Henry Tudor nor Richard III could get Lord Thomas Stanley or his brother Sir William Stanley to commit themselves, but Sir Thomas Talbot with Shropshire men and Sir Thomas Savage with Cheshire men joined Henry Tudor. They advanced on to Lichfield and then to Tamworth. They were joined by Sir Rhys ap Thomas, who had promised support earlier, with Welsh retainers, and then by Sir Walter Hungerford and Sir Thomas Bourchier, loyal servants of King Edward IV, with English recruits. Sir Rhys had made a famous promise to Richard that Henry Tudor would have to walk over his body in order to invade England; so, the Welshman sat under a bridge while the rebel forces passed over!

As he marched from Nottingham to Leicester, Richard received word that Lord Thomas Stanley was ill with the sweating sickness and could not join him. Richard knew it was treason. But many of the lords, knights, and landed gentry would not join him. Nor would they join Henry Tudor. They decided to stay home, tired of the constant quarrel over the throne and just wanting to be left in peace. In the end, among the magnates, only Norfolk was enthusiastic in his support for the king. Surrey went with his father, Northumberland stayed in the rear, and Lincoln was looking after his own interest in the crown. The Stanleys appeared noncommittal but had secretly promised Henry Tudor.

When Henry Tudor invaded England, as promised at Rennes Cathedral in December 1483, Richard III should have won the Battle of Bosworth Field on 22 August 1485, for he was by far a more experienced military commander than Henry Tudor. Plus, his army was much larger and occupied the higher ground on the Redmore Plain (Miller, 2003). But before the battle, there were troubling signs: Richard had nightmares, his camp was disorganized, the chaplains were late to celebrate the Mass, and the officers had no hot breakfast because the cooks had overslept (*Croyland Chronicle,* 1854). Many of his supporters deserted, or so it was said, and many did not fight very hard. This battle was poorly described. Over the years, there have been numerous conflicting accounts.

Ignoring the usual aggressive Yorkist strategy of King Edward IV, Richard III drew up in a very defensive position near marshy ground facing to the south-west and left primary aggression to the rebel army. Edward IV would never have done that. Empingham and Bosworth are only thirty-five miles apart. Edward would have attacked on the open plain, with fierce cannonade and longbow arrow-storm – this to soften up the rebels before they advanced too close. Unlike his older brother, Richard did not fight on the front line but remained behind the lines until it was too late (see Appendix I–K). It is unclear why Richard failed to take the initiative, but demoralization must have been setting in. Richard's own main division never really engaged with the rebel army, and his rearguard division under Northumberland was situated way to the rear. This meant that Richard made no use of his superior numbers. He also made poor use of his superior artillery. Northumberland said that his men were tired after a long march and he needed to keep watch on the Stanleys, who were positioned off to one side on the south. This was Richard's first experience as overall commander in a pitched battle; he certainly missed his brother, England's great Warrior King Edward IV.

Henry Tudor had fine commanders with him, especially the legendary earl of Oxford, John de Vere, and the experienced soldiers, Sir Edward Woodville, Sir Rhys ap Thomas, and Jasper Tudor. The rebel army was initially arranged in three close-together battles led by Oxford in the centre, with Talbot and Savage on the flanks. On the south-west side of the royal army, the rebels advanced north and then wheeled in perfect formation to face the north-east and advanced on Norfolk's vanguard division. Their discipline was superb. When attacked, the three rebel units merged into a single tightly closed formation, spiked with halberds like a porcupine. This solid mass stubbornly resisted all attempts by Norfolk's division to penetrate and destroy it. The closed formation, with every man packed close to his banner, maintained a slow but relentless advance. The royal army could not stop them. Richard failed to use his cannon to break the Tudor progress, probably because Norfolk's men, by then, were in the way. Richard's most loyal ally, John Howard, the duke of Norfolk, was killed by an arrow in the throat after his bevor was dislodged, it is said following a clash with the earl of Oxford. Howard's son, Thomas, Earl of Surrey, replaced his father in command. Not only Surrey's captains, but also Richard III must have been greatly discouraged; they must have felt that their men were not fighting hard and that too many were just watching, instead of coming to support the king. Lord Stanley and Sir William remained motionless on the south side of the battlefield, and Northumberland did not move from his position far in the rear.

As failure loomed, Richard decided on a sudden desperate charge against the Tudor guard, which was sheltered behind the right flank of the advancing rebel army but which was exposed when it moved a short distance towards the Stanleys. Richard had not laid the political groundwork for the struggle, but not for lack of trying. He was so unpopular that it had proved impossible. The morale of his men was low. Some were leaving. There were additional forces and heavy artillery on the way, for which Richard should have waited, but his self-confidence and his contempt for Henry Tudor overwhelmed his judgement – and important potential supporters failed to help him at a crucial time late in the battle. Thomas, Lord Stanley, and his brother Sir William Stanley, on the south side, waited to see who would win. They had eventually told Henry Tudor that they would enter on his side, but they needed to wait for the best opportunity. Their treason was so bad that they needed to make very sure that Richard III did not survive the battle.

When Henry Tudor took his small guard south towards the Stanleys, Richard and his guard charged at a thunderous gallop to kill the Tudor and decide the battle. The Stanleys finally entered the fray when it was seen that Richard was personally vulnerable as he closed in on the Tudor guard. Henry Percy, the fourth earl of Northumberland, in command of the rearguard, a fourth of Richard's army, never entered the battle, even when a request was signalled and even when Sir William Stanley made his move against the Yorkist king.

Richard was reckless; he ignored the important principle that the king should personally survive the battle, whether won or lost, in order to fight another day. He had forgotten the strategic flight of King Edward IV in 1470 when he had been faced with hopeless odds. Despite the advice of Sir William Catesby that it was time to escape the battlefield on a fresh horse, Richard needlessly exposed his person in an aggressive yet heroic effort to kill Henry Tudor and so win the day. It is said he almost succeeded, but Richard had out-charged his protection. Richard knocked Sir John Cheney off his horse and killed Sir William Brandon, the standard-bearer for Henry Tudor. But then the king was unhorsed, caught in boggy ground, surrounded by scores of men, and killed in combat. He had multiple wounds and finally went down with a crushing poleaxe blow delivered by Sir William Gardiner, a powerful Welshman. The Plantagenet dynasty, on the English throne since the year 1154, and the proud, independent Royal House of York both died at Bosworth Field that day, along with a valiant but reckless King Richard III.

As soon as the news spread, the fighting more or less ceased. The king's army laid down its arms, and some fled the field. The earl of Surrey is sometimes accused of surrendering, but he knew that the royal army was beaten. There was not much pursuit of the defeated Yorkists, but there was some; Henry Tudor did not wish to begin his reign with a bloodbath. Many Yorkists came to him and swore their allegiance on the battlefield. Many more followed soon after, including Thomas, Earl of Surrey, and Henry, Earl of Northumberland, who were both sent to the Tower, probably for their own protection. The earl of Lincoln survived and was also reconciled with Henry Tudor. Sir Richard Ratcliffe and Sir Robert Brackenbury were killed; Sir William Catesby was captured and executed a day later; and Viscount Lovell escaped to fight Henry Tudor another day at Stoke Field in 1487.

It was a remarkable ending to a medieval battle, heavily reflecting the extreme unpopularity of Richard III and the general relief of the English nation. Men had joined the king, but their hearts were not with him. Richard's badly mutilated body was shamefully treated; it was slung naked over a packhorse, held uncovered and on public view for two days, and buried at the Greyfriars Church of St Mary in Leicester, in an unmarked grave below the choir stalls. This severe mistreatment may not have been unusual for a king fallen in battle. King Richard's severe mistreatment was considered similar to that of Charles the Bold at Nancy in 1477 and James IV at Flodden Field in 1513 (Ashdown-Hill, 2011); but the mistreatment was in direct contrast to the respectful treatment given Warwick and Montagu after Barnet.

The victorious Henry Tudor paid for an inexpensive headstone ten years later, which means that nobody had properly marked Richard's grave in the meantime. For centuries, his burial place has remained unknown, but in the recent months of 2012–13, it was found under the remnants of the Greyfriars Church, the site now covered by a city parking lot in Leicester. It was alleged that, fifty years after his death, Richard's bones were thrown in the River Soar and that his stone coffin was used as a horse trough for many years in Leicester. This story is obviously not true, based on recent discoveries, but the fable and its acceptance is more evidence of the widespread anger against Richard III. At the time of his death, Richard III must have been one of the most disrespected kings of England. Of late, in our own times, the Richard III Society has struggled mightily to restore the better part of the king's reputation. It is a fair question to ask: What other English king has such an organization devoted to the support of his posterity? Certainly not England's great Warrior King Edward IV.

After Bosworth Field, the Tudor reign began; Henry Tudor became King Henry VII. His coronation was held on 30 October 1485, which was clearly meant to indicate that Henry claimed the throne by right of conquest and by his doubtful Beaufort family history. He did not wish to acknowledge that he needed to marry a Yorkist princess to validate his throne. Henry VII and Elizabeth of York were married on 18 January 1486. His bride's coronation did not occur until 25 November 1487. The Tudors would rule England for the next 118 years.

Mary Clive (1974) blamed Lord John Howard for the disastrous reign of Richard III. She implied that without the encouragement of Howard, Richard would not have pursued his treacherous course but would have maintained loyalty to his nephews and served his days as Lord Protector. In the Tower in 1485, Thomas Howard must have reflected on how his formidable father had caused his own death and that of Richard III, Edward V, Prince Richard, Lord Hastings, Anthony Woodville, Richard Grey, Thomas Vaughan, the duke of Buckingham, and many other good men. Surrey must have considered how a complete outsider and a wandering exile such as Henry VII had ascended the English throne, and with a relatively weak hereditary claim. King Edward IV must have rolled in his magnificent tomb at the misjudgements of his younger brother. How many men had died for the House of York, and yet to no avail? Ironically, the damage to the legacy of Edward IV was huge. It was no fault of the first Yorkist king, but, sadly, it was certainly the fault of the last Yorkist king.

Despite all of Edward IV's magnificent victories on the battlefield and, later, his prosperous reign, it was ultimately the House of Lancaster which prevailed in the War of the Roses. When the Warrior King died in 1483, the House of York proceeded literally to tear itself apart. It was left up to the Parliament, to the English people, and to Queen Elizabeth Woodville to ensure that the blood of Edward IV was passed down in the royal line. Henry VII would soon marry Edward's eldest daughter, Princess Elizabeth of York, and there would be a more than sufficient number of royal children to carry the genes of King Edward IV into the brave new world.

CHAPTER 7

The Great Mystery of the Yorkist Period

The Princes in the Tower

The mystery surrounding the fate of King Edward's sons, Edward V and his brother young Richard, remains somewhat unresolved, but the confusion is mainly related to the effort of some scholars who refuse to understand, or are unable to understand, the specific treachery of Richard III in relation to the throne, despite his reputed excellent government and his much admired modern vision. The mystery has been exhaustively analyzed by Alison Weir (1999) and Helen Maurer (2000), who seem to have reached some definite and well-founded conclusions.

During the reign of King Henry VII, Sir James Tyrell, in 1502, confessed to the murders of the princes in the Tower, admittedly while under threat of execution for treasonable assistance given to Edmund de la Pole, a Yorkist nephew of Edward IV. This threat is sometimes stated as sufficient reason not to believe his confession, but Tyrell knew with certainty that he was doomed. And, more likely, a man with heavy guilt crushing his conscience may have wished to relieve his country and himself of the burden before his death. Most important, in his confession he named precisely where the missing children were buried in the Tower, under the stair foot leading up to the Chapel of St John in the White Tower. Up to that point in time, nobody else had ever provided such specific information.

According to Sir Thomas More (2005), Tyrell stated that he received his instructions from Richard III. He described how he had stood guard outside the royal bedchamber while John Dighton and Miles Forrest smothered the princes in their bedclothes. Only then did he enter the chamber to confirm their deaths, as he knew this was an heinous crime. They buried the boys in a wooden chest lowered into a great hole that they had prepared under a staircase leading up to the Chapel of St John in the White Tower. They covered the chest with a great mass of paving stones. No doubt, they must have done well to cover the disturbance. Perhaps surprisingly, Tyrell also claimed that he did not know where the bodies remained at the time of his confession, as Richard III had planned to have Brackenbury's priest remove them from the Tower and drop them in the mouth of the River Thames. However, it is likely this never happened, probably because it would have involved much heavy work and many more people committed to secrecy and most likely because the priest died a few days after the murders. It is not unreasonable to believe that Richard inspected the burial site and decided that the bodies were adequately hidden. Certainly, subsequent general Tower searches for the Yorkist children were never successful.

And most important, at the same time in 1502, John Dighton was questioned and gave a similar but independent description of the murders. The presumed confession documents of 1502 were likely stored in the archives. Henry VII did not announce anything because his men, who had searched the Tower in 1485, had not found the dead princes – and the king did not want to draw attention to the matter anymore. He followed an ancient principle of "the least said, the soonest mended." Besides, virtually the whole world of Christendom believed that Richard III murdered the princes, so why risk disturbing the universal conclusion which suited Henry Tudor the most?

Sir James Tyrell had done well under Henry VII, at least for the first fifteen years of the reign. He had received two pardons in 1486, most likely for his support of Richard III, and had been allowed to continue in his appointment as governor of Guînes Castle at Calais. If the Tudor king had made a public announcement in 1502, he did not want it falsely suggested that the generous treatment in 1486 had been a reward for the murder of the princes in 1483. More likely, in 1502, Henry VII took it into account that Sir James Tyrell, by accomplishing the murders, had opened the way for his own ascent to the throne. It should be remembered that Henry was a Lancastrian and viewed the Yorkist kings as usurpers; he felt no reason to raise public sympathy for them, and so the less said, the better.

The presumed confession documents of 1502, long in the archives, were revealed after 1513 by Sir Thomas More when he wrote his book *The History of Richard III* (More, 2005); unfortunately, those source documents have since been lost. This has aroused the suspicion that there never were any confession documents. But the intimate details of the story as presented by Sir Thomas More strongly suggest that such documents existed at one time (Weir, 1999). It is easy to believe that Henry VII may have written nothing, but his agents sent to question Tyrell and Dighton would undoubtedly have followed protocol and made written reports.

The unpublished incomplete manuscript was discovered in his papers at home after Sir Thomas More's execution in 1535. But it was not until 1557 that his nephew William Rastell had the book published. It is interesting to note that in Sir Francis Bacon's book on the reign of King Henry VII, the author of the introduction (Rawson Lumby, a Cambridge professor of divinity) used a different title for Sir Thomas More's book, namely *The History of the Life and Death of King Edward V, and of the Usurpation of Richard III*. This appears to be a more accurate description of what Sir Thomas More actually wrote (Bacon, 1889).

Sir Thomas More (1478–1535) was a careful historian and an accomplished lawyer; he believed his account of the confessions to be true. The author probably interviewed John Dighton, who was still alive at the time. Alison Weir (1999) quotes More as saying of Dighton, "He yet walks alive and in good possibility to be hanged ere he die." In addition, More had close contact with Bishop John Morton, his mentor, another who must have known many of the details. But the relationship with Morton should not be exaggerated. In 1491, Thomas More entered Morton's service at the age of thirteen years. Morton died nine years later in 1500, so most of the contact occurred during More's formative teenage years, and close contact was probably limited by the generational difference. Sir Thomas More did not write his book until 1513, when he would have been recalling much earlier conversations; and More may not have finished his manuscript until 1518 or so. It is unlikely that Morton wrote More's book, as some have claimed, and even less likely that Sir Thomas More would have adopted it as his own and claimed authorship.

There were others at the Tudor court who Sir Thomas More would have interviewed: namely, Bishop Richard Foxe (1448–1528), later the bishop of Winchester; Christopher Urswick (1448–1522), Henry VII's confessor; and Reginald Bray (1440–1503), a close friend of Margaret Beaufort. Sir Thomas More (2005) may be quoted: "I shall rehearse you the dolorous end of those babes [the princes], not after every way that I have heard, but after that way I have so heard by such men and by such means as methinks it were hard but it should be true."

In other words, there were some unreliable accounts, but More took great pains to seek out only the most honest correspondents. There were further witnesses who could provide more information for Sir Thomas More: his own father, Sir John More (1451–1530), a London lawyer and judge, who still practiced in 1483; John Roper (1460–1524), later Attorney General for Henry VIII and the father of Sir Thomas More's son-in-law, William Roper; and Dr John Argentine (1443–1508), the physician who attended the princes frequently in the Tower and who was probably the last to see them alive. In addition, it is very likely that Sir Thomas also discussed the story with four elderly ladies resident at the Minoresses Convent in London (Weir, 1999). They were Elizabeth, the daughter of Sir Robert Brackenbury, in whom Sir Robert may possibly have confided; Mary Tyrell, the sister of Sir James Tyrell, who may also have had pertinent conversations with Sir James; Anne Montgomery, the widow of Sir Thomas Montgomery, a close friend of Edward IV, an executor of Edward IV's last will; and Elizabeth Mowbray (1443–1507), the dowager duchess of Norfolk, wife of the fourth duke of Norfolk, younger sister of Lady Eleanor Butler, mother of Anne Mowbray, and mother-in-law of the murdered Prince Richard. These elderly ladies, especially the dowager duchess of Norfolk, were in a position to know about the princes; and Sir Thomas More, who probably had long conversations with them, must have felt confident that they were in accord with his basic interpretation of the events.

Sir Thomas More believed that Tyrell rode to London from Warwick and that the murders occurred in late August. But Polydore Vergil (1844) suggested that Tyrell rode to London from York. As it is known that Richard III, during his royal progress, reached Pontefract, near York, on 27 August 1483, Tyrell may have departed for London about the same date or a little later. Alison Weir (1999) said that the princes died on or about 3 September 1483. She reached her conclusion from the analysis of the London Wardrobe Accounts of the Palace, which showed Tyrell's presence in London at that time (Kendall, 2002), and then by analyzing how long it would take for Tyrell to ride from York to London, accomplish his monstrous task, and then ride back to York in time for the investiture of King Richard's son, Edward, as Prince of Wales on 8 September 1483.

Some have criticized the work of Sir Thomas More. His account was embellished with events which were not described by Polydore Vergil (1844); but More described the events of three months in 1483, whereas Polydore Vergil described the history of three reigns from 1422 to 1483. It was natural that there was more detail in the account of Sir Thomas More. Furthermore, Sir Thomas used a classical literary device by inventing speeches to describe what he thought was said; this has suggested to some that he is not a reliable historian. But the physical events described by Sir Thomas More, Polydore Vergil, and others are broadly in agreement. Some have pointed out that nearly all of More's sources were likely Tudor supporters. While this is not quite true, it should be realized that nearly everybody living at the time believed Richard to be guilty. And Sir Thomas More, a great scholar and statesman of the age, was quite capable of detecting untruthful bias.

Giles St Aubyn (1983) has reviewed other reasons not to accept More's account, but St Aubyn clearly believes its essential truthfulness. Neither Tyrell nor Dighton was punished for the murder of the princes, but they carried out the orders of their king, who must therefore bear all the blame. And Tyrell was punished for other reasons. Dighton was not punished because many years had elapsed and a statute of limitations had been lawful since 1484. Brackenbury never suggested the king was responsible for the murders, but the constable was fiercely loyal to Richard and, like many Englishmen, knew that the princes would have to be eliminated if Richard was to reign in peace. Richard III rewarded Brackenbury for his failure, but Richard understood how difficult the decision must have been for an honest man. After all, Brackenbury did eventually hand over the keys to the Tower.

At least nine people knew about the king's orders to the Tower; they were Richard himself, his page, John Greene, James Tyrell, Miles Forrest,

John Dighton, Robert Brackenbury, the priest, and Will Slaughter. But it did not matter, for if they revealed the secret, then it would only join the flood of other rumours and theories which circulated at that time in 1483. In addition, there was never a formal investigation at which they could have been compelled to testify under oath. And several of the above people really knew very little: for instance, the page. Some were dead: for instance, Miles Forrest and the priest. So, that means only six people, including Richard himself. Really, only five people had procurable knowledge. More said that letters were carried to the Tower, which would have been very incriminating, but we do not know what happened to the letters. Very likely, it was intended that they be destroyed.

Another mystery for some critics is that Henry made no use of the Tyrell confession. He never announced to the public that the murderers had confessed and the matter was resolved. Some claim that Henry invented the story, but that is very unlikely, given that he never used it for any purpose. Henry only wanted to be sure in his own mind that the princes were dead, as he had always believed; the Tyrell confession gave him that assurance, and that is all he wanted. Henry never intended any public announcement. The whole world believed that the princes were dead and that Richard III was responsible; there was nothing further to add, especially as his men had already searched in 1485 and not found the princes. Henry believed Tyrell's claim that they had been reburied by the Tower priest; that explained why no bodies could be produced. The last thing the Tudor king wanted was for the matter to be discussed further, especially as his own claim to the throne was widely considered suspect. So far as the public was concerned, Henry's intention was to "let sleeping dogs lie" so he could reign over England in peace.

Sir Francis Bacon (1889), writing in 1622, gave another account of the murders which closely agreed with More's account. But there were some important differences, notably in the possible dates. Henry VII was much aggravated by the activities of Perkin Warbeck, the pretender, who some considered to be Richard, Duke of York, the younger of the two princes in the Tower. Henry needed to reconfirm in his own mind that young Richard had indeed been murdered in 1483, as he had always believed.

The following is from Sir Francis Bacon:

> There were but four persons who could speak upon knowledge
> to the murder of the Duke of York [young Richard]: Sir James
> Tyrell, the employed man from King Richard; John Dighton
> and Miles Forrest[,] his [Tyrell's] servants, the two butchers
> or tormentors; and the priest of the Tower that buried them
> [allegedly somewhere else]. Of which four, Miles Forrest and
> the priest were dead, and there remained alive only Sir James
> Tyrell and John Dighton. These two the king caused to be
> committed to the Tower, and examined touching the manner
> of the death of the two innocent princes. They [Tyrell and
> Dighton] agreed both in a tale, as the King [Henry VII] gave
> out to this effect.

There followed a brief account of the murders, which was the same
as that of Sir Thomas More. The date for this examination by Henry VII
does not seem at all clear, but from what follows in Bacon's narrative,
it must have been before Warbeck's execution in 1499, before the time
Warbeck campaigned in Cornwall in 1497, and before Sir William Stanley
was executed in 1495 for allegedly supporting Warbeck. All these dates
preceded the investigations described by Sir Thomas More, which are
usually dated 1501 or 1502. But it would be possible that Bacon did
not stay with a precise chronology in his history. As the tale was highly
favourable to Henry VII's claim to the throne and with the two princes
being dead, Bacon suggested that this was why the king allowed the two
murderers to go free.

As Bacon appears to relate, it was presumed that the word in political
circles was that only four men knew the facts about the death of the
princes, namely Sir James Tyrell, John Dighton, Miles Forrest, and the
Tower priest – and the latter two were known to be dead. It seems from
Bacon's account that the identity of those involved in the murders was at
least common knowledge among the king's advisors and other officials in
the Tudor government, if not among the commons.

But what Henry "gave out," or communicated, was that the two men,
Tyrell and Dighton, both held in the Tower, gave essentially the same
tale. And that tale was as follows: King Richard sent the death warrant
to Brackenbury, but the officer refused the request to put the princes to
death. King Richard then sent Sir James Tyrell, who obtained the Tower

keys for one night. Dighton and Forrest smothered the boys in bed and called Tyrell to see the dead bodies. Then, they buried the boys deep under the paving stones at the stair foot. When they reported to Richard, the king wanted the bodies moved to a better place by the Tower priest. Henry "gave out" this information probably only to his councillors and others, rather than in the form of a general public announcement. It is from those officials, or possibly from their friends and descendants, that Bacon obtained his version of the murders. Alternatively, it was from those people that Bacon was able to confirm the version given by Sir Thomas More in the publication of 1557. Bacon does not list Sir Thomas More as a primary source, but in the Introduction it is stated that Bacon derived "some few matters" from More's book. It is concluded that Bacon derived his story of the princes mainly from other sources, but he would have made comparisons with More's work.

Bacon gives the impression that it was King Henry himself who personally went to the Tower and obtained the evidence from the two men, and it was King Henry who agreed that Tyrell and Dighton corroborated the same story. Henry then felt sufficiently reassured that the princes were dead, as he had always believed. Sir Francis Bacon's and Sir Thomas More's versions of the story are essentially the same, but Bacon's version of the Tudor interrogation seems to have occurred in 1495 or thereabouts, and More's version of the Tudor interrogation seems to have occurred in 1502. Bacon's version seems to have come from Henry VII himself by word of mouth, as the king put nothing to paper, whereas More's version presumably came from examination of the presumed confession documents in the archives. The defenders of Richard III tend to question Sir Thomas More's version of history, but it appears that Sir Francis Bacon confirmed the story. All this might suggest that Tyrell and Dighton underwent interrogation twice and related the same story both times; first to Henry VII personally in about 1495, and second to the king's official agents in 1502. However, it is equally likely that Bacon, writing 120 years later, had the dates wrong, and therefore his chronology was also wrong. But the events described agreed closely with those described by Sir Thomas More.

The Bones of 1674 and 1678

Nearly two hundred years after the death of the princes, there were found in 1674, in the reign of King Charles II, during some excavation work ordered by the king, two small skeletons buried in the Tower at the exact same site named by Sir James Tyrell in his presumed confession of 1502 and thus in the account given by Sir Thomas More. The skeletons were positively identified by expert antiquaries as belonging to the two princes, and the bones were deposited in an urn designed by Sir Christopher Wren and then sent to Westminster Abbey, where they remain to this day. A formal funeral service was performed in 1678. At that time, there was no doubt about the identity of the bones: they belonged to the Yorkist princes. The doubts about the princes came later, much later, fostered by those attempting to defend Richard III. According to Giles St Aubyn (1983), Horace Walpole (1768) wrote in his *Historic Doubts* that he did not believe that the bones discovered in 1674 belonged to the princes, but then he also believed that Perkin Warbeck was Prince Richard who had escaped from the Tower.

An account of the 1674 discovery, based on the findings of John Knight, the chief surgeon of King Charles II, was published in 1677. The skeletons were found ten feet under the ground by "digging down under the stairs which led from the king's lodgings [up] to the chapel in the said [White] Tower." The bones were mixed with extraneous rubbish and other animal bones; the labourers were "caused [ordered] to sift the rubbish and by that means preserved all the [human] bones." Some of the bones were damaged by the violence of those digging. The length of the bones, "upon the survey[,] were found proportional to [the] ages of those two brothers [the princes], viz about thirteen and eleven years" ("Plantagenet of York, Edward V," 2013).

There were small pieces of velvet cloth present with the bones, indicative first of the high birth and wealth of the children, and indicative second that the date of death and burial was sometime after 1400 when velvet was first introduced into Europe (Weir, 1999). The presence of animal bones mixed with the human bones was consistent with the dogs which the princes were known to have had with them. At the present time, the princes' memorial is in the north aisle of the Henry VII Lady Chapel, near the tomb of Queen

Elizabeth Tudor. The Latin inscription on the urn leaves no doubt as to what happened to the princes (Dean and Chapter of Westminster, 2012):

> Here lie the relics of Edward V, King of England, and Richard, Duke of York. These brothers being confined in the Tower of London, and there stifled with pillows, were privately and meanly buried, by the order of their perfidious uncle, Richard the Usurper; whose bones, long enquired after and wished for, after 191 years in the rubbish of the stairs [those lately leading to the chapel of the White Tower], were, on the seventeenth day of July 1674, by undoubted proofs discovered, being buried deep in that place. Charles II, a most compassionate prince, pitying their severe fate, ordered these unhappy princes to be laid among the monuments of their predecessors; [dated] 1678, in the thirtieth year of his reign.

It is duly noted that Charles II counted his reign from 1649, when his father King Charles I was executed.

The Bones Examined in 1933

Medical examinations in 1933 were made by Professor William Wright, an expert anatomist, and by Dr George Northcroft, the president of the British Dental Association. The evidence was reviewed by Laurence E. Tanner, the keeper of monuments at Westminster Abbey, and by Professor Wright. In their publication in the journal *Archaeologia* (Tanner and Wright, 1934), they estimated the bone ages but properly thought the dental ages were far more reliable. They estimated dental ages approximating that of the two princes; the values given were very close to the known ages, but not exact. For the older child, they estimated the age as twelve or thirteen years; this compared with Edward's age of twelve years and ten months at early September 1483, as Edward was born on 2 November 1470. For the younger child, they estimated the age as nine to eleven years; this compared with Richard's age of ten years and one month at early September 1483, as Richard was born on 17 August 1473. Suggestions that the small inconsistencies meant that the remains were not those of the princes are not correct, given what we understand about biological variation. The estimates were indeed very close. Despite opinions expressed by defenders of Richard III, these experts did reach a conclusion: that the bones were consistent with belonging to the princes.

The Bone Evidence Examined in 1955 and Later

In 1955, a panel of four experts from Britain and the United States made further examinations of the evidence, not from the skulls directly, but from the photographs taken in 1933 and from the written reports of Wright, Northcroft, and Tanner (Kendall, 2002). An additional three experts have given similar opinions in 1978 (Weir, 1999), and three others gave opinions as recently as 1981 (Weir, 1999). These were experts in the fields of anatomy, orthodontics, dentistry, and surgery. Their new estimates, also based on the dental evidence, broadly agreed with the earlier estimates of 1933. They concluded that the older child was nine to thirteen years old and that the younger child was seven to eleven years old. The estimated limits were wider. However, it is noteworthy and of great importance that the upper limits for both children were similar in both the 1933 and later reports; the changes suggested by the new experts were on the lower limits, rather than on the upper limits. The upper limits correspond with the evidence that the boys were not reliably seen again after the summer season of August 1483.

Using the original 1933 data of Tanner and Wright, published in a peer-reviewed journal, together with the historical visual evidence, and assuming that the identifications were correct, we can calculate the presumptive death years as 1482 or 1483 for Edward, and 1482, 1483, or 1484 for young Richard. As it is known that the princes were alive in 1482, the year which fits with all the data is 1483. This evidence strongly suggests that the princes died in 1483, which is consistent with the conclusion that Richard III and his confederates were responsible for their deaths. Both the visual evidence and the dental evidence are consistent with this conclusion. It does not provide absolute proof, but, given the circumstances in 1483, it appears most likely. And, certainly, it is not consistent with deaths in 1485 or 1486.

From long bone measurements, the height of the children had been estimated as 57.5" for the larger child and 54.5" for the smaller child (Tanner and Wright, 1934). Although these heights fall on the twentieth and fiftieth percentile, respectively, when plotted on a modern growth chart (US Centers for Disease Control and Prevention), it was stated that these measurements suggested that the children were tall for chronological age in the fifteenth century, when humans were shorter than in modern times. This might support the notion that the upper estimates of age at death were more likely nearer to the truth. This is supported by the fact that the lower estimates of age at death coincide with strong evidence that the princes would have been very much alive in 1482 (and, obviously, earlier).

The data from 1955 and later needs to be examined in greater detail, as it was not entirely consistent and may be misunderstood. There was much disagreement among the experts, which is not at all surprising, considering the nature of professional academics. But the problems were related to many different issues, including the use of long bones to attempt determination of chronological age; the nature of the brown stain on the skull of the older child, as described by Tanner and Wright; the possibility of consanguinity, considering the wormian bones in both skulls; the gender of the two prepubertal children; the possible cause of death; the nature of the mandibular osteomyelitis found in the older child; and the importance of hypodontia, or absence of certain teeth, in both children. But there seems to have been general acceptance that the dentition gave a reliable estimate of chronological age. On that point, there was not much disagreement.

Sceptics have used the notable disagreements in an attempt to discredit all the findings, including those related to the dentition, which are generally considered by medical scientists to be quite reliable. With the clear exception of one expert, all agreed that the dental age gave the best estimate of chronological age in the children. Dr W. M. Krugman said that the dental evidence was "soundest"; he said that Tanner's estimate was too precise, meaning that the estimated limits needed to be wider, but he also stated that the dental age was "consistent with death in August 1483." The ages could have been thirteen and ten years, respectively. Dr A. Lewis stated that the older child was eleven to thirteen years old, but he favoured eleven and a half years. He gave no estimate for the younger child. Dr B. Kraus said that the older child was definitely younger than twelve years and favoured nine years. Dr R. Lyne-Perkis made no estimate based on dentition. Dr J. Rogers also made no estimate based on dental age. Dr J.

H. Musgrave said that the Tanner evidence for dental age was "strong." Dr E. W. Bradford said that the older child was more than eleven years old; his best guess was twelve years old. He also said that the younger child was seven to eleven years old, based on the teeth. There have been similar opinions expressed by Dr R. G. Harrison, Dr F. M. Lind, Dr J. Ross, and Dr T. Molleson (Weir, 1999). In relation specifically to the dental age estimates, Alison Weir has stated that "the findings of the experts were in all cases consistent with the remains being those of the Princes in the Tower; although some questioned the findings of Tanner and Wright, they did not discredit them; indeed their conclusions substantiated them."

The Failure of King Richard to Show the Princes Alive in Mid August 1483

The failure of Richard III to show the princes to the public in mid August 1483 is strong evidence of his guilt, especially considering the absolute certainty, gleaned from visual evidence, that he had them locked up in the Tower at that time. It is impossible to believe that with all the rumours spreading around the country at that time, Richard would not have considered something so simple as showing the princes at St Paul's Church one fine Sunday afternoon. It would have been proof they were still alive.

But Richard might have been afraid to produce the boys in public if he himself doubted the validity of the process by which they were declared illegitimate. Like many others, he must have lacked confidence in the marriage contract invention. A public statement by the well-educated, superbly trained Edward V, assisted by his prelate advisors, pointing out the lack of supportive evidence for the 1461 marriage contract and asking that the matter be heard by an ecclesiastical law court would have been very embarrassing for King Richard III. The failure to produce the princes in mid August 1483 and prove them to be alive is the most damning evidence against the king. The usurpation was bad enough, but previous kings had survived usurpations, for instance Henry IV. The problem was that the murders of the children greatly magnified the hostility of the English people towards Richard III. It was that specific hostility which denied him loyal support and ultimately wrecked his reign.

The Conclusion that King Richard Ordered the Murders Appears Strongly Reasonable

In Sir Thomas More's account written in the years following 1513 and published in 1557, taken from the presumed confessions of Tyrell and Dighton in 1502, it is stated that the princes' bodies were buried deep under the paving stones at the foot of the stairs leading up to the Norman Chapel of St John in the White Tower. This account was absolutely consistent with where the bodies were later excavated in 1674. It is completely reasonable to believe that only the murderers or their accomplices would have known exactly where the bodies were buried. There cannot be much doubt that Henry Tudor, on the basis of the intelligence he had obtained in 1483, believed that the boys were dead when he made his promises at Rennes Cathedral on Christmas Day 1483, since that made his prospective bride, Princess Elizabeth, the direct Yorkist heir. Despite suggestions to the contrary, history has correctly blamed Richard III for the death of King Edward V and his younger brother, Richard.

According to Commines, Louis XI, the Spider King, king of France, had no doubt about who killed the princes. The Lord Protector failed to protect young King Edward V, the son of King Edward IV. Whether or not Richard was truly guilty is finally immaterial; what mattered most was that, during the reign of Richard III, nearly all the people of England, from the highest to the lowest, came to believe that King Richard III was guilty of this monstrous crime and that his treachery could not go unpunished. Most people living in 1485, a superstitious age, believed that Richard's defeat and death at Bosworth Field reflected divine retribution for his misdeeds.

It is often claimed that the Croyland Chronicler (1854) expressed no conclusions about what happened to the princes. But in the *Croyland Chronicle*, written in 1486, there is a poem by an unknown author about the three English kings named Richard, which, in reference to Richard III, is quoted as follows:

> Edward's vast hordes of wealth consumed, the Third [Richard III]
> Was not content therewith, but must destroy
> His brother's progeny, and then proscribe
> Their partisans [supporters]. Two years had he usurp'd
> The throne, when, meeting these [partisans], he lost his life

And ill-gain'd crown, upon the battle-field.
The year one thousand, hundreds four, and five
To eighty added, when of August came
The twice eleventh day, the Boar's tusks quail'd;
And, to avenge the White, the Red Rose bloomed.

Whatever the reader may think of this, as very strange poetry or simply bad prose, nevertheless, the opinion is clearly expressed: Richard III destroyed his brother's progeny, usurped the crown, and was killed at Bosworth Field on 22 August 1483. That strange piece was put there for a reason. The chronicler did not say it directly, being fearful of the consequences, but he gave out his opinion by the use of this literary device. Some have called this material "doggerel" (Drewett and Redhead, 1984), but that does not make it false. It is perfectly clear what the chronicler intended. And the poem is consistent with the view that Richard III was responsible for the death of the princes. Since the chronicler was likely Bishop John Russell, the chancellor of England, we have the opinion of a very close observer of all these sad events.

Helen Maurer (2000), after exhaustive consideration of all the data, and when discussing the problem of whether or not Richard III needed to eliminate the already deposed and illegitimate Edward V, stated recently her conclusion: "The choice was made and the order given by the only man who had the power to give it. Someone conveyed the order to the Tower. The princes died." She could not bring herself to say that it was Richard, but that is who she meant by "the only man who had the power."

While it appears quite clear that Richard had the boys murdered, for he had the boys locked up and controlled the keys, the evidence is nevertheless circumstantial; there is no smoking gun. Several mock trials in recent years, five hundred years after the fact, have been performed. One trial at the Shakespeare Theatre in Washington, DC, another trial at the Indiana University Law School, and a third trial conducted by Channel Four Television in London (Drewett and Redhead, 1984) have, unsurprisingly, found the last Yorkist king to be not guilty of putting the princes to death. The case against him was simply not proved sufficiently. But Richard alone had the power, the motive, the means, and the opportunity to murder the boys in 1483 – and the facts are clear that they disappeared forever on his watch. The requirements for a verdict of guilty in a judicial court are much stricter than the requirements of history; yet circumstantial evidence is frequently sufficient to support a conclusion of guilt, even in the courts. It would appear that the standard used in the trials was "beyond all reasonable doubt" rather than "based on reasonable probability." Even if the judge gave the correct instructions, the juries tended to use the "beyond doubt" standard.

It is not reasonable to expect that Richard III would have left clear evidence of his guilt. Unlike many people who perform malignant deeds, Richard was a reasonable man, very capable of using his considerable power to successfully hide important evidence of his guilt. And most important, as is commonly stated, Richard astutely maintained absolute silence about the matter, never offering even the most casual comment, so he gave away no indirect evidence. Nor did he ever, with specification, confess to his crime.

Some critics have argued that Richard did not need to kill the princes in the Tower, but that argument is difficult to understand. King Edward V was a proclaimed king, but he was not an anointed king, as his coronation had been cancelled on 18 June 1483. Moreover, the Great Council had pronounced that he was illegitimate and so not eligible to be king; but there were grave doubts about that decision. Once Richard was anointed and crowned, it was suggested that there would be no rebellions against him, but history proved the critics wrong. First of all, Buckingham rebelled. Then there was the Tudor invasion, which is easily called a rebellion. And there can be little doubt that if Henry Tudor had failed at Bosworth, then there would have been further rebellions. Richard was not safe, even after his coronation. Furthermore, Richard knew there would be rebellions and so made preparations. There were several Yorkist claimants to the throne remaining alive, such as Lincoln, young Warwick, and Princess Elizabeth of York. And there were more to grow older or to be born in the near future. Plus, unless Henry Tudor, if he failed the first or the second time, was killed, then there could be no question that he would be back to try again. The notion that Richard was ever safe is quite untenable. He was widely considered an usurper, so he could expect all the trouble experienced by the usurper king Henry IV. The rebels would not be concerned about the finer points of whether or not Richard was anointed with holy oil; the rebels correctly considered him to be an unlawful king.

If we accept the notion that Richard did not murder the princes, then, by comparison, the alternative suggestions for the fate of the princes are supported by completely insufficient evidence – in fact, usually not much at all, only interesting conjecture. The theory that the princes were smuggled from London to the Tyrell family home at Gipping House in Suffolk, and thence to Flanders, is poorly supported by any reliable evidence. The idea that they were kept at Sheriff Hutton Castle is virtually unsupported; a reference to wardrobe supplies for the "Lord Bastard" means that John of Gloucester, Richard's illegitimate son, was present at that time. The English are well known for their derisive sarcasm; and it was well known that Richard looked after John of Gloucester and other of his children with great care. The notion that Richard of Shrewsbury returned as the pretender Perkin Warbeck is completely demolished by the confession that Warbeck made in 1497. That King Edward V's brother Prince Richard, facing certain execution, would have admitted to an imposture and thus denied his royal birth is utterly incomprehensible. And Perkin was unable to identify people in London who he should have known (Wroe, 2003). Moreover, King Henry VII's investigations in Flanders established clearly the identity of Warbeck. No doubt, the defenders of Richard III will come up with other fascinating theories, but these theories seem mostly designed to cause confusion and doubt.

It is, however, as a point of interest, a useful exercise to consider who else but Richard III might have killed the princes in the Tower.

Others Who May Have Killed the Princes: Buckingham, Henry VII, and Margaret Beaufort

Duke of Buckingham

There is some evidence that Henry Stafford, the second duke of Buckingham, may have been involved; he is often so accused. According to Alison Weir (1999), in the *Croyland Chronicle,* almost certainly written by Bishop John Russell or a very close associate of his, it was stated that the princes were alive at the end of August 1483, but they were certainly not seen after that. As chancellor of England in the upper echelons of the government, the bishop was in a good position to know, unlike many others who have expressed opinions but were never in a position to know. There is little doubt that the treacherous Buckingham was near or at Brecknock Castle in Wales from early August to mid October 1483 and was not in a position to carry out the murders in late August or early September 1483. The best opportunity Buckingham had to kill the princes was in July 1483, after Richard III left London for his royal progress on 22 July 1483 and before Buckingham left London to catch up with the king in late July 1483 at the town of Gloucester. But a July date for the murders would have been too early, as the princes were seen alive after that time.

However, it is possible that Buckingham sent his agents to kill the princes in late August 1483; that would be hard to disprove. But by late July 1483, after meeting with the king, Buckingham may have concluded that Richard had already put them to death, or at least sent the orders, so it is not likely he would have sent his own agents to accomplish the same task. Moreover, Buckingham's agents could not have reached the princes without passing Sir Robert Brackenbury, the constable of the Tower, and that required a warrant from Richard III. Some have claimed that since Buckingham was the newly appointed constable of England, he would have been allowed access to the Tower prison without the help of Brackenbury. But that is not true, either, as the constable of the Tower was a unique appointment. It still would have been necessary to pass Brackenbury, who was directly and solely responsible to the king.

If Buckingham killed the princes independent of the king, then Richard III would have soon known about it and seized his chance at redemption. He could have charged Buckingham with the crime, escaped the blame, and partly restored his own political credibility. When Buckingham faced execution for his treason in late October 1483, that would have been the perfect opportunity; the fact that Richard did no such thing is excellent evidence that Buckingham was not involved in the death of the princes. At the very least, that is what Richard himself believed, and he was in an excellent position to know. There were some baseless rumours circulating at the time which suggested that Buckingham was involved, but in retrospect this seems most unlikely. Buckingham probably advised the king to put the princes to death, as suggested by the much discussed document discovered in the College of Arms in 1980 (MS 2M6) and reviewed by Richard Firth Green (1981). This would be supported by the manuscript MS 1448 in the

Ashmole Collection at Oxford University. It is not likely that Buckingham or his agents committed the murders independent of the king.

If it is true that Richard followed Buckingham's advice, then Buckingham would not have been too upset when, in late July 1483, at the town of Gloucester, Richard told him the execution orders had been given. There would have been little argument, and Buckingham would have been glad that Richard had followed his advice. On the other hand, if Buckingham had nothing to do with the decision, then he may have considered the planned murders to be a very serious crime, far more serious than he had anticipated, in which case he might have been very angry with the king. This remains one possible reason for the reported argument between the two men in late July 1483 and for Buckingham's leaving the royal progress, going home to Brecknock Castle, and never seeing Richard again. This could still be true despite other reasonable suggestions, such as Richard's possible admission about the 1461 marriage contract invention.

Henry VII

There have been additional suggestions that Henry Tudor was to blame, a position supported by Josephine Tey (1951) in her well-known book and by Sir Clements Markham (1906). But Henry was in Brittany during August and September of 1483. And if Henry were able to reach the princes in the Tower, then his agents, too, would have had to get past the fiercely loyal Brackenbury. And that raises the question as to why Henry would even bother when, much earlier, his intelligence sources told him that Richard would do the monstrous deed for him and, later, that Richard had, in fact, killed the princes and was already, disastrously, taking all the blame. In late 1485, nobody was blaming Henry VII for the murders; that idea only came up when people tried to defend Richard III much later.

It is reasonable to suppose that when Henry became king in 1485, he had his men search the Tower and they found no sign of the dead princes. At that point in time, they had no idea to look under the stair foot at the Chapel of St John or in any other specific location. It was not necessary to say anything when the verdict of the nation was already in: Richard III had had the princes killed. And Richard III was dead. It was pointless looking anywhere else in England because the king's men had no idea where to start.

Nor did Henry VII need to change his policy of ignoring the question when the presumed confessions of Sir James Tyrell and John Dighton became available to him in 1502. The confessions changed nothing and only substantiated the already universally accepted verdict. It is plausible, but not proven, that Henry VII or his agents visited the staircase in 1502, thought the site looked unpromising, and believed Sir James Tyrell's account that the bodies had been removed and taken elsewhere, possibly to the deep mouth of the River Thames. Henry sent the presumed confession documents to storage in the archives and maintained his silence.

But there is another variation. A few historians, taking note of two successive pardons for Sir James Tyrell in 1486, believe that Henry VII found the princes alive at the Tower in 1485 and then later had Sir James Tyrell, who always waited for special orders, murder them and bury them under the stair foot, as described by Sir Thomas More (2005). This might explain why Sir James Tyrell was first pardoned on 15 June 1486 and then pardoned a second time on 17 July 1486, only a month later.

When Sir James Tyrell confessed in 1502, he would have said that it was Richard III who gave him the orders; it would have been foolish if he had indicated that it was Henry VII. These historians, and many others, believe that the course of events described by Sir Thomas More (2005) was near the truth; but they suggest some changes: there needed to be corrections for some of the minor errors, such as the age of King Edward IV, the length of time he was exiled in Burgundy, and the long relationship of the king with Sir James Tyrell. There needed to be a change in the date, from 1483 to 1486; and there needed to be a change in some of the important names. It was Henry VII, instead of Richard III, who gave the orders; it was still John Greene who carried the orders to the Tower; it was John de Vere, the earl of Oxford, or his deputy, instead of Sir Robert Brackenbury, who refused to kill the princes in the Tower; it was still Sir James who next organized the murders during a single night of control in the Tower, but he employed Will Slaughter and John Dighton, not Miles Forrest, who was already dead of a malignant infection; and it was Slaughter and Dighton who buried the children at the stair foot.

Such a theory would not have been consistent with the evidence that the princes died in 1483. If we use the accepted visual evidence for when the princes were last seen, the end of August 1483, combined with the 1933 dental evidence, then we can deduce when the princes died. These calculations bear repeating. If Edward V was born in 1470, then the dental evidence for an estimated age of twelve to thirteen years sets the death year as 1482 or 1483. As the visual evidence excludes 1482, then 1483 is the estimated year of death. If Prince Richard was born in 1473, then the dental evidence for the estimated age at death of nine to eleven years sets the death year as 1482, 1483, or 1484; as the visual evidence excludes 1482, then 1483 or 1484 are the estimated death years. As Henry was in France in both 1483 and 1484, he appears to be absolved. Furthermore, the princes were never seen alive in 1484.

We can put this another way. If Edward V died in 1486, then the dental evidence does not fit. The boy would have been sixteen years old, not thirteen years old. If Prince Richard died in 1486, then the dental evidence also does not fit; the boy would have been thirteen years old, not eleven years old. That supports the conclusion that it does not appear reasonable to blame Henry VII. It does not help if young Richard's birth is assigned to 1472, as some claim; in 1486, he would have been fourteen years old, not eleven years old.

More likely, it would appear that the two pardons in June and July of 1486 were routine and had no sinister meaning. The first may have been a pardon for Sir James's general support of Richard III; the second may have been to confirm his agreement to continue as governor of Guînes Castle. Others have suggested that the second pardon was a simple matter, possibly a correction for erroneous paperwork regarding the first pardon. Claims that the princes were seen after Bosworth have never been substantiated; it would be truly astonishing if the princes survived undetected in the busy Tower of London for another three years after 1483.

Margaret Beaufort

Others say that Margaret Beaufort was the guilty party, as she was well motivated. It was her desire to see her son Henry Tudor on the English throne. It is clear that the defenders of Richard III tend to suggest as many suspects as they can; it points attention away from Richard III. But Margaret's piety would never have allowed her direct involvement. Also, her agents could never have gained the necessary access to the Tower; they, too, would have had to get past Brackenbury. Richard III would have soon known about it and used it for his own ends. Nothing would have suited King Richard better than to have been able to shift the blame from himself to Buckingham or Margaret Beaufort or somebody else. Yet the fact remains that he did not even make the attempt; Richard knew who killed the princes, and he carried that knowledge to his grave.

The Possibility that the Princes Were Not Murdered but Died of Natural Causes in the Tower

The defenders of Richard III like to suggest that the princes were not murdered at all but died in the Tower of natural causes. Edward V was being seen by Dr Argentine on a regular basis and may have died of an infection. When Archbishop Bourchier went to the Tower to persuade the queen to release Prince Richard from sanctuary, she claimed that he was not well. When the boys were gravely ill, Richard could have made an announcement at Clerkenwell that Dr Argentine was attending them; he then could have had the doctor stand before the people and describe the gravity of the situation. When the boys were ultimately dead, Richard could have made another announcement and had Dr Argentine state that they had died of natural causes, such as an infection, and not from poisoning. Perhaps there could have been other medical witnesses recruited. This would have been to Richard's great advantage; it would have proven that the boys were initially alive, and later it would have strongly suggested that they were not murdered. He could have had them lie in state at St Paul's Church for the people to see, and then the princes could have had a public and respectful burial, as befitted their station. Richard could have mourned them in public and paid them respect. Especially with the help of the good doctors, this would have done a great deal to restore Richard's reputation and credibility and possibly save his reign. But it did not happen that way. Instead, the whole matter was kept secret and the princes were buried in the Tower, where later their bodies were discovered under the stair foot. This strongly suggests that they did not die of natural causes. And in the Mancini (1989) account, it is suggested that Mancini visited in France and told officials that the princes had been murdered by the king; this would explain the near certainty of the announcement in January 1484 by William de Rochefort that it was Richard who murdered the princes.

The Possibility that the Princes Escaped from the Tower

This has been considered, but it is concluded that there is no certain evidence and is most unlikely. In a land that mourned the princes for years after they disappeared and affectionately remembered their father, all the boys needed to do was stand up in the sanctuary and reveal themselves. With their credentials, they would have rapidly attracted loyal support. If they had reached Flanders or France, then the duchess of Burgundy would have had real princes, instead of pretenders, to send back to England accompanied by armed force.

As discussed by Alison Weir (1999), a recent London investigator, Mr Jack Leslau (2001), believes that Edward V appeared as Sir Edward Guildford and that Richard appeared as Dr John Clement in the household of Sir Thomas More. So far as is known, this very complicated theory awaits confirmation. In addition, he made a number of remarkable assertions: a 1461 marriage contract document existed once, but Edward IV destroyed it; Edward bribed the Talbot family to remain silent; there was a secret ecclesiastical law court hearing, but its conclusions were never made public; Clarence knew about the contract but never said so; and Richard III knew about the contract but could not produce it in 1483. Mr Leslau offered no independent evidence to support his views. It is extremely doubtful that the English people would have accepted the results of a secret ecclesiastical law court hearing. English history has demonstrated no confirmation of this idea, as all of Edward's descendants have been considered legitimate; but we shall wait and see.

CHAPTER 8

The Titulus Regius of January 1484, Richard III's Justification for the Usurpation

The statute was long. It has become one of the most infamous documents in English history. Although Henry VII very nearly suppressed it entirely, the Croyland Chronicler made one copy, which was discovered many years later during the reign of King James I. Its contents are now widely known.

According to Tracy Bryce (2008), the Titulus Regius may be divided into three parts:

(1) a prolonged and disorderly denunciation of Edward IV's reign, most of it without serious merit;

(2) a disqualification of the heirs of Edward IV and the duke of Clarence, also without serious merit. It was claimed that Edward IV's marriage was bigamous and so his children were all not legitimate, a claim which, disgracefully, was carried in the Parliament; and

(3) a probably false claim that Richard III was the only true son and heir of Richard, the third duke of York, who died in 1460. Although not clearly stated, this last claim meant that both Edward IV and Edward V were never rightful kings; nor was Clarence ever a rightful duke. It was more disgrace.

In part one of the statute, Edward IV's reign is described as a disaster for the kingdom, a period filled with poverty, oppression, death, and rape, all the fault of the allegedly wicked King Edward IV. Such exaggerations need no further discussion. There have been repeated descriptions of English life during the War of the Roses and of how little was the disturbance (Lander, 1969). Charles Ross (1997) said that the allegations represented typical dynastic propaganda common in the Middle Ages.

In part three of the statute, the right of Richard III to be king was set forth. He is "the undoubted son and heir of Richard, the third Duke of York," and "there is none other person living but [Richard] only, that by right may claim the said crown and dignity royal, by way of inheritance." By referring to "the undoubted son," Richard III was pointing to the old rumour that King Edward IV was not a legitimate son of the duke of York who died in 1460 – a rumour Richard III had always believed to be true. On the matter of the alleged illegitimate birth of Edward IV, the document is otherwise silent. Richard III knew only too well that unless his father denied Edward, then Edward was legally legitimate under the English common law and so, too, were Edward's sons; they were all able to inherit. Elsewhere in part three, the statute stated that Richard III was an Englishman and had honourably defended the kingdom on the field of battle; this was true, but it did not follow that Edward IV was French because he was born in Normandy of English parents.

To most observers, part two of the statute is the most important and interesting, as it describes why Edward IV's marriage was considered invalid. There were three considerations.

The first consideration is quoted:

> And here also we consider, how the said pretensed marriage, between the above named King Edward and Elizabeth Grey, was made of great presumption, without the knowing or assent of the lords of this land, and also by sorcery and witchcraft, committed by the said Elizabeth Woodville and her mother, Jacquetta, the Duchess of Bedford, as the common opinion of the people and the public voice, and fame [rumour] is through all the land; and hereafter, if and as the case shall require, shall be proved sufficiently in time and place convenient.

None of that invalidated the marriage (see more about canon law in Chapter 11). Neither lack of assent from the lords nor unproved charges of sorcery made the 1464 Woodville marriage invalid. The offer of proof applied to the sorcery charge only.

The second consideration is quoted:

> And here also we consider how that the said pretensed marriage was made privately and secretly with [without] edition of banns, in a private chamber, a profane place, and not openly in the face of the church, after the laws of God's church, but contrary thereunto, and the laudable custom of the Church of England.

None of that invalidated the marriage (see more about canon law in Chapter 11). Privacy and secrecy did not necessarily invalidate a marriage.

The third consideration is quoted:

> And how also, that at the time of the contract of the same pretensed marriage, and before and long time after the said King Edward was and stood married and troth plight to one Dame Eleanor Butler, daughter of the old earl of Shrewsbury, with whom the said King Edward had made a pre-contract of matrimony, long time before he made the said pretensed marriage with the said Elizabeth Grey in manner and form aforesaid. Which premises being true, as in very truth they been [being] true, it appears and follows evidently that the said King Edward during his life, and the said Elizabeth, lived together sinfully and damnably in adultery, against the law of God and his Church ... it appears evidently and follows that all the issue and children of the said King, been [being] bastards, and unable to inherit or to claim anything by inheritance, by the law and custom of England.

That last is the only reason given in the statute that explains how the 1464 marriage could possibly have been considered invalid, provided, of course, that the Lady Eleanor Butler story was true (see more about canon law in Chapter 11). Instead of providing proof, the document simply states that the marriage contract story is true, as in, "which premises being true, as in very truth they [being] true." *Now it is asked of the reader: What kind of proof, what kind of nonsense, is that?*

As in so many other reports, the marriage contract was listed last among the other lame reasons believed to invalidate the 1464 royal marriage. And so there must have been significant doubt about the alleged 1461 marriage contract that it needed prior support.

It is believed by some, in particular Alison Weir (1999), that in this 1484 document was the first time Lady Eleanor Butler was definitely mentioned to the English public at large, which might confirm that Lady Eleanor Butler was also named in Buckingham's public presentation on 25 June 1483 at Westminster Hall, when the final decision to depose Edward V was made. So, an alternative suggestion would be that 25 June 1483 was the first time the English people could ever have heard of Lady Eleanor Butler in her role as the alleged wife of Edward IV. But even then, it was not widely publicized. There were strong doubts about what was decided at that 25 June meeting, and the Titulus Regius was not passed in Parliament until seven months after King Edward V was deposed.

Thus, by implication, according to the 1484 Titulus Regius, King Edward IV was a monster, his birth was not legitimate, his marriage was not legitimate, his children were not legitimate, he was not English because he was born in France, and his military career was a failure without Richard III. It is no wonder that Edward IV's historical reputation has suffered so much, if this is the kind of nonsense that people have come to believe. And if Richard III was the great military leader largely responsible for Edward IV's multiple military victories, then Bosworth Field tells us otherwise.

Tracy Bryce (2008), mostly sympathetic to Richard III, admitted that Charles Ross (1997) described the Titulus Regius as "blatant propaganda." *It was freely admitted in the statute that King Edward V was deposed by a body which was not a lawful Parliament. In the statute, it was stated and agreed that the Great Council of 25 June 1483 was not a lawful Parliament, but its findings were then, seven months later, confirmed by the present lawful 1484 Parliament.* This fact was clearly stated in the statute in abbreviated form as follows:

> Now forasmuch as neither the said Three Estates, neither the said persons, which in their name [the three Estates], presented and delivered—the said (Parchment) Roll unto our said Sovereign Lord the King, were assembled in the form of [a]

Parliament, by occasion whereof, diverse doubts, questions and ambiguities [had] been moved and engendered in the minds of diverse persons.

It was even claimed that Edward had a formal marriage in 1461, even though not even a single witness was present. The statute indicated that Edward stood both married and in troth-plight to Lady Eleanor Butler at the time of his 1464 marriage. It is the source which first suggests that the marriage contract story was supplemented by a secret formal marriage, suggesting that Bishop Stillington was the probable author of the statute.

There was no mention of any documents to support the alleged 1461 marriage contract. Most important, there is no mention of any of the alleged diverse evidentiary proofs for the 1461 marriage contract, which were allegedly presented by Bishop Stillington at the early June 1483 meeting of the council and at the late June 1483 meeting of the Great Council. As already discussed, there is some suggestion that it was Richard who produced this documentary evidence, which means that it was certainly concocted. That makes much more sense, as surely somebody, at one or both of those meetings, would have wanted, at the very least, some stronger evidence. It would appear that even Bishop Stillington, knowing he was on dangerous ground, hesitated to include fabricated perjuries in a statute of Parliament.

Again, despite claims made, the Titulus Regius made no offer to provide evidentiary proof for the 1461 marriage contract. If a proper ecclesiastical law court had been called to examine the assertions and the supportive evidence, then Richard's supporters could have quoted and referred to the considered finding of the law court as their authority. Instead, the Titulus Regius could only restate the original unsubstantiated assertions and baldly claim that they were true. *Richard's confederates were so uncertain about the 1461 contract story that they had to include the additional story that Edward IV was born illegitimate.* This explains why Richard could not resist putting in the third section of the statute, which states that he alone was the undoubted son (and heir) of Richard, the third Duke of York. The Lord Protector believed that neither Edward IV nor Clarence was a legitimate son of his father, as suggested in Dr Shaw's sermon. The claim to be "the undoubted son," even knowing his mother's serious objections, is consistent with the notion that Richard III continued to have doubts about his primary pretext for the usurpation, namely the alleged 1461 marriage contract with Lady Eleanor.

An offer to prove at a later date was made, but it was for the sorcery charge, not the 1461 contract charge. It is notable that the Titulus Regius did offer to show evidentiary proof for the sorcery charge, since sorcery claims were indeed widely believed and there had been a formal government hearing on those charges against Jacquetta Woodville in 1470. As seen above, immediately after the statement about sorcery, the document continues: "as the common opinion of the people and the public voice, and fame is through all this land; and hereafter, if and as the case shall require, shall be proved sufficiently, in time and place convenient."

Immediately following this offer of proof for the sorcery charge was the secrecy charge, without any offer to prove it following. And then followed immediately the all-important marriage contract charge, also without any offer to prove. So, the statute offered to provide evidentiary proof for the assertion of sorcery, but not for the assertion of the alleged 1461 marriage contract. If such evidence for the 1461 marriage existed, then Stillington knew that it was perjured.

Some authors believe that the offer to prove did apply to the contract charge, not just the sorcery charge (Bryce, 2008), but a close reading of the document indicates that this is not so. The offer to prove might have included the lack-of-assent charge, since that immediately preceded the sorcery charge in the same sentence. It may be concluded that the offer to prove clearly applied to the sorcery charge; Stillington made no offer to prove the 1461 contract charge, which was so critical for invalidating the 1464 marriage with Elizabeth Woodville.

The place for proving the 1461 contract charge was in the Titulus Regius, not at some later time and place in another court. Tracy Bryce, in the mistaken belief that an offer to prove the contract charge was made, wrote in her commentary that the matter of the late king's invalid marriage could be "more thoroughly demonstrated, admitting [suggesting] that here and now was not the place to do it. It does not preclude some future ecclesiastical examination into the pre-contract [the 1461 marriage contract]."

In other words, the essence of the government argument was too complicated to discuss in the statute. In a document designed to justify the usurpation, it is extraordinarily difficult to follow the line of argument that it was too complicated to discuss. Indeed, it is incomprehensible. *In the statute intended to justify the usurpation was exactly the proper place to provide the supportive evidence which allegedly proved the 1461 marriage contract charge. But it was not provided, nor was it offered at another time in an ecclesiastical law court. What was offered was proof for the sorcery charge.*

The 1484 Parliament assumed it had powers that it did not have. Of part two, it is reasonable to ask when did the 1484 Parliament get the power to decide if the canon law was broken. The matter of the marriage contract should have been decided first by the Church. Richard III knew he would lose in an ecclesiastical law court, so he did not resolve that matter before asking the 1483 Great Council, not a Parliament, to depose King Edward V. On both counts, lack of the proper ecclesiastical law court and lack of a proper Parliament, Richard III's assumption of the throne in June 1483 was not lawful; hence, history has consistently judged him correctly as the Usurper King, much to the discontent of his defenders.

According to the *Croyland Chronicle,* the 1484 Parliament did confirm the title by which Richard had ascended the throne, as we have seen. But the *Croyland Chronicle* then went on as follows: "Although that Lay Court [Parliament] found itself [at first] unable to give a definition of his [Richard's] rights when the question of the marriage [Edward's] was discussed; still …, [Parliament] presumed to do so, and did do so."

The Croyland Chronicler was confirming his opinion that Parliament (the lay court) had no jurisdiction in the marriage matter; but Parliament went ahead anyway and declared Edward's 1464 marriage invalid. Parliament presumed that it had the power to do this. According to Charles Ross (1999), presumably quoting the chronicler, Parliament was initially reluctant to take this step. The members had to be persuaded. If they had refused, then the whole statute would have been voided, as all had long agreed that the alleged 1461 marriage contract was "the crux of the matter."

It is interesting to note how George Barnett Smith (1894) handled the 1484 Titulus Regius in his *History of the English Parliament.* He stated that a bill was introduced which "set forth the circumstances attending the invitation for Richard to assume the Crown." After passage in the House of Lords and the House of Commons, the matters were "pronounced to be true and undoubted, and the King gave the measure his assent." The proceedings "of the June Council [of 25 June 1483] were thus transformed into law, Parliament giving the force of a statute to many statements which were certainly the reverse of the truth." That last is a huge understatement.

When Henry VIII died in 1547 and was succeeded by his son Edward, the new king was titled Edward VI, in recognition of the legality of Edward V's short but valid reign. It will be interesting when another Richard becomes king in the distant future, if he will be Richard III or Richard IV. The English monarchy might be well advised not to use the name Richard ever again for any possible heir to the throne.

The Reversal and Destruction of the Titulus Regius by the 1485 English Parliament

King Henry VII believed that the princes died in 1483 – in August 1483, to be more precise. He would never have taken part in the Buckingham Rebellion of October 1483 if he did not believe that. And he would never have reversed the 1484 Titulus Regius in 1485 if he did not believe that the princes were dead. His claim to the throne would have been destroyed if the princes were alive, for they had a far superior claim; and with the reversal of the statute, they would have been legitimate in practice.

Because of the rumours, it is likely that Henry VII did make an effort to find the bodies of the princes in 1485 when he became king, but a thorough search of the Tower found nothing. If Henry's officers had questioned Sir James Tyrell in 1485, perhaps at the suggestion of Bishop Morton, then Sir James Tyrell would have denied any knowledge of the murders, since he considered his life still valuable at that time. He was not facing charges of treason for any other matters. Henry was happy to let matters lie, especially since nearly everybody blamed Richard III. And anyway, Henry considered all the Yorkist kings to be usurpers against the "true" Lancastrian line.

At his first Parliament in November 1485, the Tudor king did, however, have Richard III posthumously attainted. For this purpose, he counted the onset of his reign as the day before Bosworth. So, at the Battle of Bosworth Field, the Yorkist king committed treason against King Henry VII. This was, of course, ridiculous, untrue, and illegal, but Parliament continued the practice of doing as the king instructed, and that made it legal.

Richard III was accused of "unnatural, mischievous and great perjuries, treasons, homicides and murders in shedding of infants' blood, with many other wrongs, odious offences and abominations, against God and man." The attainder did not exactly specify Richard's crimes, but it should be pretty obvious to most observers that "great perjuries" referred to the false contract story and the associated lies; "homicides and murders, the shedding of infants' blood" referred to the death of the princes in the Tower; and "other abominations" referred to the executions of Lord Hastings and Anthony Woodville and the others of King Edward V's escort party. This kind of obscure language was not uncommon in attainders, but this bill of attainder was sure to pass in Parliament, so it was simply not necessary to be more specific. Some claim that the language was not specific because the princes might have turned up alive and embarrassed Henry, but Henry knew that they were dead. History has confirmed his opinion.

Parliament was hesitant about the right of Henry Tudor to be king, even though he had won the crown by force of arms at Bosworth Field and was the sole acceptable and surviving male Lancastrian heir. Nobody was willing to consider the descendants of Philippa Plantagenet (see Appendix B), who had married into the House of Portugal. The Tudor claim, through a third marriage of a younger son of Edward III, namely John of Gaunt (see Appendix D), was indeed weak, not even as good as the earlier Lancastrian claim through the issue of the first marriage of John of Gaunt, namely Henry IV.

The succession had departed once from the true Yorkist (Mortimer) line with ultimately disastrous consequences. It is noteworthy that Henry VII obtained papal permission to marry Princess Elizabeth of York and a papal bull to support his claim to the English throne. People were aware that there were better Yorkist heirs still available in 1485, namely the several beautiful daughters of Edward IV – and also Edward, the seventeenth earl of Warwick, and John de la Pole, the earl of Lincoln. The Act of Accord of 1460 had finally established that the throne of England could be inherited through a female of the line and that, presumably, a woman could be queen regnant. If there is doubt about this, then it should be recalled that the direct Yorkist line of inheritance went through two women, Philippa Plantagenet Mortimer and Anne Mortimer Plantagenet (see Appendix C). Because of Henry's inferior claim, both the House of

Lords and the House of Commons in 1485 petitioned Henry Tudor to marry Princess Elizabeth Plantagenet, the legal Yorkist heir to the throne, as the princes were indeed dead. Henry had promised in public, at Rennes Cathedral, to marry Elizabeth. At the new king's request, and of its own accord, Parliament reversed the Titulus Regius and so made the marriage of Edward IV to be valid and all of Edward IV's royal children to be legitimate. It was argued that Parliament was simply reversing a previous unjustifiable and illegal action; no ecclesiastical law court had ever declared Edward IV's marriage to be invalid or his children to be illegitimate. Still others might suggest that in the end, in a perverse way, the Sanctuary Plot of July 1483 was finally successful.

It is notable that not only was the statute (Titulus Regius) repealed, but also serious attempts to expunge it from the statutory record and destroy it entirely, as though it never existed, were made and were largely successful. Only a single copy survived, that in the *Croyland Chronicle,* thanks probably to Chancellor John Russell; it only came to light in the early seventeenth century during the reign of King James I. This may help to explain why Sir Francis Bacon (1889), in his history of Henry VII's reign, made no mention of the attempted destruction; nor did George Barnett Smith (1894) make any comment in his *History of the English Parliament.* It should be noted that the statute was only part of the 1484 Acts of Settlement; only the Titulus Regius statute was expunged from the record. Richard's remarkable constitutional changes remained lawful and on the rolls of the 1484 Parliament. This destructive activity must be considered extremely unusual. It is sometimes argued that this was to allow Princess Elizabeth to be legitimized for the purpose of her marriage to the king, but for that purpose only a repeal of the statute, not its attempted physical destruction, was necessary.

It is far more likely that the 1484 Titulus Regius was considered repugnant, an heinous blot upon the parliamentary record, based upon the repeated falsehoods. It is usually implied that it was Henry VII who demanded the destruction, but it is not hard to imagine that the king would have received such advice from multiple quarters: the Tudor judges, many members of Parliament, Bishop Russell, Bishop Morton, Lord Stanley, and others. They all almost certainly considered the Titulus Regius of 1484 to be a disgraceful pack of lies, a black blot on the reputation of the

Parliament, and felt that it needed to be obliterated. Some partisan authors believe that Henry VII wanted to suppress the evidence that Richard III was a rightful king, but Henry had no need to do that. At that time, people were angry with Richard, and hardly anybody thought Richard was a rightful king. It was only much later that people tried to make that case in defence of Richard III.

The repealing statute passed by the first Tudor Parliament in November 1485 is described by John Ashdown-Hill (2010), after his examination of the rolls of Parliament (*Rotuli Parliamentorum*). He excerpted the Tudor statute as follows:

> That the said Bill, Act and Record [the 1484 Titulus Regius], and all the circumstances and dependants of the same Bill and Act, for the fals [false] and seditious ymaginacions [imaginations] and untruths thereof, be void, adnulled [annulled], repelled, irrite [rid], and of no force or effect. And that it be ordained by the said auctorite [authority – the 1485 Parliament] that the said Bill be cancelled and destroyed, and that the said Act and Record shall be taken and avoided [voided] out of the Roll and Records of the said Parliament of the said late King [Richard III], and brent [burned] and utterly destroyed.

In the *Year Book of Henry VII* (2010) for 1485, it is stated as follows: That the said Bill, Act and Record [the 1484 Titulus Regius] be annulled and utterly destroyed, and that it be ordained by the same authority, that the same Act and Record be taken out of the Roll of Parliament, and be cancelled and brent [burned], and be put in perpetual oblivion.

Enough said. The destruction was ordered by the Tudor judges; they wished to interrogate Bishop Stillington, who they regarded as the primary author of the statute and responsible for the multiple falsehoods. No doubt, they thought that Stillington should have been previously cross-examined, perhaps by the Great Council of 25 June 1483 or, more likely, by an ecclesiastical law court. No doubt, they thought that legal action against him was justified. But Henry VII wanted to leave this sensitive problem untouched, so he pardoned the bishop on 22 November 1485 and put an end to the matter. After all, Henry regarded the Yorkist kings as usurpers and felt some sympathy for Stillington, who had helped bring them down. And Henry VII did not want further national debate about the legitimacy of his intended queen or about his own doubtful hereditary claim to the throne.

A major complaint against Bishop Stillington has been that he was never interrogated concerning his allegations about the 1461 marriage contract. He should have been examined properly by an ecclesiastical law court *before* Edward V was deposed and Richard was made king, not afterwards. Following Bosworth, it was too late because there could be no going back; the matter was settled on the battlefield. Henry wisely wanted no discussion of the legitimacy of his intended future queen, a point which is very easy to understand. When defenders of Richard III blame Henry VII for there being no proper examination of Stillington, they are simply attempting to obfuscate and mislead. There was no proper examination because that is what Richard III and his confederates feared the most: an ecclesiastical law court proceeding. Their case would have been entirely undone, as they did not have two witnesses to establish the alleged 1461 contract as a fact under the canon law (Helmholz, 1974), and they had no legitimate corroborative evidence with which to impress an ecclesiastical law court.

The repeal and destruction of the Titulus Regius could not reverse the dismal effect the statute had on the reputation of King Edward IV, who was a fine king deserving of much better. Also, it was particularly and unfairly damaging to the reputation of Queen Elizabeth Woodville, one of the most maligned queens in English history, whose multiple children were declared to be not legitimate. Some apologists for Richard III, attempting to support the legislation, claim that the 1484 statute established the right of Parliament to choose the king, but that was already established by the Act of Accord in 1460, if not earlier. The Titulus Regius statute of 1484 was full of falsehoods, and its reversal and suppression meant that it had no constitutional effect. The English monarchy remained an hereditary institution; Parliament could elect if it was necessary, but the choices were limited by the standard rules of inheritance.

Henry Tudor and Elizabeth of York were married on 26 January 1486, five months after Bosworth, and the inheritance problem was solved. It has never been seriously challenged since. It is noteworthy that Henry and Elizabeth did obtain papal approval for their marriage. Even though Henry believed that his title to the crown was derived from his doubtful family history and also by right of armed force, most people were happier when he did as promised and married Princess Elizabeth, who had an excellent claim to the throne. And for those who still doubt the original Yorkist claim to the throne through females of the line, Philippa Plantagenet Mortimer and Anne Mortimer Plantagenet, the Tudor accession was ultimately confirmed through yet another female of the line, Princess Elizabeth Plantagenet, the eldest daughter of King Edward IV. If the English constitutional succession depended on precedent, then that precedent was finally and firmly enshrined; it can never be reversed. It is interesting to reflect that England's present beautiful queen, Elizabeth II, on the throne now sixty-two years, is a direct descendant of all those "bad girls": Henry VII's queen consort who is sometimes, in some quarters, still accused of being illegitimate; her much maligned mother, the benevolent Queen Elizabeth Woodville, who is often accused falsely of greed and rapacity; and Elizabeth Woodville's mother, Jacquetta, the alleged sorceress, the dowager duchess of Bedford, who, with her attendants, was witness to King Edward IV's valid marriage. May they all three rest in peace.

CHAPTER 9

Blaming the Dead Man

King Edward IV is often blamed for his failure to ensure the proper Yorkist succession to the throne and the survival of the Yorkist dynasty ("Blaming the Dead Guy," 2008). This explains why an excellent king still has a somewhat tarnished reputation and why later historians could criticize him for his so-called lack of accomplishment. Charles Ross (1997), who was generally sympathetic to Edward IV, surprisingly made this claim at the end of his excellent book. It is hard to be sure about this claim, as the king's modified last will of 1483 with added codicils did not survive and cannot be further examined. What remains is the king's careful and detailed last will drawn up in 1475, before the expedition to France. The principal executor of his last will, Bishop John Morton, who would have seen the added codicils appointing a Lord Protector, never made any suggestion that Edward was derelict in his duty to make proper arrangements and never contradicted Richard's right to be the Lord Protector, even though the bishop disliked Richard. Moreover, it is extremely unlikely that Hastings failed to communicate to Richard that Edward IV had appointed him as Lord Protector. There seems little doubt that Edward IV appointed Gloucester as Lord Protector, that Gloucester knew it, that the council confirmed the appointment on 10 May 1483, and that Richard initially accepted the position. It is hard to understand how that could be faulted. Even the critics do not suggest that the decision was wrong. If Richard had persisted with that plan, if he had honoured his brother's request, as was to be reasonably expected, then things would have been very different. Edward IV had no reason to suspect that Richard would be so grossly unfaithful, except that his politically astute queen might have suggested to him otherwise.

It is possible that the Woodvilles may have resisted the protectorate, but, at the time of the accession, there is no evidence that they would have taken up arms against the powerful dukes of Gloucester and Buckingham. At the least, they might have considered it initially, but then rejected it as a bad idea. If they had been seriously considering a strike against the dukes, then they would have brought Edward V to London with a considerable armed force, perhaps five thousand men, put together in Wales and the Welsh Marches, where the new king was respected and popular. The queen would not have backed down and agreed so readily with Hastings that a limited force to accompany Edward V would be more appropriate. Anthony Woodville, with far superior forces at his command, would not have been so cooperative with Gloucester and Buckingham at Northampton, and the soldiers would not have been so easily dismissed at Stony Stratford. Anthony probably considered more aggressive armed support for the boy king and had previously confirmed his powers to raise troops in the Welsh Marches. But he was not the kind of man to place England in such jeopardy. He was in no hurry to reach London in April 1483. It took him ten days to make his preparations; he deliberately delayed his departure from Ludlow so he could celebrate St George Day on 23 April 1483. That would not be consistent with a determination to support the new king more aggressively. Queen Elizabeth Woodville probably did initially suggest a larger force to accompany Edward V to London, but more moderate voices on the council prevailed, and the Queen Mother did not hesitate to give way, in the interests of harmony. In fact, in retrospect, she was almost certainly right, if we consider what actually happened. But both Anthony and Elizabeth Woodville realized their faction was not popular, the queen's tentative appeals for support in London had met with little enthusiasm, and neither wished to risk civil war again.

In any case, and most important, the Woodvilles were soundly defeated by early May 1483 and became, in effect, powerless. Richard, Duke of Gloucester, controlled the boy king; Anthony Woodville and Richard Grey were in prison; Elizabeth, young Prince Richard, the marquis of Dorset, and other Woodvilles were in the sanctuary; and Sir Edward Woodville had fled over the sea to Brittany. The often-mentioned exaggerated power of the Woodville faction collapsed in a matter of three weeks; their power was entirely dependent on a living, breathing King Edward IV, as was proper. And, aside from Gloucester, not much was heard from any other of the so-called overmighty factions, especially as Hastings had not made any firm decision. In another month, he would be dead and his men would join those of Buckingham and Gloucester. It should also be noted that Buckingham was most definitely not one of the overmighty magnates in the reign of King Edward IV, yet he played a major role in the usurpation. Richard's unfortunate decision to abuse his position as Lord Protector was quite out of character, given his previous flawless loyalty to his older brother, King Edward IV. And there lies the blame for what happened. When a headstone was finally placed on Richard's grave at Leicester, it bore the Latin inscription stating that Richard had come to the throne "By his betrayal of the trust placed in him, as Lord Protector of his nephew, King Edward V." And that was the truth.

As an unusual aside, Michael Miller (2003) suggested in his otherwise fine account that Queen Elizabeth Woodville, in order to protect herself, might have gathered all amended copies of Edward's last will with added codicils and had them destroyed. If we believe the propaganda that Elizabeth was a foolish woman, then that may be so, but there is no proof. Many people knew about the changes already, and, in fact, Elizabeth was far too experienced and far too loyal to her beloved husband to have done such a thing. It is dismaying that so many continue to hold Elizabeth Woodville in such low esteem.

To continue the argument in defence of Edward IV, the king followed the usual royal custom of making all his nobles swear to support his Prince of Wales at the succession, and that included Richard, Duke of Gloucester. Richard repeated his oath at York soon after Edward IV was dead. Again, soon after his arrival in London with Edward V, he repeated his oath of loyalty to the boy king. Richard's repeated word proved worthless.

Edward IV made extraordinary efforts to train the future Edward V in the art of kingship. According to Alison Weir (1999), this was clearly evidenced in the *Ordinances of Edward IV,* where instructions for the training of the Prince of Wales were clearly set out in minute detail. Probably no king in English history was better prepared for the throne than Edward IV's son. Anthony Woodville was a superb scholar; he and the tutor

Bishop John Alcock had trained the prince well in philosophy, literature, history, law, logic, personal habits, conversation, and government. Young Edward was an excellent student. Dominic Mancini (1969) was outspoken in his praise for the education of Prince Edward. If the Italian Mancini was unqualified in some of his opinions, then there can be no doubt that he was more than qualified on the matter of the new king's education.

It is entirely possible that Edward V would have made a very good king, and Richard would have made a very good Lord Protector or regent and taught the young king much that was worthwhile. The fine legislation that Richard eventually passed in 1484 would have been just as possible without the assassination of Hastings, without the judicial murders at Pontefract, and without the secret murders of the princes in the Tower. It is not unreasonable to suggest that Richard, given time and a little work, would have had the strong support of his well-educated nephew King Edward V. Then, the House of York would have prospered. But, for the admirers of the Tudor dynasty, there would have been no King Henry VIII and no Virgin Queen Elizabeth Tudor.

According to his critics, Edward IV was supposed to have reduced the power of the Woodvilles before he died, but they were loyal and accomplished servants of the Crown. He would have deprived his government of considerable talent. Perhaps he should have reduced the power of Richard or the power of Hastings; but that, too, would have been completely unjustifiable, as both were faithful to Edward IV's government. England at this time was not an easy country to rule; it needed firm hands, as both Richard III and Henry VII were soon to discover.

Even when Richard usurped the throne and even when it appeared that the princes in the Tower were dead, Elizabeth Woodville still made her peace with Richard, at least in public, and appeared to accept him as her husband's successor. She wanted no more civil war. It is hard to imagine that she was not furious with Richard III for his failure to protect Edward V and his brother, but she kept her feelings to herself, made no complaints on the public stage, and pursued the plans for her daughter Elizabeth and Henry Tudor in secret. She made reconciliation with Richard because it was the correct thing for England; but she made other plans for the succession. She was a worldly woman, not stupid, as Richard may have supposed. She had played power politics with the best, namely the sixteenth earl of Warwick and the duke of Clarence, and had often prevailed. She realized that overtly opposing Richard would not make any sense, since her position was so weak and her political support lacking. She knew that Richard's position would be challenged sooner or later, and she knew from where that challenge would come. She sensed that Richard was unpopular enough among his subjects that it would be best to wait and see how events developed. It is not hard to understand what she thought of the Usurper King; it is apparent that this unfortunate but talented and resourceful woman had her own plans for the House of York, despite her extremely vulnerable position. It is not unreasonable to suggest that she played her weak hand with patience, consummate skill, and more than a little luck.

Through the rear-vision mirror, it must be concluded that Richard should have accepted the role that Edward IV chose for him. Edward IV left any number of healthy heirs, including two handsome boys, Edward and Richard, and two beautiful, intelligent girls of near suitable age, namely Elizabeth and Cecily. Furthermore, Princess Elizabeth soon proved to be an excellent Tudor queen, and there were three younger daughters waiting in the wings. There were also several male nephews, of whom one, the earl of Lincoln, was old enough already to be king and had an excellent claim, better than that of Richard III. It seems clear that Edward should not be faulted; the fertile productivity of Edward IV and Queen Elizabeth Woodville, and of others in the family, gave England multiple possible Yorkist successors. We should compare their performance with that of other monarchs. Most of the Tudors spring to mind. The last three, Edward VI, Mary I, and Elizabeth I, produced not a single direct heir between them. To blame Edward IV is to ask the impossible. What followed Edward's death was the result alone of Richard III's unexpected, uncharacteristic, and uncalled for treachery.

CHAPTER 10

The 1461 Marriage Contract Story, Believed in 1483, Discarded in 1485, and Now Impossible to Believe, but which Marked the Death Knell of the House of York

This whole miserable tale was only possible because the magnates believed the 1461 marriage contract story or pretended they did; it was a convenient way to avoid another minority government and avoid a repeat of the disastrous minority reign of King Henry VI. This was especially so because the alternative presented was a powerful and successful lord, namely Richard, Duke of Gloucester, in the prime of his life, with a distinguished military career, a record of flawless loyalty to King Edward IV, and a long record of highly successful government in the north country.

But in 1483, few in the government seemed to understand that the great good man was making a very serious mistake and that it would lead to a disastrous final reckoning in a few short years. The marriage contract story did not stand up to proper examination. Any support was unsubstantiated in that there was no documented proof, there was only a single unsupported witness, and there was no decision by a proper ecclesiastical law court. This can best be understood by a close consideration of the two most important people involved, Lady Eleanor Butler and Bishop Robert Stillington. Some or much of the information was available to the magnates, but they chose to ignore it.

Lady Eleanor Butler (1435–1468)

Eleanor was the daughter of John Talbot, the first earl of Shrewsbury, the famous commander who died at Castillon in 1453. Eleanor was a distant cousin of Edward IV since her great-great-great-grandfather was also the great-great-great-great-grandfather of Edward IV. Their common ancestor was Roger Mortimer, the first earl of March, who died in 1330 (Ashdown-Hill, 2010). Edward and Eleanor were fourth cousins, one generation removed, but they were not so close in kinship that they needed a papal dispensation for their alleged formal marriage. Eleanor's younger sister, Elizabeth Talbot, married John Mowbray, the fourth duke of Norfolk. After Eleanor died in 1468, Elizabeth had a daughter, Anne Mowbray (1472–1481), who, as a child, married young Prince Richard in 1478 and was therefore Edward IV's daughter-in-law. And, most important, Lady Eleanor's mother was Margaret Beauchamp, whose sister, Anne Beauchamp, was married to Richard Neville, the illustrious sixteenth earl of Warwick. *This means that Lady Eleanor Butler was the niece by marriage of Warwick, the Kingmaker; he was her uncle.*

So, we are asked to believe that while the great Kingmaker, the sixteenth earl of Warwick, was trying to arrange a French bride for Edward IV in 1463 and 1464, and while he had his sights set on the sister-in-law of indeed the king of France, the Yorkist King Edward IV was already allegedly married to Warwick's very own niece – and had been so for several years. It is interesting to speculate what Warwick's wife, Anne, who must have been aware, would have said to him. This made the French marriage treaty planned by Warwick utterly impossible. This situation defies comprehension. Warwick would have been very surprised to hear about any marriage contract involving his own niece and his Yorkist royal master. The earl would have undoubtedly said that such a marriage did not exist; otherwise, it would be hard to explain what he was trying to accomplish in France.

In addition, it should be noted that Warwick was trying to arrange a marriage with Princess Bona, having first obtained the permission of King Edward. It would be surprising if Edward gave his permission if he knew he was already committed in marriage to Lady Eleanor Butler, Warwick's own niece. Some might argue that the king may have forgotten about the contract, but this would not be consistent with Edward's well-known attention to details, like contracts and marriages, or with his sharp memory and amazing ability to recall names and places and social details about the families he had met. Even when the king spent time at play, his power of recall, the cornerstone of his later political success, was always brilliant. It is very unlikely that Edward had forgotten about any alleged marriage contract. He gave his permission for Warwick to arrange a power marriage in France, with the understanding that he was quite free to do so. In the absence of any French marriage, Edward married Elizabeth Woodville in 1464 with the same understanding.

The royal marriage to Elizabeth was so unpopular with the magnates, and Warwick was so infuriated by the collapse of his plans for a French marriage treaty, that it is hard to imagine that efforts were not made to discover some reason that would invalidate the 1464 marriage with Elizabeth Woodville and allow it to be set aside immediately. The young king would no doubt have discouraged such efforts, but it would be difficult to believe there was no serious discussion of the matter. If there really was a 1461 marriage contract between Edward and Lady Eleanor, then the lords, especially Warwick, would have found it. Given this situation, it becomes very likely that the contract did not exist; otherwise, it could have been used as a powerful weapon against the king's Woodville marriage – or, at the very least, the young king could have been questioned and seriously challenged.

Sir Thomas More (2005) stated that the king's mother, Cecily, the dowager duchess of York, and some lords of the king's company questioned Dame Elizabeth Lucy about a possible marriage contract with Edward IV, but Dame Elizabeth Lucy flatly denied it. That was the end of that possible reason to prevent or set aside the king's Woodville marriage. This activity occurred before the 1464 Woodville marriage, not afterwards. Edward's mother did not want Edward to marry Elizabeth Woodville if there was a previous marriage contract; the savvy duchess sensed there was danger. Cecily challenged Edward about his choice of a bride. This means that Edward IV did not believe there was a previous marriage contract. It means that the subject had been seriously considered and was rejected; it is known that the king spent time to justify his choice with his mother and elaborated on the many assets of Elizabeth Woodville. It also suggests that the 1464 marriage was not as hurried as many have suggested;

nor was it such a complete secret. It does confirm that the nobles were indeed suspicious of the king, as they were not happy about the Woodville marriage and were asking the right questions. It is not unreasonable to believe that they might also have questioned other ladies, among them Lady Eleanor Butler, along similar lines; after all, it was well known that the womanizing king had multiple relationships, and any of them could possibly have been accompanied by a marriage contract. However, there is no solid evidence that Lady Eleanor was ever interrogated in this way. Discovery of a marriage contract with Lady Eleanor would have been a great coup for the magnates opposed to the Woodville marriage, but such a discovery never occurred. One very probable reason is that no such contract ever existed.

In 1483, the sixteenth earl of Warwick might have had many negative things to say about the alleged marriage contract of 1461, but he was dead. That was fortunate for Richard, Duke of Gloucester. Also, at the time in 1483, Dominic Mancini (1989) implied that he did not believe the marriage contract story; Mancini implied that the nobles accepted the usurpation not because of the force of the contract argument but because of the threats posed by Gloucester and Buckingham (St Aubyn, 1983).

Sir Thomas More (2005), a fine legal mind, writing thirty years after the usurpation, stated clearly that Richard III was "on slipper [unstable] ground when he pretended King Edward's children to be bastards." He described the story as a "convenient pretext" for Richard's seizure of the throne. Those who are more sympathetic to Richard spend much effort attempting to deny the account of Sir Thomas More; in fact, they sometimes imply that this honourable man was a liar. Sir Thomas More later died for what he considered the truth about the English Church; his reputation far exceeds that of his critics. Sir Francis Bacon (1889), also a great legal mind, a superb analyst of evidence, writing 130 years after the usurpation, said of the marriage contract story, "That fable was ever exploded." John Rous, the author of the *Warwick Roll*, described the arguments put forth by Richard as "feigned for his own advancement" (St Aubyn, 1983).

It is usually stated that Edward married Elizabeth Woodville on 1 May 1464 and thereafter made repeated secret conjugal visits to Grafton. Susan Higginbotham (2008) has suggested that it was later, based on the assertion by Michael Hicks that Edward IV granted the wardship of Elizabeth's young son, nine-year-old Thomas Grey, to Lord William Hastings on 10 August 1464. This would have been very unusual if Edward had already married Elizabeth.

The king's marriage was revealed to the public in September 1464. At that time, not one member of the Talbot family, notably including Eleanor herself, not young John Talbot, the third earl of Shrewsbury (1448–73), and not their advisors or other members of the family said anything about a marriage contract between Lady Eleanor and the king. It would be reasonable to ask why Eleanor, nearly thirty years old, was not already living in the same household with the twenty-two-year-old king and sharing the same domestic quarters, since the invented contract story included the allegation that Stillington performed their formal, but unwitnessed, marriage. As the king did not insist that Eleanor live with him in the same household at Westminster Palace, or at Ludlow, Eltham, Greenwich, Sheen, or Windsor, obviously Edward did not believe that he had made a marriage with Eleanor. And there is no certain evidence that he paid her matrimonial support or, indeed, even continued his intimate association with her. Their close relationship began in the spring of 1461 and was more or less finished by the fall of 1461, when Edward favoured Dame Elizabeth Lucy.

John Ashdown-Hill (2010) suggested that Edward IV might have given Eleanor some estates in Wiltshire during 1462 from which she derived income, but she never lived there. When she died, there was no public hearing to settle the legal transfer of her title as there was for other of her properties. This could mean that the properties were simply loaned for the purpose of rental income; a loan would have been a very unsuitable reward for her alleged silence in such a crucial matter. It was certainly a case of the always generous Edward IV looking after his friends. John Ashdown-Hill went into minute detail about where Eleanor lived during the various stages of her life, from her birth to her death, but there was no mention of her living with the king in the same household. People may think what they want of Edward IV, but he had a fine reputation for honouring commercial contracts. In medieval times, that could have included a marriage contract. The deep Christian faith of Lady Eleanor Butler has been heavily emphasized; she would have taken a formal marriage very seriously, and yet she made no effort to defend her alleged marriage to King Edward IV, either in private or in public.

The Talbot family would have seized the moment if they had decided that Lady Eleanor was the rightful queen of England. They and the earl of Warwick would have settled the matter, and the king's Woodville marriage would have been annulled by the Church. Eleanor's younger sister, Elizabeth Talbot (1442–1507), the duchess of Norfolk, was very supportive of her older sister through the tribulations of Eleanor's often sad life, but the duchess never suggested, either in public life or in private, that Lady Eleanor was married to Edward IV. This remained so even after Eleanor died in 1468. And it remained true after the king died in 1483, when supportive evidence would have greatly interested the duke of Gloucester, who badly needed a more solid pretext for his intended usurpation. It seems reasonable to believe that Richard was not entirely satisfied with Bishop Stillington's concocted story; his advisors always mentioned it last, after all the other nonsense. Duchess Elizabeth would have been Richard's saviour had she supported Stillington's tall tale. It could have been argued that Richard had two witnesses for the 1461 marriage contract, one direct and one indirect, so an approach to an ecclesiastical law court might have been considered. Finally, and most telling, neither Eleanor nor Edward ever said in public that they were married to each other.

Stillington's answer to such criticism might have been that the marriage contract was secret, but that was what made it nearly impossible to prove its validity. It was entirely dependent on the bishop's unsubstantiated word. There was no second witness needed to prove a fact under the canon law (Helmholz, 1974), and satisfactory supportive evidentiary proof has remained elusive for five hundred years. Nobody in Eleanor's family ever came forward to support the contract allegation. In the time before 1513 when Sir Thomas More was researching his book, Elizabeth Mowbray, a resident at the Minoresses Convent, had ample opportunity to give her side of the story, if indeed she had anything to say about the matter, either to her friends at the convent or directly to Sir Thomas More. But her time with Sir Thomas may have been limited because she died in 1507.

The last legal decision about the alleged marriage contract between Edward and Eleanor was made in 1485 after Bosworth Field. By its repeal and destruction of the 1484 Titulus Regius, the first Tudor Parliament concluded that in the absence of any ecclesiastical law court decision, the 1461 alleged marriage contract must never have existed; the marriage of Edward and Elizabeth Woodville was therefore valid, as had been recognized by the Church for nineteen years. Others have suggested that Parliament merely reversed what it should not have done in the first place. The 1461 contract fabrication was pushed forward by Gloucester and Buckingham in 1483 because it suited their shameful purpose to usurp the crown. It was later championed by Richard III because he needed from his one and only Parliament some form of justification for his usurpation. In 1483, Richard's supporters were assured by Bishop Stillington that it would be hard to prove that the 1461 alleged marriage did not exist. It was a very clever strategy.

Some sceptics might suggest that the above arguments are not convincing, as it is always difficult to prove that something did not happen; but under those circumstances, to prove it did happen, it becomes imperative that the allegation be supported with proper witnesses and adequate collateral evidence. At that time, and at that time only, did the story carry the day; it was sufficient to put Richard III on the throne. And in twenty-six miserable months, it spelled the doom of the grand Royal House of York and nearly destroyed the fine reputation, achievement, and legacy of King Edward IV.

Robert Stillington (1420–1491), the Bishop of Bath and Wells

Robert Stillington was a member of the king's council from the year 1449, when Henry VI still reigned. Under Edward IV, he was the keeper of the privy seal from 1460 to 1467, one of the highest positions in the land. He held office at the time of the alleged 1461 verbal contract with Lady Eleanor Butler, at the time of the alleged private marriage to Lady Eleanor Butler, and at the time of the valid royal marriage of Edward and Elizabeth in 1464. Stillington was made the bishop of Bath and Wells in 1465. He was chancellor of England from 1467 to 1470 and again from 1471 to 1473. Never once during that extended time in high office did he say anything about a legal problem with the royal marriage; yet it is alleged that he knew that there was such a problem, in which case he was grossly derelict in his duty to the king.

When Edward IV recovered his kingdom in 1471, Bishop Stillington was restored as Lord Chancellor; but ill health caused the bishop to be increasingly ineffective, according to the Croyland Chronicler (1854). The king was annoyed that the bishop defended the countess of Warwick and opposed her virtual disinheritance following the treason and death of her husband, the Kingmaker. Edward was determined to punish Warwick even when the earl was dead. This sounds unreasonable, but it was common among rulers in the Middle Ages. In 1473, Edward IV dismissed Stillington; it is said that the bishop did not lose favour entirely, as he continued to act as a trustee for the king and was also sent on several diplomatic missions. However, it is likely that Stillington deeply resented his fall from power; in 1475, he was summoned to the Vatican to face secret accusations, possibly related to his well-known neglect of his ecclesiastical duties as the bishop of Bath and Wells. Stillington never recovered from his fall from grace.

Some have suggested that Stillington mentioned the 1461 marriage contract to the duke of Clarence in the years before 1478, but Clarence never used this argument to threaten the king's 1464 marriage; in which case it is extremely unlikely, many would say impossible, knowing the treacherous nature of Clarence, that Stillington imparted any such information. Clarence was already spreading the notion that Edward was a bastard at birth and that his marriage was invalid because Elizabeth was a widow. Adding the 1461 contract story to his propaganda would have been no problem for Clarence. If Stillington had imparted such information in 1478, then he would have faced execution for treason; King Edward IV would not have tolerated this threat to the succession; and the queen, mother of the Prince of Wales, certainly would have insisted on a solution. No doubt, the bishop, sympathetic with Clarence, was critical of the king for any of several reasons, most likely the story that the king himself was a bastard; but the bishop was examined in the Tower, made to pay a large fine, and released from custody. There is no good evidence that Stillington ever mentioned any marriage contract story before June of 1483.

At the time of the alleged marriage contract, Edward IV was already the king of England. The year of the alleged contract is not known for certain, but it is likely to have been 1461. As there was no precise date or place for the alleged contract, that alone should have cast considerable doubt on its validity. It is not likely that a forty-one-year-old man in the prime of his career, already the Lord Privy Seal and soon to be the bishop of Bath and Wells, already a theologian with a well-developed knowledge of canon and civil law, would have been witness to a marriage contract and then performed a formal marriage ceremony for the king of England, no less. It would be even less likely if he did this in secret with no second witness for the contract, or no witnesses at all for the formal marriage and no documentation whatsoever. It would be impossible that he kept the secret for twenty-two years through the king's announcement of his marriage to Elizabeth Woodville, through her enthronement performed by the bishops, through her coronation performed by the Archbishop of Canterbury, and through the birth of ten royal children with ten royal baptisms and wide publicity. It is reasonable to suggest that if Bishop Stillington thought the 1464 marriage was invalid, he had a moral obligation to discuss the matter with the bishops and the Archbishop of Canterbury. Yet, so far as we know, he did no such thing, because the prelates went ahead with all of the above-mentioned sacraments.

It is also unlikely that Stillington could have remained silent during the time when Warwick was attempting to arrange the marriage of Edward IV to the French princess Bona of Savoy in the years 1463–64. Such a French marriage treaty would not have been possible if the alleged 1461 contract story was true. If the arranged state marriage had occurred and an earlier 1461 marriage was discovered, then the diplomatic storm with France would have been unimaginable. Stillington, sitting in the council chamber, would have been compelled to warn Warwick against his marriage plan with Princess Bona; yet, clearly, he did not do so. Or, if Stillington did warn Warwick, the earl would have questioned his Beauchamp family, including his niece Lady Eleanor, and then concluded that there was no marriage.

As it was, there was considerable dismay when the king announced in September 1464 that he was already married to Elizabeth Woodville. Many would have loved to hear about the alleged 1461 marriage to Lady Eleanor at that time. Stillington would have received widespread support among the magnates if the royal marriage to Elizabeth Woodville could have been quietly annulled in 1464 and if any proven contract with Lady Eleanor could later have been secretly set aside by the Church authorities with payment of a suitable annuity. The great magnates could then have met their hearts' desire and arranged a great marriage of state for their Yorkist king.

It must be concluded that the contract story was not true. Philippe de Commines, writing in 1493, only repeated what he had heard in 1483 and 1484. Commines expressed his own opinion of Bishop Stillington as follows: that for many years, "this malicious prelate smothered this revenge in his heart." Stillington's claim that he witnessed the 1461 marriage contract was never confirmed by a supportive witness, and his alleged formal marriage of the king was not witnessed at all, not by anybody. As some have pointed out, a marriage with no witnesses is no marriage at all (Okerlund, 2005). Sir Clements Markham's suggestion that there was documentary evidence for the 1461 marriage contract was never confirmed. Giles St Aubyn (1983) wrote that "the most compelling reason for rejecting the story of Edward IV's contract is that there is not a shred of evidence to support it; it was based on a series of assertions, almost certainly invented, intended to justify the unlawful deposition of the rightful King." It is impossible to disagree with his conclusion.

Most likely, Stillington invented the contract story after Edward IV was dead, perhaps in early June 1483, when Gloucester was in serious consideration of deposing King Edward V and was looking for a reliable pretext. Hoping for favour with Gloucester, Stillington used his serious but flawed knowledge of canon law in an attempt to invalidate the marriage of Edward IV. There followed the abject failure of the initial and preferred tale presented by Dr Shaw on 22 June 1483, that Edward IV himself was illegitimate, that he was not the biological son of Richard Plantagenet, the third duke of York who died in 1460, and, by inference, that he should not have been king in the first place. Because of the dowager duchess of York's loud complaints, it was decided on 23 June 1483, before Buckingham's address on 24 June 1483, to use the 1461 marriage contract story alone. Despite this, it should be obvious that, in fact, the contract story was always their second choice, as suggested by Alison Weir (1999). It was based upon the unsupported word of Bishop Stillington, upon the useful ambiguity of both the contract custom and the canon law, and upon Edward's well-known promiscuity. It would be hard to prove that the alleged 1461 marriage contract did not exist when both parties were dead and when most of those likely to support Edward V were executed, imprisoned, or intimidated.

Regardless, Richard used the contract story to delegitimize the boy king Edward V, a king the duke had repeatedly sworn to protect and support. Richard followed the advice of his lawyer, Sir William Catesby, which was to throw sufficient muck against the wall and hope that some would stick. The 1461 contract fabrication stuck just long enough for Richard to successfully claim the crown, after which the story came demonstrably unstuck. But most important, unlike the timid and confused lords, the English people were not fooled for a moment; they recognized a false story when they saw one (Clive, 1974).

It is notable that during the reign of Richard III there was no modern democratic process to work its will; it took time for the people's hostility to hasten the downfall of the Usurper King. Surprisingly, perhaps, it took only two years. Richard III did not heap rewards upon Stillington. If the bishop had revealed a legitimate 1461 marriage contract, then the king would have been very grateful, but the king remained uneasy about the contract story. He suspected that Stillington had lied, so the king issued no rewards.

Before Edward IV married Elizabeth Woodville in 1464, Richard's mother, the dowager duchess Cecily, had considered the possibility of an earlier marriage contract, concluded there was no evidence (Ellis, Grafton, and Hall, 1809), and, in 1483, may even have told Richard of her opinion, although there is no confirmation for this. Richard would have preferred to use the story that Edward IV himself was not legitimate, even though it aroused his mother's anger; he could not resist suggesting this again in the Titulus Regius, claiming that he himself was "the undoubted son [and heir] of Richard, the third Duke of York." Although not much is known of Richard's subsequent relationship with Duchess Cecily, his mother's last will suggests that she did not favour him. She never mentioned him (Okerlund, 2010)! And it is important to note that she did not attend his coronation. Richard's defenders claim that he would never have done such a thing, accuse his own mother of adultery, when he lived for a while in the same house, namely at Baynard Castle in London, but that feeble suggestion only makes it doubly despicable. And besides, on 5 June 1483 or soon after, Richard moved abode to Crosby Hall to be with his wife,

Duchess Anne; and it was only later, on 22 June 1483, that the despicable story was first put forward on the public stage by Dr Shaw.

Since Richard III never presented the princes in public, as was so desperately needed if he was to save his credibility and thus his reign, that, too, would be consistent with the notion that even Richard himself did not believe the contract story. The risk that Edward V would speak up and demand a church court hearing was too great. It is also likely that Catesby, Richard's lawyer, did not believe the story either, as he never supported a church hearing, which could have supplied powerful support if the Stillington story was true. If such an ecclesiastical law court had invalidated Edward's 1464 marriage, as was likely if the contract story was true, then Richard's case would have been that much stronger in public opinion. He would not have felt the need to execute the prisoners at Pontefract, assassinate Lord Hastings, or murder the princes in the Tower – and he would not have suffered such a disastrous loss of credibility in the eyes of his subjects. But both Richard III and Sir William Catesby knew that the story was a fabrication; the invention just fitted with Richard's desperate need to be the king of England. And yet it is amazing how long has been the life of this shameful fabrication. It is simply incomprehensible; it is utterly impossible that it could be true. Richard saw his chance for supreme power and took advantage; it was a huge and fatal mistake, the biggest of Richard's career. The rest indeed is very sad English history. It was a contemptible insult laid upon the House of York and the English people, and it was disastrous for the proud legacy of King Edward IV.

CHAPTER 11

The Canon Law and Its Relationship to the Marriage of King Edward IV

Contract, Marriage, and Legitimacy

It is important to understand what constituted a valid marriage contract under canon law in the fifteenth century; this has been extensively discussed by Christopher Brooke (1989) and Mary O'Regan (1973), among others. It is sometimes suggested that marriage contracts required only present-tense conversational statements of action, such as "I do marry you," which may or may not have been followed by sexual intercourse. The essence of a marriage under the canon law was that the two parties each consented to the marriage. Apparently, no witness or document was required; if the two persons said they were married, then that was sufficient. For such an informal marriage to be valid, a marriage licence was not required. Indeed, such a document did not exist in medieval times, only later. Any other kind of signed document was not required, either. It was a surprisingly loose arrangement. So long as there was no challenge to the marriage, there was no problem and all the children were considered legitimate.

In that case, marriage contracts were so informal that any reasonable or unreasonable suggestion of a prior marriage contract could be made in order to invalidate any subsequent marriage as bigamous. That sometimes happened, usually in cases of disputed inheritance. Under such circumstances, a marriage contract could be totally fabricated by a third party and used against anyone; so, Stillington, Catesby, and Gloucester knew what they were doing with this blunt instrument.

However, once the matter was taken to an ecclesiastical law court, there arose a difficult problem. Legal proof of a prior marriage or marriage contract in an ecclesiastical law court, for the purpose of setting aside a later marriage, required a proper document or other proper evidence, or it required at least two witnesses who were present at the prior marriage contract agreement (Helmholz, 1974). This was so in England in the fifteenth century, and this would be especially so for a crowned king of England. It is no wonder that Gloucester did not take his case to an ecclesiastical law court. After his bishops had probably explained, he knew he could not meet the requirements and could not possibly win his case. No supportive documentary evidence has ever been found for the alleged 1461 marriage contract between King Edward and Lady Eleanor; the allegation was entirely dependent on the claim of a single person, and an alienated one at that. Most important, there was no second witness to support Bishop Stillington. This explains why the matter of Edward's 1464 marriage was never taken to an ecclesiastical law court. It is absolutely reasonable to conclude that the valid 1464 marriage of Edward IV and Elizabeth Woodville was challenged and illegally set aside using a completely unsubstantiated assertion which could not be supported in an ecclesiastical law court.

There was another concern. If one or both parties were dead, then there could be a problem, as the matter of mutual consent might be difficult to show in an ecclesiastical law court without secondary evidence. In the matter of Edward IV's alleged 1461 marriage contract, as the bride and the bridegroom were both dead in June 1483, Stillington thought that it would be impossible for anybody to prove conclusively that a prior marriage contract never existed, especially if it had been kept secret, as he claimed. But that was not the point or purpose in an ecclesiastical law court, where it would be necessary to prove the existence of the prior marriage contract with evidence or witnesses.

Furthermore, although the very informal contract arrangement may have been not infrequent among the commons, it was invariably followed by cohabitation in the same household; in fact, that was the usual purpose for the agreement. Many couples lived together and claimed they were married by contract without going through a formal church ceremony. But it is very unlikely that such an arrangement occurred among the magnates, who had far too much wealth, title, and property at stake to afford taking such an enormous legal risk. Both Edward and Eleanor belonged to the propertied magnate class. This is another reason to be very suspicious of Stillington's allegation of a prior marriage contract.

In the fifteenth century, it was not the custom for Parliament to decide about the validity or the invalidity of a marriage. From the twelfth century or soon after, marriage law in Christendom was exclusively the province of the Church (O'Regan, 1976). The proper procedure was followed in dealing with the Beaufort family in the last decade of the fourteenth century (see Appendix D). In 1396, Pope Boniface IX first pronounced the legitimacy of John of Gaunt's third marriage, to Katherine Swynford, and hence the legitimacy of their children, the Beauforts, born out of wedlock. Then, Parliament decided the matter of inheritance in the affirmative for the Beaufort children in 1397.

To bolster their difficult case, Richard's confederates claimed other reasons to invalidate the 1464 marriage to Elizabeth; they suggested lack of official assent, involvement of sorcery, the matter of privacy and secrecy, lack of published banns, and lack of a proper church. But none of these certainly caused invalidity. It was definitely not necessary to have a priest perform a public ceremony in a consecrated church, although this was common and considered desirable. Clandestine marriages were not favoured, but they were valid and only required penance. The public issue of banns was encouraged in order to give people the opportunity to object to the union, but banns were not mandatory. This raises the question of why Eleanor did not object in 1464. She must have known from her famous Talbot family that her uncle Warwick was looking for a French bride for Edward IV, and she must have heard the news when Edward admitted that he was married to Elizabeth Woodville in 1464; yet Eleanor never suggested there was a problem. She was more than sophisticated enough to know that the king could not have two wives.

If she was a shy and shrinking commoner, as some have suggested, then her silence might be explained, but Eleanor was no commoner. She was the daughter of a great magnate, one of the most famous of the age. She could have gone to Bishop Stillington or to her young step-nephew John Talbot, the third earl of Shrewsbury (1448–73), or to both, and together they could have raised the matter with the lords. If Eleanor had wished, a satisfactory solution could then have been found. For one, although unlikely, an ecclesiastical law court could have validated the 1461 alleged marriage contract, although by 1464, Lady Eleanor had probably given up on Edward's close affections. But in 1464, the magnates would have been delighted with Lady Eleanor's story and persuaded the court that the 1464 Woodville marriage should be voided before there were any children. On the other hand, and much more likely, the ecclesiastical law court could have invalidated the alleged 1461 marriage contract for lack of proof. It could have made an official declaration that it never happened, that it was annulled. This would have validated the king's 1464 Woodville marriage. The fact that Lady Eleanor and Bishop Stillington did nothing suggests that there was no 1461 marriage contract. She did not think that there was a problem in 1464, and neither, apparently, did Bishop Stillington.

For Richard, Duke of Gloucester, the obvious question was, given these loose contract arrangements, how anyone was to provide proof of a marriage contract in a law court. How was Richard's government to prove in court that Edward IV was contracted to Lady Eleanor in 1461? Stillington said he married them, but there was no conclusive proof. Given the above-described situation, it may be that conclusive proof could never be found. Richard's party simply decided to ignore the problem and press ahead, believing that, equally, it would be impossible for opponents to prove that there was not a 1461 marriage contract. In his recent book, referring to the alleged marriage, John Ashdown-Hill (2010) wondered aloud what proof indeed could be offered. He believed that there was a marriage contract in 1461, but he was prepared to believe this in the absence of good evidence, presumably on the basis of Edward's alleged promiscuity. Under the circumstances, it is not unreasonable to believe that the allegation by Stillington was a clever fabrication.

However, according to Christopher Brooke (1989), discussing the views of the great theologian Peter the Lombard, there were further possibilities which could be examined by an ecclesiastical law court in looking for validation of the 1461 contract. This was the concept of a putative marriage. If it could be shown that the couple lived together as man and wife, then that might have been sufficient to support evidence for a 1461 marriage contract. If there were children of the union, then that would undoubtedly have helped. If one party had gone to an ecclesiastical law court to establish validity, then that would definitely have been useful. If there was public recognition of a marriage, including recognition by the Church or by the civil authorities, then that, too, would have helped prove validity. Or if both Edward and Eleanor were known to have acknowledged the marriage while they were still alive, that would have been more than sufficient. But that never happened. If witnesses could be found who said that Edward or Eleanor or both told them that they were married, that might have helped. It should be obvious from the foregoing that the matter was very complex; that is why only an ecclesiastical law court could render a reasonable determination of validity versus invalidity of an alleged marriage contract, especially concerning a king's marriage and especially after the king and his alleged bride were both dead.

Some have argued that Richard had no standing before an ecclesiastical law court since he was not party to the alleged marriage, but, of course, Richard and his protectorate government would have had standing before the court, because the question of validity or invalidity depended upon who occupied the English throne – a serious matter of inheritance and a problem that the prelates understood with considerable sympathy. Furthermore, a civil law court could have heard the case and then asked that the matter of the alleged 1461 contract be heard by an ecclesiastical law court; in fact, that is what the Great Council that met on 25 June 1483 should have requested. If the ecclesiastical law court decided on invalidity of the 1464 Woodville marriage, then Parliament could subsequently decide the inheritance question. This was the long-established precedent starting as far back as the eleventh century, when the secular courts began to abdicate their authority in these sensitive matrimonial matters.

The Opinion of the Experts in the Matter of the King's Marriage. They Needed an Ecclesiastical Law Court to Make a Legal Decision

In relation to the alleged marriage contract, there have been a number of scholarly papers published with a discussion of canon law in the medieval period. Mortimer Levine (1958) said there were four reasons to dismiss Richard's case for deposing King Edward V and seizing the throne:

(1) Edward V and Prince Richard were born in 1470 and 1473, respectively, after Lady Eleanor had died in 1468. Upon her death,

the 1464 marriage became valid, and so Edward V and Richard could not be declared illegitimate. But this would probably not have been widely accepted. Some, however, have accepted this line of argument; if the alleged 1461 agreement was similar to a standard contract, as agreed in other matters during life, then it would have been void with the death of Lady Eleanor in 1468. That would have made all the children legitimate, except for Princess Elizabeth and Princess Mary, who were both born before Lady Eleanor died. There is some evidence that people in medieval times were inclined to accept marriage as a contract, perhaps like a commercial contract, much more so than in our own modern times.

(2) Referring to the Woodville marriage, a clandestine marriage was valid and binding, although such a marriage was considered sinful and required penance.

(3) Referring to the Woodville marriage, the passage of time and public recognition of the marriage by both Church and State resulted in validity.

(4) Only an ecclesiastical law court could declare invalidity of the 1464 Woodville marriage – not the council, not the Great Council, and not even a proper Parliament.

But R. H. Helmholz (1986) disagreed with the first three reasons as follows:

(1) True, but there would need to be a remarriage before the princes were conceived; however, that would have been forbidden because the partners were already "polluted by adultery." And in any case, it did not happen.

(2) True, a clandestine marriage was valid, but only if the 1464 marriage was performed before the congregation (in facie ecclesiæ). As that was not clearly defined, this might have proved hard to establish. If the congregation had to be large, more than just a few, then it would no longer be clandestine. It is frequently claimed that the 1464 marriage was clandestine; it can reasonably be stated that a clandestine marriage was not necessarily invalid at all (Levine, 1958; Helmholz, 1986).

(3) True, public recognition led to validity, but again only if the 1464 marriage was performed before the congregation (in facie ecclesiæ). But, again, this phrase needed to be exactly defined by an ecclesiastical law court.

However, highly significant, R. H. Helmholz agreed with the last assertion by Mortimer Levine as follows:

(4) True, period, with no disagreement whatsoever; under the canon law, an ecclesiastical law court was without question required to establish validity or invalidity of the 1464 Woodville marriage.

In her academic discussion of the marriage contract matter, Mary O'Regan (1973) added her agreement with Levine and Helmholz, saying that an ecclesiastical law court was required to resolve properly the matter of Edward's 1464 marriage; then, the Parliament, the civil court, had the authority to decide the matter of inheritance and the royal succession. She stated clearly that from the twelfth century, matrimonial law had become the exclusive province of the Church. In the last paragraph of her complex paper, she admits that Richard was initially an usurper, indicating her probable rejection of the marriage contract story for lack of adequate proof, but after a period of time holding the crown, coupled with a supportive statute of Parliament in January 1484, Richard became a lawful king. In other words, the Titulus Regius removed the taint of usurpation. As a practical matter, this line of argument may be reasonable – and perhaps acceptable to many who still believe that Richard was initially an usurper. But by 1484, Richard had so alienated the English people by his treatment of his nephews that his ultimate fate was already determined. The line of argument was subtle and academic. There was no way the English people would accept such an elaborate conclusion; they considered Richard III to be an usurper king.

Mary O'Regan admired Richard III; she regretted that he died too early and left no heir to uphold his specific claim, as distinct from his brother's heir, Princess Elizabeth Plantagenet. But the English people had no such regrets; even in the North Country and even in the town of York, they only briefly mourned him after his death at Bosworth Field.

Thus, there were major problems with the Stillington position in 1483:

(1) An ecclesiastical law court was required to determine validity or invalidity of the 1464 marriage; in other words, the civil power (the Great Council or even Parliament) had no jurisdiction in the matter.

(2) But there was insufficient evidence to uphold the government's case in an ecclesiastical law court hearing; there was no second witness and there was no proper supportive documentation. Knowing this, Richard's government did not even make the attempt.

An ecclesiastical law court was needed to decide on the definition of the phrase "in facie ecclesiæ" before a decision could be made about a clandestine marriage and about public recognition of a marriage. And a court was needed to decide whether Edward and Eleanor ever appeared to be married. These things could not be decided by a body of confused and frightened lords who had little understanding of the complexities of the canon law.

On the matter of "in facie ecclesiæ," such an ecclesiastical law court might have ruled that there were sufficient people present at the 1464 marriage to satisfy the canon law, for Jesus of Nazareth is quoted in the New Testament of the Bible (Matthew 18: 20) as follows: "For where two or three are gathered together in my name, there am I in the midst of them." Thus, according to the traditional Christian teaching of the Trinity, Edward's 1464 Woodville marriage was performed before God (Christ) and at least three witnesses; this could have been considered "in facie ecclesiæ." It may be difficult for secularists to accept this, but the bishops might have had no such problem. It is not unreasonable to believe that an ecclesiastical law court could have reached the same conclusion, especially if the court was free of political threat from Richard's government. Furthermore, the painting of the king's 1464 wedding, published in the late fifteenth century in the *Chroniques d'Angleterre* (Wavrin, 2005), reveals at least eight other people, besides the priest, with Edward and Elizabeth in the church.

Such an ecclesiastical law court might have ruled that Stillington's solitary allegation needed additional supportive evidence; it would then have been a huge problem for Gloucester, since no such evidence was easy to find.

Furthermore, there was nothing else to suggest that Edward and Eleanor were married, nothing to suggest a putative marriage. There was absolutely no public acknowledgement of a marriage by either party; there was no admitted offspring of the alleged union; it was never claimed that they lived together as man and wife in the same household; and there was never public civil or Church acknowledgement of the marriage. Neither Eleanor nor her family ever took her case to any ecclesiastical law court to defend the validity of her alleged marriage; she may have had good reasons for not doing this, but it remains true that there was no public acknowledgement of this alleged marriage, at least while the couple were alive. And when public acknowledgement was belatedly made by Stillington, one man, in 1483, twenty-two years later, it was widely disbelieved.

On the other hand, Edward and Elizabeth gave every appearance of being married. There was obvious public acknowledgement a few months (no more than five months) after the marriage. The couple lived together as man and wife for nineteen years in the same household, and there was constant public and Church acknowledgement through the enthronement of Elizabeth at Reading Abbey, the coronation of Elizabeth at Westminster Abbey, and the multiple holy baptisms of the ten royal children. It can be strongly suggested that an ecclesiastical law court would never have found in favour of Richard, Duke of Gloucester.

In summary, it is difficult to understand how the alleged 1461 procedure could be considered a valid marriage for the king of England, whereas Edward and Elizabeth gave every appearance of being married. The matter should never have been raised, or, if it was, it should have been resolved in an ecclesiastical law court.

That there was no good evidence with a document, or a second witness, for the marriage contract explains why no ecclesiastical law court ever heard the matter. The bishops and the lawyers knew that an ecclesiastical law court was required to determine the validity of the 1464 Woodville marriage. A court could have been formed; there was plenty of time for such a court, as Richard, Duke of Gloucester, had all of his likely opponents intimidated, imprisoned, exiled, or executed. He remained virtually unchallenged as the all-powerful Lord Protector; he held firm control of the government; he held all the cards in this miserable game. But Sir William Catesby must have concluded that there was no sense in risking an adverse ecclesiastical law court decision, and thus he advised the Lord Protector on how to proceed.

Further Arguments about the Alleged 1461 Marriage Contract: The Absolute Need for an Ecclesiastical Law Court Hearing in the Matter of Edward's 1464 Woodville Marriage

In the fascinating London television trial of Richard III (Drewett and Redhead, 1984), the archivist Dr Anne Sutton stated correctly that the 1461 contract of matrimony was "the crux of the matter." It should be obvious that it was this which eventually led to the unfortunate deposition of King Edward V and the usurpation by King Richard III.

Between Dr Sutton and her attorney, it was claimed that the 1464 Woodville marriage was adulterous. Adultery was an heinous crime in the Middle Ages. But adultery was not uncommon and, in the historical record, did not make a marriage invalid. It was obviously not cause for deposing a king or his heir. It can be readily observed that the Church enthroned Elizabeth in 1464 *after* the marriage and crowned Elizabeth in 1465 *after* the marriage. What is more, on ten later occasions, the Church baptized the successive children of Edward and Elizabeth *after* the marriage. None of these multiple actions by the Church would have been appropriate if the 1464 marriage was considered invalid. Dr Sutton and her attorney may have considered Edward's 1464 marriage adulterous, based on their 1984 belief in the 1461 contract; but, clearly, the contemporaneous Orthodox Church did not. One further argument could be made, perverse as it sounds: Edward's later unfaithful behaviour could only be called adultery if the 1464 marriage was valid. His behaviour before 1464 could only be considered adultery if the 1461 marriage contract was true, a matter for very considerable debate and a matter by no means established.

Dr Sutton then made the claim that the 1461 contract, with its effect on the 1464 marriage, was "notorious," as doubtfully suggested in the Titulus Regius of 1484. The apparent statement in the statute may be quoted as follows:

> And here also we consider, how the said pretensed marriage between the above named King Edward and Elizabeth Grey was made of great presumption without the knowing or assent of the lords of this land, and also by sorcery and witchcraft, committed

by the said Elizabeth and her mother, Jacquetta, Duchess of
Bedford, as the common opinion of the people and the public
voice, and fame [rumour] is through all this land; and hereafter,
if and as the case shall require, shall be proved sufficiently in time
and place convenient.

The significant decretal by Pope Alexander III stated that "if the crime
is so public that it might rightly be called notorious, in that case neither
accuser nor witness is necessary." So, if no witness was required, then
Stillington's position was much improved and Richard's defenders were
greatly encouraged. But Pope Alexander still intended that the Church
should make any decision.

Allegedly, the effect of the 1461 contract on the 1464 marriage was in
a state of being generally well known and long accepted. But the bishops
and the people had never heard of the 1461 contract until Stillington
introduced his tale in June 1483. Only a cursory examination of the facts
reveals that the 1461 contract was hardly notorious; it was maybe first
revealed on 8 June 1483, privately before the council; it was not mentioned
in public until the multiple addresses of 22, 24, and 25 June 1483 in
London, as previously described; and King Edward V was deposed on 26
June 1483. Thus, it was known in preliminary fashion by a limited portion
of the public for only one to three days before the usurpation occurred,
but prior to that time the alleged contract had been kept absolutely secret
for all of twenty-two years and could not possibly have been considered
"notorious." The argument for notoriety, which negated the need for proof
and witnesses, is very doubtful indeed. The story of Lady Eleanor Butler
was not well known for many years after 1483, in fact, not until the reign
of King James I, and still it was not widely known. That Edward's marriage
was considered invalid at the time of the usurpation was not notorious in
any sense of the word. Nobody seriously questioned its validity for nineteen
years. Through June 1483 and for a long time thereafter in English history,
the 1464 Woodville marriage was widely regarded as valid, and all the
children and their descendants were considered legitimate. Never mind
Richard III's false claim.

Furthermore, and most important, a careful reading of the 1484
statute indicates that the penultimate phrase in the above quotation – "the
common opinion of the people and the public voice, and fame is through all

this land" – in other words, the "notoriety," referred not to the "pretensed marriage" but, instead, to the alleged sorcery committed by the queen and her mother. It was this latter allegation of sorcery which was "notorious," as it was indeed widely believed by the people in the superstitious fifteenth century and had been the subject of a court proceeding in 1470. It was so notorious that, according to the papal decretal, neither accuser nor witness was necessary. Nevertheless, the earlier court, possibly having heard from accuser and witness, dismissed the charges entirely.

Another mysterious suggestion was that since the "pretensed" 1461 marriage was allegedly "notorious," it was the responsibility of the royal children to appeal against the deposition of the king. It is difficult to follow that line of argument, for it took no account of the children's confinement in the Tower or the sanctuary. The suggestion opens the way for some speculation. The princes and their family were not invited to attend the Great Council meeting on 25 June 1483; Magna Carta afforded the barons such rights to be heard, but apparently that did not include the imprisoned king of England. It is not unreasonable to suggest that the well-trained King Edward V would have handled himself well in such a hearing; he only needed to ask simply that a church court hear the matter. His appearance may well have turned the tide, considering that the lords had all taken the oath of allegiance to him. But it should be obvious that a proper ecclesiastical law court hearing was the last thing that Richard ever planned, knowing full well what it would conclude.

Dr Sutton was also asked if it was appropriate for Parliament to rule on the matter of the matrimonial status of Edward IV. She replied that in the case of the depositions of Edward II, Richard II, and Henry VI, the Parliament had confirmed the deposition of the king each time. So, she questioned why it was not appropriate for Parliament to make a similar decision in the case of Edward V and his father. All of the previous kings were deposed for reasons of misrule under the civil law, without any issue under the canon law. In the specific case of Edward V, there was no misrule, but there were alleged matrimonial matters of legitimacy which needed a preliminary decision under the canon law, which was necessary before Parliament could make a decision on inheritance under the civil law. If any legal body had a responsibility for properly questioning Edward V and hearing the counterarguments, it was a legally assembled Parliament, not a Great Council, which should have referred the matrimonial issue to an ecclesiastical law court for an appropriate decision. It should be recalled that the writs for Parliament were cancelled on 17 June 1483 and that no Parliament is listed as having occurred during the short reign of King Edward V ("List of Parliaments of England," 2014).

Finally, and most important, Dr Sutton eventually admitted, "Strictly speaking[,] the matter of the [1464] marriage and the 1461 pre-contract, the [allegedly] clandestine marriage and the pre-contract together, should have gone before an ecclesiastical court." After that admission, in the face of no such known court hearing, her arguments become even more difficult to understand.

Following a discussion about the allegation made by only a single witness, namely the bishop of Bath, it was claimed that a single allegation was all that was necessary under the canon law, "Because you [the law] acted on the presumption of truth." Under that premise, a postulated but very likely reply by the boy king, after consultation with his prelate advisors, that King Edward never married Lady Eleanor would also have been considered the absolute truth by the court. So, it would have been a drawn game. And yet again, it should be obvious that this complicated doctrine about the "truth" could only be decided by an ecclesiastical law court, and by none other. The idea was that we should distinguish between what Richard's defenders *knew* to be the truth and what could be established in an ecclesiastical law court as being the truth; the latter could apparently be disregarded.

In the same vein, in reference to the 1461 contract, Dr Sutton made a startling claim, that "*if* people generally accepted it to be true, that was more important than any evidence that could be presented in a court of law, under the canon law as they understood it." There has never been any evidence that the 1461 contract was generally accepted as being true. Perhaps it is so in a meeting of the Richard III Society! The reader should review the conclusions of Dominic Mancini, the Croyland Chronicler, Sir Thomas More, and Sir Francis Bacon, none of whom believed the 1461 contract story to be true and none of whom thought that the English people generally believed the story, either. In fact, it was widely disbelieved. Nor has such a claim been supported by the subsequent course of English history. Starting with Henry VII's 1485 Parliament, all of Edward

IV's descendants were considered legitimate. That includes England's present beautiful Queen Elizabeth II. As Dr Sutton made this peculiar suggestion, that public opinion should take precedence over the findings of an ecclesiastical law court, this author concludes that the matter should have been resolved by a public referendum! King Edward IV, winsome, charming, and popular, even in his grave, would undoubtedly have won that round in the contest!

After hearing all these arguments advanced by Dr Sutton, especially if the reader agrees with her views, it becomes clearly obvious that the matter was extraordinarily complex, even more so than everybody realized. It should have been referred to an ecclesiastical law court for decision and judgement. Indeed, Dr Sutton herself testified as follows: "They were confused by what was presented to them, and therefore they fell back on the old story of Edward IV [himself] being a bastard, because they couldn't comprehend the rather complicated Canon Law that came into play to make the princes illegitimate." It was not entirely clear, but it would appear that by "they," she was referring to those at the Great Council meeting of 25 June 1483. They should have asked Cecily, the dowager duchess of York, about the truth of the matter of the illegitimacy of Edward IV. She could have started by reading to the Great Council her not yet composed last will and testament: "I, Cecily, wife unto the right noble prince, Richard late Duke of York, father unto the most Christian Prince, my Lord and Son, King Edward IV ... make and ordain my testament." Before she died, Duchess Cecily settled the truth for all time.

As discussed by R. H. Helmholz (1974), England had a well-developed system of ecclesiastical law courts; one of the most common litigations handled by the system was very similar to the presently discussed problem, namely the validation and possible enforcement of an alleged private marriage contract. In this matter of evidence and proof, the standards set by the courts were high. It is postulated that Gloucester's party needed to prove that the 1464 Woodville marriage was invalid on the basis of the alleged 1461 contract. Usually, both parties to the contract appeared in court and gave sworn testimony. That was in response to a plaintiff's suit or in response to an examination by the court acting ex officio at the request of a third party, such as Gloucester's government. Neither party to the 1461 alleged contract could appear in court in 1483, as they were both deceased. The court might then have issued a summary judgement and dismissed the case for lack of a proper plaintiff; or it might have considered other evidence for such things as a putative marriage.

As repeatedly stated in this text, the alleged 1461 marriage contract had only one witness, namely Bishop Stillington. But that was a huge problem. R. H. Helmholz (1974) wrote unambiguously: "The [canon] law required 2 witnesses to prove a contract" (p. 41). R. H. Helmholz repeated words to the same effect a second time in his book, so there can be no possible confusion: "In canon law the testimony of one witness was insufficient evidence of any fact" (p. 62). These statements about the need for two or more witnesses accompanied a discourse on how the canon law made contracting a marriage easy, ridiculously easy, but it also made proving a contract difficult. On that basis alone, the court would not have found in favour of the government of Richard, Duke of Gloucester. And it should be obvious that the Lord Protector was well aware of this problem; it is hard to imagine that the many bishops on his council did not inform him of this situation. So, Richard and his advisors did not ask an ecclesiastical law court to hear the matter. They proceeded unlawfully without a church court decision. On the other hand, if the ecclesiastical law court had agreed with Richard III, then his case would have been made and he would no longer be regarded in English history as an usurper king.

CHAPTER 12

The Multiple Achievements of King Edward IV

The Court of Edward IV

In contrast to the drab Lancastrian court of Henry VI, the Yorkist court of King Edward IV was spectacular, filled with beautifully dressed courtiers, dazzling entertainment, great music, and brilliant feasting and festivity. Henry VI's queen, Elizabeth, was considered one of the most beautiful women in all England. Edward was a very handsome man, nearly six-foot-four in height, towering over his friends and attendants. He had a wonderful masculine physique, which he showed off to advantage by the fashionable and beautiful clothes he wore. His court followed his brilliant example. The *Croyland Chronicle* (1854) noted how Edward "collected vessels of silver and gold, tapestries and decorations of the most precious nature." In Europe at that time, the finest royal court was that of the duchy of Burgundy in Bruges. The Yorkist court became at least comparable, if not more gorgeous. The Yorkist court closely followed the procedures of that in Bruges with its excellent organization, formal protocol, and dazzling ceremonies. The offices, the duties, the wages, and the procedures were described in meticulous detail in *The Black Book of the Household of Edward IV,* a version of which was published by A. R. Myers (1959). Although Edward ran a spectacular court, he was careful to control his own expenditure and that of his queen. He was not miserly, but he was cautious; he spent much less than Henry VI and somewhat less, even, than the parsimonious Henry VII. According to the *Croyland Chronicle* (1854), we "might have seen in those days the Royal Court presenting no other appearance than such befits a most mighty kingdom."

Architecture

Edward IV was a great builder. He made significant additions to the royal palaces at Nottingham, Fotheringhay, Westminster, Sheen, and Greenwich. At Eltham Palace, he built a splendid Great Hall, which remains to this day. But his architectural masterpiece was the Chapel of St George at Windsor Castle, headquarters for the Order of the Garter and the intended burial site of his Yorkist dynasty, himself included.

The Royal Library

The king was probably the first monarch in England to assemble a royal library, which he accumulated progressively throughout his reign. Although William Caxton introduced the printing press into England during his reign, Edward preferred the more lavish, older style of hand-embellished books and illuminated manuscripts. It is possible that Edward did not appreciate what the printer would do for the Age of Enlightenment and the coming Renaissance, but then most others in his company did not, either. Elite historians have been critical of him for this reason, unjustifiably; for Edward's queen, Elizabeth Woodville, was a cultured, literate woman and a faithful patron of William Caxton. She gave him considerable encouragement and financial support. She more than compensated for Edward's lack of interest, and Edward was more than willing to learn from her. The queen's brother, Anthony Woodville, was also a devoted patron of Caxton. The King's Library became one of the premier collections in the modern British Museum.

Commerce and Trade

The king greatly expanded English trade, encouraging growth with Denmark, the Hanseatic League (Germany), and Burgundy (Netherlands, Belgium), and also with other parts of Europe, such as Italy and Spain and, eventually, France. In this, he was greatly assisted by the relative peace which existed later in his reign. In 1474, he made peace with the Hanseatic League at the Treaty of Utrecht; it settled the terms of trade and gave the Hanse properties in London and King's Lynn to use for warehousing. While Edward IV was king, the merchant capitalist class prospered and the wealth of the English State grew rapidly, despite the civil war. The king encouraged the growth of commercial shipping to carry the expanded trade. His pro-business policies were a great boost for the developing capitalist system of the nation, heralding the approaching decline of the feudal social order.

Edward IV, the Merchant King, used his own private resources to join in the general commercial advance; he was especially successful in the wool trade with Burgundy and the tin trade with Italy. The king used his own immense profits to supplement the public purse, to ensure that taxation of his subjects usually remained relatively low, although not always so. During his reign, Edward issued a handsome and much admired new coinage, and at the same time he modestly devalued the English currency; this encouraged the expansion of English exports, improved the balance of trade, and contributed greatly to the level of prosperity. But, as described by Charles Ross (1997), Edward did have some protectionist policies, which he considered necessary for a small nation faced with competition from powerful European interests. In 1463, there were laws limiting the importation of corn, which encouraged English farming; in 1464–66, there were laws which limited the importation of manufactured goods, which encouraged the growth of domestic industries; in 1465, there were laws which encouraged the English weaving industry, to use more home-grown wool rather than wool imported from overseas and to export more finished wool products.

The City of London

During the reign of Edward IV, London became one of the wealthiest cities in the world as a result of increased international trade. The River Thames became crowded with ships, docks, and warehouses filled with great loads of goods from over the seas. The city was filled with German, Burgundian, and Italian merchants negotiating multiple mercantile deals. This was the beginning of London as one of the paramount financial centres of the world, a position it held until well into the twentieth century, and perhaps still. London did not have the opulence of Paris or Milan, but for commercial activity, it was unequalled; perhaps this was the birth of Napoleon's "nation of shopkeepers."

Financial Policies

When Edward assumed the crown, his level of support in England was relatively poor; he and his advisors knew that they needed to keep the levels of taxation low so as not to impose a burden on his newfound subjects. Edward IV's motto was "method and order"; he prided himself on sound financial management. When he died, the treasury was in good condition. The national debt was fully paid with a significant annual surplus, unusual in an age of profligate spending and, unfortunately, rare in our own times. He had numerous royal estates as a source of income, including the Duchy of Lancaster, and made sure that the funds were efficiently collected, properly tabulated, securely stored, and wisely spent. He developed the notion of accountability among those who administered the royal estates, and he put an end to the widespread corruption and graft of the preceding regime. Instead of funding the disorganized Treasury Exchequer, controlled by Parliament, he accumulated wealth in the Chamber of the Royal Court at Westminster Palace, where he exercised better control over the financial accounts.

One of his best sources of income was from the custom duties, which increased at a steady rate with the expansion of trade and his organization of an efficient customs department. Edward sent permanent commissioners to all the ports in England to make sure that the customs taxes were efficiently collected. Parliament never actually granted him the customs privilege, but Edward IV took it anyway, and Parliament never objected. Another source of income was the Benevolence, a subsidy paid to the king as a gift or free loan by some of the wealthiest subjects, in effect voluntary taxation of wealth. Of course, it was resented in some quarters, but the commons and the middle class had no objections and considered it to be reasonable and fair. But it should also be noted that Edward had a fine reputation for repaying loans when promised, although, by modern standards, interest was not usually paid. Many of the general revenue collection functions of the exchequer were transferred to the Royal Chamber during Edward's reign, again so the king could better maintain closer supervision. To his everlasting credit and to the benefit of the nation, many of his financial policies were followed by King Henry VII. Edward's policies set the country back on a sound footing after the near bankruptcy under Henry VI. Things stayed the same under Henry

VII, but under Edward's grandson, the big-spending Henry VIII, the national debt exploded.

However, the Benevolence remained controversial, despite Edward's generally cautious approach; Richard III made it illegal but used it himself when money was desperately needed late in his reign. Henry VII used tactics which were equivalent; he suppressed his baronage, holding them with constant threats of legal action, extorting financial support, and subjecting them to constant reappointment or dismissal, so he was immensely unpopular. His people were no less burdened than under Edward IV. Charles Ross (1997) quoted Lord Dudley, the Tudor king's chief extortionist, as saying that Henry VII "kept his peers feeling danger at the King's own pleasure." It is difficult to believe this was proper behaviour for a king; it worked for Henry VII, but his people loved Edward IV much better.

Edward IV, at many times during his reign, no longer depended on Parliament for funding. On the whole, during his reign, his excellent financial management added to the national prosperity. The only exception was in the late 1460s when numerous Lancastrian rebellions were a problem and money had to be raised by taxation. Warwick complained about it in 1469, but it was he who was causing the problems, and it was Parliament which made the final decision about raising taxes.

In 1475, Edward invaded France in support of Burgundy and Brittany, but he was always reluctant about the campaign, so when his allies proved unreliable, the king completely lost interest in the project and signed the Treaty of Picquigny. Under its terms, King Louis XI undertook to pay Edward a handsome pension, front-loaded and then followed on an annual basis, in effect a major financial accomplishment for the king of England. In addition, Louis paid a large ransom for Margaret of Anjou, who was still confined in England. Furthermore, Louis paid generous pensions to many of Edward's ministers, including Lord Hastings, Anthony Woodville, the marquis of Dorset, John Howard, and others. This financial success was criticized at the time, especially by Richard, Duke of Gloucester, but it meant that Edward did not need to raise taxes. In our own age, financial conservatives would have loved King Edward IV for his low tax policies and balanced budgets; but perhaps the financial progressives would not have liked Edward at all, as he did not favour social spending.

Unfortunately for Edward, it was the latter who often wrote the history of his reign. In 1484, Richard III would compensate for Edward's disinterest with benevolent social legislation.

Relations with His Peerage

A medieval king had no police force or standing army with which to maintain order. When Edward became king, he had a vast patronage to bestow as a result of attainders and resumptions following Towton in 1461. Charles Ross (1997) estimated that he had patronage worth thirty thousand pounds sterling at his disposal, an incredible sum five hundred and fifty years ago. In 1471, he had similar patronage available with the fall of Warwick; and in 1478, there was still more available with the fall of Clarence. The king was able to elevate many of his baronial supporters to the higher ranks of the peerage, with the associated gains in landed property. In addition, the king made use of land grants, offices, wardships, marriages, pensions, and annuities to further empower his supporters. In return, he expected them to maintain the peace and properly administer the judicial system. Some did this by practicing debauched feudalism; they controlled the people by maintaining permanent retainers or private armies on the payroll. In other words, they paid their men with cash, not land. The king is often criticized for creating the so-called overmighty magnates: he controlled the northern counties with Warwick and, later, Gloucester; the Midlands with Clarence and Hastings; the Welsh Marches with Lord Herbert and, later, Anthony Woodville, the second Earl Rivers at Ludlow; and the West Country with Humphrey Stafford and, later, Lord John Dinham. It is suggested that these overmighty magnates caused problems at the end of Edward's reign; but in fact, only one caused the trouble in 1483, namely Gloucester. Nevertheless, it appears true that Edward IV also over-rewarded Warwick, trying to maintain his loyalty, but, unfortunately, the earl continued to be greedy and rapacious, and hostile to Edward until Warwick died at Barnet in 1483.

Parliament did complain about the practice of maintenance and livery, suggesting that it was often oppressive to the commons. Edward often promised to ban it and had statutes passed, but he did little in the way of enforcement, since it was a variant of his very own policy. Furthermore, only a few magnates actually practiced it; it was too expensive to keep men at arms all the time. It proved difficult to enforce the abolition of maintenance and livery. It should be noted that Richard III had passed similar legislation, as did Henry VII later, but they, too, found it difficult to enforce. Edward IV was not the only king who failed to suppress the practice. But more often, the magnates gave land lots to their tenants in return for promises to supply men, so-called enfeoffments, when needed. This was the more traditional form of feudalism.

Conciliation Policy

After Edward assumed the crown in 1461, a large proportion of the baronage remained faithful to the Lancastrian cause, at least for ten years. They had increased their considerable power during the reign of Henry VI and were reluctant to give it up. The new king needed powerful magnates to help restore law and order in England, but they had to be Yorkists – and Edward needed to turn some of the Lancastrians to his own side. Although his policy of conciliation was often successful as he tried to consolidate his support, there were some notable exceptions after pardons and benefactions had been granted: Sir Ralph Percy surrendered several of the Northumberland castles in 1463 and died at Hedgeley Moor fighting for Henry VI in 1464; Sir Humphrey Neville of Brancepeth rebelled in Northumberland in 1469 and was executed after Edward escaped from Middleham Castle; Henry Beaufort, the third duke of Somerset, was killed at Hexham in 1464 after the king had tried very hard to enlist his support; John de Vere, the earl of Oxford, remained implacably opposed to Edward despite generous treatment of his initial inheritance with the execution of his father; Henry Courtenay, the brother of the Lancastrian sixth earl of Devon, was tried and executed for treason in 1468 after multiple pardons; and William Lord Beaumont (1438–1507), a friend of Oxford, was imprisoned from 1474 to 1483 for repeated rebellions.

Following his triumph in 1471, Edward was again surprisingly lenient with the peerage, many of whom had not supported him. There were few attainders. The king's preferred mode of punishment was the extraction of money in the form of gifts or free loans, rather than the appropriation of title and property. The exceptions were those who opposed him at Tewkesbury, but they had demonstrated implacable opposition and Edward had finally realized he needed to be rid of them for the sake of peace in his kingdom.

For those who only offended by showing consistent loyalty to Henry VI, Edward once more gave pardons. Under Edward, attainders were often easily reversed. Many lords took advantage, as Edward did not use attainders as attacks on private power, as Henry VII did later. Edward was a magnanimous king and consistently tried to persuade, not force, people to support his rule. Many of the decisions for which he was criticized were made because he followed this policy of conciliation with his subjects; and there were times, as mentioned, when it went terribly wrong. It was, however, misleading of George Barnett Smith (1894) to suggest that the reign of Edward IV developed into a "reign of terror." There were many battlefield deaths in the civil war, especially at Towton in 1461, but there was nothing which remotely resembled wholesale atrocities committed against innocent English people, even on a small scale.

The Prestige of the English Crown

By the extensive exercise of personal power, Edward greatly restored the wealth and prestige of the English Crown, which had reached a pitiful state during the reign of Henry VI. Many of his procedures were followed and continued by King Henry VII, who seems to have been given more of the credit than Edward IV. But they were both fine administrators. The contemporaneous and early Tudor historians, in general, admired Edward IV greatly and gave him considerable credit for his excellent financial management. The exception was Commines, who did not live in England and was critical of Edward for his alleged debauchery. The suggestion of later historians, much separated in time and much influenced by Victorian morality, that Edward IV was a king with limited accomplishments was never justified and has proved to be biased propaganda in light of more modern research. Charles Ross (1997) wrote: "In shorthand, he [Edward IV] could be described as the king who took the country out of the Middle Ages." Edward's "variable temper and sharp oversight worked an extraordinary change in the country of England." According to Winston Churchill, underneath all of Edward's human faults, the king "shrouded a profound political ability." J. R. Lander (1969) wrote: "Edward established the foundation of a proud national state." When we consider the long civil war, we see that Edward achieved this in the peaceful last decade of his reign.

Relations with the House of Commons

Charles Ross (1997) has made a detailed assessment of the king's experience with Parliament. Edward had six Parliaments in a reign of twenty-two years; they sat for a total of eighty-four weeks and passed only fifty-four statutes. Historians have considered this to be a poor record; others might have considered this desirably limited government. Half of these statutes dealt with matters of industry and commerce, a particular concern of the Merchant King; another 25 per cent were mainly legal in nature, another concern of the king, but perhaps less so. Most bills originated with Edward IV, few with the House of Commons. This contrasted with the previous Lancastrian rule under which the House of Commons was much angrier and far more active. The Parliament of 1461–62 dealt mainly with attainders and resumptions against the supporters of Lancaster; that of 1463–65 dealt mainly with subsidies for the suppression of rebellion in the north country; that in 1467–68 provided subsidies for the suppression of rebellions by Warwick and Clarence; that in 1472–75 was to vote subsidy for the popular invasion of France; that in 1478 was called to deal with the treason of the duke of Clarence; and that in 1483 was to vote subsidy for war against France, about which Edward was reluctant and which did not eventuate because the king died.

As noted by some, there were few statutes dealing with the expansion of civil rights; some might say that England had not reached sufficient social development for those questions to be considered. When Richard III passed much social legislation in 1484, it was a long time before it was appreciated. Parliaments were generally manipulated to support the king or the magnates; Edward's government proved adept at seating who it wanted. It would be another three hundred and fifty years before the Reform Acts of 1832, 1867, and 1884 began to change all that. But Edward's Parliaments did not always grant him subsidies in the way he wanted; they often granted less than requested, and sometimes they required restitution when he did not spend the money as they wished. The king was meant to "live on his own" by the income from his estates and from the customs; the generous pension from the king of France meant that Edward called few Parliaments after 1475.

The Judicial System

Edward took great interest in the judicial court system; he travelled the country to sit on the assize courts in the same way as the Angevin kings had. He frequently sat on the bench himself, heard the evidence, and helped render a judgement. Edward insisted on the proper administration of justice, especially for the common people of his realm. When he ascended the throne, the courts were thoroughly corrupted by the magnates and long delays were common. Although he made few changes to the structure of the judicial system, he greatly improved the decision-making process. He started the practice of referring those indicted in the sheriff's court to be tried in the lower courts, then supervised by the Justice of the Peace, in order to overcome the backlog of cases held waiting. The king believed that justice delayed was not justice at all. He sent commissioners to every county in England to speed up the administration of the law; of course, this depended on the people he sent, so it was not always effective. Despite his best efforts, the problem of civil disorder did not always greatly improve during his early troubled reign. Edward made heavy use of commissions of oyer and terminer ("hear and determine"). These were headed by one or more nobles, employed judges and lawyers, and were very flexible in settling complicated problems. Edward's early encouragement of the legal process and his personal involvement heralded the development of commercial law, so important for the emerging modern industrial system. To assist poor people who could not afford legal action in the courts, Edward IV formed a commission of his advisors to hear their petitions and reach a decision. It was this court which Richard III later developed into the court of requests.

The King's Popularity

Edward was a popular, respected, and beloved king; this was the almost universal conclusion of those writing at the time. Only centuries later did historians attempt to modify his excellent reputation. Edward stands out, especially when compared with the incompetent Henry VI or the talented but widely disliked Richard III. Edward's critics seem to forget the many tumultuous welcomes he received each time he entered London; the English capital was always Edward's town. Even the great Warwick, who tried hard to undermine him, was successful only for a very short time. Edward suffered unpopularity for a time in 1468–69, related to the propaganda of Warwick and Clarence. Most of the time, the people loved their magnificent king, especially the womenfolk; they understood and forgave his human weaknesses. Edward was always over-friendly with his ladies and was criticized for this, but he never forced himself with them. Many adored him for his attentions. It cannot be denied that he was unusually promiscuous; however, it should not be exaggerated. Mary Clive (1974) has counted the illegitimate children of other rulers at the time – those of Scotland, Burgundy, and France – and Edward compared quite favourably. And as we have seen, Richard III was really no better than Edward IV in this regard. The prolific author J. R. Lander (1969) wrote that despite all his personal faults, King Edward IV "did not lose his hold on the hearts of his people." We have already mentioned Edward's remarkable ability to recall names and faces and family details; that made him immensely popular with the lower gentry and the common folk. According to Sir Francis Bacon (1889), Henry VII was not respected or liked until he married Edward's daughter Elizabeth in 1486; the people had not forgotten their beloved King Edward IV.

William Shakespeare wrote famous plays with titles *Henry VI* and *Richard III*. The great good successful king in between those two sad reigns was largely ignored as only a minor player. One protracted series of disasters, in the case of Henry VI, or one short massive disaster, in the case of Richard III, obviously made better dramatic plays than did Edward's solid mercantile activity with its steady creation of national wealth and prosperity. King Edward IV's reputation deserves to be restored to something nearer the truth.

The Yorkist Propaganda Machine

When Edward IV came to the throne, England was still largely a Lancastrian country. The level of support for Henry VI was amazingly high, despite his failed reign. At most of the major battles, the peers turned out for the old king, probably because of their oaths of loyalty. The size of the armies hardly ever favoured the Yorkists. It was not surprising, therefore, that the Yorkists tried to change minds by placing heavy emphasis on their own perceived assets. As described by Leslie Coote (2011), Edward emphasized the Mortimer heritage, long inhabiting the Welsh Marches. Edward liked to think of his house as heavily admixed with the Britons, the early inhabitants of Britain, driven to the west by the Roman invasion. Although the Mortimers were Norman, their seat of power was among the Britons in the west. Edward considered himself the second coming of King Arthur; he and his queen placed strong emphasis on the Arthurian legend at the Yorkist court. They pushed a sense of belonging to Britain, of original possession of the land; their forefathers arose out of the mists of time from the ancient legends. There was something magical about the House of York, hence the three suns in the sky at Mortimer's Cross and the statue of St Anne at the Daventry church. Much of the propaganda was formulated by George Ripley, the canon of Bridlington, who was closely associated with Edward IV and the Yorkist reign.

Military Leadership

Edward was a great military leader, certainly one of the best, if not the best, in English history. He never lost a battle at which he was present, and he was present at many. His enemies greatly feared him on the battlefield. He was not present at Edgecote in 1469 when Warwick and Clarence rebelled; it is not unreasonable to claim that if he had been present, the result would have been different. His strategy was always to attack early and suddenly – if possible, unexpectedly – never mind the difficulties, such as the driving rain at Northampton, the rear location of the River Lugg at Mortimer's Cross, the blowing snow at Towton, the open plain at Empingham, the heavy fog at Barnet, or the hedgerows at Tewkesbury. Unlike most leaders, he always led from the front line, sharing with his men the extreme dangers of mortal combat; he did not remain behind the lines as did Warwick and many others. He seldom used defensive tactics, as was common at that time, for instance, by the Lancastrians at Northampton or by the Yorkists at Second St Albans – and, it should be added, to a large extent by Richard III at Bosworth Field in 1485. Edward set an heroic example: fierce in battle and a great inspiration to his men. Once the battle was joined, his men knew there would be no retreat while the king lived; and they always knew him to be up front in the thick of the battle. His men always followed the Warrior King, so it is no wonder that Edward mostly managed to win, often in spectacular fashion. When he died, he had greatly strengthened and restored the English Crown, which had reached a very low ebb when he was crowned. Although wavering sometimes, the English monarchy has lasted for another five hundred and fifty years, a superb legacy. It is unfair to describe Edward as a king of limited achievements. Admittedly, the Crown wobbled during the short reign of Richard III, but there is little doubt that Edward IV prepared the way for the Tudor dynasty.

Gunpowder

Although Edward was slow to recognize the value of printing, he was quick to see the value of gunpowder, which was introduced into Europe at the end of the Hundred Years War. Edward made widespread use of cannons, especially at battles like Empingham (1470), on the open plain, where his ferocious cannonade put the rebels quickly to flight; and at Tewkesbury (1471), in the initial assault against superior forces holding an advantaged position. His brother Richard III failed to use his cannon effectively at Bosworth Field, especially when we consider the initial tightly closed and therefore vulnerable ranks of Lancaster. Richard III paid a heavy price for his tactical failure.

The King's Foreign Wars

Edward did not generally waste time, money, or lives on futile wars in France or Scotland, as did many of his predecessors, such as Edward I, Edward III, and Henry V. Much has been made of great English victories like Dunbar (1296), Crecy (1346), and Agincourt (1415), but that road led ultimately to humiliating disasters at Bannockburn (1314), Formigny (1450), and Castillon (1453). One does not read much about these later events in popular English history. Scotland and France were simply not permanently subdued, and the military expenditure only retarded the commercial development of England and prolonged the inefficient feudal system. Edward's single invasion of France in 1475 proved to be benign and very profitable; he took his army home and banked the cash. Edward sent his younger brother, Richard, Duke of Gloucester, into Scotland in 1482, but he maintained close communications by horse-rider relay, quickly reached accommodation, reclaimed Berwick, and withdrew. Of course, Edward was often involved in the civil war, the War of the Roses, so it could be claimed that his foreign war policy was the result of circumstances. But Edward never enjoyed the battlefield, even though he was always so successful. He greatly preferred to develop peace and prosperity. His short period of passivity and inactivity after Edgecote in 1469 was a reflection of his weariness with rebellion and civil strife; but belatedly, he realized that a medieval king must face the challenge at home or else be overthrown.

Naval Policy

Edward built or purchased many warships; he expanded and developed the English navy and began the restoration of English control over the waters of the English Channel. He used his own warships and the warships of his Burgundian allies to blockade the French coast in order to thwart his enemies and defend his kingdom. The best example would be his blockade of Warwick in 1470 and of Queen Margaret in 1471; it was only the forces of nature which broke up his defence. This was a king who early understood the value of sea power, especially for an island nation, a development which later was to see a small country like England expand its influence around the world. The Tudor monarchs received most of the credit, but, again, it was Edward IV and Richard III who established the process.

Edward's Reputation and That of His Queen

Edward's reputation has suffered because of the criticisms advanced by Clarence, Warwick, and Gloucester and the sometimes unjustified attention given to these men by historians. In particular, Edward's reputation has suffered because of the attacks on his queen, Elizabeth Woodville. But Elizabeth, by the standards of the age, was a well-educated woman like the other Woodvilles. She took an interest in public affairs, she supported her husband, and the king remained close to her, despite his promiscuous misadventures. For her involvement in public affairs, she was ferociously slandered; the magnates were not accustomed to an active queen like Elizabeth. They had hated Queen Margaret Anjou and they resented the commoner Elizabeth Woodville.

When Henry VII became king, he kept his wife and Elizabeth's eldest daughter, also named Elizabeth, under much stricter control. Edward IV would never have done that to his beautiful queen. Edward was a powerful personality. He was larger than life, was charming and affable, had that great political asset called charisma, and inspired great confidence. He was a born leader of men. The Merchant King had a remarkable capacity to remember names and small details about personal lives, family, and business; this was especially amazing because the king led a vigorous social life for which he was severely criticized. It is not possible to claim that Edward was a feminist, but he loved his womenfolk and treated them with the utmost respect. There were exceptions, of course, as in the case of Warwick's Beauchamp wife, who was disinherited, but then Edward probably considered that she deserved it, based on the constant treachery of her husband. Edward's promiscuity was a relentless problem, but it should be noted that his sexual misadventures were always consensual. Despite this, and thanks to his queen, Edward's reign represented the climax of knightly chivalry and the Arthurian legend in England. Executing women did not become the English custom until Tudor times; Henry VIII did not follow the fine example set by his grandfather Edward IV.

Another problem was that when Edward IV died, there was great difficulty with the succession. Although Edward made the proper arrangements, if belatedly, the execution by his government was faulty, with Richard, Duke of Gloucester, rapidly making the decision to usurp the throne and murder Edward's legal heir, the boy King Edward V. It is not reasonable to blame Edward IV for this, as few would deny that Richard was an appropriate choice as Lord Protector. Perhaps only the much maligned but astute Queen Elizabeth Woodville saw this early as a likely problem. The great magnates were simply taken completely by surprise by the usurpation.

Historians of the early Tudor times, such as Sir Thomas More, were admirers of Edward IV; they considered him to be a king of considerable achievement. They emphasized his business acumen, the peace and prosperity of his later reign, and his general popularity. They understood the difficulties he had in the first ten years of his reign, with plots and rebellions from the very persistent Lancastrian loyalists. But historians of the eighteenth and nineteenth centuries emphasized his so-called debauchery, cruelty, and rapacity. Some of this may be true, but not much. Modern historians such as Charles Ross (1997) have reached far different conclusions; Edward IV eventually rescued England from continued civil war and imposed order, wealth, and prosperity.

Effect on the Institution of Marriage

Edward and Elizabeth married because they were in love with each other. As stated by Okerlund (2005), "They were in the vanguard of a movement that allowed love to become a factor in marriage." So, "The institution of marriage began to change from a business liaison into a personal engagement."

The Council and Government of King Edward IV

Edward was no autocrat; he relied heavily on the collective wisdom of his council. The chief members were the chancellor, the treasurer, and the keeper of the privy seal, together with a number of bishops. The most prominent treasurer was Henry Bourchier, the earl of Essex, who held the office from 1460 to 1462, and then from 1471 to 1483. Another treasurer, Richard Woodville, the first Earl Rivers, held the office from 1466 to 1469. Others for short periods were John Tiptoft, Edmund Grey of Ruthin, and Walter Blount.

Early in the reign, the bishops tended to be men of high birth, like Thomas Bourchier, Archbishop of Canterbury, and George Neville, Archbishop of York, an overhang from the Lancastrian regime. Later in the reign, the bishops tended to be men of more humble birth, like Thomas Rotherham of York, John Russell of Lincoln, Robert Stillington of Bath and Wells, John Alcock of Rochester, and John Morton of Ely. Stillington, Rotherham, and Russell, between them, shared the position of Lord Privy Seal for the whole reign. Stillington and Rotherham held the office of chancellor for much of the reign, but other chancellors were George Neville, the bishop of Exeter, later the Archbishop of York; and Lawrence Booth, the bishop of Durham.

Among Edward's most trusted advisors on the council were William Hastings, John Howard, John Dinham, and Walter Blount, the Lord Mountjoy. The office of steward of the royal household was held successively by William Neville, Lord Fauconberg, the earl of Kent; John Tiptoft, the earl of Worcester; Henry Bourchier, the earl of Essex; and Lord Thomas Stanley. These men also sat on the council. Taking the reign as a whole, over a hundred men held positions on the council, which is a reflection of how widely the king sought advice. There were some prominent exceptions, however. Edward never trusted Henry Stafford, the second duke of

Buckingham. Because John Mowbray, the fourth duke of Norfolk, was the subject of many complaints for private warfare activity, he was given little responsibility. John de la Pole, the second duke of Suffolk, despite being related by marriage to the king, was not reliable and not admired.

But the king accumulated a large number of men of more humble birth who carried out the various executive functions of the Crown and were prominent members of his household, men such as Sir John Fogge, Sir John Scott, Sir John Elrington, Sir William Parr, and Sir Thomas Vaughan. They often served on the council, as well. By bringing these so-called "new men," mostly men from the upper middle class, into the government of England, Edward IV initiated the English civil service. J. R. Lander (1969) wrote that "Edward admired and made full use of the learned accomplishments of men of the common rank." Before Edward IV, the use of laymen, knights, and gentry to administer the country was comparatively small; Edward greatly expanded their role. His construction of this early civil service led the way for its domination in the governments of Henry VII and the Tudor dynasty. These officials felt great loyalty to the king, rather than to the magnates; many shared in the king's exile in Burgundy. And, after Edward died, some joined the October Rebellion of 1483 to support the accession of Edward V. Others joined Henry Tudor in Brittany.

The classic example of "new men" would be Richard Woodville and his son Anthony Woodville. Both were talented, cultured, literate men; they were on the cusp of a great change about to take place in England. Political status would no longer depend on birth and station, as society was no longer composed only of the rich and the poor. Edward's reign was characterized by the rise of the middle class, which was composed of people with talent, education, and intellect. The old order was being pushed aside by the new class of bankers, merchants, capitalists, manufacturers, lawyers, and professionals – people with new wealth. These changes did not occur suddenly with the Tudor dynasty; they were already developing under Edward IV and during the short reign of Richard III.

The Overmighty Magnates

Edward's expansion of the civil service and the middle class allowed the later reduction in power of the overmighty magnates who often proved so troublesome during his reign, especially the earl of Warwick and the duke of Clarence. Edward has been criticized for these overmighty magnates, but in turbulent times, without a standing royal army or police force, he had no choice but to use them. A replacement took time to develop, but Edward began the process of pushing the magnates aside. This had everything to do with the resentment of the Woodvilles by men of the old order, such as Clarence, Warwick, and Gloucester. And this had much to do with the constant stream of criticism directed against Edward's beautiful and well-educated queen and the other Woodvilles. In the end, Edward executed Clarence for treason, killed Warwick in battle, and was happy to have Gloucester spend much of his time away from London in the North Country. But it was Gloucester who nearly ruined Edward's legacy by overthrowing Edward V, the rightful Yorkist heir.

Changes to the Laws of Inheritance

The House of York made it possible for inheritance to proceed through females of the line. Although it met with resistance, Edward interpreted the laws of inheritance consistent with the Act of Accord and tended to favour females of the line when it was necessary. This was most obvious in the Exeter and Norfolk settlements, which Edward had confirmed by acts of Parliament. This was a necessary change. Had it not been made, the problems of the Tudor dynasty would have been greatly aggravated; in fact, the Tudor dynasty would have been destroyed.

The Beginning of the End of Birthright in England

By his promotion of people with talent, such as the Woodvilles, Edward IV began the downfall of the old nobility in England; this was a revolution which progressed further under the Tudors and later. But initially, the magnates struck back with anger and resentment. This self-destructive behaviour only opened the way for more people of lesser rank to enter positions of power and influence, a change which has never been reversed. But one of the earliest victims of this conflict, with its attack on the Woodvilles, unfortunately proved to be the Royal House of York.

PART THREE

The People

CHAPTER 13

The Family of King Edward IV

The Parents of King Edward IV

Cecily Neville (1415–1495), the duchess of York, was one of the younger daughters of Ralph Neville and Joan Beaufort (see Appendix E); she was the sister of Richard Neville, the fifth earl of Salisbury, and the aunt of Richard Neville, the sixteenth earl of Warwick. Cecily had a reputation for pride and piety; as she was also beautiful, she was known as the Rose of Raby, after the northern castle in which she was born. Cecily was betrothed early and married Richard Plantagenet, the duke of York, in 1429. When the duke served in France as lieutenant for Henry VI from 1436 to 1447, the couple lived in Rouen, where Edward IV was born in 1442. When her husband was lieutenant in Ireland, she resided in Dublin. During the early stages of the civil war in England, she resided at Ludlow Castle, the headquarters of her husband. And when her son Edward became king, she lived at Baynard Castle in London. It is notable that she stayed close to her husband wherever he resided, such was her great loyalty to her marriage. After the Act of Accord in 1460, she considered herself to be royalty, destined to be the rightful queen consort of England. Later, she retired to Berkhamstead Abbey.

When Edward IV married Elizabeth Woodville in 1464, it was rumoured that Cecily was angry with her son for not choosing a wealthy royal heiress. She may also have been supporting Warwick in his efforts to find a French queen for Edward. She questioned Edward about possible marriage contracts and concluded there were none (More, 2005; Ellis, Grafton, and Hall, 1809). It was also rumoured that in 1469 and 1470, she may have supported her son George in his surreptitious claim to the throne, a claim difficult to believe, as it was made largely on the basis of the alleged bastardy of Edward IV. There is some evidence that she loved George over her other sons. It is claimed that she pleaded with Edward IV to spare the life of George, Duke of Clarence, when he was found guilty of treason, but to no avail. Both the council and Parliament insisted on carrying out the well-deserved death sentence. No doubt, Cecily was upset by the feuding which was tearing apart her family. After the execution of Clarence in 1478, Cecily left court and had much less contact with Edward IV thereafter; but it should be realized that she was nearly sixty-four years old, considered quite elderly in the Middle Ages, and looked forward to her retirement. It has also been claimed that in 1483 she may have supported the desire of her son Richard, Duke of Gloucester, to ascend the throne over her grandson Edward V, who she may have considered too young to be king. Or maybe she saw what was inevitable. Given her reputation for piety, these allegations about her preferences are all difficult to believe, especially as they are poorly documented and tarnish Cecily's otherwise upstanding reputation.

After Dr Shaw's sermon on 22 June 1483, in which he claimed that both Edward and George were not legitimate sons of the third duke of York, and that the younger son, Richard, Duke of Gloucester, who looked like his father, short and spare, should be king, Cecily complained bitterly about the insult to herself. Cecily was immensely loyal to her husband, so the stories about adultery are impossible to believe. She remained at her husband's side through all his trials and tribulations. She did not attend the coronation of Richard III for reasons that any mother could understand; other sons might also understand if they accused their own mothers of adultery. It would be amazing if Richard had any subsequent relationship with his mother; it is unlikely that Cecily would have believed what Richard probably claimed, that he had nothing to do with Dr Shaw's speech of 22 June 1483, and likewise with all the others that day, as well. In the controversies of later June 1483, because of Cecily's attitude, the notion that Edward IV was illegitimate at birth was dropped. The strategy to achieve the overthrow of Edward V became one of declaring young Edward V illegitimate based on the invalidity of Edward IV's marriage.

But Richard's supporters would bring it back again in the statute of 1484, namely the notion that Edward IV was not legitimate at birth.

According to Arlene Okerlund (2005), when Cecily died in 1495, she expressed herself plainly in her last will and testament. She declared, "I, Cecily, wife unto the right noble prince, Richard, late Duke of York, father unto the most Christian Prince, my Lord and son, King Edward IV, the first day of April in the year of our Lord 1495, make," etc. It could not be much clearer: Richard, the third duke of York, was the father of her son Edward IV; those repeated allegations about the illegitimacy of Edward IV were without foundation. No doubt, those allegations could be traced to the vicious propaganda of Clarence, Warwick, and Gloucester. Cecily's last will also made clear how she felt about the marriage of King Edward IV; she made specific bequests to her living granddaughters, referring separately to each and every one by name as "my daughter," distinct from "my granddaughter," implying total hereditary possession. If she ever resented Elizabeth Woodville, then that feeling was long gone. Although she had initially doubted Edward's choice, she came to realize what a fine queen her daughter-in-law became. Cecily's last will also made clear how she felt about her other sons; she never mentioned them, neither George, Duke of Clarence, nor Richard, Duke of Gloucester, with whom she must have remained very angry for their foolish destruction of the grand Royal House of York.

Richard Plantagenet (1411–1460), the third duke of York, was the son of Anne Mortimer and Richard Plantagenet, the earl of Cambridge (see Appendix C). The earl was executed in 1415 for plotting against the Lancastrian King Henry V in the so-called Southampton Conspiracy. Richard inherited his family name of Plantagenet from his father, the earl of Cambridge. He also inherited the title "Duke of York" from his paternal uncle Edward of Norwich, the second duke of York, who was killed at Agincourt in 1415. However, the title was not transferred to Richard until 1425. On the death of his maternal uncle, the fifth earl of March, Richard became the sixth earl of March, also in 1425.

Richard's mother, Anne Mortimer, died at his birth. As an orphan, he was made a ward of Ralph Neville, the earl of Westmoreland. Richard was betrothed to Cecily Neville, one of the younger daughters of Ralph Neville; Richard and Cecily were married in 1429. From 1436 to 1439,

Richard served his first term as lieutenant in France for Henry VI. The duke had some military success, notably at Fecamp in the Pays de Caux, but the English star in France was in progressive decline following the exploits of Joan of Arc in 1429, the slow but progressive recovery of King Charles VII, and the loss of the Burgundian alliance with England in 1435. And Richard found that he had to pay most of the expenses, as there was little support from the corrupt government in London. In 1440, he was reappointed for a five-year term with the aim of negotiating a peace with France; his term was later extended by two years to 1447. In 1443, the expedition to Gascony led by John Beaufort, the first duke of Somerset, angered York, as he could have used the money and resources for the defence of Normandy. From 1445, there began a two-year truce arranged under the 1444 Treaty of Tours. But in 1447, Edmund Beaufort, the second duke of Somerset, replaced Richard as lieutenant in France and soon proved to be ineffective. The relationship between Edmund Beaufort and Richard, Duke of York, was a bad one and would contribute much to the future problem between the Houses of Lancaster and York. Richard was then made Lord Lieutenant of Ireland in 1447, but he took up the appointment only in 1449. In the meantime, the earl of Kildare substituted for him. Richard suspected that the appointment was a device to remove him from English politics.

Returning to England in 1450 and again in 1452, Richard made serious but unsuccessful attempts to reform the corrupt government of Henry VI, but he was frustrated by the efforts of Queen Margaret and twice had to retreat to Ludlow. In 1453, as disasters in France proliferated, Henry VI was disabled by insanity. Richard was made Lord Protector in 1454. Henry VI briefly recovered and took over the government again in early 1455, but later in 1455, there was a further episode of insanity and Richard was again Lord Protector. But the king, once more, recovered. Then, York gathered his forces; he was supported by the earls of Salisbury and Warwick, and they defeated the royal forces at the First Battle of St Albans in 1455. Edmund Beaufort, the second duke of Somerset, Richard's hated rival, was killed at St Albans. This was the opening battle of the civil conflict to be known as the War of the Roses.

Queen Margaret then exerted her power in defence of the king and her newborn son, Edward of Westminster, the new Prince of Wales.

The Great Council, meeting at Coventry in 1456, dismissed the duke of York as Lord Protector. The queen then ruled in the name of the king. York's appointment in Ireland was renewed, presumably for another ten years, obviously intended to keep him out of England. During a fragile peace, both sides gathered political and military strength as the road led inevitably to further warfare. The earl of Salisbury was the Yorkist victor at Blore Heath in 1459, but the Lancastrians won the skirmish at Ludford Bridge, also in 1459, so Richard fled back to Ireland. The Yorkist earls of Warwick and Salisbury, together with York's oldest son and heir, Edward, the seventh earl of March, fled to Calais. Duchess Cecily and her young sons, who remained in Ludlow, experienced hard times as the Lancastrians celebrated their victory. Then, in 1460, the earls of Warwick, Salisbury, and March invaded England, defeated the royal army at Northampton, and imprisoned the king in the Tower. Soon after, York returned from Ireland and, at Westminster, claimed the throne of England. This was met with a total lack of enthusiasm. Richard was not widely loved, and most nobles maintained their loyalty to Henry VI. But complex negotiations began. These lasted for several weeks.

Richard's mother, Anne Mortimer, was descended from the third son of Edward III, Lionel, Duke of Clarence, and his father was descended from the fifth son of Edward III, Edmund, Duke of York. According to the custom of primogeniture, this was superior to the claim of Henry VI, who was descended from the fourth son of Edward III, John of Gaunt, the duke of Lancaster. This was only true if inheritance through a female of the line was accepted as lawful.

By the Act of Accord in 1460, Henry VI remained king by right of possession, but York was declared heir to the throne by right of inheritance and was appointed as Lord Protector again. It must be concluded that inheritance through the female line was lawful in England, unlike in France. The Lancastrians rose once more under Henry, the third duke of Somerset. York was defeated and killed at the Battle of Wakefield on 30 December 1460. Queen Margaret defeated Warwick at Second St Albans in early 1461. But Edward, Earl of March, the new heir to the throne, won a decisive victory at Mortimer's Cross, marched into London with the earl of Warwick, and was proclaimed King Edward IV. People in London were tired of Henry VI and his French queen, and they adored the handsome

Yorkist prince. Some authors insist that Edward was made king by a small and unrepresentative band of Yorkist lords, and so they describe Edward as an usurper. But Parliament made the decision and deposed Henry VI. The people joyfully acclaimed Edward IV at Clerkenwell.

Richard, Duke of York, was short, small, and spare, whereas his two older surviving sons, Edward and George, were both fair and well built. The youngest son, Richard, resembled his father, being also short and spare. This was later taken as evidence that Edward and George were not legitimate. Any modern student of Mendelian genetics can tell the reader that this is simply not necessarily so, but this was not understood at the time. After Edward IV died in April 1483, Dr Ralph Shaw, in his speech of 22 June 1483, said that neither Edward nor George was legitimate, for the same reason: neither looked like his father.

As Edward IV's 1464 marriage to Elizabeth Woodville was claimed to be bigamous, Richard, Duke of Gloucester, the youngest brother, usurped the throne of Edward's son and heir, King Edward V, and became Richard III in June 1483. The boy King Edward V and his younger brother, Richard of Shrewsbury, both imprisoned in the Tower, were murdered in late August or early September 1483 at the orders of Richard III. As a result of widespread rumours about the fate of the princes, never contradicted by his government, Richard III was deeply unpopular in England and was defeated and killed by rebel forces under Henry Tudor, the last of the Beaufort line in the House of Lancaster, at Bosworth Field in 1485. Henry Tudor married Elizabeth, the Yorkist heir, the oldest daughter of Edward IV, in 1486, thus combining York and Lancaster and beginning the Tudor dynasty.

The Brothers and Sisters of King Edward IV

Anne Plantagenet (1439–1476) was the oldest child of Richard, the third duke of York, and Cecily Neville (see Appendix C). Anne married the Lancastrian Henry Holland, the duke of Exeter, in 1455. They had a daughter named Anne Holland (1455–1474), Edward IV's niece, who, in 1466, married Thomas Grey, the eldest son of Queen Elizabeth Woodville by her first marriage to Sir John Grey. Thomas, later the marquis of Dorset, served both Edward IV and Henry VII, but he rebelled openly against Richard III.

Exeter commanded at the great Lancastrian victories of Wakefield and Second St Albans in 1460 and 1461, respectively. He was on the losing side at Towton later in 1461, after which he was attainted in Parliament. Following the attainder, Anne legally separated from Exeter in 1464. In 1467, the duke's title and estates were settled on Anne in her own right, with their daughter Anne Holland as the heiress.

Warwick restored the duke's title and estates in 1470 at the Readoption of Henry VI, and Parliament reversed his attainder. The duke commanded at Barnet in 1471, where he was severely wounded and left for dead on the battlefield, but his men must have returned and he miraculously survived. He reached sanctuary at Westminster but was later sent to the Tower, where he remained until 1475. With Edward IV back as the king, Exeter's attainder was restored. The duke's title and estates were removed again and settled once more on his wife, Duchess Anne, the king's sister, in 1471. Anne then succeeded in divorcing Henry Holland in 1472, an unusual achievement for a woman in those times, but one easily explained on the basis of Exeter's constant treason. It left Anne holding the title and estate of the duchy in her own name. This must have caused the lawyers a significant headache.

The young heiress Anne Holland died in 1474 at the age of nineteen years, without issue and without inheriting. Henry Holland later drowned at sea in 1475 while returning home from the king's expedition to France. It was rumoured that Henry was pushed overboard. In the meantime, Anne Plantagenet had married again, this time with Sir Thomas St Leger, in 1474. The duchess Anne and Thomas St Leger had a daughter, Anne St Leger, with whom Anne died in childbirth in 1476. So, by 1477, Anne Holland, the original heiress; her mother, the duchess of Exeter; and her father, the former duke of Exeter, were all dead. In 1483, before Edward IV died, Parliament settled the entire Exeter estate on Duchess Anne's new daughter, Anne St Leger, with a modest annuity given to Richard Grey, the king's younger stepson from Elizabeth Woodville. Anne St Leger was contracted to marry young Thomas Grey, the son and heir of his father, also Thomas Grey, the marquis of Dorset. The boy was the issue of Dorset's second marriage, with Cecily Bonville. For this arrangement, Queen Elizabeth Woodville paid the king the sum of five thousand marks. This complex settlement meant that the Woodville family acquired considerable further wealth, but it was not for long. It completely ignored the rights of Henry Holland's nephew and heir, Lord Ralph Neville, who soon after became the third earl of Westmoreland, and it greatly offended much of the English peerage, who feared how the king might treat their own heirs. Obviously, Edward IV, consistent with the Act of Accord, believed that females of the line could inherit.

This example is often used to explain why Queen Elizabeth Woodville was unpopular, despite the fact that the settlement occurred so near the end of the reign. But it may help explain why so few of the magnates sprang to the defence of her son, the boy King Edward V, later in 1483. However, it is not clear what were the rights of Ralph Neville, since Exeter, attainted in 1461, had lost his title and estates to his wife, Anne, in 1467, in her own right. That loss would be passed by law through to Exeter's descendants, although Parliament could reverse it. In any event, Parliament apparently agreed that Duchess Anne, not Henry Holland, had the title and the estates. Parliament settled the inheritance, but not the title, on Anne's new daughter and heir, Anne St Leger (1476–1526). To the modern mind, this seems more than reasonable, as it was not uncommon for estates and titles to be permanently lost following attainder. Although Sir Ralph Neville did support Gloucester after Edward IV died, he did not play a very important role in the usurpation. Being a Neville from the North Country, he probably would have supported Gloucester anyway. The Exeter title had become extinct at the death of Anne, the duchess of Exeter, in 1476, and the Exeter estate was inherited by the ancestors of Anne St Leger after she died in 1526. Thomas St Leger, Duchess Anne's second husband, was executed for his part in the Buckingham Rebellion of October 1483.

Historians have suggested that the Exeter arrangements proved to be another example of Edward IV's failure to follow the laws of inheritance when it suited him. But knowing that it was doubtful, the king had Parliament make it legal. So, in addition, it is an example of how, in those days, Parliament usually did what the king wished. But Parliament's interpretation of the complex legal events may have been correct. There was also a perfectly understandable reason why the king treated Exeter so harshly, namely his constant treason. Edward probably deeply regretted not having him executed after Barnet; it was Edward's way of punishing the memory of Exeter for not supporting his wife's House of York. And, as usual, no doubt, the queen supported her husband. The contract between Anne St Leger and the younger Thomas Grey, for which Queen Elizabeth paid the king, never culminated in marriage. It was later cancelled. Anne St Leger then married Sir George Manners, and their heirs inherited the Exeter estates, but not, of course, the extinct title. The younger Thomas Grey later married Eleanor St John. It remains an example of how inheritance can be carried through the females of the line. England needed to accept the idea.

There has been recent publicity concerning Anne of York. In 2012, the remains of King Richard III were found under a parking lot in Leicester. To prove the body was that of Richard, his mitochondrial genetic material (DNA, which is the acronym for desoxyribose nucleic acid) was compared with that of Michael Ibsen, a proven seventeenth-generation living descendant of Anne of York. Because the result in 2013 was a match, it proved that the body under the parking lot was that of Richard III, a younger brother of Anne of York, the duchess of Exeter.

Edward IV (1442–1483), the seventh earl of March and the duke of York, was the first surviving son of Richard, Duke of York, and Cecily Neville. This book is his amazing story.

The second surviving son was *Edmund, the earl of Rutland (1443–1460),* who died with his father, Richard, the third duke of York, at the disastrous Battle of Wakefield in the last days of 1460. Edmund's baptism in Rouen was described as lavish, in contrast to that of Edward IV, which was private and modest. This aroused speculation that Richard and Cecily were less proud of Edward, so he might not have been legitimate. This, of course, was not true if we believe what Cecily stated in her 1495 last will, that Edward's father was indeed her husband. Edmund was described as "maidenlike," so there may have been little resemblance to the muscular King Edward, but that is not uncommon in families. The young earl's battlefield death at Wakefield in 1460 was blamed on John, the ninth Lord Clifford, subsequently known as Bloody Clifford, against whom the Yorkists took their revenge at Ferrybridge in a skirmish that occurred the day before Towton, in 1461. Several accounts suggest that Rutland was captured and disarmed when Clifford discovered his identity at Wakefield and promptly killed him with his dagger; this may explain Clifford's name and why the Yorkists were determined to take revenge. Sir Clements

Markham (1906) did not believe this account and said that Edmund was killed while fighting heroically in the thick of the battle. Edmund's head was displayed on the gates of the town of York, along with the heads of his father, the duke of York, and his uncle, the earl of Salisbury. Edmund was roughly buried at Pontefract Priory, but, along with his father, he was reburied with great pomp and circumstance at Fotheringhay Castle on 29 July 1476, in the family vault. This was one of those glorious ceremonials for which the House of York was later celebrated.

Elizabeth Plantagenet (1444–1503) was the second daughter of Richard, Duke of York, and Cecily Neville (see Appendix C). She was married to John de la Pole (1442–1491), the second duke of Suffolk, in 1458. The duke was known as the Trimming Duke because he supported both Lancastrian and Yorkist causes, depending on the circumstances, and thus he took little part in the Yorkist government. His father, William de la Pole, the first duke of Suffolk, was the infamous magnate who was blamed for the losses in France during the Hundred Years War, notably at the Battle of Formigny in 1450. William was imprisoned in the Tower, attainted, exiled by Parliament, and murdered at sea; he was decapitated by multiple strokes with a rusty sword. Hopefully he lost consciousness with the first blow.

Following the attainder of the first duke, the duchy of Suffolk was restored to Elizabeth's husband in 1463 by her brother King Edward IV, so Elizabeth became the duchess of Suffolk. This marriage produced the younger John de la Pole, the earl of Lincoln, the oldest nephew of Edward IV. John had an excellent claim to the throne when King Edward V and his brother young Richard died in the Tower in 1483. John had an inferior claim compared to Edward's daughters and an inferior claim compared to the seventeenth earl of Warwick, the heir of Clarence, but he had a superior claim compared with that of Richard, Duke of Gloucester, who became King Richard III. John's claim was never taken seriously because Gloucester dominated as Lord Protector and because John's claim was through a female of the line, namely his mother, Elizabeth. Lincoln sided with Richard III, perhaps reluctantly, and was rewarded by his appointment as president of the Council of the North. Lincoln was made heir to the throne soon after the death of Queen Anne, and he fought on Richard's side at the Battle of Bosworth Field in 1485. Although he then supported Henry VII, he later rebelled against the Tudor king in 1487;

no doubt, he would have pressed his claim to the throne had the results at Stoke Field been different.

There were multiple other children, eleven in all, from the marriage between Elizabeth Plantagenet and the elder John de la Pole. Among the males, Edmund, the third earl of Suffolk, and his younger brothers, Richard and William, all nephews of Edward IV, maintained the Yorkist claims to the English throne after the death of the earl of Lincoln in 1487. When the princes periodically departed to France, Henry VII, and later Henry VIII, became greatly alarmed, but the Tudor kings expertly controlled the situation by leading diplomatic offensives, which cut off potential foreign support for possible rebellions in the name of Edward IV's Suffolk nephews.

Of Elizabeth's many other children, some were sons who entered the church and were not considered threats to the Tudor throne, others died in infancy or childhood, and some were daughters who escaped the dangers of being significant heirs.

Margaret Plantagenet (1446–1503) was the third daughter of Richard, Duke of York, and Cecily Neville; she became the duchess of Burgundy. Her departure for Burgundy in 1468 was celebrated with magnificence in London, another one of those glorious occasions of the Yorkist court. Her marriage to Charles the Bold, the duke of Burgundy, his third marriage, was also a massive celebration in Bruges, apparently still celebrated today. There was no issue from this marriage, but Margaret became the devoted stepmother of Mary of Burgundy, the daughter of her husband by his second wife. Mary succeeded to the duchy of Burgundy when Charles died at the Siege of Nancy in 1477; she married Maximillian, the archduke of Austria, the son of the Holy Roman Emperor Frederick III, and died in an unfortunate horse-riding accident in 1482.

Margaret may have supported her nephew Lincoln when he raised troops in Flanders prior to joining the Lambert Simnel Rebellion in 1487; but Lincoln died at Stoke Field. Also, Margaret, mistakenly, more likely knowingly, acknowledged Perkin Warbeck as her nephew, Richard, Duke of York, the brother of King Edward V, the son of King Edward IV, and unsuccessfully supported Warbeck's demonstrably false claims to the English throne later during the reign of Henry VII. It should be obvious that Margaret detested the Tudor king for his overthrow of the House of York. She foolishly allowed that to colour her political alignment.

If the deposed King Edward V and his brother Prince Richard had ever reached safety in Flanders in 1484, as supposed by some, then there can be no doubt that proud, powerful Margaret would have known about it and would have organized an invasion of England to remove Henry VII and restore the proper Yorkist line. It never happened. The evidence that the princes in the Tower ever reached Flanders is imaginary; if they had reached Flanders, the publicity would have extended to the four corners of Christendom. And Margaret would have informed Henry VII that his days as king of England were indeed numbered.

George Plantagenet (1449–1478), the duke of Clarence, was born in Dublin; he was the third surviving son of Richard and Cecily. George married Isabel Neville, the older daughter of Richard Neville, the sixteenth earl of Warwick. Isabel died in childbirth in 1476, and her last infant died a week or so later. George and Isabel had several other children: Anne, who died at her birth off Calais in 1470 and was buried at sea; Edward, the seventeenth earl of Warwick; and Margaret, later the countess of Salisbury. Margaret's title and estate came to her much later during the reign of Henry VIII, as the earldom of Salisbury had passed to Clarence after the fall of the sixteenth earl of Warwick in 1471.

Clarence was never happy; he resented that his younger brother Richard, Duke of Gloucester, had so much power in the North Country and that the Woodvilles had so much power in London and in the Welsh Marches. Especially, he resented Edward's refusal to allow him to marry Mary of Burgundy after his first wife, Isabel, died in 1476 and Mary was widowed in 1477. It seemed that he was rich, single, and without much power. He attacked the king, claiming that the king was not a legitimate son of his father; he attacked the queen, claiming, mistakenly, that her marriage to the king was not valid because she was a widow and no longer a virgin, and, soon, that she had helped poison his wife, Isabel. This all meant that he was a threat to the royal succession of the king's children. He joined Warwick in rebellion during the years 1468–70. He made numerous silly complaints against Edward and Elizabeth, and all led to fully justifiable charges of treason. He joined further rebellions in the period after Tewkesbury, which also involved the earl of Oxford and

George Neville, who were both imprisoned for their treason. The king had forgiven him repeatedly, but finally the king's patience was exhausted. Clarence was arrested, imprisoned, tried for treason in Parliament, found guilty, and executed in 1478.

Many people blamed the queen for the execution of Clarence. It was known that the Woodvilles blamed Clarence for the executions of Richard and John Woodville after Edgecote in 1469. It is hard to see how Clarence could avoid sharing the blame with Warwick for that atrocity. It was suggested that the execution of Clarence was the Woodville revenge, which completely ignored the primary role of the king himself. The case against Clarence was open-and-shut. It was undoubted treason on many fronts. It was the king's decision to try him. The king gave most of the evidence in Parliament, and Parliament insisted that the sentence be carried out when the king hesitated to execute his own brother. There is repeated nonsense that none of the magnates spoke against Clarence at his trial, the implication being that they sympathized with him. As the king's testimony was overwhelming, their silence meant that the result was considered a foregone conclusion.

But the enemies of the commoner Queen Elizabeth Woodville never ceased their propaganda; Elizabeth saw clearly that Clarence was a threat to the royal succession. Her judgement was correct, whereas the king took some time to convince and hesitated to carry out the execution until Parliament demanded it. But Richard, Duke of Gloucester, would not forget the queen's limited role in the fall of his older brother Clarence.

It should also be noted here that, despite Edward IV's association with Bishop Stillington, no suggestion about Edward's alleged 1461 marriage contract was ever mentioned by the treacherous Clarence in his attacks on the king's 1464 Woodville marriage. It must be concluded that Stillington never said anything about such a supposed contract; there can be no doubt that Clarence would not have restrained himself in using such an alleged story for his own ends, especially as he was accused of treason and very likely to suffer the death penalty.

George's son Edward Plantagenet, the seventeenth earl of Warwick, was another nephew of King Edward IV. Despite his intellectual disabilities, he was considered the heir of Richard III in 1484 when Edward of Middleham died in April. This honour was probably to please Queen Anne, who had looked after him following the death of Clarence in 1478 and was very attached to him. But when Queen Anne died in 1485, young Edward was replaced as heir to the throne by the earl of Lincoln, a much more suitable choice. Richard clearly did not consider young Edward to be too competent; this was before Edward was locked in the Tower for the rest of his life by Henry VII and presumably became even less competent as a result of prolonged social isolation.

Richard Plantagenet (1452–1485), the duke of Gloucester, was the youngest son of Richard, Duke of York, and Cecily Neville. He proved wonderfully loyal to his brother King Edward IV during his reign. After the fall of Warwick in 1471, the earl's extensive estates were divided between Clarence and Gloucester. Because both brothers wanted a better deal for themselves and competed aggressively with each other, the earl of Warwick's wife, Anne Beauchamp, lost everything and was effectively disinherited by Parliament. King Edward IV allowed it to happen. Richard wanted to marry Anne Neville, the younger daughter of Warwick, but Clarence was opposed to this. Richard had to give up much of his share of the Warwick estates before he could go ahead and marry Anne in 1472. Clarence was the beneficiary. Richard took Anne's mother into his own household following the disposal of Warwick's estate. This was generous and respectful. Some have claimed that Richard and Anne needed a papal dispensation for their marriage, as Richard was a great-great-great-great-grandson of Edward III and Anne was a great-great-great-granddaughter of Edward III, but the canon law had become much more flexible by the late fifteenth century and neither party reached the prohibited four degrees of affinity or closer. Others have claimed that Richard did obtain a papal consent. Richard and Anne had a son, Edward of Middleham, who was never robust and who died in 1484.

The duke was a fine military commander and proved a superb administrator of the northern counties of England; he probably took more powers for himself than King Edward IV might have intended, and for this he was not trusted by Queen Elizabeth Woodville. But the king needed a strong executive in the North Country.

There were two acknowledged illegitimate children of Richard: John of Gloucester (1470–1491), whose mother was probably Alice Burgh, and Katherine Plantagenet (1471–1487), whose mother was Katherine Haute, the daughter of Sir William Haute and Joan Woodville. The latter was an aunt of Queen Elizabeth Woodville. Richard was very careful to look after these children and always remained affectionate and considerate towards them. Richard's daughter Katherine Plantagenet married William Herbert, the second earl of Pembroke, in 1484, after the earl's first wife, Mary Woodville, died in 1481. John of Gloucester supported his father and remained a loyal Yorkist; he was knighted in 1483 and made captain of Calais briefly in 1485. John was imprisoned and executed by Henry VII in 1491, presumably on trumped-up charges of treason. Another unacknowledged son was Richard Plantagenet of Eastwell (1469–1550). He was reared by his nurse, received domestic supplies that were mysteriously delivered every quarter, and was sent to a good school where he learned Latin. It is said that the king gave him a bag of gold before Bosworth Field. There have been unsuccessful attempts to convince people that he was Richard of Shrewsbury, one of the princes in the Tower. Richard III disapproved of Edward IV's promiscuity, but the record suggests that Richard III might have been hypocritical in this matter. However, there is no evidence for adultery after Richard married Anne Neville.

Richard was exposed to a great deal of violence in the War of the Roses. At the age of nineteen years, he commanded the right battle at Barnet and the left battle at Tewkesbury. It has been suggested that Richard was present at the violent death of Henry VI in the Tower on 21 May 1471. The evidence is conclusive that Richard was at the Tower on that occasion. However, Richard cannot be blamed for the murder. Edward IV certainly gave the order, but he would not have wanted his younger brother to be responsible for murdering an anointed king. The constable of the Tower, the elderly John Sutton, the first Baron Dudley (1400–1487), or more likely his deputies, probably carried out the royal warrant; but the true identity of the assassins remains a well-kept secret to this day. Before that event, Richard was present at the death of many of the Lancastrian lords following the Battle of Tewkesbury, when his older brother Edward IV at last decided to remove those who constantly threatened his Yorkist throne. Some consider that his experience may have influenced Richard later when he deposed King Edward V; but it should be obvious that if a man makes a decision and deposes a king, it becomes necessary to eliminate those who oppose him and also to kill the king and other of his heirs. Richard made a big mistake in deposing Edward V; as a result, he found himself needing to do things which were contrary to his nature, and he must have suffered feelings of great guilt and regret. His promising career, after a brief triumph, deteriorated rapidly as a result.

After Edward IV's unexpected, but not premature, death in 1483, Richard, as Lord Protector, disastrously imprisoned Edward IV's two sons in the Tower and had what might be considered a Great Council of the Realm declare the 1464 Woodville marriage of Edward IV invalid and all the royal children therefore illegitimate. Before that, Richard executed Lord Hastings on 13 June 1483; following which he executed Anthony Woodville, the queen's brother; Richard Grey, the queen's son by her first marriage; and Thomas Vaughan, on 25 June 1483. Richard then proceeded to usurp the throne of his own nephew, King Edward V, on 26 June 1483. Soon after, it was widely believed, he had the two princes in the Tower, Edward and Richard, put to death on or about 3 September 1483. Soon after that, on 2 November 1483, he had executed the duke of Buckingham for the October (1483) Rebellion. For all of this, Richard III was intensely unpopular in his kingdom in his own time, although he retained some measure of popularity in the north of England. Queen Elizabeth and her Woodville family proved powerless in the face of Richard's ruthless seizure of the Yorkist throne.

Some have argued that Richard had nothing to fear from the princes and so had no need to murder them; they had been declared illegitimate by the Great Council. But that was of doubtful legality, and Richard himself was probably not convinced of the evidence on which the decision was based, which was just the solitary, unsupported testimony of a bitter Bishop Stillington. The king decided on this course soon after the early rebellions of July 1483 had occurred; all previous deposed kings of England, Richard II, Edward II, and Henry VI, had ultimately been murdered because it was feared that there would be constant rebellion in their name. Richard knew this history only too well and already felt the hostility from many parts of the country.

Richard intensely disliked Elizabeth Woodville and her family, mainly because he regarded them all as commoners, but also because they were previously Lancastrians. He was angered by the many beneficial Woodville marriages in the years 1464–66 and by the power and influence they were given. But in particular, Richard was angry because he believed, probably without much justification, that Elizabeth played a vital role in the imprisonment, trial, and death of the duke of Clarence, Richard's older brother. His antipathy could also be explained by the queen's limited role in the earlier execution of the earl of Desmond in Ireland.

Richard spent the last four years of Edward IV's reign in the North Country, seldom attending the court in London. This did not mean that he knew little of what happened in London, as he certainly had his representatives and attorneys, who kept him constantly informed. Edward IV did not see a problem with Richard's absence, as he was needed at the northern frontier, but Queen Elizabeth Woodville deeply distrusted the duke. And, as was not unusual, the queen's political acumen proved correct in the end.

As king of England, Richard III introduced several much needed reforms: a system for legal aid to assist the poor, a statute of limitations, jury qualification reform, land tenure reform, and a system for promoting a more just bail procedure for those charged with crimes. For these reforms, he was later greatly admired. Now, five hundred years later, many continue to defend his reputation. But Richard could not overcome the conviction of his subjects that he murdered Edward V and his brother Richard in the Tower. Some claim that his enlightened social legislation was only an attempt to promote favour with his subjects. With time, his credibility plummeted, and by rumour and innuendo he was called usurper and murderer. The path was set for his inevitable destruction. Richard's defenders often appear to argue that because he was such a good man in many respects, he did not murder his nephews; that would not necessarily be so, and the evidence makes the argument doubtful.

Before Queen Elizabeth Woodville would leave sanctuary in March 1484, Richard had to make an humiliating promise in public, that he would not harm the Yorkist princesses; he made no such promise for the two princes in the Tower, who obviously were already dead. The death of his only son, Edward of Middleham, the Prince of Wales, provoked a serious crisis for the House of York. Richard drew away from his faithful but seriously ill wife and looked for a more fertile substitute, a new queen.

Edward Plantagenet, the seventeenth earl of Warwick, the son of Clarence, was considered to be heir apparent in 1484 after the Prince of

Wales died; young Warwick was aged nine years. But young Warwick was replaced by John de la Pole, the earl of Lincoln, the son of Richard's older sister Elizabeth, in 1485, after Queen Anne died in March. At one point, Richard considered marrying his niece Princess Elizabeth Plantagenet, who had newly arrived at court after her months in sanctuary. But this liaison with his niece was fraught with political problems, and papal consent was needed. He suffered further humiliation when he was forced to make a public announcement that he did not intend to marry Princess Elizabeth and planned to send her away from his court to Sherriff Hutton Castle in Yorkshire.

Sir Francis Bacon (1889), writing in 1622, recounted Richard's many alleged faults. Richard (1) murdered Henry VI, (2) contrived the death of Clarence, (3) poisoned his own wife Queen Anne, (4) ordered the murder of Edward V and his brother Richard in the Tower, and (5) planned to marry his very own niece Elizabeth. While much of this was not true, namely the first three alleged misdeeds, the fact that the famous historian would say such things reflects what the English people believed and is powerful evidence of Richard III's extreme unpopularity. The English people grew disgusted with their king. Some authors claim that support for Henry Tudor grew rapidly, although this was never translated into significant military assistance. Richard III was killed at the Battle of Bosworth in 1485, and Henry Tudor succeeded him as King Henry VII. Sir Francis Bacon said that Henry Tudor gave instructions that Richard was to be buried with all honour at Leicester, but even the friars did not follow these instructions; Richard's body was treated badly, and his grave in Leicester was unmarked for many years. Later, it was claimed wrongly that his bones were thrown in the River Soar at the time of the English Reformation. His bones were recovered recently in 2012 from the place where the king was buried, under the now degraded Greyfriars Church of St Mary in Leicester.

There is much propaganda about Richard III, thanks to William Shakespeare and some of the Tudor historians. He was not born by abdominal section after a gestation of two years, he was not born with teeth and hair, he was not a hunchback (he had only the mildest shoulder deformity), and he did not have a withered arm. A considerable amount of literature attests to these facts. When his skeleton was discovered in 2012, it became obvious that he did have scoliosis, a curvature of the spine; this may have set one shoulder slightly higher than the other, but it does not seem to have affected his considerable ability in armed combat.

Horace Walpole (2013), writing in 1767, made a reasonably balanced but flawed assessment of Richard's multiple faults and crimes. He did not think that Richard was guilty of murder in the death of Edward of Westminster at Tewkesbury. He did not believe that Richard murdered Henry VI in the Tower. He thought that Richard had nothing to do with the execution of Clarence, did not order the murder of the princes in the Tower (but he did think that Buckingham was the guilty party), and did not poison Queen Anne. Walpole believed the 1461 marriage contract to be true, but he mentioned no evidence to support it. He was convinced that Prince Richard survived the Tower and later appeared as Perkin Warbeck, a suggestion disproved by the Warbeck confession in 1497. The only crime committed by Richard, according to Walpole, was the judicial execution of Anthony Woodville and his party at Pontefract without proper trial – and this he attributed to the violence of the Yorkist age. Walpole condoned the execution of Hastings without trial, on the basis of self-defence and, again, the custom of the times. He also appeared to believe that the queen's party took up arms against Richard, despite her early precipitous flight into the sanctuary at Westminster.

Richard was a good family man, mostly kind and thoughtful. He looked after his mother-in-law, the countess of Warwick, when she was effectively disinherited in 1472 after the death of her husband at Barnet. Richard was responsible for a great body of enlightened social legislation during his short reign as king of England; he goes down in English history as a good reformer, a capable ruler, and a fine military commander. He did have illegitimate children who he acknowledged and looked after. Also, he was benevolently religious and tried hard to win the affection of his subjects. But, unfortunately for him, it was much too difficult and proved to be in vain.

It must be emphasized that he could never overcome the dismal results of deposing his nephew King Edward V. Once he set his course for seizing the throne, he had to execute his presumed opponents. Once he had deposed the king, he had to put both of the princes in the Tower to death. Historians still argue about this, but there is no solid evidence that the princes ever left the Tower. Their bones were discovered in the Tower in 1674. On the balance of evidence, they were likely murdered at the orders of Richard, which was what nearly all his subjects believed at the time.

In brief summary: Richard locked the princes in the Tower and usurped the throne. In English history, on three previous occasions, kings who deposed kings were responsible for the murder of the deposed kings; so, the people fully expected the princes to be murdered based on the historical record. The princes disappeared forever at the end of August 1483; the people believed that they were murdered. Their bones were discovered in the Tower in 1674. The chances that they were not murdered are negligibly small. And Richard III is nearly certainly the guilty king responsible for their deaths.

Queen Anne Neville, the younger daughter of Richard Neville, the sixteenth earl of Warwick, was married twice, first to the heir of Henry VI, Edward of Westminster, who was killed at Tewkesbury, and second to Richard, Duke of Gloucester, later Richard III, who was killed at Bosworth. After he was dead in 1471, the sixteenth earl of Warwick, the Kingmaker, got what he had always wanted: a daughter who was queen of England, even if only for two very unfortunate years.

Other Short-Lived Children of Richard, Duke of York

There were other children of Richard, Duke of York, and Cecily Neville who did not survive infancy: Henry, born 1441; William, born 1447; John, born 1448; Thomas, born 1451; and Ursula, born 1454.

The Notable Nephews and Nieces of King Edward IV

John de la Pole (1464–1487), the earl of Lincoln, was the eldest son of Elizabeth Plantagenet and the second duke of Suffolk. After the deaths of the princes in the Tower, Lincoln had the best claim to the English throne, better than that of the duke of Gloucester. The Act of Accord had established that the Lincoln claim could be transmitted by his mother, Elizabeth, but as Gloucester was Lord Protector and dominated national affairs, nobody advanced Lincoln's claim. Instead, John de la Pole was a supporter of King Richard III on the council. He was appointed president of the Council of the North in 1483, which had the effect of alienating the fourth earl of Northumberland, who considered he needed no help. This must be the primary reason why Northumberland did not support Richard III at Bosworth in 1485. After the death of Edward of Middleham, the Prince of Wales, in 1484, Lincoln was made Lord Lieutenant of Ireland in his place, but he was mostly absent. The earl of Kildare substituted for him. The earl of Lincoln was the heir of King Richard III after the death of Richard's wife Queen Anne in 1485: previously, Richard had made the seventeenth earl of Warwick his heir to please Queen Anne. Lincoln was young, energetic, mature, and intelligent; he would probably have made a reasonable king if the occasion had arisen. Lincoln was on the side of Richard III at Bosworth, but he reconciled with Henry VII after the battle and the death of Richard. In view of the Yorkist defeat, Lincoln could make no claim to the throne. The Tudor king appointed him as a commissioner of justice, but Lincoln was by no means a favourite, presumably because of his claim to the crown. In 1487, the young earl, no doubt anxious to seize the throne, rebelled against Henry VII. He raised troops in Flanders, where he probably communicated with his aunt Margaret, the duchess of Burgundy. He joined the Lambert Simnel Rebellion, invaded England with the earl of Kildare, died at the Battle of Stoke Field in 1487, and was posthumously attainted. While he was in Flanders, nothing in his behaviour suggested that he knew that Princes Edward and Richard were living in Flanders or nearby. He went ahead and supported an obvious imposter, perhaps thinking that he could later seize the throne himself. Like Henry Tudor and the whole world around him, he had concluded that the princes in the Tower were long dead.

Edmund de la Pole (1471–1513), the third earl of Suffolk, was the fourth son of Elizabeth Plantagenet and her husband, the second duke of Suffolk. Edmund swore allegiance to Henry VII after Bosworth and attended the Tudor court. When his father, Suffolk, died in 1491, Edmund succeeded to his title, but his inheritance was diminished by the attainder of his older brother, Lincoln, so Edmund was demoted from duke to earl. Many of his properties were removed to the Crown, and he had to pay huge sums of money for their restoration. As a result, he spent much of his life heavily indebted. This treatment was not uncommon during the reign of Henry VII.

Edmund became worried about the 1499 execution of Edward Plantagenet, the seventeenth earl of Warwick, which seemed to him to indicate the progressive destruction of the House of York. As we shall see later, Edmund was correct in his interpretation of these events. He left England in 1499 and conferred with Sir James Tyrell at Calais, but he soon returned to England at the orders of King Henry VII. It was this meeting which resulted in Tyrell's being accused of treason, ultimately leading to his execution in 1502. Edmund again left England in 1501 and reached agreement with Maximillian I, the Holy Roman Emperor; Edmund was promised money and troops to mount an invasion of England aimed at restoring the House of York. Edmund repaired to Aix-la-Chapelle to await further events. For this treason, Edmund was outlawed by Parliament in 1502. As Edmund was in Europe, he could not be arrested, so Henry VII instead imprisoned his younger brother, William de la Pole, and executed several of his Yorkist associates, including Sir James Tyrell. Before he died in 1502, Tyrell, possibly under the influence of torture, confessed to the murders of King Edward V and his brother Richard in the Tower. It seems likely that the confession documents were not reported at the time but were stored in the archives, later examined by Sir Thomas More, and, still later, lost for all time.

Henry VII concluded a peace treaty with Maximillian, who promised not to support any English rebels, so the planned invasion of England never happened. Edmund, along with his younger brothers, William and Richard, was attainted in 1504 by the English Parliament. In the same year, Edmund departed from Aix-la-Chapelle, leaving his brother Richard as hostage for his unpaid debts. But Edmund was captured by the duke of Gueldres, who Henry VII paid to keep Edmund safe in prison. In 1506, Edmund was sent back to England by Philip, the king of Castile, who extracted a promise from Henry VII that Edmund was to be imprisoned but not executed. It is likely that Henry paid handsomely for the transfer and recovery of Edmund. At the accession of Henry VIII in 1509, Edmund was excluded from the general pardon which commenced the reign. He remained in the Tower. When Richard de la Pole threatened invasion from Brittany in 1513, King Henry VIII executed Edmund and concluded a peace treaty with France in 1514; this effectively blocked Richard de la Pole's plans for invading England.

Richard de la Pole (1480–1525) was the seventh son of Elizabeth Plantagenet and the second duke of Suffolk. He became the fourth earl of Suffolk at the death of Edmund, but not in practice, as he was in exile and attainted since 1504. He was the last Yorkist open pretender to the English throne; he escaped England after his attainder and joined his brother Edmund at Aix-la-Chapelle. When Edmund departed for parts unknown, Richard remained in Aix-la-Chapelle as hostage for Edmund's debts. Henry VII negotiated with France for his return to England, so Richard took refuge in Hungary. Richard negotiated with Louis XII, the king of France, who, in 1513, allowed Richard to raise an army in Brittany and muster at St Malo. But Henry VIII made peace with France in the Anglo-French Treaty of 1514, and Richard's plans had to be abandoned. Richard negotiated next with Francis I, the new king of France; preparations for an invasion of England were made in 1523, but there were other conflicts, chiefly the Italian War of 1521–26, and again the plans for an English invasion were abandoned. Richard died fighting for the king of France at the Battle of Pavia in 1525.

The second youngest brother, *Sir William de la Pole (1478–1539),* knight of Wingfield Castle, the sixth son of the duchess of Suffolk, lived to a reasonable age but suffered prolonged imprisonment for the treason of his brothers. Not much else is known about him, but he avoided execution and apparently died peacefully in the Tower of London. He was never the earl of Suffolk, no doubt because of his attainder in 1504.

There were other brothers of Edmund, Richard, and William. Among these were Edward, the archdeacon of Richmond; Geoffrey, who died young; and Humphrey, who took holy orders. The Tudors apparently left these nephews of Edward IV alone, not feeling that they were a threat to the Tudor throne. There were also sisters: Elizabeth, who married the eighth Baron Morley and had no issue; Dorothy, who died young; Anne, who entered a convent; and Catherine, who married the fifth Baron Stourton and had no issue.

Edward Plantagenet (1475–1499), the seventeenth earl of Warwick, was the son of George Plantagenet, the duke of Clarence. Edward was born at Warwick, the family home of his mother, Isabel Neville, the elder daughter of the sixteenth earl of Warwick who was the famous Kingmaker. Edward's mother died in 1476. When his father was executed in 1478, Edward was made the seventeenth earl of Warwick, his inheritance through his mother. As he was only three years old, he probably remained in the household at Warwick. But by 1481, he was a ward of the marquis of Dorset and probably lived in Dorset's household. In June 1483, when Edward was aged eight years, Richard, Duke of Gloucester, took charge of him. For a short time, he was with Duchess Anne at Crosby Hall in London, but soon, maybe in September 1483, he was moved to Sheriff Hutton Castle in Yorkshire until August 1485. With the disappearance and deaths of Edward V and Prince Richard, the seventeenth earl of Warwick was a possible heir to the throne; based on the attainder and execution of his father, Edward's claim had to be disqualified by the Great Council which met on 25 June 1483 at the time of the usurpation. The young earl had quite marked intellectual disabilities; he was considered weak-minded and unlikely ever to attain the throne of England. After Duchess Anne Neville became queen consort of England in 1483, her husband, King Richard III, made Edward the heir to the throne following the death of Edward of Middleham, the Prince of Wales, in 1484. But following the death of Queen Anne in 1485, Edward was replaced as heir to the throne by the earl of Lincoln, an older and more mature prince.

When Henry VII succeeded to the throne after Bosworth in August 1485, he sent the ten-year-old Edward to the Tower as a precaution against any attempted rebellion in his name. During the Lambert Simnel Rebellion in 1487, in which young Warwick was impersonated, Henry VII demonstrated Edward in public at St Paul's Church to assure people that Lambert Simnel in Ireland was an imposter. The rebels claimed that they had the true prince and Henry VII had the imposter. Edward remained in the Tower for the rest of his life. When Perkin Warbeck joined him in the Tower in 1499, after another failed impersonation, this time of Richard of Shrewsbury, Warwick and Warbeck together plotted an escape from the Tower and the overthrow of Henry VII. For this, they were both executed for treason; Warwick was beheaded as a magnate, and Warbeck was hanged as a commoner.

Margaret Plantagenet Pole (1473–1541), later the countess of Salisbury, was the daughter of George, Duke of Clarence, and Isabel Neville. Margaret's mother was the daughter of Richard, the sixteenth earl of Warwick, who died at Barnet in 1471, and the granddaughter of Richard, Earl of Salisbury, who died at Wakefield in the last days of 1460. In 1483, Richard III held Margaret and her brother, the seventeenth earl of Warwick, under close supervision at Sheriff Hutton Castle in Yorkshire.

When records during the reign of Richard III refer to "the children at Sheriff Hutton Castle," this includes Margaret and her brother Edward, as well as the younger daughters of Edward IV and Queen Elizabeth, namely Anne, Katherine, and Bridget, along with the illegitimate children of Richard, namely young John of Gloucester and young Katherine Plantagenet. There is no good reason or evidence to think that Edward V and his brother Richard ever kept them company.

In 1487, Margaret married Sir Richard Pole, whose mother, Edith St John, was a maternal half-sister of Margaret Beaufort. Margaret and Richard Pole had five children: Henry Pole, Reginald Pole, Geoffrey, Arthur, and Ursula. When her husband died in 1504, Margaret was a widow with five children. She was nearly destitute and received limited support from Henry VII. The Pole children were related to Edward IV as his grand-nephews and grand-niece.

When Henry VIII ascended the throne in 1509, he married Katherine of Aragon. Margaret became one of the new queen's ladies-in-waiting. In 1513, the Salisbury and Warwick lands were restored to her and she was made the countess of Salisbury in her own right. By good care, she became one of the wealthiest magnates in England.

Her oldest son, Henry Pole, was made Baron Montagu, a title long held by the Neville family. Henry became a close associate and favourite of Henry VIII. Henry married Jane Neville in 1510, and the couple had five children: three daughters named Catherine, Lucy, and Winifred, and two sons: Thomas, who died early, and young Henry (1427–1442).

Another son of Margaret, Reginald Pole, entered the church and eventually became a cardinal of Rome during the reign of Henry VIII. He was the last Catholic Archbishop of Canterbury during the reign of Queen Mary I. He was also the grandson of George, Duke of Clarence.

Margaret became the governess for Princess Mary, the daughter of Queen Katherine and King Henry VIII. But that position was lost in 1533 when the king asked the Tudor Church of England to annul his marriage to Queen Katherine and declare Princess Mary to be illegitimate. It should be noted that the Church, not the civil government, made this latter final decision.

In 1532, Reginald Pole left England to further his studies; in 1536, he broke relations with the king over the English Reformation and remained in voluntary exile serving the Vatican. Also in 1532, it was suggested by the Holy Roman Emperor Charles V that Reginald should marry Princess Mary and claim the English throne in place of Henry VIII. Reginald Pole recommended that Henry VIII be deposed and wrote a pamphlet to the king suggesting that the royal position on the Church of England was unlawful. It is not difficult to imagine the king's anger. Reginald also wrote to Margaret, explaining his opposition to the king, and Margaret, sensing the danger to her family, replied very carefully with her clear and sensible disapproval. In 1537, Reginald was made a cardinal of Rome. The Pope had him encourage the rebellion known as the Pilgrimage of Grace, a failed attempt to slow both the changes in the Mass and the dissolution of the monasteries.

In 1538, a number of people were arrested and imprisoned in the Tower on charges of conspiracy. They were Henry Courtenay, the marquis of Exeter, a grandson of King Edward IV through his daughter Katherine (see the section dealing with the grandchildren of Edward IV); Exeter's young son Edward Courtenay; Henry Pole, known as Baron Montagu, a grand-nephew of King Edward IV; Henry Pole's young son, also named Henry Pole (1527–1542); Geoffrey Pole, also a grand-nephew of Edward IV; and Margaret herself, the countess of Salisbury, the niece of King Edward IV. In 1539, the Pope sent Reginald Pole to Emperor Charles V to request a trade embargo against England. Later in the same year, 1539, Exeter and Montagu were found guilty of treason and beheaded in the Tower; the main charge was their alleged correspondence with Reginald Pole and their involvement in a conspiracy arising in the West Country, known in history as the Exeter Plot. Geoffrey Pole was pardoned, perhaps because he turned state's evidence and helped condemn Exeter and Montagu; however, Geoffrey later regretted his testimony and spent the rest of his life in a miserable exile.

Margaret Pole remained in the Tower with young Edward Courtenay, the great-grandson of Edward IV, and young Henry Pole, the great-grand-nephew of Edward IV. It was thought that Margaret had supported the idea of Reginald Pole and Princess Mary's claiming the throne, but under severe questioning, she never admitted it. The countess was never properly tried, but she was executed on 27 May 1541. The decapitation procedure was widely condemned for its brutality. It was conducted by an inexperienced headsman who needed eleven blows with the axe to accomplish his task. There was a storm of protest, which must have worried the king. King Edward IV would never have condoned the execution of a woman, let alone in such a manner. Margaret Pole was beatified as a martyr by the Pope on 29 December 1886.

Young Henry Pole, the son of Baron Montagu, remained in the Tower and died in 1542, probably of neglect and starvation. For those who wonder why such a boy would be treated thus, it reflects the determination of Henry VIII to stamp out all the Plantagenets. Young Edward Courtenay, the son of Exeter, the great-grandson of Edward IV, was not released until Queen Mary ascended the throne in 1553. She created him the new earl of Devon in succession after his father. However, he was regarded as a threat to Queen Mary's throne, so she sent him to the Continent and would not allow him to return to England. He died in exile three years later in 1556, with high fever and throat obstruction thought to be caused by the bubonic plague. Young Edward carried the last trace of the genes of that very legitimate king, England's Warrior King Edward IV.

Edward Plantagenet of Middleham (1474–1484) was the son of Richard, Duke of Gloucester, and Anne Neville. After Richard became king, Edward was invested as Prince of Wales on 8 September 1483. Edward of Middleham was always sickly. When he died exactly one year after his uncle King Edward IV, the Yorkist succession was badly threatened and his parents were heartbroken. As his mother, Queen Anne, had tuberculosis, it seems not unreasonable to believe that young Edward died of the same infection.

The Woodville Family and the Advantage They Gained with the Marriage of Elizabeth Woodville to King Edward IV; the Probable Cause of the Later Treachery of Warwick; and the Alienation of Clarence and, Later, Gloucester

Richard Woodville (1405–1469), the father of Queen Elizabeth Woodville, was knighted in 1426. He was made Baron Rivers in 1448 during the reign of Henry VI, and he was made Earl Rivers in 1466 during the reign of Edward IV. During the years 1433–41, he often served in France with the English army, fighting in the Hundred Years War. Richard married Jacquetta of Luxembourg in 1436. As this marriage was not sanctioned by Henry VI, the young couple had to pay a heavy fine to the king. Together, they had many children, variously estimated at twelve to sixteen in number. Richard was strikingly handsome and athletic; he was a superb and famous jouster and represented England on many occasions. Jousting tournaments in medieval times were the equivalent of modern Olympic Games. They were splendid exhibitions of chivalry, athleticism, and festivity. In 1444, Richard and Jacquetta went to France to help escort the fifteen-year-old Margaret of Anjou back to England for her wedding with Henry VI; they gave enormous support to the nervous French princess. From 1450, Richard Woodville was constable of England and a Knight of the Garter, and he was appointed to the king's council. Later, he was lieutenant at Calais and seneschal of Aquitaine.

When recalled from Calais at the appointment of Warwick in 1455, Richard did not vacate the post until the government had paid his men. This was much to the annoyance of Warwick, but to the pleasure of his troops. Of course, Warwick bore the grudge forever and would later have his revenge. In response to Warwick's piracy in the English Channel, Richard was appointed by the Lancastrian government to head a royal commission to investigate in 1458. Warwick was infuriated at being called to appear before a man who did not have the "noble blood," and this increased his already well-developed hatred for all the Woodvilles, not just Lord Rivers. It is not unreasonable to believe that Warwick was determined to sully the Woodville reputation. At this he proved very efficient. In 1459, Warwick captured Richard Woodville and his son Anthony during a raid on Sandwich, took them back to Calais, and famously bullied them at a formal hearing, again over this problem of lack of the "noble blood." In this shameful episode, Warwick was joined by his father, the earl of Salisbury, and his cousin the seventeen-year-old seventh earl of March, later King Edward IV, who, at that time, apparently did not yet know any better.

Initially a Lancastrian, Richard was at Towton in 1461 and fled north with Henry VI as far as Newcastle, but then he acknowledged Edward IV as the rightful king and was later pardoned. Richard became a confirmed Yorkist when his daughter Elizabeth married Edward IV in 1464. He did not attend the wedding, which was kept secret, even from him, the father of the bride. Richard gave faithful service to Edward IV. In 1466, Lord Rivers was made treasurer of England, a position which earned him further malicious resentment from Warwick, who could see his power over the king slipping away. In 1467, Richard Woodville was made constable of England for a short time. After Edgecote in 1469, Richard Woodville, along with his son John, was captured. They were both executed by order of the earl of Warwick following a summary trial using trumped-up evidence; Warwick stopped at nothing. It is not surprising that thereafter, Queen Elizabeth Woodville remained hostile towards the earl of Warwick, not only for his general antipathy towards her, but also – and especially – for his role in the death of her father and brother. Richard Woodville was a classic example of the commoner men who Edward IV introduced into his government, the so-called new men. Few served the English monarchy better than Richard, Lord Rivers. He was buried at the Norman church of St Mary the Virgin at Grafton Regis. He was the great-great-grandfather of Queen Elizabeth I, later one of England's most famous rulers.

Jacquetta de St Pol (of Luxembourg) Woodville (1416–1472), later the mother of Queen Elizabeth Woodville, was the widow of John, Duke of Bedford, who was the brother of Henry V and regent in France for Henry VI. This marriage made Jacquetta the aunt of Henry VI. She was described as charming, lively, cultured, and beautiful. Some suggestions have been made that there was no shortage of the "noble blood" in her family. She was the daughter of Peter, the count of St Pol; her mother was the daughter of the Duke of Andrea in the kingdom of Naples. Much farther back, she was descended from King John (Richardson, 2011), the infamous Plantagenet king who signed the Magna Carta in 1215. It can be calculated that she was a great-great-great-great-great-great-granddaughter of King John. Moving forward, Jacquetta was a great-great-great-great-great-granddaughter of the famous Simon de Montfort, the protagonist of the early English Parliament assembled in 1265 during the reign of King Henry III ("Jacquetta of Luxembourg," 2014). It is also claimed that she was descended from Charlemagne, the king of the Franks.

Jacquetta's relevant family line began with Eleanor, a daughter of King John of England. Eleanor married Simon de Montfort, the earl of Leicester. There followed in successive generations Guy de Montfort, the count of Nola in right of his wife, and then Anastasia de Montfort, the countess of Nola in her own right. Anastasia married Romano Orsini, who became the next count of Nola. There followed three successive

Orsini generations: Roberto, then Nicholas, both counts of Nola, and then Sueva. Sueva married Francesco, the son and heir of Bertrand, the duke of Andrea. Sueva and Francesco had a daughter named Margaret de Baux who married Peter, the count of St Pol. Margaret and Peter had a daughter named Jacquetta, who later married Richard Woodville and became the mother of Queen Elizabeth Woodville. In the veins of this Woodville family ran the blood of Plantagenet kings, a famous earl, an Italian duke, and multiple European counts (earls in England). There was no shortage of the so-called noble blood; Warwick simply was not aware of the genealogical table.

The regent John, Duke of Bedford, died in 1435, but Jacquetta retained all her dower properties. At the royal court of Henry VI, she preceded all ladies in the land, with the exception of Queen Margaret Anjou. In 1436, Jacquetta married Richard Woodville without the permission of Henry VI; the young couple was much in love. They paid a large fine to the king and subsequently produced a very large family. Jacquetta's eldest daughter, the future Queen Elizabeth Woodville, aged eight years, was probably a flower girl for Queen Margaret at her wedding in 1445, although this is often questioned. In terms of the notion of "noble blood" espoused by the arrogant Warwick, Jacquetta was only too well endowed. And it should be noted that she endowed her daughter Queen Elizabeth Woodville and her other Woodville children with the same hereditary genes. With the Yorkist ascendancy in 1461, the Lancastrian Woodvilles had fallen on relatively hard times.

Jacquetta passed on to her children her love of literature, art, and music, the importance she attached to family life, her appreciation of the world around her, and her deep religious faith. Her delightful adherence to the Burgundian myth concerning her family and the water goddess Melusina made her a loving storyteller for her many children. Her decision to marry for love was followed by her future son-in-law King Edward IV, who himself was born into a troubled, dysfunctional family and had a lasting admiration for the unity and cohesion of the Woodville family.

Jacquetta was sent by the Lord Mayor of London to dissuade Queen Margaret Anjou and her ravaging Scots from entering London after the Lancastrian victory at Second St Albans in 1461. For this, Jacquetta earned the lasting gratitude of the citizens of London. She gave considerable encouragement to her daughter Elizabeth. As the love affair with Edward IV evolved, she quickly realized the advantages and was present at the secret royal wedding at Grafton Regis. By her presence and that of her attendants, she made sure the marriage was properly witnessed and legal. Also, there is no way she would have allowed her daughter to marry anywhere but in a church and in front of a Catholic priest. During the reign of Edward IV, it was Jacquetta who arranged many of her daughters' marriages. Even though Elizabeth took much of the blame, Edward was always agreeable and the married couples were mostly happy. When Warwick executed her husband, Richard, after Edgecote in 1469, Jacquetta was heartbroken. Not many marriages were as successful as theirs.

At the time of the Warwick Rebellion in 1469, the ever-vengeful Warwick had Jacquetta indicted for sorcery, but she was acquitted in early 1470, soon after Edward IV escaped from Middleham Castle. Much has been made of the sorcery charges against Jacquetta Woodville. Sorcery was an important part of the historical novel *The White Queen* by Philippa Gregory (2009) and the associated recent BBC television series of the same name. After the death of Edward IV in 1483, Richard, Duke of Gloucester, accused her again, posthumously, this time along with Queen Elizabeth Woodville, of using witchcraft to induce the king to marry Elizabeth. The argument was meant to support the alleged invalidity of the royal marriage and the bastardy of the royal children. This nonsense also appeared in the Titulus Regius of 1484, along with much other nonsense, which belatedly confirmed Richard III's reasons for usurping the crown in 1483. The statute was promptly repealed by the Tudor government of Henry VII. Justifiably serious and nearly successful attempts were made to expunge it entirely from the shameful parliamentary record. Thanks to the jealousy of Richard, Earl of Warwick, and the specific villainy of Richard, Duke of Gloucester, history has not always judged Jacquetta as well as she deserves. The Woodville children are considered as follows:

Elizabeth Grey Woodville (1437–1492), accompanied by her two young sons, Thomas and Richard Grey, met the young King Edward IV while he was on royal progress, it is assumed in 1463. He was out hunting in the forest at Grafton Regis; when Elizabeth encountered him, she requested the return of her late husband's forfeited property for the benefit of her children. The king fell in love with her, allegedly at first sight, and visited her family home often. A common view is that he lusted after her and was initially rebuffed. Subsequently, on 1 May 1464 or possibly in August 1464, Elizabeth and Edward were married in secret by the king's chaplain priest at a chapel near her mother's home. There were only a few witnesses: her mother, Jacquetta; two of Jacquetta's lady attendants; a clerk to sing the office; and possibly several others. It is not certain where the marriage occurred, but it was probably at the Norman church of St Mary the Virgin located on the Woodville estate or, more likely, at the smaller Hermitage Chapel, then adjacent to the Church of St Mary but now degraded. Some claim that the marriage did not take place in a house of worship, not that it really mattered in terms of validity; but that suggestion is almost impossible in view of the firm religious beliefs of the Woodville family and the proximity of the two chapels. Some claimed that Edward was tricked into the marriage, but Edward always loved Elizabeth and placed great confidence in her. Elizabeth later had seven daughters and three sons during the marriage, which lasted from 1464 to Edward's death in 1483, a period of nineteen years. It is easy to calculate that Elizabeth spent at least half her marriage to Edward in a pregnant or post-partum state. She should have been considered the perfect queen in a monarchy that was very dependent on a large family for inheritance, succession, and survival.

Elizabeth was born and lived at Grafton Regis in Northamptonshire. At the marriage of Henry VI and Margaret of Anjou in 1445, the eight-year-old Elizabeth was probably in the bridal procession for the queen, no doubt courtesy of her mother, Jacquetta of Luxembourg, who, because of her royal blood, was very influential at the English court. Elizabeth had married Sir John Grey in 1452 and with him had two sons, Thomas Grey, later the marquis of Dorset, and Richard Grey. Her first husband, Sir John Grey, a Lancastrian in charge of the king's cavalry, was killed at Second St Albans in 1461. Her brother-in-law Edward Grey was later Lord Lisle. All members of the Woodville family were initially Lancastrians. No doubt, this aroused the suspicions of many Yorkists. When Edward IV was forced to reveal the marriage to his council, later in 1464, Elizabeth was recognized as queen consort and was enthroned at Reading Abbey by the bishops; an illustration of this ceremony has been published (Board, 2012). Soon after, she was crowned as queen of England at Westminster Abbey on 26 May 1465 by Thomas Bourchier, the Archbishop of Canterbury.

She was England's first commoner queen and, for the privilege, was widely criticized, often without justification, for much of her reign. The traditional description of the queen was that she was greedy, grasping, and rapacious; this has been repeated so many times that it has become accepted as true. Yet if one reads the more recent historical novels of Susan Higginbotham (2010), Philippa Gregory (2009), or Anne Easter Smith (2009), all women authors and talented historians, one will find that the queen is often portrayed as warm, motherly, and sensible. Likewise, Arlene Okerlund (2005) and Anne Sutton with Livia Visser-Fuchs (1995) have given us a much more sympathetic view of Queen Elizabeth Woodville. Obviously, Edward IV loved and respected her; this would be unlikely if she was as malignant as described. The description of her as greedy and rapacious must at least be seriously questioned, if not completely ignored (Higginbotham, 2011B). It is clear that our female historians do not believe the propaganda repeated by so many male historians, even Charles Ross (1997).

When Edward IV revealed his marriage in 1464, there was much unhappiness; a group of magnates went to the king and told him that his bride was "not his match." By this, they meant that the king should have married a wealthy royal heiress with an associated splendid dowry and a rich political or commercial marriage treaty. But Elizabeth had considerable assets, as enumerated by David Baldwin (2002): she was beautiful and virtuous and had demonstrable strength of character and a calm, mature personality, which are wonderful qualities in a queen. She also had proven fertility – very desirable for an hereditary monarchy. She was Lancastrian, so a conciliation policy was necessary to heal the kingdom. Elizabeth had political advantages in that the king would not offend one Yorkist family versus another, and she also had propaganda value, as the Yorkists loved to compare the king's marriage to that of the Black Prince, who had also married a beautiful woman, Joan of Kent, for love, in 1361.

Elizabeth's strength of character had been demonstrated in her family dealings when her first husband died. Her mother-in-law, Lady Ferrers, attempted to take back some properties given at the time of her marriage to Sir John Grey. Elizabeth had not surrendered but made an agreement with Lord Hastings, the chief magnate of the region, and maintained the inheritance of her two young sons. She asked that King Edward IV endorse the agreement and was later delighted to marry the king.

In 1464, the magnates soon realized that this marriage would stand; there would be no quick annulment. The successful attack on Elizabeth's marriage came nineteen years later, thanks to the treachery of her brother-in-law Richard, Duke of Gloucester. Also thanks to him, it virtually destroyed the grand Royal House of York, through no fault of Elizabeth.

After Edward IV died, it was alleged that Elizabeth's marriage to the king was bigamous and that all of her many children were therefore illegitimate. It was alleged that the king was earlier married by contract to Lady Eleanor Butler. It is impossible to imagine the distress this must have caused the dowager queen. At the time when Edward revealed the Woodville marriage in 1464, the earl of Warwick had been arranging for Edward to marry Princess Bona of Savoy and was furious about having to abandon these plans. It would be curious if Warwick, a savvy politician with a considerable reputation at stake, had not taken steps to confirm the king's marriage, perhaps by interviewing the priest who performed the ceremony or by questioning other possible attendants, such as the dowager duchess of Bedford, Jacquetta Woodville. It would also be amazing if Warwick had not been aware of any contract that allegedly already bound Edward to Lady Eleanor Butler, his very own niece. It should be noted that a coronation is a ritual sacrament performed by the church; Elizabeth was crowned by the Archbishop of Canterbury Thomas Bourchier. Nobody, including the archbishop, questioned the validity of the royal marriage in 1465. That question was only seriously raised eighteen years later, after Edward IV had died and all the many royal children had been born and baptized in the Church, usually with splendid ceremony and wide publicity. Some have even suggested that if there was any impediment to her marriage to the king, it was completely removed by her coronation.

Elizabeth and her Woodville family were viciously scorned by the English aristocracy, most especially by Richard, Earl of Warwick, George, Duke of Clarence, and Richard, Duke of Gloucester. Those three men persevered in trying to discredit Elizabeth and the others. The commoner Woodvilles were considered interlopers, belonging at best to the class of country gentry and not thought to be in possession of the "noble blood." This was despite the royal descent of Elizabeth's mother, Jacquetta, both in the English line and in the Burgundian line. Elizabeth was the great-great-great-great-great-great-great-granddaughter of King John who died in 1216; she carried the genes of Henry II, the very first Plantagenet king, and the father of King John. As Elizabeth's father, her first husband, and the rest of her family were all Lancastrians, there was an element of mistrust on the part of the many Yorkist partisans; and there was intense jealousy, as the Woodvilles clearly had the support of King Edward IV and made good headway in the Yorkist government. In addition, there was the suspicion that Jacquetta was a witch, no doubt related to the mythical legend that her Burgundian family was descended from the water goddess Melusina – not a problem in modern secular times, when magic is much enjoyed, but a huge problem in the superstitious Middle Ages. Another source of criticism was that Elizabeth's marriage to King Edward was her second marriage; the king did not marry a virgin, as might be expected of a handsome young prince. But this was only sometimes considered a problem, and certainly not by the Church. Yet another source of criticism was that Elizabeth and Edward married for love, not for concerns of State. This was a revolutionary idea at the time, a departure from common practice for monarchs, and was widely resented. Never mind the precedent set by the Black Prince. It should be noted that Edward's heir presumptive was George, Duke of Clarence; if Elizabeth had a son by the king, then Clarence would be set one step back in the line of inheritance. The new queen represented a serious danger to the Clarence ambition. This does much to explain the duke's persistent hostility towards Elizabeth.

But the marriage to Edward IV was a wonderful success by the admittedly low standards of the age. Elizabeth appears to have tolerated the frequent infidelities of her husband, at least in public; she performed her duties as queen with faultless grace. Over time, tales have been told and repeated which are meant to discredit Elizabeth. The most famous tale is recounted by David Baldwin (2002), who clearly had a favourable opinion of Elizabeth. After the birth of Princess Elizabeth, following the churching of the queen, there was a strange ceremony in which the queen sat alone at a table on a golden chair in a beautifully decorated chamber. The ladies who served the queen had to remain kneeling until the queen had finished eating. The meal apparently lasted over a period of three hours; there was total silence and nobody spoke. A variation of this story is that nobody was allowed to eat until the queen and her guests had finished. The ladies had to keep their heads bowed and not make eye contact with the queen. Later, the queen made her own mother, Jacquetta, and her sister-in-law, possibly Anne, remain kneeling before her for a long time, to the point of considerable physical discomfort for all concerned – this despite the fact that the queen is known to have repeatedly bid the ladies to rise. This was one of those curious rituals of the Yorkist court, almost certainly derived from the Burgundian court, but not in any way the preference of Elizabeth. Still, she showed that she was capable of following the protocol in her new role as queen. From this story arose the notion that Elizabeth was haughty and arrogant, which could not have been further from the truth. Charles Ross (1997) had a rather unfavourable opinion of Elizabeth, who he had never met, obviously, but he nevertheless defended her in several of those instances which had brought her reputation so low.

There were several other occasions in which the queen's startling beauty, warmth, and charm shone through, as when Louis de Gruthuuse, the king's Burgundian friend and supporter, visited Edward in 1472. *Edward Hall's Chronicle* (Ellis, Grafton, and Hall, 1809), reporting the view of contemporaries, described Queen Elizabeth Woodville as "lovely, sober, cultured, ravishing and eloquent." According to David Baldwin (2002), Mancini described her as having "beauty of person and charm of manner." Sir Thomas More (2005), quoting people who knew her, described her as "both fair, of good favour, moderate of stature, well made, and very wise." The Croyland Chronicler (1854), who knew her well but seldom exaggerated, described her as "a most benevolent Queen" – a theme recently taken up by Anne Sutton and Livia Visser-Fuchs (1995). And yet she was widely disliked, thanks to the propaganda of her jealous enemies. It was Elizabeth who caused to prosper at Edward's court the Yorkist tradition of chivalry, with fair-maiden damsels courted by knights in shining armour, seemingly at the court of Camelot. As Elizabeth was an extremely literate queen, she must certainly have been familiar with the Arthurian and associated legends, although it was a few years before the publication of Sir Thomas Mallory's *Le Morte d'Arthur* in 1485.

There were other stories designed to discredit the Woodville queen. During the troubled times of 1468, a London merchant named Thomas Cook was accused, falsely, of giving money to support Queen Margaret

Anjou. Her agent approached him, but he refused to donate. Cook was tried, found guilty of treason, and imprisoned. Subsequently, the charge was reduced to not reporting treason to the authorities, namely misprision, and Cook was released with a considerable fine owed to the king. While he was in prison, servants of the Crown, searching for evidence, caused considerable damage to his property, so a compensatory amount was deducted from his fine. The amount was calculated by an independent panel, but it was perhaps not sufficient to adequately cover the damage. The queen tried to collect queen's gold, a 10 per cent addition to the fine, but Cook petitioned and the queen forgave the additional money. Some historians have described this episode as evidence of the queen's greed, forgetting that the queen forgave the additional payment and neglecting to mention that queen's gold had been standard practice among English queens since the days of Eleanor of Aquitaine, the wife of Henry II. There is no doubt that Edward IV considered Cook to be disloyal; the merchant's Lancastrian sympathies were on full display during the Readoption in 1470. The queen was also accused of causing the 1469 downfall of Chief Justice John Markham, who had advised the jury to find Cook not guilty of treason but, rather, guilty of misprision. Markham resigned six months later because he was seventy years old and was feeling in poor health; he held no antipathy towards the queen.

There were other episodes in which the queen stood accused of malevolence. In the Desmond affair in Ireland, the earl of Desmond was correctly found guilty of treason by the Irish Parliament and was executed, but it was claimed that his two innocent sons were executed along with him. This may have been one of Sir John Tiptoft's cruel procedures for which he was renowned; it would be extremely doubtful if the queen, a faithful mother, would have condoned the execution of the boys or was even aware of it. It was alleged that Elizabeth signed the death warrant for the earl of Desmond using the king's signet seal. It was implied that she did this without the king's knowledge, but the king never complained. Indeed, for all we know, he may have instructed her to go ahead. This affair is discussed further under consideration of John Tiptoft (see in the section on the friends of Edward IV in Chapter 16). Susan Higginbotham (2013) has considered the matter in great detail and remains unimpressed with the evidence that the queen was involved. Richard III blamed "those who had the governance and rule of Ireland"; he made no mention of the queen and encouraged Desmond's son to pursue the matter in the justice system. At the time, in 1464, nobody took much notice of the affair, at least not in England. In 1538, during the reign of Henry VIII, when Desmond's grandson tried to recover property, he allegedly criticized Elizabeth for her role. This, of course, was long after her death, but, as discussed by Arlene Okerlund (2005), others believed that the fault lay with the Irish Parliament and completely exonerated the queen.

In another episode, some believed that Clarence was executed in 1478 because of the hostility of the queen, but Clarence was richly deserving. He clearly committed treason on multiple occasions, including rebellion at least four times; and this despite many pardons. The principal accuser was the king himself. Edward testified in Parliament, and, when the king procrastinated about the death sentence, the House of Commons petitioned hard for the execution to be carried out. The queen played the role of a supportive wife for the troubled king, not happy about having to execute his own natural brother. Gloucester blamed Elizabeth for the death of Clarence, but he took advantage by having Edward adjust the settlement of the Warwick estate to his own advantage. Richard justified this by noting how he was deprived in favour of Clarence in the earlier 1472–73 settlement.

In 1479, when the Merchant Adventurers were punished with a large fine for non-payment of back taxes, tonnage, and poundage, they petitioned the queen for a remedy. They also petitioned Hastings, Rivers, and others; but these latter men all referred the matter to the queen, explaining that she would be more effective. The king reduced the fine for the merchants, who expressed their gratitude to the queen. This tale was somehow meant to discredit Elizabeth, but what it shows is the positive involvement of the queen in public affairs and that her opinions were deeply respected by others in the government. Most likely, those who spread this contemptible tale thought the queen was meddling in the king's affairs and should have confined herself to her embroidery or else stayed barefoot and pregnant!

Elizabeth had conventional well-developed Christian beliefs. She made frequent pilgrimages within England, and she founded the St Erasmus Chapel at Westminster Abbey, which was later incorporated into the Henry VII Lady Chapel. The queen was a member of multiple religious fraternities designed to foster the use of prayer: the Fraternity of the Virgin Mary; the Fraternity of Canterbury Cathedral; a specific royal fraternity of the Holy Trinity, which she founded at Leadenhall so that sixty priests could pray daily for the welfare of the king, the queen, and the Archbishop of York, forever; and the Fraternity of the Worshipful Company of Skinners. Elizabeth and Edward were strong financial supporters of the Syon Abbey and the Carthusian charterhouse at Sheen. The queen obtained a papal indulgence for people who knelt and recited the Angelic Salutation three times a day; this may be dismissed in our secular age as inconsequential, but it was of enormous comfort to all Christian folk in medieval times.

Elizabeth was always publicly calm when danger presented; this was well demonstrated at the time of the Readoption of Henry VI and again at the time of the usurpation by Richard, Duke of Gloucester. But in private, her emotional reaction was often on display, as when she had to give up Prince Richard in the sanctuary and, later, when she was told her boys were certainly dead. It is clear that she was not cold and calculating. In addition, after the defence of London in 1471, in an anonymous poem, the queen was praised: "O queen Elizabeth, O blessed creature, O glorious God, what pain had she, what languor and anguish did she endure, when her lord and sovereign was in adversity." The speaker of the House of Commons, Sir William Alyngton, praised her for "womanly behaviour" and "great constancy" during the fighting.

Elizabeth was a patron of William Caxton; she understood the importance of the new development of printing, and she purchased many of the early printed books to support Caxton's enterprise at Westminster. Some historians give Edward IV credit for supporting Caxton, but it was really his queen and Anthony Woodville who were the driving forces. The books that she purchased, read, and gave away have been reviewed by Anne Sutton and Livia Visser-Fuchs (1995).

Elizabeth took over the unfinished founding of the Queen's College at Cambridge University. This had been started by Queen Margaret Anjou in the previous reign, but Edward IV seemed not very interested until his queen persuaded him otherwise with her enthusiasm and financial support. The Queen's College at Cambridge has recognized that it had two founders, the Lancastrian Margaret and the Yorkist Elizabeth. The ugly civil war did not entirely destroy beautiful attempts at reconciliation.

Elizabeth was also a strong supporter and benefactor of Eton College, founded during the reign of Henry VI; here, too, King Edward was not initially sympathetic, but again Elizabeth persuaded him to change his mind.

During her life, she twice had to flee into sanctuary; first at the Readoption of Henry VI in 1470, because she feared the earl of Warwick, and later at the usurpation of the crown in 1483, because she feared the duke of Gloucester. These men were allegedly her friends. Her life was filled with sadness, loss, and reversal, but she bore it all with dignity, faith, and grace. Queen Elizabeth Woodville was a remarkable woman and does not deserve the incessant criticism and foul judgements of history.

To summarize, the propaganda war against the commoner queen was persistent and successful, for she had many "faults." Among these were that she was beautiful, eloquent, and effective. She could do magical things, was a good and faithful wife to the king, took a keen interest in the affairs of state, defended the monarchy against the arrogant magnates, never committed treason against Edward IV, encouraged the spread of the new printed literature, was responsible for much of the knightly romance associated with the Yorkist court, and, most of all, defended her Christian church. During the reign of Edward IV, the power of the monarchy began to advance and that of the Parliament began to recede; this process continued under the Tudors and did not reverse until the Stuart dynasty, at which time the Parliament finally reasserted itself. Queen Elizabeth Woodville was present at and instrumental in the return of the monarchy after the disaster of Henry VI's reign.

At the time of Edward's death, it is believed that Elizabeth may have sent instructions that the new king, Edward V, was to be brought to London with a significant armed force for his support. But when Hastings feared that this might lead to renewed civil war and threatened to withdraw to Calais, the queen agreed immediately and instructed Anthony Woodville to bring no more than two thousand soldiers, a number which suited Hastings better. The Croyland Chronicler described how the queen was desirous of smoothing out all disagreements in the divided council. But, in retrospect, the queen's judgement of the situation may have been correct. Elizabeth graciously gave way to Hastings over the size of Edward V's escort; the only problem was that she proved right and he proved wrong.

Horace Walpole (1768) accused Elizabeth of "taking up arms" against the duke of Gloucester at the time of the usurpation; it was claimed that this provocation was the reason why the Woodvilles were imprisoned on 30 April 1483. It was probably true that some people appeared on the streets of London carrying arms and that a small number supported the queen, but they dispersed to their homes when reassured by Lord Hastings. Perhaps Walpole may have had in mind the size of the royal escort for Edward V, which promptly went home when Richard gave it the order. Walpole had the usual low opinion of Elizabeth; this would explain his exaggeration of the events.

When the plans of Richard, Duke of Gloucester, to usurp the throne became clear to her, on 2 May 1483, the queen took prolonged sanctuary in Westminster Abbey with her young family and did not leave until March 1484. At that time, there was apparent, but not real, reconciliation with Richard III, after the new king had publicly promised Elizabeth's own safety and that of her daughters. Her two sons in the Tower were not mentioned in the agreement; as they were long dead, the reason was clear.

The threats posed by the Woodvilles, frequently mentioned and exaggerated by historians, never materialized. By early May 1483, the queen was in sanctuary, Rivers was in prison, Dorset was in sanctuary with his mother, and Edward Woodville had sailed to join Henry Tudor in Brittany. At least one of the so-called overmighty factions had all but disappeared. And Hastings, the leader of another so-called overmighty faction, was soon, fleetingly during execution, to discover that he had failed to adequately back the right party. Hastings would be murdered at the hands of the ruthless Richard, Duke of Gloucester. Some historians have placed great emphasis on the ill feeling between Elizabeth and Lord Hastings; the queen resented Hastings because he frequently joined Edward in "wanton company with the ladies." Most reasonable people could sympathize with the queen, who tolerated the king's mischief with dignified silence, at least in public. We shall never know what she said to him in the royal bed.

Elizabeth had to survive a long series of adverse events at the time of the usurpation: the sermon of Dr Shaw on 22 June; the similar sermons delivered that same day in London by other clerics; the speech by the duke of Buckingham at the London Guildhall on 24 June; the presentation to the Great Council at Westminster on 25 June; the shocking decision to depose her son Edward V; the swearing-in of Richard III on 26 June; Richard's coronation on 6 July; and the outright lies and half-truths eventually inserted into the Titulus Regius in January 1484. In the face of the magnates at Westminster Abbey on 16 June 1483, her magnificent and eloquent defence of her right to retain her son Prince Richard in sanctuary was memorable. And later, in September 1483, her hysterical response to the news certain that her boys were dead, and her angry cry to God for vengeance were reactions that perhaps only mothers could comprehend. There are few women in English history who tolerated as much as Queen Elizabeth Woodville; she deserved much better.

Richard III was responsible for the death of no fewer than three of Elizabeth's sons of her body: Princes Edward and Richard in the Tower and Richard Grey at Pontefract. In addition, Richard was responsible for the death of her very own brother, Anthony Woodville. She had every right to mistrust King Richard III. If some modern historians continue to think that Richard was innocent of these crimes, Elizabeth Woodville was under no such illusion. Despite her apparent rapprochement with Richard III, which she made for the sake of her severely compromised and socially isolated daughters, it is clear that Elizabeth did not forgive Richard. Some supporters of Richard III have argued that Elizabeth would never have reached agreement with Richard if she believed that the king had killed the princes; but that is simply not so. It just shows that the former queen was a realist and a skilled negotiator. She knew for certain, without a shadow of doubt, that Richard had killed Anthony Woodville and Richard Grey at Pontefract, and yet she still made the agreement. This was for the benefit of her daughters; it was not for the benefit of Richard, against whom she continued her conspiracy with the Tudors.

Elizabeth had for some time been involved in secret arrangements with Margaret Beaufort, mother of Henry Tudor, for the betrothal and eventual marriage of Henry Tudor with Princess Elizabeth, her own eldest royal daughter. In response, on 25 December 1483, Henry Tudor made an announcement at Rennes Cathedral in Brittany of his promise to marry Princess Elizabeth once he recovered the English throne for the House of Lancaster. This eventually strengthened Henry's claim to the throne. It is clear that Elizabeth Woodville wanted both a betrothal and a public announcement. Thus, when Princess Elizabeth eventually married Henry VII in 1486, she passed the legitimacy of her father, King Edward IV, to the House of Tudor and to all subsequent English monarchs. Elizabeth Woodville eventually had the satisfaction of securing for all time the royal legacy of her dead husband's blood. From a very vulnerable position in sanctuary, by her skill and determination, she managed to preserve forever the posterity of the House of York in the royal line of England.

The last years in the life of Queen Elizabeth Woodville have been reviewed by Arlene Okerlund (2005). Under the rule of Henry VII, the dowager queen was at first respected and comfortable as the mother of Henry's queen; during late 1485 and 1486, most of her dower estates were restored to her by the Tudor government. She attended the wedding of her daughter Elizabeth on 18 January 1486; she was sole godmother to Prince Arthur at his baptism in late 1486. During 1486–87, Henry even suggested that she marry the Scottish king, James III, as part of a three-year peace treaty with Scotland. The proposal remained on the books without conclusion, but James was killed in 1488 at the Battle of Sauchiburn. And Henry VII knew only too well that Elizabeth had been supporting his own claim to the throne, along with his own mother. Elizabeth was fortunate, for the arrogant Scottish lords would have treated her even worse than the jealous English magnates.

But in early 1487, the government appeared to reverse course. They decided to take Elizabeth's estates away and transfer them to her daughter Queen Elizabeth York; however, it is clear that the estates remained in Elizabeth's family. In return, Elizabeth was given an annuity of four hundred marks per annum. The stated official reason for this seeming fall from grace was her apparent reconciliation with Richard III, but this had allegedly happened three years before. It seemed rather late for Elizabeth to be punished. She and the king's own mother, Margaret Beaufort, had been encouraging Yorkist supporters to leave England and join Henry in Brittany and France. And the dowager queen's daughter Queen Elizabeth York apparently never felt it necessary to try and protect her mother from this allegedly harsh treatment by the Tudor government.

In late 1486, the pretender Lambert Simnel had made his appearance. Some historians have suggested that Elizabeth gave him her secret support, even though there is no documentary evidence to buttress this assertion.

There are many reasons to seriously doubt such nonsense: Elizabeth would hardly support a rebellion against her own daughter, the Tudor queen, and Elizabeth would not likely support a pretender claiming to be Edward, the seventeenth earl of Warwick, the son of Clarence, when she detested Clarence for good reason. And Elizabeth would never have supported a pretender backed by Bishop Stillington, who had invented the marriage contract story and brought down the Royal House of York. It is unlikely that Henry VII would have sponsored somebody he suspected of treason, as part of a marriage treaty with Scotland. Henry knew only too well that Elizabeth was supporting his own claim to the throne.

On 12 February 1487, Elizabeth retired to live a contemplative life among the nuns at the Benedictine Abbey of Bermondsey, across the Thames River from the Tower; this was as close as she could be to her murdered sons. This did not mean that she took the veil; she still took part occasionally in royal court functions. Her comfortable rooms at Bermondsey were former royal apartments. Her room and board was paid by an endowment derived from the Benedictine Abbey of Cluny, which was founded in the tenth century by the duke of Aquitaine, from whom Edward IV was descended on the Plantagenet side of his family. Elizabeth's annuity paid by the Tudor government was sufficient to meet her other modest needs; but it was insufficient for her to leave much for her children when she died.

In 1487–88, Henry VII gave her multiple additional grants to help with her court expenses. In November 1489, Elizabeth attended her daughter Elizabeth in confinement for the birth of her second child, Margaret Tudor, daughter of the king himself. Also in 1489, Elizabeth helped her daughter Queen Elizabeth hold a sumptuous reception for the French ambassador. In early 1490, the king again increased her annuity and made her a special payment for Christmas that year. It does not sound like Elizabeth was excluded from the royal favour. Much more likely, it may be that Elizabeth, deeply religious and in failing health, may have decided in 1487 that she needed to be rid of her possessions and the considerable administrative responsibilities they entailed. She had never left such matters to her assistants.

The only daughters who visited the former queen frequently were Cecily, her third daughter, and, surprisingly, Grace, a former lady-in-waiting, an illegitimate daughter of her husband. Anne Easter Smith (2009) suggested that Grace may have attended Elizabeth at Bermondsey Abbey. The Tudor queen visited sometimes, but not as often as she should. She was frequently pregnant and in confinement. When Queen Elizabeth Woodville died on 8 June 1492, there was little left for her to give away in her last will. Grace was one of the few who rode in the funeral barge, which took Elizabeth's body up the River Thames to Windsor Castle. This confirms that Grace and Elizabeth were very close friends and that Elizabeth had forgiven Edward for his transgressions. The dowager queen's body was received late at night at Windsor and rapidly interred with King Edward IV.

Elizabeth's funeral service a few days later was a subdued and inexpensive affair at her own request, but it was by no means neglected by her family. Those who attended the funeral service included her eldest son by her first marriage, the marquis of Dorset, who paid for the funeral Mass; her daughter-in-law Cecily, the marchioness of Dorset; her nephew Henry Bourchier, the second earl of Essex, the son of the deceased sister Anne Woodville; Edmund de la Pole, the earl of Suffolk, her nephew by marriage; Viscount Lord Welles, the husband of Elizabeth's daughter Cecily; Elizabeth Stafford, the countess of Sussex, the daughter of Katherine Woodville and hence Elizabeth's niece; the other Plantagenet princesses – Anne, Katherine, and Bridget – with many other ladies; and her above-mentioned stepdaughter Grace Plantagenet. The Tudor Queen Elizabeth did not attend the funeral of her mother because she was in confinement with her fourth child. Nor did Henry VII attend.

The former queen was buried in the St George Chapel with her beloved husband, King Edward IV, in a magnificent tomb. There were no bells tolled for her, and there were only a few Masses sung for the preservation of her soul. By the standards of the time, for a former queen of England, this was considered a poor funeral, much to the shame of the Tudor government. But it was Elizabeth's request, and it was characteristic of the parsimonious King Henry VII. Elizabeth was probably one of England's most beautiful, cultured, and literate queens, ever faithful to her liege lord, King Edward IV, during one of the most turbulent periods in English history. She has been ruthlessly berated by many, but her posterity should have been treated much better. Her three most vile detractors, Warwick, Clarence, and Gloucester, all proved ultimately to be villains in one way or another. Elizabeth was no saint, but, unlike the three magnates, she never committed treason against King Edward IV or soiled his legacy. She did commit treason against Richard III, but then, in view of her story, who would blame her for that? Referring to her tomb at Windsor, the poet Robert Southey wrote in admiration for Elizabeth, "Lightly let this ground be pressed. A broken heart is here at rest."

Anne Woodville (1438–1489) was a lady-in-waiting for her older sister, Queen Elizabeth Woodville. In 1466, Anne married William, Viscount Bourchier, heir to Henry Bourchier, the first earl of Essex. William sided with Edward IV at Barnet in 1471; he died in 1480 before he inherited the earldom, so Anne was never the countess of Essex. Anne and William had three children, Henry, Cecily, and Isabel. Young Henry became the second earl of Essex in 1483 when his grandfather Henry Bourchier died. Henry attended the funeral of his aunt Queen Elizabeth Woodville in 1492.

Shortly after her first husband's death in 1480, Anne married George Grey, heir to Lord Grey of Ruthin, the Yorkist first earl of Kent. But Anne died in 1489, before George became the second earl of Kent in 1490, so she was never the countess of Kent, either. Her son by this second marriage, Richard Grey, eventually became the third earl of Kent in 1503, a position he apparently wasted by gambling and accruing heavy debt.

Margaret Woodville (1439–1491) was married in October 1464 to William FitzAlan, Lord Maltravers, heir to the sixteenth earl of Arundel. She became the countess of Arundel when her father-in-law died in 1487, at which time also her husband became the seventeenth earl of Arundel. Lord and Lady Maltravers assisted at the christening of Bridget, the youngest daughter of Edward IV and Queen Elizabeth Woodville, in 1480. Margaret Woodville's son, also named William, became the eighteenth earl of Arundel in 1487 when his father died. A daughter of Margaret, Joan, married Lord Abergavenny. Another daughter, Margaret, married John de la Pole, the earl of Lincoln, who was considered the heir to King Richard III after Queen Anne died in 1485. The earl of Lincoln was reconciled with Henry VII after Bosworth, but he rebelled against the Tudor king and died at the Battle of Stoke Field in 1487.

Anthony Woodville (1442–1483) was a well-educated man whose translation from the French of *The Dictes and Sayes of the Philosophers* was one of the first books printed by William Caxton in England in the year

1477. Other translations by Anthony Woodville and printed by Caxton include *The Moral Proverbs of Christine de Pisan* in 1478 and *The Cordyale* in 1479.

At Towton with his father in 1461, Anthony was on the defeated Lancastrian side, but then he pledged allegiance to Edward IV as the rightful king and was later pardoned. He married Lady Elizabeth Scales (1436–1473), the heir of the seventh Baron Scales, in 1461, before Edward could have had much influence on his behalf. Anthony added considerably to his wealth by this marriage. This may have resulted in the claims that he was greedy and grasping, but not much else in his career supports this notion. Nevertheless, Clarence and Gloucester complained about it. As women could not sit in the Parliament, in 1462, after the murder of his father-in-law in 1460, Anthony attended Parliament as Lord Scales in right of his wife. Also in 1462, Anthony attended the siege of Alnwick Castle. Anthony became the second Earl Rivers in 1469, when his father was executed at the orders of Warwick after the Battle of Edgecote Moor.

Anthony served Edward as a successful diplomat in Burgundy during the negotiations which preceded the marriage of the king's sister Margaret in 1468. No doubt, this earned him the continued enmity of Warwick, who instead favoured a French marriage treaty. Anthony was made captain of the king's fleet in 1468. Since Warwick considered himself the pre-eminent naval commander of the age, this appointment must have contributed further to Warwick's hostility. During Warwick's initial rebellion in 1469, when Edward IV was released from Middleham Castle in September, Anthony quickly rejoined the king at Pontefract. As naval commander, Anthony successfully defended the port of Southampton against Warwick in 1470. As the traitor earl fled England, Anthony inflicted considerable damage as he pursued Warwick's small fleet across the Channel. These were yet more reasons for Warwick's hostility. Anthony shared the king's exile in Flanders and participated in the triumphant return of Edward IV in March 1471. He was wounded at Barnet. Anthony was in charge in London while the king was at Tewkesbury; he held London against the attacks of the Bastard of Fauconberg, ably assisted by the gallant Lord Mayor of London, Sir John Stockton, and many other brave citizens.

Also in 1471, along with many lords of the realm, Anthony took the oath to support the succession rights of the king's new infant son and heir,

Edward, the Yorkist Prince of Wales. Anthony kept his word, unlike quite a few others. After a brief pilgrimage to Portugal and Spain, Anthony went to Brittany to fight the French. In 1472, he negotiated with Brittany for the extradition of Henry Tudor. The negotiations were initially successful, but the duke of Brittany changed his mind before Henry reached a ship bound for England. During the 1475 campaign in France, Anthony was sent by the king to persuade Charles the Bold to join the English, as he had promised. The duke complied, but when he joined Edward, his exhausted force was nearly useless for further warfare. In 1476, Anthony went on a pilgrimage to Italy; on the way home, he visited Charles the Bold at the Siege of Morat, but he soon headed back to England. Charles, irritated that Anthony did not stay to help him, complained in public about him. But Anthony did not trust the erratic duke who took huge losses at Morat; Charles was killed soon after while recklessly besieging Nancy in the dead of winter in 1477. So, Anthony had made the right choice.

Anthony Woodville, appointed in 1476 as governor of Ludlow Castle, was responsible, along with Bishop John Alcock, for the excellent education and training of Edward, the Yorkist Prince of Wales, later the unfortunate King Edward V. As a result of his residence together with Edward at Ludlow Castle in Shropshire, Anthony Woodville was responsible for much of the good government and prosperity of the Welsh Marches. Thanks to his excellent education, many consider that Edward V might have been an excellent king if he had not been deposed by his uncle the duke of Gloucester.

Anthony was made lieutenant of Calais in 1482, but the king apparently changed his mind and appointed Hastings soon after. This caused a dispute which is considered the main reason for the hostility between the two men. It appears unlikely that Anthony ever took up the appointment at Calais. Anthony Woodville and Hastings then engaged in a very public condemnation of each other, which produced little respect for either of them from the commons.

Edward IV is often criticized for the four power bases he allowed in his kingdom: his own in London; Anthony Woodville's in Ludlow; that of Hastings in the Midlands; and that of Richard, Duke of Gloucester, in the northern counties. In a reign filled with threats of constant rebellion, this situation was hardly surprising. It is doubtful, though, that this caused all the problems when Edward IV died. As Anthony was quickly imprisoned by Richard, Duke of Gloucester, and the queen fled into sanctuary, the Woodvilles were effectively and rapidly defeated. Lord Hastings was almost as quickly murdered. There was really only one overmighty magnate in 1483; the problems were caused by the unexpected treacherous conduct of Richard, Duke of Gloucester, not by any overmighty Woodville faction, as frequently supposed. Gloucester accused Anthony Woodville of planning to murder him on the way to London. No evidence for such a conspiracy has ever been produced, nor does this notion make any sense based on Anthony's behaviour. The fact that he went to his execution without much complaint does not prove that he conspired against Gloucester. After the outrageous murder of Hastings, Anthony knew there was no point in defending himself, and so he wrote his last will and asked that Gloucester favour his executors.

Throughout his life, Anthony remained an enthusiastic performer with lance and shield at the jousts, following in the footsteps of his famous father. Anthony fought the Bastard of Burgundy to a draw in 1471, before the king called an end to the match to avoid an unnecessary death. In 1479, King James III of Scotland proposed a marriage between his sister Margaret and the widowed Anthony Woodville, but it was cancelled when Margaret became pregnant and was therefore deemed unsuitable. In 1480, Anthony married Mary FitzLewis, a thirteen-year-old heiress descended from the second duke of Somerset.

When Edward IV died in 1483, Anthony helped escort Edward V from Ludlow Castle towards London, but the boy king was intercepted at Stony Stratford by Richard, Duke of Gloucester, and Henry, Duke of Buckingham. The dukes feared Anthony's power over the new king and claimed, falsely, that Anthony intended to ambush and kill them. So, they arrested him at Northampton and held him in prison, later along with Richard Grey and Thomas Vaughan. Anthony was one of the very few Woodvilles who could have raised a significant army and supported by force the succession of Edward V.

In 1483, Anthony gave serious consideration to raising an army for the new king, but he agreed with final instructions from the council in London that limited the new king's armed escort to two thousand men. He did nothing to risk the possible renewal of civil war; he certainly did not make haste to get Edward V to London. In fact, Anthony was quite favourably disposed towards Richard, Duke of Gloucester, as only a few months previously he had used Richard as an arbitrator in a Norfolk land dispute. On the day before his arrest at Northampton, Anthony had spent a pleasant evening over dinner with Gloucester and Buckingham. He appeared to have no inkling of what was in store for him the next day. Certainly, his behaviour was not consistent with any plan to kill Gloucester, of which the duke subsequently accused him. Anthony was beheaded at Pontefract Castle for no obvious legal reason, at the orders of Richard, Duke of Gloucester, during the latter's shameful usurpation in June 1483. Some authors appear to believe that Anthony was guilty of a conspiracy against Richard, with a plan to murder him on the road to London, but these authors never present any objective evidence for such a plot. Maybe Richard believed that Anthony should have remained at Ludlow and waited for Gloucester to arrive and escort the new king. But, in fact, Anthony was only too willing to cooperate with Richard; he deviated from his planned route in order to meet Richard at Northampton. One further suggestion has been that Richard thought that he, not Anthony, should have controlled the education of the Prince of Wales, since Edward had previously given him some responsibility for his young nephew. The addition of Richard Grey to assist Anthony meant that the Woodvilles had far too much control over the Yorkist heir to the throne. This might explain Richard's specific hostility. Still, that would have meant sending the prince far away to the North Country where Richard was sorely needed.

Anthony Woodville provided King Edward IV good and faithful service as military commander, political leader, foreign diplomat, skilled administrator, and brilliant scholar. He had a close association with William Caxton, who printed many of his translations. Anthony Woodville and Queen Elizabeth gave Caxton considerable financial and intellectual support. They understood the significance of the coming printed word and the effect it would have on medieval life, even if Edward did not. Anthony was charming, urbane, and immensely talented; the king placed enormous confidence in him. Both he and his father were the prototype of the upper-middle-class royal servant favoured by Edward IV and soon to be favoured by the Tudor monarchs as the Middle Ages ended and the Renaissance took hold in England. When Anthony's body was thrown in a common grave at Pontefract, it was noted that he was wearing a hair shirt, a sign of his great personal humility.

Anthony's advantage with the king's favour earned him the unjustified enmity of the magnates, mainly Warwick, Clarence, and Gloucester, who were jealous of his position. They slandered him and his family with false charges of grasping greed and self-aggrandizement. Some historians have repeated the propaganda. In a recent movie production, Anthony was displayed as an amiable moron. Nothing could be further from the truth. It appears that the only example of Anthony's grasping greed is his marriage to Lady Elizabeth Scales, but there was not much unusual about that. Also, the marriage was a happy one. Anthony's big problem was that he was considered not to possess the "noble blood," even though, through his mother, Jacquetta, he was descended from King John of Magna Carta fame. Anthony Woodville's distinguished career deserves re-evaluation by historians.

Mary Woodville (1443–1481), in 1466, married William Herbert, Lord Dunster, the older son and heir of the senior William Herbert, who was created the Yorkist first earl of Pembroke in 1468 after the fall of Harlech Castle. The earl did not enjoy his earldom for long because he was executed after Edgecote in 1469 at the orders of Warwick. It is hard to feel sympathy for Warwick, well known for his ruthless savagery. The marriage of Mary and the young William was performed in the St George Chapel at Windsor Castle with great celebration and excitement. Mary's husband succeeded as the second earl of Pembroke with the execution of his father, when Mary became titled the countess of Pembroke.

Warwick considered this marriage particularly noxious; but then, the Herberts and Warwick previously had fierce quarrels over properties in Wales and had long remained mortal enemies. Warwick's criticism was possibly not surprising. Lord Herbert negotiated several land grants from the king before he would give his consent to the marriage. The first Earl Rivers made the appropriate arrangements. No doubt, the insufferable Warwick was upset.

Mary and William had one daughter named Elizabeth. William was not successful in South Wales, which generally remained loyal to Lancaster, so, in 1475, William and Mary were forced to exchange Pembroke for the lesser earldom of Huntingdon. Thomas Grey gave up the earldom of

Huntingdon and became the marquis of Dorset instead. The earldom of Pembroke was later, in 1479, given to Edward, the Yorkist Prince of Wales, the future Edward V. After Mary Woodville died in 1481, young William married Katherine Plantagenet, the illegitimate daughter of Richard, Duke of Gloucester. Some authors suggest that as young William Herbert was loyal to Richard III and finally exerted control in South Wales, Henry Tudor was forced to take a more northerly course through Wales as he invaded England in 1485.

Jacquetta Woodville (1444–1509) was most likely named after her mother. Jacquetta married John le Strange, the eighth Baron Strange of Knockyn, in 1460 or thereabouts, before Edward was king. Their daughter Joan married George Stanley, the older son and heir of Thomas, Lord Stanley, who served Edward IV and Richard III as steward of the royal household. Joan and George had a son, young Thomas Stanley. But George died in 1503 before his father died in 1504. It was Joan's son young Thomas Stanley who became the heir of the elder Thomas, Lord Stanley.

The elder Thomas deserted Richard III at Bosworth and so helped gain victory for Henry Tudor. George Stanley, Joan's husband, Jacquetta's son-in-law, was held hostage by Richard III before Bosworth in a vain attempt to hold his father's loyalty. Richard III actually ordered George's execution at Bosworth just before the king's fatal charge against Henry Tudor, but the order was not carried out because Richard's men stared defeat in the eyes and the king was killed in combat. As a reward for his support, Henry VII made the elder Thomas Stanley the first earl of Derby. Joan's son, Jacquetta's grandson, the young Thomas Stanley, eventually became the second earl of Derby in 1504.

John Woodville (1445–1469), when aged only twenty years in January 1465, married Katherine Neville (1397–1483), the sixty-eight-year-old wealthy and often married dowager duchess of Norfolk. The duchess was a daughter of Ralph Neville and Joan Beaufort (see Appendix E), an aunt of Richard Neville, the sixteenth earl of Warwick, and the mother of John Mowbray, the third duke of Norfolk, the Earl Marshal, the great supporter of Edward IV. Ironically, the marriage made young John Woodville the uncle of Warwick by marriage. This was considered one of the most egregious power grabs made by the Woodville family, according to Warwick. But Katherine raised no public objections and may well have been only too happy with her young steed husband, who was handsome and charming. By her multiple marriages, Katherine proved adept at holding onto her wealth and property; there were already lawsuits over the matter. Her Mowbray heirs, descended from the first duke of Norfolk, were waiting impatiently for her to die. By her marriage to the brother-in-law of King Edward IV, she made it unlikely that she would have to give up many of her holdings. It may even have been the duchess who first suggested the match with John; it is not unusual for older rich women to be attracted to handsome young men. Charles Ross (1997) said that such marriages were not all that uncommon in the fifteenth century. Like his brother Anthony, John Woodville was a fine performer with lance and shield at the jousts. Unfortunately, along with his father, Richard Woodville, John was executed following Edgecote in 1469, at the orders of his nephew by marriage, the vengeful earl of Warwick. It was ironic that the duchess outlived even her young fourth husband. Also, it is difficult to find much sympathy for Warwick's hostile attitude.

Richard Woodville (1446–1491), the third male of the family, was pardoned, along with the other male members of the family, by Edward IV for his early adherence to the Lancastrian cause. He gave notable performances at the jousts in celebration of the creation of Prince Richard as the duke of York in 1474, and again at the marriage of Prince Richard to Anne Mowbray in 1478. He served on several judicial commissions in the Welsh Marches. Late in Edward IV's reign, Richard was constable of Chester and Wallingford Castles. He may have given limited assistance to his brother Anthony in the supervision of the Prince of Wales at Ludlow Castle. Richard became the third Earl Rivers at the death of Anthony Woodville in 1483, but his estate was withheld by Richard III; nevertheless, his inheritance was his own right, not granted through any special privilege bestowed by Edward IV. Richard took part in the Buckingham Rebellion and was attainted in 1484, but he was pardoned in 1485 by Richard III because the king was attempting to strengthen his political support. It would appear that Richard's properties were not restored. Some claim that the earl deserted to the Lancastrian side at Bosworth so as to avoid fighting against his younger brother, Edward Woodville; this may well be true, since the earl's inheritance was eventually restored after Bosworth by a grateful Henry VII. Richard later performed legal administrative work for the Tudor king. He attended the coronation of his niece Queen Elizabeth York and the christening of her son Prince Arthur. Richard never married. He died in 1491.

Lionel Woodville (1447–1484) was reputed to be the first person granted an honorary degree at Oxford University. In 1478, he was the dean of Exeter Cathedral; from 1479 to 1483, he was chancellor of Oxford University; and in 1482, he was appointed bishop of Salisbury, a position he richly deserved. In early May 1483, he fled with his mother into sanctuary at Westminster Abbey. After the murder of Hastings in mid June, he left sanctuary, believing that the Church would not protect him from Richard, Duke of Gloucester, and went into hiding elsewhere in England. Sir Clements Markham (1906) listed him as attending the coronation of Richard III in early July 1483. In late July 1483, Lionel was at Oxford in his capacity as chancellor to welcome Richard III on his first royal progress. This must have been awkward, as the king had recently executed Lionel's brother Anthony and his nephew Richard Grey at Pontefract. In October 1483, Lionel joined the Buckingham Rebellion with a rising at Salisbury; when it failed, he fled into sanctuary at Beaulieu Abbey. Lionel was attainted, so Oxford University promptly replaced him as chancellor. Richard III tried but failed to remove him from the sanctuary. The bishop died in 1484, it is thought from natural causes, probably at Beaulieu Abbey. It is likely that the bishop of Salisbury is buried in a tomb, now somewhat dilapidated, at Salisbury Cathedral.

Martha Woodville (1450–1500) married Sir John Bromley (1410–1489), a Lancastrian knight who survived the Battle of Blore Heath in 1459. The marriage may not have been valid, as she is not listed in the *Peerage of England* as the wife of Sir John. They had a son named Thomas, but not much else is known. Her dates are very uncertain. It is possible that no favourable marriage was arranged for her because her liaison with Sir John Bromley was illicit and she thereafter lost favour in the close-knit Woodville family.

Joan Woodville (1452–1491), often known as Eleanor, in 1466 married Sir Anthony Grey, heir to Edmund, Lord Grey of Ruthin, the Yorkist first earl of Kent. Joan apparently had no children. The earldom of Kent had reverted to the Crown when Lord Fauconberg died in 1463, but it was newly created for Edmund Grey in 1465, apparently for his service rendered to Edward IV at Northampton in 1460. Edmund Grey, on the side of Henry VI, ordered his men to lay down their arms, which contributed greatly to the Yorkist victory. Joan's husband, Sir Anthony Grey, died in 1480 without inheriting, so Joan was never the countess of Kent. Sir Anthony's younger brother, George Grey, became the second earl of Kent when their father died in 1490. George Grey had married the widowed Anne Woodville in about 1481; she died in 1489 before George inherited. Their son Richard became the third earl of Kent in 1503.

Edward Woodville (1455–1488) was a famous warrior knight. He was given no special privileges by Edward IV, his brother-in-law, but he remained a loyal military and naval commander in support of Edward IV. He did not support Richard III and instead served Henry Tudor especially well at Bosworth Field in 1485 and again at Stoke Field in 1487. During the usurpation, Edward Woodville took the English fleet out to sea after the Woodvilles on the council ordered him to resist French attacks on English shipping. Gloucester then ordered most of the ships to return, but Edward, with few remaining loyal ships, sailed on to exile in Brittany, taking with him a small part of Edward IV's treasure collection. It is thought that he used these limited funds to pay his sailors. Edward, an experienced soldier, commanded under the earl of Oxford at Bosworth in 1485; a grateful Henry VII appointed Edward Woodville as the captain of the Isle of Wight. In 1487, Edward commanded the Tudor vanguard at Stoke Field and won a decisive victory for the Tudor king. Edward then went to Spain to fight the Moors and was hailed by a grateful Ferdinand and Isabella. In 1488, without Henry VII's permission, Edward took a small army, raised in the Isle of Wight, to Brittany to fight for the duke there. At the Battle of St Aubin, he was killed by the French. It is notable that soon after Edward Woodville was dead, King Henry VII decided that it was in the national interest to support Brittany against the French. Sir Edward's judgement was confirmed.

Katherine Woodville (1458–1497), the youngest sister of the queen, married Henry Stafford, the second duke of Buckingham, in 1465, at the age of seven years. At the coronation of Queen Elizabeth Woodville later in 1465, the married couple were children who were carried in the procession by attendants. Katherine's birthdate is often misstated as 1449, which made her six years older than her husband and old enough to walk by herself in the coronation procession. Henry was alone among the spouses in resenting his marriage to a low-born Woodville. It is said that he assumed an almost pathological hatred for his wife's Woodville family. Warwick objected to the marriage for his usual reasons, mostly unjustified and somehow related to Katherine's lack of the "noble blood." Warwick regarded the queen as excessively greedy, which is a perfect example of the pot calling the kettle black. Still, Warwick was successful in ruining the reputation of the queen and her family. Because his father died early and never inherited, Henry Stafford became the second duke of Buckingham when his grandfather, the first duke of Buckingham, died at Northampton in 1460. Henry played little role during the reign of Edward IV, at first because he was too young, and later because the king, wisely, did not trust him. Edward IV was not always such a bad judge of character. About the only thing that Edward let Buckingham do in his role as seneschal of England was pronounce the death sentence on the duke of Clarence in 1478.

When Edward IV died, Henry played a pivotal and destructive role in supporting Richard III in his usurpation of the crown; it was his way of seeking revenge against the Woodvilles. But soon, the untrustworthy duke turned against the new king, probably because of the lies promulgated by Richard III and his other confederates. Henry was executed in 1483 for his disastrous treason and the failed October Rebellion. Buckingham may have disliked the Woodvilles, but he ended his life by joining them against Richard III. The eldest son of Katherine and Henry, named Edward, the third duke of Buckingham, intrigued against King Henry VIII. He, too, was executed for treason, in 1521.

Katherine was hostile to Richard III for obvious reasons and did not attend his coronation. She would have been outspoken in defence of her sister's marriage to King Edward IV, and it is easy to suggest that she must have contributed to her husband's change of mind about the alleged 1461 marriage contract. It is interesting to note that King Richard did help her after her husband's execution; this would be consistent with Richard's considerable regret about, and guilt over, the deposition of Katherine's nephew King Edward V.

The beautiful and charming Katherine later married Jasper Tudor, the Lancastrian earl of Pembroke, in 1485, after Bosworth. Jasper was then created the duke of Bedford in 1488. Katherine certainly benefitted greatly from her marriage arrangements and eventually was titled both the countess of Pembroke and the duchess of Bedford. But her success in life could not always be assigned to Elizabeth Woodville, who was long out of power when Katherine married Jasper Tudor. Katherine attracted husbands on her own. When Jasper died in 1495, Katherine married Sir Richard Wingfield, her long-patient servant, in 1496. He survived her and later served Henry VIII as a fine diplomat.

There may have been two other children of Richard and Jacquetta. *Lewis Woodville* was born in 1438 and died at the age of two years. *Agnes Woodville* married William Dormer. It is not clear that she belonged to the family. Edward IV gave her no special treatment. Her birthdate is not known; she died in 1506. A Thomas Woodville is sometimes mistakenly listed as a Woodville sibling who married Anne Holland, but that was Thomas Grey, the elder son of Elizabeth Woodville by her first husband, Sir John Grey.

The Stepsons of Edward IV

Elizabeth Woodville had two sons by her first husband, Sir John Grey of Groby, the son of Elizabeth, Baroness Ferrers.

Thomas Grey (1455–1501) married, in October 1466, the eleven-year-old Anne Holland, the daughter of Anne Plantagenet, the king's older sister, and Henry Holland, the duke of Exeter, much to the anger of Warwick and Clarence. Anne Holland was already marriage-contracted to George Neville, the son of John Neville, and thus the nephew of Warwick, so perhaps the earl of Warwick's anger was justified in this instance. But the fact is that from 1464 to his death in 1471, Warwick was always offended by Edward and Elizabeth, no matter what they did. Queen Elizabeth Woodville paid Duchess Anne four thousand marks to cancel the marriage contract, a perfectly legal procedure. It is assumed that John Neville was then paid for his consent, although this seems not to be confirmed. Edward IV was happy with the arrangement, as the Holland family were Lancastrians and the king frequently pursued a policy of conciliation, even though the policy in this case was notably unsuccessful. However, the nineteen-year-old Anne Holland died without issue in 1474 and never inherited the Exeter estates; so, neither did Thomas Grey.

At the age of sixteen years, Thomas fought for Edward IV with distinction at Tewkesbury in 1471 under the command of Lord Hastings. Thomas was made the earl of Huntingdon in 1472, but he surrendered the title to the Crown in 1475 and was promoted to be the marquis of Dorset instead. He was always close to King Edward and was frequently criticized for his promiscuous misadventures with the king in "wanton company with the ladies." Thomas served King Edward during the invasion of France in 1475. Soon after his return, he was given a place on the council. Also in 1475, Thomas married Cecily Bonville, a stepdaughter of Lord Hastings, who was paid twenty-five hundred marks. This marriage proved a fertile union which produced seven sons and eight daughters, but it did not resolve Thomas's bad relationship with Lord Hastings. In 1482, Dorset, along with his uncle Edward Woodville, served under Richard, Duke of Gloucester, in the successful invasion of Scotland. There were no reports of family conflict.

In early 1483, Thomas Grey's oldest son, also named Thomas Grey, was contracted to marry Anne St Leger, the daughter of Anne Plantagenet, the duchess of Exeter by her second husband, Thomas St Leger. Also in early 1483, Anne St Leger was made heiress to the Exeter estates, an arrangement also widely disparaged by the English peerage. But Queen Elizabeth Woodville paid her husband five thousand marks for this arrangement; Parliament apparently agreed with the legal arguments made by the king and confirmed the inheritance. The contract between young Thomas Grey and Anne St Leger did not end in a marriage, as it was later cancelled.

On his deathbed, Edward IV made Dorset and Hastings promise to settle a long-standing feud between them and to cooperate in support of King Edward V. The feud was mainly over land holdings in Leicestershire, but it was also over a common mistress at court and the close favour of the king. Dorset had been made deputy constable of the Tower in the month before Edward IV died, so the king's treasure was under Dorset's control. This may explain why Mancini alleged that Dorset seized the treasure for his own purpose, which was not true. At meetings of the council, Dorset favoured making decisions as necessary because Gloucester was still far away in the north. This is sometimes interpreted to mean that he did not favour the Lord Protector, but he knew full well that Edward IV had made the appointment. Dorset proved ineffective at defending the short reign of Edward V. Soon after Gloucester took control over Edward V at Stony Stratford, Dorset, aged twenty-eight years, fled into sanctuary with his mother. Later, upset by the illegal execution of Hastings, he fled from the sanctuary for fear that the Church would not protect him from the duke of Gloucester. The Lord Protector's men hunted for Dorset with bloodhounds near the abbey. Dorset went into hiding, probably in Yorkshire, and soon joined the Buckingham Rebellion of October 1483. When the rebellion failed, he fled to Brittany to join Henry Tudor and was attainted by Parliament in 1484.

In March 1484, Elizabeth Woodville appeared to make amends with Richard III, mostly for the sake of her daughters, but also because of her considerable discomfort in the sanctuary. Much later, in March 1485, she asked Thomas to return to England, presumably because she needed his support. Richard III, anxious about the political situation, may have promised a pardon for him. Loyal to his mother, in July 1485, Thomas started the journey, but Henry Tudor sent troops to arrest him. He did not accompany Henry's invasion force on 1 August 1485 because Henry did not trust him, as he suspected that Thomas may have turned his coat. This might confirm that Richard III had indeed offered a pardon. Thomas remained in France as security for a loan made to Henry Tudor by the French government. But after Bosworth Field and the death of Richard III, he was recalled to England, his attainder was reversed, and his titles were confirmed.

During the Simnel Rebellion in 1487, Thomas was sent to the Tower as a precaution against his joining the rebellion. He was released after Stoke Field. After that, he remained loyal to the Tudor king. Dorset assisted in the suppression of the 1497 Cornish rebellions. In 1492, he was made to sign an indenture which made it clear that the king would take his lands for the Crown if he committed treason or misprision. This was a common procedure under the suspicious Henry VII. In the same year, Thomas attended and paid for the funeral of his mother in the St George Chapel at Windsor. Dorset befriended a young Thomas Wolsey, later cardinal chancellor, to whom he gave the rectory at Limington in Somersetshire.

Thomas began building Bradgate Manor on the Groby estates of his father, Sir John Grey. After Thomas died in 1501, his son and heir, young Thomas Grey, completed the project. In turn, the son of the younger

Thomas Grey, named Henry Grey, married Frances Brandon, a daughter of Mary Tudor Brandon and therefore a granddaughter of Henry VII and Queen Elizabeth York. Henry Grey and Frances produced Lady Jane Grey, apparent queen of England for nine days after the death of King Edward VI. Lady Jane Grey was the great-great-granddaughter of both Queen Elizabeth Woodville and Edward IV.

Richard Grey (1458–1483) was knighted in 1475 and was later granted several properties and offices by Edward IV, but there was nothing unusual or excessive. He did receive a modest annuity taken from the inheritance of Anne Holland, his stepsister-in-law, which some considered very unreasonable. Richard never married. He was a notable performer at the jousts celebrating the creation of Richard of Shrewsbury, Edward's second son, as the duke of York in 1474, and again at the jousts for the marriage of Richard, Duke of York, to Anne Mowbray in 1478. Richard Grey assisted Anthony Woodville in the tutelage of Edward, the Prince of Wales, at Ludlow Castle and was active in the related administrative duties. At the death of Edward IV, he was in the escort taking Edward V to London for the accession ceremonial. He was arrested at the orders of the Lord Protector, Richard, Duke of Gloucester. He was imprisoned, falsely accused of conspiring to ambush and murder the Lord Protector, and later executed at Pontefract Castle without a serious trial, along with Anthony Woodville and Thomas Vaughan. Richard III intensely disliked the Woodville family; no other motive for this disgraceful behaviour has ever been proposed. In much of the historical record, the usual attempt to justify this judicial murder amounts to a constant stream of vitriol directed against the Woodville family. No one has ever produced any evidence that the Woodvilles conspired to murder Richard, Duke of Gloucester. That the Woodvilles would attempt to do so makes absolutely no sense, since they knew early that King Edward IV had appointed Gloucester as the Lord Protector. Even Horace Walpole (2013), a stalwart defender of Richard III, said that the execution was not justified.

The Woodville Marriages which Caused Much Unhappiness among Certain Nobles

Many of the marriages which occurred between 1464 and 1466 greatly enhanced the influence, wealth, and social standing of the Woodvilles, especially for the females. This was alleged to be much to the chagrin of the established peerage, particularly Warwick, Clarence, and Gloucester. However, Elizabeth was a beautiful queen married to a generous king; it is not surprising that she was so successful in providing for her sisters. Nor was there anything unusual in a queen's taking steps to promote her family. It has been suggested that the problem was that there were so many Woodvilles, which seems very likely. Another problem may have been that most of the marriages occurred in rapid succession in the years 1464–66.

It was sometimes alleged that the marriages greatly reduced the supply of eligible male spouses, but in view of the endless armed conflicts during this period of history, there were surely other explanations. Warwick needed to make arrangements for his daughters, Isabel and Anne; he felt that the supply of eligible males was diminished. But the king's own brothers, George and Richard, were clearly still available to him, and both brothers eventually married the earl's daughters, although Warwick was dead before Anne and Richard of Gloucester were espoused in 1472.

The Woodville marriages also served another purpose for Edward IV. By taking many eligible males out of the marriage market, the king blocked potential attempts by some magnates to increase their wealth and power and establish themselves as counterweights to the new king (Clive, 1974). The earldoms of Essex, Arundel, and Pembroke, and the duchies of Buckingham and Norfolk, would have added considerably to the power of already wealthy men like Warwick, Gloucester, and Clarence. Edward IV believed what Sir John Fortesque wrote, that the king should take care to be the richest man in England. Edward's attitude may simply have been good policy for political reasons.

Warwick, Clarence, and Gloucester were all greedy, arrogant power-grabbers. It is not surprising they resented the queen, who was their often successful rival at playing the power games. What mattered was that Elizabeth was a good and faithful wife to Edward IV, whereas Warwick and Clarence both committed demonstrable treason against the king multiple times; and Gloucester was ultimately responsible for the fall of Edward's son and heir, King Edward V. By supporting the opinion of Warwick, Clarence, and Gloucester, all traitors to their king, history may well have judged Queen Elizabeth and her Woodville family unfairly.

Most of the Woodville women (some when they were girls) were married into families which supported Edward IV. It should not be forgotten that England was still largely Lancastrian and that the king needed to retain the loyalty of his Yorkist supporters. It can be assumed that the family heads gave their happy assent. Most of these families were Yorkists and no doubt had little problem with the arrangements. The king retained their loyalty, kept them in the family, and built the political strength of the House of York. It was unfortunate that such family strength was wasted by the internecine conflict which occurred after Edward IV was dead.

The female Woodvilles were all attractive, lively young women, and all of the chosen young men were happy with their spouses, as far as we know. In the case of the seven-year-old Katherine, who married the ten-year-old duke of Buckingham, it was Buckingham who was the exception. He was never happy and complained throughout his life, but the marriage was successful by the standards of the time. The couple had five children together. Buckingham had much to learn from his well-informed wife; Katherine knew Gloucester too well and, along with her mother, did not trust him. It is sad that it took Buckingham so long to reach agreement with her judgement. In the meantime, he had done a great deal of harm to the Royal House of York.

Many of the Woodville males, Richard, Lionel, and Edward, were never married. Anthony made his own advantageous marriage to Lady Elizabeth Scales in 1461, well before Elizabeth was queen and a little before Edward was king. Of the two Grey boys, Richard never married, either.

So, the important question to ask is why there were so many complaints. The real reason why Warwick, Clarence, and Gloucester complained was that they considered Queen Elizabeth a commoner, not of the royal blood. They were against her from the day they found that she was married to the king, when they determined not to give her a chance. There were other reasons: she was cultured, literate, and clever, her family had been Lancastrian, they suspected her of sorcery, and she was not a virgin at the time she married the king. It is not unreasonable to accuse those three magnates of blatant hypocrisy in the matter of Edward's beautiful queen. And some authors have said that apart from Warwick, Clarence, and Gloucester, most of the nobility were not unhappy at all. Furthermore, Edward accomplished his purpose for the queen with only minor expenditure for the Crown. It seems reasonable to discount all the controversy surrounding the Woodville marriages; the magnates had bad reasons for their opposition, and Edward exercised the discretion to which a king was entitled. It should have been the end of the matter. But, unfortunately for the Royal House of York, it was not.

The General Reasons Why the Woodvilles Were Unpopular

The Woodvilles were favoured by the king and given advancement that many considered undeserved. They took the place of people who otherwise would have been advanced and who then became jealous of them. It was likely that they were considered greedy and grasping, even though there were only a few instances in which this could be considered the case. Accusations of greed and rapacity were common in the fifteenth century. Such accusations were made against many. To name just a few, those accused of greed and rapacity were: Edward IV, Henry VII, Clarence, Gloucester, Warwick, Margaret, Duchess of Burgundy, Richard, the third duke of York, Sir William Hastings, Sir John Howard, Lord Thomas Stanley, Henry, the second duke of Buckingham, Lord William Herbert of Pembroke, Thomas Courtenay, the sixth earl of Devon, and John Tuchet, the sixth Baron Audley. The list goes on and on; it is hard to find somebody not so accused. Similar accusations against the Woodvilles need to be taken in context. Also, not much supportive evidence was ever suggested.

In the past, governments had been run by people from the upper noble class. As Edward promoted people lower on the social scale to the new civil service, the Woodvilles benefitted greatly, so people were quick to accuse them. It was never forgotten that earlier, most of the Woodvilles had Lancastrian sympathies, so they were never considered to be true Yorkists, despite their faithful service to the king. Some of the Woodvilles, perhaps Dorset being the best example, were a bad influence on Edward and accompanied him on many of his promiscuous misadventures. Gloucester appears to have felt that Dorset needed to be restrained – and he may have been right. How much the question of sorcery was involved is difficult to evaluate, but the Woodville success was sometimes attributed to magical events. Clarence seems to have believed that sorcery was used against his wife, Isabel, near the time of her death. And finally, Clarence had high hopes of inheriting the throne, but the fertile queen produced many children, and each one made Clarence's path to the crown one step more difficult.

The Children of King Edward IV and Queen Elizabeth Woodville, and Their Descendants

Elizabeth Plantagenet of York (1466–1503) in 1469 was briefly betrothed to George Neville, the young son of John Neville, the marquis of Montagu, but the arrangement was cancelled when John Neville turned Lancastrian in the next year and joined with his brother the earl of Warwick in rebellion (Clive, 1974). In 1475, at Picquigny, Elizabeth was promised in marriage to the dauphin of France, later King Charles VIII, but the marriage never occurred when relations between England and France deteriorated in 1482. Instead, Charles VIII married Anne of Brittany and swallowed the duchy. After the death of Edward IV in 1483, the seventeen-year-old Elizabeth accompanied her mother into the sanctuary at Westminster Abbey. At the usurpation by Elizabeth's uncle Richard, Duke of Gloucester, all the children of Edward IV were declared illegitimate by the Great Council of 25 June 1483, including Elizabeth. This was confirmed by the Titulus Regius of January 1484, but it is reasonable to claim that this statute was not lawful since no ecclesiastical law court had ruled on the matter of Elizabeth's legitimacy. When her mother reached accommodation with Richard III and left sanctuary in March 1484, Elizabeth and the other princesses were often sent to Richard III's court. After Queen Anne Neville died in 1485, and maybe before, Elizabeth of York and King Richard were attracted to each other. It was rumoured that they would marry, especially as the king desperately needed new heirs. But such a marriage between an uncle and a niece needed papal dispensation. The rumours about such a proposed incestuous marriage contributed greatly to Richard's accelerated loss of credibility. The mere request for a dispensation would have meant acknowledging the legitimacy of Edward IV's birth, something which Richard had always doubted, and also acknowledging the validity of Edward IV's marriage. Faced with this conundrum, and on the advice of his council, Richard made a public announcement that he was not considering such a marriage and never had, and that he planned to send Elizabeth to Sheriff Hutton Castle to keep the young seventeenth earl of Warwick company. The king's advisors knew well that the king was lying; they had been forced to bring a conference of twelve clerics, doctors of divinity, to consider the question and persuade the king to drop the whole idea.

Once she was convinced that the princes in the Tower were dead, Queen Elizabeth Woodville secretly supported Henry Tudor and approved the marriage of her daughter Elizabeth to Henry VII. When Henry VII ascended the throne in 1485, the Tudor government reversed the Titulus Regius and legitimized Elizabeth and her sisters. Since matters of legitimacy were the province of the Church, not the Parliament, it can be argued that Elizabeth never was illegitimate. Elizabeth and King Henry VII were married on 18 January 1486; their marriage combined the Houses of Lancaster and York into the House of Tudor. It should be noted that a dispensation was obtained from the Pope, as Henry and Elizabeth were distantly related; they were fourth cousins, two generations removed, which presented a possible impediment, but it was outside the prohibited fourth degree of affinity. Like the English people, they recognized that the Church had the power over the validity of marriage. This remained true even after the English Reformation in 1534–35. The difference by then was that the king, not the Pope, controlled the English Church, and the king also had significant control over the Parliament.

There were multiple children from Elizabeth's marriage: Arthur (1486–1502), who was the Tudor Prince of Wales; Margaret (1489–1541), who married King James IV of Scotland; Henry VIII (1491–1547), who succeeded King Henry VII in 1509; Elizabeth (1492–1495), who died in early childhood; Mary (1496–1533), who first married King Louis XII of France and, after her husband's death, married Charles Brandon, the duke of Suffolk; Edmund (1499–1500), who died at less than one year of age; and Katherine (1503), who died at age one week.

Elizabeth of York's coronation did not occur until 25 November 1487, over twenty-two months after she was married to the king. Henry VII did not want to emphasize his wife's superior claim to the throne, which everybody knew was much stronger than his own. According to Sir Francis Bacon (1889), there was considerable unhappiness among the English people because Henry VII delayed Elizabeth's coronation for so long. But once it was done, the English people warmed to the Tudor king. The marriage was not a passionate one, but Henry was kind and respectful to his Yorkist wife, and Elizabeth was an accomplished queen. They drew closer to each other when Prince Arthur died and when several of their later children died early. Queen Elizabeth York died in 1503, it is thought with a post-partum infection following the birth of her last child, Katherine. The same infection probably also caused the infant Katherine to die.

It is often stated that Elizabeth was the model for the queen in the modern deck of playing cards; this was derived from her love of card and dice games. Some believe that she and Henry were the subjects of the nursery rhyme with these lyrics: "Sing a song of sixpence, a pocket full of rye. Four and twenty blackbirds baked in a pie; the king was in the counting house counting out his money, and the queen was in the parlour eating bread and honey," etc. The *Great Chronicle of London* had high praise for Elizabeth and described her as "the Gracious Queen" (Arlene Okerlund, 2005).

On 14 November 1501, Prince Arthur married Katherine of Aragon; Arthur was fifteen and Katherine was sixteen years old. They were sent to live at Ludlow, the traditional home of the Prince of Wales, where Arthur tragically died in April 1502. Prince Henry, when he became King Henry VIII in 1509, married the widowed Princess Katherine of Aragon, but later, when she produced no surviving male children, he wished to annul his marriage to her. Initially, this was based on the alleged proscription in the Old Testament book of Leviticus (chapter 20: verse 21) against marrying a brother's wife. This controversy and the failure of Pope Clement VII to grant the king's wish eventually resulted in the break with the Church of Rome, the English Reformation of 1535, and the birth of the Tudor Church of England (see the section on Henry VIII, a grandson of Edward IV).

Mary Plantagenet (1467–1482) was the second daughter of Edward IV. In 1481, she was promised in marriage to King Frederick I of Denmark, the heir of the king of Norway. But she died a year later at the age of fifteen years, in a year which turned out badly for her father, King Edward IV. She had a sumptuous funeral and was buried in the St George Chapel at Windsor Castle, presumably in the same large vault with Edward and Elizabeth.

Three hundred years later, in 1789, during repairs of Edward IV's tomb at Windsor Castle, a second, smaller vault was discovered containing two unmarked coffins, thought to contain two children (Mary of York,

2012). Neither coffin was opened or moved. The small vault was resealed and the larger tomb was marked, presumably on the outside, with the names George, Duke of Bedford, and Princess Mary Plantagenet. As neither coffin was opened, we are left to infer that neither coffin was individually marked with the supposed name of the unknown deceased. In 1810, during further work near the tomb, two more coffins were found in what was presumably a third vault. Each coffin had been individually and clearly marked as belonging to George, Duke of Bedford, or Princess Mary Plantagenet. These were removed to the main vault with Edward IV and Queen Elizabeth Woodville. Mary's marked coffin was briefly opened. A shock of pale golden hair and pale blue eyes were identified, consistent with Princess Mary. Although the report is poorly worded and therefore ambiguous, it appears that there may still remain two unidentified coffins in the adjoining vault found in 1789. There has been no permission from the Crown to carry out any further examination. The defenders of Richard III are most anxious to determine if the two unidentified coffins belong to the princes in the Tower, but so far no permission for examination has been granted. But even if it could be proved that those unidentified coffins contain the remains of King Edward V and his young brother, Richard, the conclusion of history would not be changed. The boys were certainly not seen after the summer of 1483. Nor were they seen in 1484 or in the first eight months of 1485. Richard III was still king during all that time, still controlled the Tower, and would still be called usurper and murderer. Obviously, by its refusal to further investigate, the Crown has grown to accept the unfortunate historical reputation of the last Yorkist king.

Cecily Plantagenet (1469–1507) was considered the most beautiful of Edward's beautiful daughters. She was widely promised in marriage, most especially to the heir of James III of Scotland, eventually King James IV, and later to Alexander, Duke of Albany, the younger brother of James III. Cecily played reserve in the marriage market for her sister Elizabeth; in the 1475 agreement at Picquigny, she was promised to the dauphin of France in the place of Elizabeth, if necessary. And Henry Tudor said he would marry Cecily if Elizabeth died. Edward IV paid her dowry for the Scottish Prince James in instalments, but the Scots were against the marriage. Edward IV sent Gloucester into Scotland in 1482 with a very large army; part of the dowry was recovered, and Edward cancelled the marriage arrangement.

Alexander, Duke of Albany, was briefly lieutenant in Scotland, but he was forced out and arrived in England. With the assistance of Richard III, he invaded Scotland with English cavalry, lost the Battle of Lochmaben in 1484, and died in France in 1485, before there was any marriage to Cecily.

By the arrangement of Richard III, Cecily was first briefly married to Lord Ralph Scrope, a much older man and a supporter of Richard III, in 1484, but the marriage was quickly annulled in 1485 after the death of King Richard. It is noted that Henry VII intended to marry Cecily if he could not marry her sister Elizabeth. In 1487, Cecily married John, Viscount Welles, not to be confused with his younger brother, Richard, Lord Welles, who was executed before the Battle of Empingham in 1470. John Welles, twenty years older than Cecily, was a half-brother of Margaret Beaufort, who probably suggested the marriage; the Tudors obviously considered Cecily's birth to be perfectly legitimate, consistent with the reversal of the 1484 Titulus Regius by the first Tudor Parliament.

Cecily attended her sister Elizabeth at her coronation in 1487. Cecily carried Prince Arthur at his christening and the train of Katherine of Aragon when Katherine later married Prince Arthur. Cecily remained faithful to her mother, Elizabeth Woodville, with frequent visits at Bermondsey. She did not attend the funeral of her mother in 1492 for unknown reasons, but she sent her husband, Lord Welles, instead. Cecily had two children by this marriage, Elizabeth and Anne, granddaughters of Edward IV, but not much is known of them, as they probably died at an early age. Young Elizabeth in 1498 was affianced to young Thomas Stanley, later the second earl of Derby, but Elizabeth died in the same year and the two were never married. The second daughter, Anne, was buried at the Church of the Austin Friars in London.

After her second husband, John Welles, died in 1499, Cecily fell in love with and married a squire named Thomas Kyme in 1503. This angered Henry VII, who had not given his permission. Cecily lost her dower properties, which were only partially restored at the request of her good friend Margaret Beaufort, the Queen Mother. Cecily retreated to the Isle of Wight and had two more children. Richard was born in 1505, and Margaret was born in 1507. They were never recognized by the royal family, not even by Cecily's sister Queen Elizabeth York. This, of course, was a perfect example of what happened in medieval times when a member of the royal family married a commoner; Cecily's mother, Queen Elizabeth Woodville, knew all about that. It is stated that both children survived, married, and had children, but nothing further is known. Cecily was buried at the Quarr Abbey on the Isle of Wight, but the abbey was destroyed during the English Reformation and Cecily's remains have not been found.

Edward V (1470–1483) was born on 2 November 1470 and was made the Prince of Wales in 1471. In 1473, he was made nominal president of the governing council of Wales and the Welsh Marches under the supervision of Anthony Woodville. In 1480, he was betrothed to Anne of Brittany, but they were never married. He succeeded Edward IV as king of England on 9 April 1483, but his throne was usurped by his uncle Richard III on 26 June 1483, after a nominal reign of only seventy-seven days. He disappeared in the Tower of London in 1483 and was almost certainly murdered, although defenders of Richard III continue to deny that Richard was responsible. Richard needed to justify his usurpation. For this, he had four choices for dealing with young Edward: attaint him in Parliament, declare him to be incompetent, accuse him of egregious misrule, or make his birth illegitimate. As Edward could not be accused of treason, incompetence, or misrule, the last became the favoured approach, a strategy well known in the Middle Ages. The marriage of his parents was declared invalid by the Great Council; Edward V and all his brothers and sisters were declared illegitimate, so none could ascend the throne, which allegedly made Richard the only lawful king. But the matter should have been lawfully decided by an ecclesiastical law court, not the Great Council.

Edward was born while Edward IV was in exile in Burgundy and while his mother was in the sanctuary at Westminster Abbey. He was taught the art of kingship and governance by his tutor, Bishop John Alcock, and by Anthony Woodville, under precise and detailed instructions from Edward IV as given in a royal letter, as described by Alison Weir (1999). When Edward IV died on 9 April 1483, young Edward was proclaimed in London as King Edward V. The prince might have made a fine king, especially had he been mentored and encouraged by a faithful Lord Protector, his uncle Richard, Duke of Gloucester.

When Edward was on his way to London for his accession ceremonial, the duke of Gloucester arrested his supervisors at Northampton and Stony

Stratford. The twelve-year-old prince made a determined defence of his mother's Woodville family, but to no avail. In the Tower, he was apparently very worried and depressed. He spent many hours praying and became convinced that he would die. From his knowledge of English history, he well knew the fate of deposed kings of England, namely Edward II, who was murdered with a spear in the rectum; Richard II, who was starved to death in prison at Pontefract; and Henry VI, who was stabbed and then killed with a crushing blow to the head while imprisoned in the Tower. In addition, Edward probably knew the fate of Prince Arthur, the duke of Brittany, heir to King Richard I. Arthur was murdered by his uncle King John, and his body was thrown into the River Seine in France.

Dr John Argentine attended Edward V frequently in the Tower, most likely for treatment of what might have been considered a common toothache. However, it was probably osteomyelitis, evidence for which was later found when Edward's skeleton was examined in 1933. According to the *Croyland Chronicle,* Edward V was not seen after the end of August 1483. According to Alison Weir (1999), he was murdered by suffocation, along with his younger brother, Richard, on or about 3 September 1483, and then was buried in the Tower. He was never lodged at Sheriff Hutton Castle and never found his way to Flanders.

Margaret Plantagenet was born on 19 April 1472, died on 11 December 1472, and was buried at Westminster Abbey at the age of eight months.

Richard of Shrewsbury (1473–1483) was born on 17 August 1473 at Ludlow Castle. He was created the duke of York in 1474. The king's critics considered this to be an unnecessary benefit for his own family, even though the king himself held the duchy of York from his father. In modern times, it has become traditional for the second son of the royal family to be made the duke of York; this is no longer considered an unnecessary benefit for the royal family.

When the fourth duke of Norfolk died in 1476, his only daughter, Anne Mowbray (1472–1481), became the countess of Norfolk in her own right. Prince Richard was given several of the duke's other titles, the earl of Nottingham and the earl of Warenne. In 1478, Richard and Anne, both children, were married with great ceremony and celebration, after which they were titled the duke and duchess of Norfolk. But the estate remained with the duchess. However, in 1481, Anne died at the age of nearly ten years. It was argued that her inheritance should have passed to her Mowbray heirs, Viscount William Berkeley and Lord John Howard, as Prince Richard, aged eight years, might have been considered too young to inherit by marriage. Both Berkeley and Howard were grandsons of Thomas Mowbray, the first duke of Norfolk, who was also the great-great-grandfather of Anne Mowbray.

The king knew that there was a problem, so he had the Parliament pass a law which gave Prince Richard the entire duchy of Norfolk, both the title and the estate, for life. In effect, Edward IV took the duchy from the Mowbray heirs and gave it to his own son Richard. The king obtained Viscount Berkeley's consent by paying off his very considerable debt, but for Howard he made no provision. The reason for this remains obscure, but, apparently, he and his advisors thought it was not necessary. This is considered one of the several times when the king may have abused the laws of inheritance. The injured party, Lord John Howard, was one of the king's most trusted advisors, but the inheritance problem may explain why he did not support King Edward V; instead, Lord Howard supported the usurpation by Richard III.

Nevertheless, if Parliament could control inheritance, as most authorities agree, then the king was perfectly justified, as marriage sometimes changes the line of inheritance. A good example would be the sixteenth earl of Warwick. He, his father, and his grandfather successively inherited through their respective marriages. Parliament and the king may well have been correct in their assessment of the situation in the case of Norfolk.

The common ancestor of Anne Mowbray, John Howard, and William Berkeley was Thomas Mowbray (1366–1399), the first duke of Norfolk. His duchy was confiscated in 1398 during the disturbance at the end of the reign of Richard II. The duke had two sons, Thomas Mowbray (1385–1405) and John Mowbray (1392–1432). The older son, Thomas, was executed in 1405, so the younger son, John, became the second duke of Norfolk when the duchy was restored to the Mowbray family by King Edward II in 1325. The second duke was succeeded by his single son, another John Mowbray, the third duke of Norfolk, the Earl Marshal who was decisive for Edward IV at the Battle of Towton in 1461. The third duke was succeeded by his single son, yet another John Mowbray, the fourth duke of Norfolk, who alienated King Edward, died in 1476, and was succeeded by his daughter Anne Mowbray, the countess of Norfolk in her own right. She was later married to Edward IV's younger son, Prince Richard.

The first duke of Norfolk also had two daughters, Margaret (1388–1459) and the younger Isabel. Margaret married Sir John Howard. Their son, also John Howard, was Edward IV's fine supporter. Isabel married James Berkeley, and their son was Viscount William Berkeley. The line from the first duke of Norfolk to Anne Mowbray was the direct line; it left Howard and Berkeley two generations behind. Edward probably considered them eliminated; on the other hand, Howard and Berkeley considered that Anne had no direct heir, so their claim was viable. After their marriage in 1478, Prince Richard and Countess Anne became the duke and duchess of Norfolk, with Anne still holding the estate. When Anne died in 1481, the king and Parliament ruled that young Richard should inherit the estate from his deceased wife.

The king was unhappy with the fourth duke of Norfolk for his continued regional disputes and private warfare activity, especially with the Paston family over Caister Castle in Norfolk. No doubt, the king took this belated opportunity to reduce the Norfolk power and incorporate it into his own family. He followed the suggestion of Sir John Fortesque that the king should be the wealthiest man in the kingdom.

Some historians claim that Anne Mowbray's mother, Elizabeth Talbot, the duchess of Norfolk, the younger sister of Lady Eleanor Butler, supported Richard III at the usurpation because Edward was allegedly so unkind to her older sister (Eleanor), in 1461. But a far more likely reason is the king's later treatment of the Norfolk inheritance.

After the death of Edward IV in 1483, young Richard was taken by his mother to the sanctuary at Westminster. On 16 June 1483, he was sent to join his brother, Edward V, in the Tower. The two princes were not seen again after the end of August 1483. According to Alison Weir (1999), they were murdered on or about 3 September 1483, at the orders of Richard III. There were claims that Prince Richard was smuggled out of England, that he was taken from the sanctuary, and that it was a changeling boy who was sent to the Tower in his place. This was one of the themes of Philippa Gregory's story *The White Queen* (2009). It has been claimed that Richard later returned from Flanders as Perkin Warbeck, but there is no good evidence for any of this. A much better suggestion about Warbeck's ancestry has been made: that he was the son of a Tournai merchant boatman.

When the Archbishop of Canterbury went to the sanctuary to request young Richard's presence with his brother, Edward V, in the Tower, the Queen Mother made a magnificent defence of her right to keep her younger son. Later, when Elizabeth was told that the princes in the Tower were certainly missing and therefore dead, her reaction was mortified grief. She regretted sending Prince Richard to the Tower and knew that it was a big mistake. From her eloquent resistance to the transfer of Richard out of the sanctuary, and from her hysterical grief when she was later told of his certain death, it can be readily argued that there was no transfer of young Richard to Flanders or any other place, and no substitution with a changeling boy. Either that or else Elizabeth was a magnificent actress.

Anne Plantagenet (1475–1511), in 1480, was promised to two-year-old Philip the Handsome, the heir to Maximillian, the Holy Roman Emperor, and Mary, the duchess of Burgundy. But the marriage of Anne and Philip never occurred, as the European marriage policies of Edward IV proved less than successful in 1482. Edward died the following year. Anne wore the chrisom at the christenings of Prince Arthur in 1486 and Princess Margaret in 1489.

In 1495, long after Edward IV was dead, Anne married young *Thomas Howard (1473–1554),* the grandson of John Howard. Thomas was the second earl of Surrey. Much later, in 1524, after Anne died, he was the third duke of Norfolk. He was a prolonged survivor; much later, he was called the Old Duke, and became a controversial elder statesman during the Tudor period.

The father of Anne's husband, her father-in-law, also named Thomas Howard (1443–1524), the first earl of Surrey and, later, the second duke of Norfolk, commanded under Richard III at Bosworth Field in 1485 and took over when his father, John Howard, was killed. His reputation has been besmirched because it was alleged that he did not fight hard at Bosworth. Some claim that he saw defeat early and may even have surrendered, although this would be hard to prove. Later, this same Thomas Howard was the famous victor at Flodden Field over the invading Scots in 1513, which happened while King Henry VIII was engaged in fruitless military operations in France. With his reputation restored, Thomas was made the second duke of Norfolk by a grateful Henry VIII.

The grandfather of Anne's husband was John Howard (1425–1485), one of Edward IV's most loyal followers who, later, was also a loyal ally of Richard III. The last Yorkist king made John Howard the Earl Marshal and the Yorkist first duke of Norfolk after the usurpation. John Howard died fighting for Richard III at Bosworth in 1485. There was never any question that he remained loyal to King Richard, nor any question that he fought hard at Bosworth. According to the numeric sequence of the dukes of Norfolk, the Tudor rulers were apparently happy to ignore the reign of Richard III and describe the first duke of Norfolk in King Richard's reign as in the Tudor line, given that he was still alive on the day before Bosworth, when Henry claimed he was already king of England!

By her marriage to the second earl of Surrey, later the third duke of Norfolk, Anne had four children. Three died in infancy, and one, a boy, not surprisingly also named Thomas Howard, died in 1508 at age twelve years. These were grandchildren of King Edward IV. Anne was titled the countess of Surrey, but she was never the duchess of Norfolk, as she died before her husband acceded to the duchy in 1524. Anne did attend the funeral of her mother, Dowager Queen Elizabeth Woodville, in 1492. Anne was first buried at Thetford Priory, but her remains were later removed to the Church of St Michael the Archangel in Framlingham, Norfolk, which is the burial site of many of the Howard family and where her husband, the Old Duke, was also later buried. If twelve-year-old Thomas had survived, then it seems clear that he, too, would have been watched closely by the suspicious Tudor government. He was considered legitimate and might have been a Yorkist king.

Anne's husband, later the third duke of Norfolk, had an active life after his wife was dead in 1511. Thomas was a good soldier and also a big help to his father, the victor at Flodden Field in 1513. He became a close friend of Henry VIII and was on the Privy Council from 1516. In 1521, he crushed an Irish rebellion. He led efforts to annul the king's marriage to Queen Katherine and was made Earl Marshal and Lord High Steward. His second marriage to Elizabeth Stafford was a disastrous failure, ending in scandal and a permanent separation. Thomas put down the Pilgrimage of Grace Rebellion; authored the more Catholic Six Articles of Religion; and quarrelled with Chancellor Thomas Cromwell. Thomas Howard was at the height of his power when King Henry VIII married his niece Katherine Howard. However, at the fall of the young queen, he was attainted and sent to the Tower, where only the king's death in 1447 saved him from execution. He remained in the Tower for the complete six-year reign of King Edward VI. After Queen Mary released him and restored him to favour, he put down the Wyatt Rebellion. Not long after that, in 1554, he died and was buried at Framlingham in Norfolk, it is assumed near his first wife, Anne of York, the dowager countess of Surrey.

George Plantagenet (1477–1479) was the Yorkist duke of Bedford; he died in early childhood and was buried in the St George Chapel at Windsor Castle.

Katherine Plantagenet (1479–1527) was betrothed in 1482 to John, heir to the king of Castile, but the marriage never happened following the death of Edward IV in 1483, when Katherine was only four years old. In 1487, there was a complicated marriage negotiation between Henry VII and James III of Scotland: Katherine was to be betrothed to James Stewart, the duke of Ross, the second son of James III; the Scottish king was to marry Katherine's mother, Dowager Queen Elizabeth Woodville; and another sister, the beautiful Cecily, was promised to James Stewart, the duke of Rothesay, the future James IV. None of this happened, as James III died at the Battle of Sauchiburn in 1488. James IV did not continue the negotiations but would later marry Margaret Tudor, a granddaughter of Edward IV.

In 1492, Katherine, aged thirteen years, attended the funeral of her mother, Elizabeth, the former queen. Later, in 1495, the sixteen-year-old Katherine married Sir William Courtenay (1475–1511), heir to Edward Courtenay, the Tudor earl of Devon, who had worked so hard against Richard III in favour of Henry Tudor. Katherine had three children, Henry Courtenay (1496–1539), Edward (1497–1502), and Margaret (1499–1512), all grandchildren of Edward IV. Young Edward died early, and young Margaret choked to death on a fish bone. Only Henry Courtenay survived past childhood. He became a serious Yorkist claimant to the throne; he was an earl of Devon but was better known as the marquis of Exeter.

William's father and Katherine's father-in-law, Edward Courtenay, took part in the Buckingham Rebellion and was attainted after it failed.

During the years 1483–85, Edward Courtenay took part in the secret negotiations between Elizabeth Woodville and Margaret Beaufort about the planned marriage of Henry VII to Princess Elizabeth of York. It appears that, despite his attainder for his part in the Buckingham Rebellion, he was never captured. He had played the dangerous role of courier in the conspiracy. Edward Courtenay fought for Henry VII at Bosworth and was created the Tudor first earl of Devon for his service.

In 1504, during the reign of Henry VII, Katherine's husband, William, was attainted and confined in the Tower on charges of Yorkist association. Allegedly, he corresponded with Edmund, the third earl of Suffolk, who planned to seize the throne. With her husband incarcerated, Katherine was destitute and had to be largely supported by her sister Queen Elizabeth York. When his father, Edward, died in 1509, William did not inherit the title earl of Devon because of his attainder. He was released from the Tower later in 1509 at the accession of Henry VIII and restored to his title in 1511 as Henry VIII's first earl of Devon. But William died one month later, at which time Katherine's eldest son, Henry Courtenay, became Henry VIII's second earl of Devon. Henry was a devoted servant to Henry VIII, who made him the marquis of Exeter in 1525. But later, there would be a big problem, due to what is known as the Exeter Plot.

Katherine never married again; she took vows of chastity in 1511, soon after her beloved William died. Katherine Courtenay was godmother to Prince Henry, the firstborn son of Henry VIII and Queen Katherine of Aragon, but the boy died at the age of not quite two months in 1511. Katherine died in 1527; she was buried at St Peter's Church in Tiverton, Devon, where there is a fine statue of her in the garden. Katherine's surviving son, Henry Courtenay (1496–1539), the (Henry VIII) second earl of Devon, the marquis of Exeter, married first Elizabeth Grey (1505–1519), and second Gertrude Blount (1502–1558), who was a devout Catholic. By his second marriage, Henry Courtenay had a son named Edward Courtenay (1527–1556), who was later Queen Mary's first earl of Devon. Because of their Catholic allegiance, Henry and Gertrude fell afoul of Thomas Cromwell, the Lord Chancellor. In 1438, Henry, Gertrude, and their eleven-year-old son, Edward, were all sent to the Tower, along with Margaret, the countess of Salisbury, the daughter of Clarence, her son Henry Pole, known as Baron Montagu, and her grandson young Henry Pole.

Henry Courtenay, the marquis of Exeter, was executed in 1439, along with Baron Montagu. Gertrude was released in 1540; young Henry Pole died of starvation in the Tower in 1542; and young Edward Courtenay was only released by Queen Mary I in 1553 after a prolonged imprisonment. Their crime was association and correspondence with Cardinal Reginald Pole, who was self-exiled in Europe and who had become a fierce opponent of Henry VIII and the English Reformation. The countess of Salisbury, never released from the Tower, was brutally executed in 1541; her additional crime was that she gave birth to Reginald Pole!

The Tudor monarchs, Henry VII and Henry VIII especially, were relentless in their determination to control the Yorkists. It mattered not whether they were Courtenays (descendants of Edward's daughter Katherine) or Poles (descendants of Edward's niece Margaret, the countess of Salisbury) or De la Poles (descendants of Edward's sister Elizabeth), as long as they were part of the family of King Edward IV. All were considered threats to the Tudor throne. It became very serious after the death of Queen Elizabeth York in 1503. The ghost of England's great King Edward IV, who was long dead but much alive in the minds of many, haunted the Tudor monarchs for over a century. In the case of Katherine Courtenay especially, a daughter of Edward IV, nobody, not anybody, considered the king's Woodville marriage to be invalid. Katherine's descendants were considered dangerous threats to the Tudor throne.

Bridget Plantagenet (1480–1517), the last daughter of Edward IV, entered a Dominican convent at Dartmouth Priory at the age of ten years. She was never married. Her mother, Elizabeth, tired of the unjust world, must have decided that she wanted Bridget to be reared by the nuns. Bridget maintained correspondence with her oldest sister, Queen Elizabeth York, who paid for much of her upkeep. The young princess left the convent only once, which was to attend the funeral of her mother, Dowager Queen Elizabeth Woodville, in 1492. It can be presumed that when she was old enough, she took the vows. She was later buried at the Dartmouth Priory.

The Concubines of Edward IV, Who Might Have Been Part of the Family of the King

Jane Shore (1445–late age) was the daughter of a London merchant. Her proper name was Elizabeth, and her maiden name was Lambert. She married a London mercer named William Shore, but the marriage was annulled in 1476 on grounds of her husband's impotency. The Pope had three bishops hear the evidence and decide the case; it should be noted that the case was decided by a church court, not by the civil authorities. Jane's liaison with Edward IV began in 1476 after his return from France and lasted until the king's death in 1483; there was no known issue of this relationship. As the king said, he had three mistresses: "one merry, one holy and one wily." Jane was undoubtedly the merry mistress, beautiful, charming, fun-loving, and quick-witted. Aside from the king, she seduced many other men with her charm, including Lord William Hastings; Thomas Grey, the marquis of Dorset; and even the solicitor Thomas Lynom, who Richard III appointed to investigate her. After the death of Hastings, Richard, Duke of Gloucester, imprisoned her and made her do public penance for her alleged multiple moral transgressions and for her alleged role in the Hastings Conspiracy with the Woodvilles. But her public appearance in scanty clothing only aroused more sympathy for her – and more antagonism against the duke of Gloucester. She was thought to have carried messages between Hastings and the Queen Mother Elizabeth in sanctuary; this seems improbable, since Elizabeth did not trust Jane, for obvious reasons. But it cannot be excluded and may help explain Jane's public penance and brief imprisonment at Ludgate.

In 1484, she married Thomas Lynom with the reluctant permission of Richard III. Under Henry VII, Thomas was clerk controller for Arthur, Prince of Wales, at Ludlow Castle. Jane had one child and lived out her days as a respectable married woman. Sir Thomas More saw her when she was much older and remarked favourably upon her residual beauty.

Elizabeth Lucy (1444–1502) was sometimes known as Elizabeth Waite, possibly her married name. She became the king's mistress in the fall of 1461, succeeding Lady Eleanor Butler in the king's affections. There were multiple children associated with Edward IV, who gave the children his acknowledgement. Elizabeth Plantagenet was born in 1462; she married Sir Thomas Lumley in 1477. Arthur Plantagenet, later the Viscount Lisle, was born about 1463. He held important posts under Henry VIII: squire of the body; vice admiral of England; warden of the Cinque Ports; and governor of Calais. He was created Viscount Lisle in 1523, was later wrongly accused of treason, and died in the Tower in 1542. Grace Plantagenet, born about 1465, was a lady-in-waiting at the Yorkist court; she alone among her father's biological daughters visited Elizabeth Woodville frequently during the reign of Henry VII as the star of the former queen faded. In fact, Anne Easter Smith (2009) claimed that she lived with Elizabeth at Bermondsey Abbey. We know for certain that Grace was one of the few who accompanied Elizabeth's funeral barge upriver to Windsor Castle, which confirms a very close relationship with the dowager queen.

Elizabeth Lucy may have been the wisest or wiliest mistress, but, like many other women, she must have loved the king. She maintained a very low profile, remained obscured in the background, and kept out of trouble. Dr Shaw, other prelates, and the duke of Buckingham said in 1483 that Edward had a marriage contract with her, but, like most liars, they were confused and could not keep their concocted story straight. Elizabeth Lucy is known to have denied any marriage contract with Edward when in 1464 she was questioned by Cecily, the dowager duchess of York, and other of the unhappy magnates before Edward IV married Elizabeth Woodville (More, 2005; Ellis, Grafton, and Hall, 1809). Those sympathetic to Richard III often accuse Sir Thomas More of deliberately confusing Dame Elizabeth Lucy with Lady Eleanor Butler as part of an alleged Tudor conspiracy to suppress the name of Lady Eleanor. But Sir Thomas More based his story on the testimonies of his father, John More, a London judge; John Roper, his son-in-law, who was later Attorney General for Henry VIII; Bishop Morton; and others who very likely attended the Shaw speech on 22 June 1483 and the Buckingham speech on 24 June 1483. We cannot be sure of this, but neither can we be sure of the alleged Tudor conspiracy, which seems to have been an invention of the later defenders of Richard III.

Lady Eleanor Butler (1435–1468) was the older sister of Elizabeth Talbot, who married John Mowbray, the fourth duke of Norfolk. Eleanor's father was the heroic John Talbot, the twice-married Lancastrian first earl of Shrewsbury who died at Castillon in 1453. Her half-brother was the second earl of Shrewsbury, who died in 1460 defending Henry VI at the Battle of Northampton. Her half-nephew was the third earl of Shrewsbury

(1448–1473), who joined Warwick in 1470 at the Readoption of Henry VI and who later died unexpectedly at the age of twenty-five years. Her half-grand-nephew was George Talbot, the fourth earl of Shrewsbury (1468–1538), who was alive in 1483, aged fifteen years. It was the latter, or his relatives and advisors, who might have confirmed Bishop Stillington's tale about the 1461 marriage contract. But so far as anybody knows, they did not.

Eleanor was the widow of a London merchant named Thomas Butler. According to John Ashdown-Hill (2010), there is no evidence that she ever had any children of her own. When Eleanor married Thomas Butler in 1449, his father, Lord Sudeley, gave the couple three manor houses. When her husband died in 1459, Eleanor returned one manor house to Lord Sudeley but retained the other two manors, both in Warwickshire. It is not known how Eleanor met Edward IV. One common story is that soon after he became king, she asked him to restore a dower property for her. But some believe that this story is not true (Ashdown-Hill, 2010). Another story is that she met the king as he returned from Towton in 1461, passing through Norwich.

It was alleged that Eleanor refused Edward's sexual advances until a marriage contract arrangement had been made. There was no documentation, so far as we know, only Stillington's unsupported statement twenty-two years later that he was the single witness to a marriage contract. According to R. H. Helmholz (1974), under canon law it would have taken a second witness to prove this contract in an ecclesiastical law court. This would be of critical importance, as many critics believed that Stillington lied. Some have claimed that Lady Eleanor had a child named Edward de Wigmore who was born and died in 1468, the same year when she died of an unknown illness. It was suggested that Edward IV was the father, but their intimate relationship was long over by late 1461. Edward never paid Lady Eleanor an annuity, but it is alleged that he did give her rental property in Wiltshire in 1462 (Ashdown-Hill, 2010). Some historians interpret this to mean that Edward paid her to keep quiet about the alleged marriage contract, but he may also have done this for any number of routine reasons. He was a generous king who frequently awarded properties to any number of his subjects, especially to friends. Before she died in 1468, Eleanor deeded some property to her sister, the duchess of Norfolk.

After she died, her will passed other property to other heirs (Armstrong-Hill, 2010). Susan Higginbotham (2013), always sceptical about the 1461 contract, has stated that Eleanor could make neither assignment under English law without the consent of her husband. This suggests that Eleanor did not consider herself to be married at that time.

Lady Eleanor Butler may have been the king's holy mistress. Some have unfairly called her the Holy Harlot. So far as we know, she did not have multiple sexual affairs. She was a patron of the Corpus Christi College at Cambridge University, and she endowed a priestly fellowship there. She became a lay member of a tertiary order of the Carmelite Priory at Norwich in 1463. This did not mean that she became a nun, but she did follow a devout religious life. When she died in 1468, she was buried under the choir stall of the Carmelite Priory Church in Norwich. Eleanor's alleged marriage contract with Edward IV in 1461 played a major role in the downfall of the Royal House of York, especially in the hands of Richard III and Bishop Stillington. No doubt, Lady Eleanor's Lancastrian father would have cheered from the grave, but Edward IV in his tomb at Windsor would have reached for his sword.

It was claimed that Lady Eleanor was named in the 1461 marriage contract discussed at council in early June 1483, but the claim was poorly documented and appeared doubtful. On two different occasions, 22 June and 24 June, Elizabeth Lucy was named in discussions of the alleged 1461 marriage contract (More, 2005). Surprisingly, Mancini (1989), quoting Richard, Duke of Gloucester, in late June, even suggested that Edward could have been married to Princess Bona of Savoy. It was suggested that the earl of Warwick, standing in as proxy, married her to Edward IV, but Warwick never confirmed this. On 25 June 1483, it is considered that Lady Eleanor was named for the first time in discussions of the 1461 contract, but again the documentation was poor. However, in the Parliamentary Act of 1484, the Titulus Regius, Eleanor was definitely named as the alleged bride in the 1461 marriage contract. This probably confirmed that she was also named at the meeting of the Great Council on 25 June 1483. Elizabeth Lucy was known to have denied a contract when questioned in 1464. She was alive in 1483, as was Princess Bona, and it was possible that the French court could have denied a contract or a proxy marriage. Although it is possible that Lady Eleanor may have been named in early June 1483, it is also possible that Gloucester's advisors only decided to name Lady Eleanor on 25 June 1483 when they understood that she had died in 1468 and could not be expected to deny involvement in the alleged 1461 contract.

The Pretenders Who Impersonated the Heirs of Edward IV

Lambert Simnel (1477–1525) was not an issue of Edward IV but was of humble birth. Under the guidance of Richard Symonds, an Oxford priest, Simnel impersonated Edward Plantagenet, the seventeenth earl of Warwick, the son of the duke of Clarence and his wife, Isabel, and the nephew of Edward IV. Soon after Bosworth, Henry VII imprisoned the seventeenth earl of Warwick in the Tower as a precautionary measure against rebellion in his name. Because Edward V, Prince Richard, and Richard III were all dead, Edward was the male Yorkist heir to the throne. It was alleged that Lambert Simnel was Warwick who had escaped from the Tower; but the real Warwick remained in the Tower, which fact Henry VII had little trouble demonstrating by his public exhibition of the prince at St Paul's Church. On 24 May 1487, Simnel was crowned as Edward VI in Dublin, where the Irish had always supported the House of York and were only too willing to be duped. The earl of Lincoln supported Simnel, raised forces in Burgundy, and conferred with his aunt Margaret, the dowager duchess of Burgundy, who supplied fifteen hundred mercenaries together with transport ships. Lincoln then joined the rebels in Ireland. It is said that Bishop Stillington also supported Lambert Simnel, as illogical as that sounds. But Stillington had destroyed the princes by his invented tale, and ill fate had destroyed Richard III, so the seventeenth earl of Warwick was all that remained for an embittered Yorkist who was largely ignored by both Richard III and Henry VII.

Simnel's forces under the Lord Lieutenant, the earl of Kildare, landed in Lancashire. Near Newark, they were defeated at Stoke Field on 16 June 1487. Simnel was pardoned by Henry VII, as he was only a ten-year-old boy manipulated by adults, and was given a position in the palace kitchens. Later, he became a falconer in the royal household. Lords Kildare and Lincoln and Sir Thomas Broughton were killed in the battle; Richard Symonds was captured and imprisoned for life; and Lord Lovell escaped across the River Trent and was never seen again. Some claim that soldiers walled up Lovell in his domestic wine cellar and left him to die of starvation. As for Stillington, the bishop of Bath, he died a lonely man in prison at Windsor.

Perkin Warbeck (1474–1499) had a striking physical resemblance to Edward IV, George, Duke of Clarence, and Richard of Shrewsbury, noted by many observers. He claimed to be Richard of Shrewsbury, the younger of the princes in the Tower. It was claimed that he was smuggled out of England in 1483 and that a changeling boy was sent to the Tower to join Edward V, but there is no good evidence for such a fascinating story. Perkin was supported by Margaret, the dowager duchess of Burgundy, Edward IV's younger sister, who should have known him but who may simply have chosen to be deceived by him; such was her hatred for Henry VII. In Margaret's defence, she left England in 1468, well before Richard was born in 1473. But Margaret visited for three months in 1480 and should have been familiar with the prince. Sir Robert Clifford, a diplomat sent by Henry VII, reported back that the young man was undoubtedly Prince Richard; that report must have upset King Henry VII. Margaret supplied Warbeck with men and ships; he later led unsuccessful rebellions against King Henry VII, much to Margaret's disappointment.

In 1495, Perkin Warbeck landed at Deal in Kent. His forces were immediately routed by royal troops, and he fled back to sea. In Ireland, he besieged Waterford, a town loyal to Henry Tudor. Warbeck failed to take the town and fled to Scotland. He was welcomed by King James IV and married the king's cousin, the beautiful Lady Catherine Gordon. In 1496, he invaded Northumberland with Scottish forces but aroused no English support and so retreated. He was forced to leave Scotland when Henry VII made peace with James IV. Back in Ireland, he again besieged Waterford but failed once more. In 1497, he landed in Cornwall, was welcomed, was proclaimed King Richard IV at Bodmin Moor, and, with a Cornish army of six thousand, advanced on Exeter and then on Taunton. But as the royal army advanced, he lost his nerve. He deserted his Cornish army, fled for his life, and was soon captured while seeking sanctuary at Beaulieu Abbey.

In his confession, Perkin Warbeck identified by name his father, mother, paternal grandfather, and maternal grandfather, all residents of Tournai in Flanders. His family confirmed his identity (Wroe, 2003). In addition, he could not identify the marquis of Dorset or the earl of Arundel, both of whom he should have known if he was Prince Richard. Warbeck was imprisoned in the Tower, joining the seventeenth earl of Warwick. It is then alleged that Warbeck and Warwick formed a conspiracy to take over the Tower, escape the prison, and overthrow Henry VII; for this, they were both executed for treason in 1499.

Records in Tournai revealed that Warbeck was indeed the son of Jehan de Warbecque, a boatman and, later, a municipal official. There seems to be no actual proof that Perkin was born in Tournai, but in those days, such records were seldom kept properly. It leaves open the question of whether or not he was born in Flanders.

But there have been alternatives to this story, given Warbeck's striking resemblance to the Yorkist princes and also his courtly manners and knowledge of Latin. Anne Easter Smith (2009) claims that he was an illegitimate son of George, Duke of Clarence, Edward's younger brother. George had acknowledged him and paid the boy's maternal grandparents for his support in England. When Clarence was executed in 1478, Edward IV sent the four-year-old boy to live with his mother, Katherine de Faro, who had married Jehan de Warbecque in Tournai, where apparently the child was not treated well. This version of the story may explain why Warbeck had such a resemblance to the Yorkist princes. Margaret, the dowager duchess of Burgundy, was made aware of the boy. Having no children of her own, she paid his mother and took him to her palace at Binche. There, he learned to ride horses well, became a proficient swordsman, and learned French, English, and Latin. In 1485, he was sent to Antwerp to hide him from the Tudor court in England. He was often at sea in the merchant marine service. In 1489, he was employed by Sir Edward Brampton, a famous Jewish merchant operating out of Lisbon. In 1491, in the service of a silk merchant named Pierre Jean Meno, Warbeck was at Cork in Ireland, where Yorkist partisans noted how much he resembled the younger son of Edward IV, namely Prince Richard. Also in 1491, he was at the French court of Charles VIII, where the king was convinced that he was Prince Richard. But after the Treaty of Etaples between France and England, Perkin left France and went to Burgundy in 1492.

Duchess Margaret also claimed that he was indeed Richard, even though allegedly she may have known from London that he was a royal bastard. Margaret had Perkin better learn English, familiarize himself with his alleged Yorkist family, and trained in courtly manners and the knightly arts so that he could reclaim his royal inheritance in England. Margaret provided him with ships and soldiers. He landed at Deal in 1495, as previously described. An additional twist to this story is that he was rather an illegitimate son of Edward IV, not of Clarence. We shall never know, except that Edward never acknowledged him – although he acknowledged three others.

The evidence strongly suggests that Warbeck was not Prince Richard. A few doubters, forced to accept this conclusion, have suggested that Warbeck was the stalking horse for the princes, who were alleged to remain safe in Flanders. If the princes in the Tower survived and went to Flanders, then Duchess Margaret, the arch-enemy of Henry VII, never heard about them, never found them, and never attempted to restore them to their rightful place. Considering the hatred Margaret bore for Henry Tudor and her repeated attempts to overthrow him using pretenders, this means, almost certainly, that the princes never reached Flanders.

The Famous Grandchildren of Edward IV, and Their Descendants

Margaret Tudor (1489–1541) was the oldest daughter of King Henry VII and Queen Elizabeth York. Following the ill-named Treaty of Perpetual Peace between England and Scotland in 1502 and an initial proxy marriage, Margaret married King James IV in 1503 and was queen consort of Scotland. There were six children of this marriage; all except James V (1510–1542) died in infancy. When Henry VIII went to war in France, James IV invaded England with a large army. He suffered ignominious defeat and his own death at Flodden Field in 1513. Margaret was regent for her three-year-old son, King James V, but in 1514, she married Archibald Douglas, the sixth earl of Angus, and was replaced as regent by the brother of James IV, John Stewart, the duke of Albany, in 1515. Margaret gave up custody of her son James V to the new regent and fled to England, where she gave birth to Lady Margaret Douglas. In 1517, Margaret Tudor returned to Scotland and was reconciled with Albany; she decided that she wanted to divorce Angus and made application to Rome. There was constant feuding among the Scottish lords. Border wars with England resumed.

In 1524, the Scottish Parliament declared the regency ended, so James V, aged fourteen years, ruled Scotland with Margaret as his chief advisor.

Unfortunately, Angus took control of James V and ruled instead. In 1527, the Pope granted Margaret's divorce from Angus. In 1528, she married Henry Stewart, a distant cousin of her first husband, James IV. James V then forced Angus out, and Margaret, with Henry Stewart, ruled Scotland in the name of James V. There was a renewed Anglo-Scottish Treaty in 1534; but a planned meeting between Henry VIII and James V in 1536, designed to discuss church reforms, failed when James V did not attend, much to the annoyance of Henry VIII. In 1536, James V married Madeleine, the daughter of Francis I, the king of France, but the princess died. In 1538, James V married Mary of Guise. They had two children who died in infancy, and then a famous daughter, Mary Queen of Scots, in 1542. Meanwhile, Margaret Tudor, weary of unruly Scotland, had died in 1541.

Margaret's daughter Lady Margaret Douglas (1515–1578) married Matthew Stuart, the fourth earl of Lennox, at which time she was titled the countess of Lennox. She became the mother of Lord Henry Darnley (1545–1567), who later married Mary Queen of Scots, the daughter of James V.

James V died in 1542, a year after Margaret had died; and the six-day-old infant Mary, the great-great-granddaughter of King Edward IV, was Queen of Scots. As Scotland was unruly, Mary was sent to France for safety. Her mother, Mary of Guise, was regent for her in Scotland. At the age of sixteen years in France, Mary married the dauphin and was very soon the queen of France. But her husband died and Mary was alone.

The Protestant Reformation occurred in Scotland in the years 1559–60. Despite warnings, the Catholic Mary returned to Scotland in 1461. At first, she was welcomed and did well as queen regnant, but her Catholic faith was always a problem in a newly Protestant land. She made two unfortunate marriages, first to Lord Darnley, who was murdered in 1567, and second to James Hepburn, the earl of Bothwell, the probable murderer of Darnley, also in 1567. The young queen needed protection from the arrogant magnates. This second marriage was forced upon her by Bothwell's sexual assault. Her son James, fathered by Lord Darnley, was born in 1566, so then Scotland had a prince who could be king. As a result of her unpopular marriage to Bothwell, Mary was forced to abdicate and was deposed by the Protestant lords; her loyal forces were defeated at the

Battle of Langside, near Glasgow. She fled to England in 1568, where she was imprisoned for nineteen years by Queen Elizabeth Tudor and executed in 1587 for plotting against the English Crown. After her abdication, her son, James VI, ruled Scotland, initially with regents, but later in his own name. Only gradually did he gain control of Scotland. However, Scottish politics continued to be turbulent. Following the death of Queen Elizabeth Tudor in 1603, James VI was probably glad to travel south at the invitation of the English government and rule as King James I of England. He was a great-great-great-grandson of King Edward IV. It should be obvious that, like all of Edward's direct descendants, James was not considered to be illegitimate.

Henry VIII (1491–1547) was the third child of Henry VII and Queen Elizabeth York. In 1505, Henry was betrothed to Katherine of Aragon, the widow of Henry's older brother, Prince Arthur. But King Henry VII did not allow the marriage because the dowry remained not fully paid. The marriage had to wait until 1509, when Henry was king following the death of his father. Between 1510 and 1519, Queen Katherine had eight pregnancies, but many ended in miscarriage or stillbirth. A young prince named Henry died at the age of two months. There was only a single survivor, Princess Mary, later Queen Mary I.

Henry VIII renewed the claim of English kings to the French throne in 1510. His campaign against Bayonne in 1511 was an ignominious failure, but his campaign against Therouanne in 1512 was more successful. The English won the Battle of the Spurs, so named because the French forces fled on their horses without a fight. While the king was busy in France, in 1513, the English won the great Battle of Flodden Field over the Scots. King James IV was killed. Queen Katherine, acting as regent, played a significant organizational role in assisting the English commander, Thomas Howard, the first earl of Surrey, the son of John Howard who died at Bosworth. Cardinal Thomas Wolsey came to power by 1514; he was charged with repairing the damage caused by Henry's bad policy in France. In 1520, Henry made peace with Francis I, the king of France, at the famous Field of the Cloth of Gold meeting organized by Cardinal Wolsey.

Henry VIII became obsessed with his lack of a male heir. He sent his bishops, including Bishop Stephen Gardiner and Bishop Edward Foxe, to

Rome to ask for an annulment of his marriage to Queen Katherine. The bishops argued from the Old Testament book of Leviticus (Chapter 20: verse 21), saying that a man may not marry his brother's wife. In fact, the passage only says that the marriage should be without children; it does not forbid the marriage. Katherine's representatives argued that her first marriage to young Prince Arthur was not consummated and was therefore invalid, so her second marriage to Henry was lawful. It was also argued that the alleged proscription in the book of Leviticus was based on King Henry's brother's being still alive, which was not so in the case of Prince Arthur. In Rome, the cardinals leaned in favour of Queen Katherine, while the Pope, Clement VII, was politically beholden to Emperor Charles V, the nephew of Queen Katherine. The Church did not favour Henry VIII and feared alienating the emperor. But it was plain: Henry VIII had accepted that the Church had predominant power over such matrimonial matters. The supporters of King Richard III should take note: in the absence of any change, this was the custom and the precedent in 1483, when the English civil government unlawfully invalidated the valid marriage of King Edward IV.

The Pope sent to England his legate, Cardinal Campeggio, to hold a church court in the London Convent at Blackfriars in 1529. Bishop John Fisher pleaded Queen Katherine's case; the papal bull of 1505 had given permission for Henry to marry Katherine, based on Katherine's sworn testimony that her marriage to Arthur had not been consummated. So, her marriage to Henry VIII was lawful. A document signed by many English bishops supported the king's case, but several signatures were considered forgeries. When the court failed to reach a decision, as probably planned by the procrastinating Pope, the king was very angry. Wolsey was removed from office and charged with praemunire, meaning failure to support the king's authority over that of a foreign agent, in this case the Church in Rome. Cardinal Wolsey was sent to prison, but he died at Leicester on 29 November 1530, before he reached the Tower of London. Sir Thomas More replaced him as chancellor and served from 1529 to 1532. He eventually resigned because he could not agree with the proceedings against Queen Katherine.

Sir Thomas More was replaced with Thomas Cromwell, a Protestant lawyer, who made the first suggestion that the king should make himself the

Supreme Head of the Church of England, in place of the Pope. Archbishop Thomas Cranmer argued that the Pope should not have the pre-eminent authority over marriage in England. Students of Edward IV should again take note of this; for, up to this time, the Church did have authority over such matters, as in the reign of King Edward V. The king's mistress Anne Boleyn argued with the king and suggested that Cranmer was correct. She was in favour of the Protestant Reformation, but the king was not convinced, for all he really wanted was his annulment. He did not want a break from the Orthodox Catholic Church. In 1532, Thomas Cromwell had Parliament pass two important acts: the Supplications against the Ordinaries Act and the Submission of the Clergy Act. These acts were designed to petition against alleged abuses by the prelates and to establish the king's right to declare his supremacy over the Church of England.

In 1533, Anne Boleyn was pregnant with the future Queen Elizabeth Tudor, so Anne and the king were secretly married by Archbishop Cranmer. The Pope responded later by threatening the excommunication of Henry VIII, a step he would take when it was too late. In the meantime, Archbishop Cranmer, after an ecclesiastical law court proceeding at Dunstable Priory, declared on 23 May 1533 that the king's marriage to Queen Katherine was null and void and that the king's marriage to Anne Boleyn was valid. This made Princess Mary not legitimate and the unborn Princess Elizabeth legitimate. It was the Church of England which made this decision, obviously without consulting Rome. It was not the civil government that ruled in this matter.

On 1 June 1533, Anne was crowned queen of England. Princess Elizabeth was born alive and well on 7 September 1533 and remained seriously healthy! On 23 March 1534, Parliament passed the first Act of Succession; this made Princess Mary ineligible to inherit the throne, due to her alleged illegitimacy, and made Princess Elizabeth the rightful heir, since she had been declared legitimate by the Tudor Church. For the students of King Edward IV, again it should be noted that, first, Archbishop Cranmer and the ecclesiastical court at Dunstable Priory ruled on the marriage between Henry and Katherine, and then the Parliament acted on the matter of inheritance. Further, this act included an Oath of Supremacy to be sworn by prominent citizens; this meant that the king could control the Church of England. The act authorized a charge of treason for praemunire against those who refused to take the oath. In this web, Sir Thomas More would soon be caught.

In November 1534, Parliament passed the Act of Supremacy, which made the king the Supreme Head of the Church of England, excluding the power of the Church in Rome. Sir Thomas More, "the teller of tales" in recent Yorkist history, refused to sign the oath accepting the king's supremacy and so, along with Bishop John Fisher, was imprisoned, tried, and beheaded for his orthodox faith in 1535. For the first time in English history, the civil power, as represented by the king, was in control of the Church of England and could exercise the powers of the Church in matters of marriage. It could lawfully determine the validity of a marriage and, therefore, the legitimacy of any children. The protagonists of King Richard III should yet again take note: this fundamental change occurred in November 1534, not in June 1483, when the civil power, as represented by the Lord Protector and the Great Council, could not legally invalidate the marriage of Edward IV and declare Edward V to be illegitimate. That power still resided in the hands of the Orthodox Church. But the Act of Supremacy did not change the order of procedure; it would remain the same as it was since the thirteenth century. First, the Church, now controlled by the civil power, would decide on matters of validity and legitimacy, and then, the Parliament, also controlled by the civil power, would decide on matters of inheritance in England.

Queen Anne Boleyn, after having become pregnant again, miscarried with a boy. A hugely disappointed Henry was furious and charged her, falsely, with adultery. She was tried, found guilty, and, in 1536, executed for treason in the Tower of London. But two days before Queen Anne died, Archbishop Cranmer declared her marriage to the king invalid on the basis of an earlier marriage contract with Henry Percy, the sixth earl of Northumberland. This made Princess Elizabeth illegitimate. It is likely that Henry VIII requested this so he could marry again and remove Elizabeth from the line of inheritance. Still in 1536, the king married Lady Jane Seymour. Then, the second Act of Succession reversed the first Act of Succession; it made Princess Mary and Princess Elizabeth, both declared illegitimate by the Tudor Church of England, unable to inherit and settled the succession on the unborn heirs of Lady Jane Seymour. Again, it should be noted: first, the Church of England made Elizabeth illegitimate, and then the Parliament ruled that neither she nor Mary could inherit the throne. There were multiple executions as the tyrannical king attempted to force people to agree with his position.

Unfortunately, Lady Jane Seymour died at the birth of her son, Prince Edward, who was later Henry's immediate successor, King Edward VI. As young Edward appeared to be unhealthy and as Henry needed insurance, Henry married Anne of Cleaves by proxy. But when she arrived in England, he was not satisfied with her and divorced her on grounds of non-consummation and a previous marriage contract. This was the proximate cause of the fall of Thomas Cromwell, who had made the proxy marriage arrangements. Anne of Cleves remained in England, relieved and happy with the divorce, and apparently soon prospered in her new country. Then, Henry married the nineteen-year-old Catherine Howard in 1540. She was never pregnant despite the king's best efforts, so he charged her correctly with adultery and executed her in 1542. Finally, Henry married Catherine Parr in 1543. She was mature and calmed the king. Eventually, she survived him.

There was a third Act of Succession in 1544, which named as heirs to the throne in order: Edward VI and his descendants, Mary and her descendants, Elizabeth and her descendants, and then the heirs of Mary Tudor Brandon: first, Lady Jane Grey and her descendants, and then Lady Catherine Grey and her descendants. This was the lawful order followed after Henry VIII died in 1547 and until Queen Elizabeth Tudor died in 1603. Some have pointed out that neither Mary nor Elizabeth was made legitimate by any specific clause in the third Act of Succession, but that would have been a decision to be made by the Tudor Church of England, headed by the king. However, others have argued that – because in England after 1535, the civil power controlled both matters of legitimacy and inheritance – the 1544 third Act of Succession in effect legitimized both Mary and Elizabeth by its decision on their inheritance.

The dissolution of the monasteries began in 1535 and continued through 1541. A great deal of Church property was confiscated by the Crown. There was a first Act of Suppression in 1536 which encompassed the smaller houses of religion, and then in 1539 a second Act of Suppression which was directed against the larger religious institutions. Monasteries, priories, friaries, chantries, and convents were disbanded, their income appropriated, and their assets sold. The Crown was greatly strengthened, but English history was greatly weakened by the destruction of books, manuscripts, and works of art.

Changes in the mode of worship at the parish-church level were made; at first, the Ten Articles of 1536 were modestly more Protestant, but Henry relaxed them in the Six Articles of 1539, which were considered more Orthodox Catholic. The Pilgrimage of Grace in 1536 was a rebellion by Catholics in the north of England, primarily made against changes in the Mass. The king's commanders made promises and secured the disbandment of the rebel armies, and then the king broke most of the promises, except the Six Articles, which was his attempt at compromise.

Henry was a despotic king. He had to make revolutionary changes in the Church of England to get his marriage to Katherine of Aragon annulled. By his Act of Supremacy, he took for the English Crown, through the Tudor Church of England, the powers over marriage previously exercised ultimately by the Church in Rome. For the students of King Edward IV, Henry's revolution demonstrates clearly how it was the Church in 1483 which had the authority over matrimonial matters, not the Parliament or the Great Council or the king's Privy Council. The 1484 Titulus Regius, which invalidated Edward IV's 1464 marriage to Queen Elizabeth Woodville, had no authority and no standing beyond King Richard III. Therefore, its repeal and destruction in 1485, when Richard was dead, had a solid foundation.

It is plain that Edward IV's 1464 marriage to Queen Elizabeth Woodville was always valid; it was never invalidated by any ecclesiastical law court of the Church of England, and certainly not by any pope or any church in Rome. So, the question arises as to why the English bishops in 1483 did nothing to defend the lawful king, Edward V. Both Richard III and Henry VIII demonstrated that the Church could do very little if a king of England made up his mind and decided that he wanted control over the institution of marriage. Richard III exerted control unlawfully, whereas Henry VIII had the law changed in his own favour. A few might argue unreasonably that King Richard III's 1484 Parliament did give the king the authority to invalidate the marriage of Edward IV and Queen Elizabeth Woodville – never mind that it came seven months after Richard had taken the throne. And, if that alleged authority was valid for all time, then it is impossible to understand why King Henry VIII had to go to so much trouble and why so many people had to suffer as a result.

Mary Tudor (1496–1533) was the fifth child of Henry VII and Queen Elizabeth York. She and her older brother Henry were devoted to each other. Mary was considered exceptionally beautiful. It was intended that Mary should marry Charles, later Charles V, the Holy Roman Emperor, when he reached the age of fourteen years. But it did not happen. Instead, the daughter of Louis XII, King of France, married young Charles, and Mary was married to King Louis XII himself. Mary was crowned as queen of France in 1514. Mary was eighteen years and Louis was fifty-two years old. It was a very bad match. A few months later, the French king died on 1 January 1515, allegedly in the bedchamber doing his best for France!

Many French suitors claimed the beautiful English widow, including the new king of France, Francis I. To escape them all, Mary Tudor, still in Paris, rapidly and secretly married Charles Brandon, the duke of Suffolk, the man she had always loved. Suffolk was a good friend of Henry VIII and had been sent to France to bring Mary home to England. He had promised not to marry her. Henry VIII was furious because his permission had not been obtained and Suffolk had broken his promise. With Wolsey as the broker, Henry finally accepted the situation but made the couple pay a huge fine.

Mary and Charles Brandon had four children: Henry, Frances, Eleanor, and young Henry. The two boys died in childhood; then, Frances Brandon, a great-granddaughter of Edward IV, married Henry Grey, a great-grandson of Queen Elizabeth Woodville. Henry Grey and Frances Brandon Grey had a daughter named Lady Jane Grey, who appeared to be queen of England for nine days following the death of King Edward VI. In his last will, Edward VI had named the Protestant Lady Jane Grey as his successor. Jane Grey was a great-great-granddaughter of King Edward IV and a granddaughter of Princess Mary Tudor. Lady Jane Grey was executed after Queen Mary Tudor, a great-granddaughter of Edward IV, ascended the throne. This was following the Wyatt Rebellion, in which Jane took no part. Lady Catherine Grey, the younger sister of Lady Jane Grey, became the heir of Queen Mary Tudor. During all this, no thought was given that the direct descendants of Edward IV might not be legitimate; nobody believed such nonsense.

In 1560, without royal permission, Lady Catherine secretly married Edward Seymour, the earl of Hertford. She hid a pregnancy until the eighth month, when she was forced to reveal it. Queen Elizabeth Tudor was furious and sent her to the Tower, where her husband soon joined her. Catherine's first son, also named Edward Seymour (1561–1612), was born in the Tower. Despite separation from her husband as ordered by the queen, Catherine had secret conjugal visits. Her second son, Thomas Seymour (1563–1600), was also born in the Tower. In late 1462, Queen Elizabeth had the Tudor Church of England annul Catherine's marriage to Edward Seymour. The bishops made it null and void as though it never happened. This meant that the two boys were not legitimate, so the Tudor Parliament declared them unable to inherit. Notice, again, students of Edward IV and Richard III: first, there was the annulment by the Church, and then there was the disinheritance by the Parliament. Even Queen Elizabeth Tudor and the Tudor Church of England followed the orthodoxy of the medieval church, established for over three hundred years. Catherine was never allowed to see her husband again; she died of tuberculosis in 1568 while still in close custody at a manor house in Suffolk.

Henry Courtenay (1496–1539), the Henry VIII second earl of Devon, later the marquis of Exeter, was the son of Edward IV's second-youngest daughter, Katherine. Henry's father, William Courtenay, had been attainted in 1504 for corresponding with Edmund de la Pole, the exiled Yorkist earl of Suffolk. Henry VIII made William his first earl of Devon in 1511, but William died within the month. Henry Courtenay acceded to the earldom when his father, William, died. Henry was in naval operations against France in 1513. He became a favourite of Henry VIII, as they frequently hunted together. In 1520, he was in the Privy Council; he accompanied Henry VIII to the Field of the Cloth of Gold meeting with Francis I, the king of France. Henry was made the marquis of Exeter in 1525.

When Edward Stafford, the third duke of Buckingham, was executed for treason in 1521, Henry Courtenay acquired considerable additional lands in Somerset and Cornwall. He was sent to negotiate the release of King Francis I after the French king was defeated and captured at the

Battle of Pavia by Emperor Charles V in 1525. Henry did much legal work for the king. He helped with the proceedings against Queen Katherine, signed the letter to Pope Clement VII asking for the marriage annulment, served on the parliamentary commission which deposed Queen Katherine, composed the articles against Cardinal Wolsey, and served in the trial of Queen Anne Boleyn. In 1536, he was commander, with the third duke of Norfolk, of the royal forces sent to deal with the Pilgrimage of Grace Rebellion, but he was not particularly effective.

Henry Courtenay's second wife, Gertrude Blount (1502–1558), was a strong Catholic who remained very close to Queen Katherine and Princess Mary. This aroused the suspicions of Thomas Cromwell, the king's chief minister, who was also vicar general in the new Tudor Church of England. There arose a plot against the king in Cornwall and nearby western counties; this is known in history as the Exeter Plot. As well as Exeter himself, the plot may have involved Exeter's wife, Gertrude, the marchioness of Exeter; Cardinal Reginald Pole (1500–1558); Henry Pole, Baron Montagu (1492–1539); Geoffrey Pole, a younger brother of Henry and Reginald; and Sir Nicholas Carew, the king's master of the horse. It is thought that one plan was to depose Henry VIII and replace him with Henry Courtenay, the marquis of Exeter, a grandson of Edward IV. There was not much thought, meaning that there was no thought, given to the possible problem of illegitimacy allegedly handed down from Edward IV. Others have considered that the plan was to put Reginald Pole on the throne. It is not clear, but the marquis of Exeter seems more likely, as he was a direct descendant of Edward IV, whereas Reginald was descended from Clarence.

In 1538, the marquis of Exeter; his wife, Gertrude; his eleven-year-old son and heir, Edward Courtenay (1527–1556); Margaret Pole, the countess of Salisbury; her son Henry Pole (1492–1539), known as Baron Montagu; and his son, young Henry Pole (1527–1542), were all sent to the Tower. Exeter and Montagu were tried at Westminster and executed on Tower Hill in early 1539. Gertrude was released in 1540; Margaret was brutishly executed in 1541; and young Henry Pole died of starvation in the Tower sometime in 1542. But young Edward, a great-grandson of Edward IV, was excluded from the general amnesty at the accession of Edward VI in 1547 and was not released until 1553, when Princess Mary was queen. These were all descendants of Richard, Duke of York, who died in 1460. Such was the continued ill fate of the Yorkist remnant.

Edward Courtenay (1527–1556), a great-grandson of Edward IV, was considered an uncontaminated Yorkist by the loyal remnant and a seriously possible Yorkist king of England in place of Queen Mary. At the request of Edward's mother, Gertrude Blount Courtenay, Queen Mary restored young Edward Courtenay to his title as the earl of Devon in 1553. There was talk of his marrying Queen Mary, but she was eleven years older than he and, it was rumoured, preferred the younger Princess Elizabeth. In any case, Queen Mary seems to have been determined to marry Philip II, the king of Spain. This arrangement was more consistent with Mary's hopes to reverse the English Reformation. The Wyatt Rebellion of 1554 aimed to overthrow Queen Mary and place Princess Elizabeth, with young Edward Courtenay, on the throne. After the Wyatt Rebellion failed, young Edward Courtenay was imprisoned once again, at first in the Tower, but later at Fotheringhay. He was strongly suspected of involvement in the Wyatt Rebellion and also of an unsanctioned flirtation with Princess Elizabeth. As no evidence could be found or invented, and as Queen Mary did not wish to execute him, he was released and, at the suggestion of King Philip, was sent on a diplomatic mission to Brussels in 1555. After the Wyatt Rebellion, Princess Elizabeth was also sent to the Tower. Attempts to prove that Elizabeth had prior knowledge of the Wyatt Rebellion also proved unsuccessful, but for many months, the future queen, Elizabeth Tudor, was in grave danger of execution for treason. She blamed young Edward for her predicament and remained permanently alienated from him. Later, the Virgin Queen remained permanently alienated from the institution of marriage!

Despite his requests, young Edward Courtenay was not allowed to return to England. Queen Mary was adamant that he should stay away, presumably because of his strong Yorkist descent and the threat of rebellion in his name. So, in practice, he was exiled. Edward, who never married, was, according to King Philip of Spain, "the last sprig of the White Rose." Edward Courtenay died at Padua in 1556 of fever, probably caused by the bubonic plague, at the age of twenty-nine years; this happened seventy-three years after the death of King Edward IV. Young Edward's was indeed a very sad life; some even claimed that he committed suicide. But for a man who carried the genes of his great-grandfather King Edward IV, that seems rather improbable. For those who have difficulty, the direct line of descent from Edward IV was as follows: Katherine Plantagenet, who married William Courtenay; Henry Courtenay, the marquis of Exeter; and young Edward Courtenay, the earl of Devon.

The Tudor Succession Following the Death of Queen Elizabeth York in 1503 and the Death of Henry VII in 1509

While some authors still insist that Edward IV's marriage was invalid and his children were therefore not legitimate, the course of English history after Bosworth, as we can see, does not provide the slightest support for their position. It is high time they gave it up. With the exception of Henry VII, who married Edward's eldest daughter, the descendants of King Edward IV continued to occupy the English throne. This was despite the dubious claims of illegitimacy of their common ancestor, the great Warrior Merchant King. Edward IV was grandfather to Henry VIII and great-grandfather to the successive monarchs Edward VI, Mary I, and Elizabeth I. No church, whether in Rome or in England, ever ruled that Edward IV was not legitimate at his birth; nor did any church ever rule that his 1464 marriage to Elizabeth Woodville was invalid and all of his children were illegitimate. There would be profound consequences if Edward IV's daughter Queen Elizabeth York, wife of Henry VII, had not been legitimate.

It has been argued that if Edward IV himself was not legitimate and his 1464 marriage was not valid, then his children, including Queen Elizabeth York, were also not legitimate. In this case, the complete royal line to the present day in the twenty-first century is likely not legitimate, either (*Britain's Real Monarch*, 2004). The notion is, of course, ridiculous and universally rejected. If Queen Elizabeth York was legitimate by examination of her descendants, then so also was King Edward V, her younger brother, legitimate. It must be concluded that Richard III was never a rightful king of England; history has judged him correctly as an usurper king. All of the direct descendants of Edward IV have been considered legitimate by the Church, either in Rome or in England – or in both.

Parliament gave Henry VIII the power to decide the succession after his own death. It should be noted that by the time he died, Henry represented both the civil power and the ecclesiastical power in England. The tyrant controlled everything when he pleased. In his last will of 20 December 1546, Henry VIII named his successors in order: first, King Edward VI and his descendants; then, Queen Mary Tudor and her descendants; then, Queen Elizabeth Tudor and her descendants; and then, the descendants of his younger sister, Mary Tudor. And that order was indeed followed until Queen Elizabeth Tudor was dead without a direct heir, in 1603. Henry VIII had sought to exclude the Scottish royals, descendants of his older sister, Margaret Tudor; they had greatly offended him with the invasion of England by James IV and the failure of James V to meet him at York to discuss church reforms. In accordance with the king's wishes, the Scottish descendants of Margaret Tudor were not mentioned in the 1544 third Act of Succession.

In 1553, at the death of Edward VI, who had no children, there were multiple possible heirs to the English throne, every last one of them a female of the line: (1) Princess Mary Tudor, daughter of Henry VIII and Queen Katherine of Aragon, (2) Princess Elizabeth Tudor, daughter of Henry VIII and Queen Anne Boleyn, (3) Mary Queen of Scots, great-great-granddaughter of Edward IV (she was still in France), (4) Lady Margaret Douglas, daughter of Margaret Tudor, great-granddaughter of Edward IV, and (5) Lady Jane Grey and her younger sister, Lady Catherine Grey, both daughters of Mary Tudor Brandon and great-great-granddaughters of King Edward IV. Henry VIII's last will, made on 30 December 1546 and backed by the 1544 third Act of Succession, established the line of succession as previously described. Although Margaret Tudor and her descendants were excluded, Queen Elizabeth Tudor would later restore them to their proper place.

In the meantime, Edward VI's last will named Lady Jane Grey as his successor in 1553, excluding Mary and Elizabeth in hopes of a strong Protestant succession. But there was no parliamentary act in support, and it was not consistent with the 1544 Act of Succession. The Privy Council decided to support Princess Mary, who, with her many Catholic supporters, successfully exerted her rightful claim. But Queen Mary I died in 1558 without children.

After Lady Jane Grey was executed in 1554, her sister, Lady Catherine Grey (1540–1568), was considered for many years to be the heir of Princess Elizabeth Tudor, who succeeded Queen Mary in 1558 as Queen Elizabeth I. Every last one of these above-mentioned women was a direct descendant of King Edward IV, and every last one was ultimately considered legitimate at her birth.

Before she died in 1603 without children, Queen Elizabeth must have decided the obvious. She decided in favour of the descendants of the older sister of her father, Henry VIII, namely Margaret Tudor. She also decided that James VI, King of Scotland, the son of Mary Queen of Scots, should be King James I of England. The Tudor queen must have said so in secrecy and her government proceeded with that assumption. In the direct line, James VI of Scotland was the great-great-great-grandson of King Edward IV. For those who have difficulty with this long line, the direct sequence is as follows: King Edward IV, Queen Elizabeth York, Margaret Tudor, King James V, Mary Queen of Scots, and King James VI of Scotland.

All the heirs to the throne carried the genes of England's great Warrior King Edward IV and his daughter Queen Elizabeth York. History had long judged that King Edward IV's marriage to Elizabeth Woodville was valid and that their descendants were all legitimate. No church court had ever ruled otherwise. Only a few people ever recognized any truth in Richard III's 1484 Titulus Regius, long in the dustbin of English history.

It should be noted that England was thankful that the House of York had settled the issue in 1460 by the Act of Accord: females could transmit claims to the English throne, and females could be queens regnant. Henry Stafford, the second duke of Buckingham, the great persuader at Westminster on 25 June 1483, must have rolled in his grave at Salisbury. That change in the laws of inheritance alone shows us how important was the legacy of King Edward IV and the Royal House of York.

The problem in 1483 was that it was only the English people who openly considered their beloved King Edward's marriage to be valid and all his children legitimate; but, initially, their opinion was not important in the councils of the English government. The lords, the magnates, and apparently also the bishops were frightened and confused; they were terrified by the thought of another minority government like that under Henry VI. And they were in awe of Richard, Duke of Gloucester, who was allowed unlawfully to seize the throne. Then, as time passed and ruin descended upon his reign, Richard III probably realized in his heart, but never admitted, that he had made a terrible mistake when he deposed and murdered Edward V, the last lawful Yorkist king of England.

CHAPTER 14

The Other Great Royal Families at the Time of King Edward IV

The House of Beaufort

This famous family was descended from King Edward III and the king's fourth son, John of Gaunt, the duke of Lancaster. Prior to his third marriage, Gaunt had illegitimate children with his mistress, Katherine Swynford. They were John Beaufort (1371–1410), the first earl of Somerset; Henry Beaufort (1374–1447); Thomas Beaufort (1377–1426); and Joan Beaufort (1379–1440).

The Beaufort line was so named because John Beaufort, the first earl of Somerset, was born at Beaufort Castle in France. His two brothers, Henry and Thomas, had no issue. Henry was a powerful Lancastrian politician, both cardinal of Rome and chancellor of England during the reign of Henry VI. Thomas had a distinguished military career in France and was later an interloper duke of Exeter. The abbreviated family tree of the Beauforts is shown in Appendix D. Joan Beaufort married Ralph Neville, the earl of Westmoreland, and started the Neville line with no fewer than fourteen children. Their family tree (abbreviated) is shown in Appendix E.

John of Gaunt married the mother of his Beaufort children, namely Katherine Swynford, on 13 January 1396. The Beaufort offspring were legitimized by Pope Boniface IX on 1 September 1396 and were allowed to inherit by an act of Parliament made on 9 February 1397. There was added to the 1397 act in 1407 a letter patent by King Henry IV, which specifically excluded the Beaufort line from inheriting the English throne. However, the later addition of a letter patent to an act of Parliament was obviously not legal, so the Beaufort line could, in fact, inherit the throne, as indeed happened in 1485.

Concerning the matter of the Beaufort right to inherit, it should be noted again that first, the Church acted on the matter of legitimacy, and then the Parliament followed on the matter of inheritance. This was the custom and precedent in all Christendom, including England, during the thirteenth to sixteenth centuries and beyond. Many historians would call this part of the English constitution – not a written document as in the United States of America and other countries – but the conclusion reached by long precedent, custom, and legislation.

John Beaufort, the first earl of Somerset, had three sons. The first son was *Henry Beaufort (1401–1418), the second earl of Somerset,* who had no issue; the second son was *John Beaufort (1403–1444), the first duke of Somerset,* whose only issue was a daughter, the famous *Lady Margaret Beaufort (1443–1509);* and the third son was *Edmund Beaufort (1406– 1455), the second duke of Somerset,* who had multiple children (see below). There was also a daughter, another *Joan Beaufort (1404–1445),* who married King James I of Scotland and became the queen consort of Scotland.

John Beaufort, the first duke of Somerset, was the commander of the English expedition to Gascony in 1443; he failed to restore order, went home to England, and died in 1444. The expedition offended Richard, Duke of York, who thought that it deprived him of much needed material support in Normandy.

Edmund Beaufort, the second duke of Somerset, the infamous favourite of Henry VI, was the magnate blamed for the final military losses in France. He was bitterly hated by Richard, the third duke of York, and by Richard, the sixteenth earl of Warwick. He died at the First Battle of St Albans in 1455. Edmund Beaufort, the second duke of Somerset, had three sons: *Henry Beaufort (1436–1464), the third duke of Somerset; Edmund Beaufort (1439–1471), the fourth duke of Somerset;* and *Sir John Beaufort (1455–1471).* There was also a daughter, *Margaret Beaufort Stafford (1439–1474),* who married Humphrey Stafford, the heir of the first duke of Buckingham, and continued in the Stafford line.

Henry Beaufort, the third duke of Somerset, was executed after Hexham in 1464, and Edmund Beaufort, the fourth duke of Somerset, was executed after Tewkesbury in 1471, along with his brother Sir John

Beaufort. This sequence was a startling example of how some families were devastated by the War of the Roses. It was Henry Beaufort, the third duke of Somerset, who Edward IV befriended and tried without success to turn to the side of York. It was Edmund Beaufort, the fourth duke of Somerset, who greatly mistrusted Warwick. He did not attend Warwick at the Battle of Barnet in 1471, but instead met Queen Margaret Anjou when she landed at Weymouth on the same day as Barnet. Edmund led the Lancastrian forces in the disastrous defeat at Tewkesbury, but he made a great effort by his famous charge in the woods.

The well-known *Margaret Beaufort (Tudor),* the daughter of John Beaufort, the first duke of Somerset, first married, in October 1455, Edmund Tudor (1430–1456), the first earl of Richmond, who died of the plague in a Yorkist prison in 1456. Second, Margaret married Henry Stafford, who fought on the Yorkist side and died of his wounds soon after Barnet in 1471. Third, Margaret married Lord Thomas Stanley, who betrayed Richard III at Bosworth in 1485.

With her first husband, Edmund Tudor, Margaret had a son, *Henry Tudor, the second earl of Richmond,* who later, after Bosworth Field in 1485, became *King Henry VII.* Henry's claim to the throne through his mother, Margaret Beaufort, and his great-great-grandfather John of Gaunt was considered weak, at least in comparison to quite a few others. And it should be noted that it was through a female, his mother. This became more accepted following the Act of Accord in 1460. But Henry's claim was augmented by his force of arms at Bosworth and, soon, by his marriage to Princess Elizabeth Plantagenet, the eldest daughter and later heir of King Edward IV.

Edmund Tudor had a powerful younger brother, Jasper Tudor, the Lancastrian earl of Pembroke. The mother of Edmund and Jasper was Catherine of Valois, the widowed queen of King Henry V, who their father, Owen Tudor, married secretly in 1429. Edmund and Jasper were therefore half-brothers of Henry VI, who made no secret of his affection for them and bestowed on them their respective earldoms of Richmond and Pembroke.

Margaret Beaufort (1444–1509) was a pious woman who was greatly respected in later life and who was very wealthy. She seems to have spent her life conspiring to promote the career of her son Henry Tudor, first to end his exile in Brittany after Tewkesbury, and second to seize the English crown following the 1483 usurpation. She negotiated with Elizabeth Woodville, who was in sanctuary at Westminster, and arranged the betrothal of her son Henry Tudor to Princess Elizabeth of York. The betrothal was announced in public at Rennes Cathedral on Christmas Day in 1483.

After her first husband, Edmund Tudor, died in 1456, Margaret Beaufort gave birth to Henry Tudor in 1457 and became a very young mother at the age of thirteen years. Jasper Tudor, the boy's uncle, played a large role in looking after Henry Tudor during his childhood. In 1461, Jasper fled abroad after Towton. William Herbert became the Yorkist earl of Pembroke. Henry Tudor, aged four years, was found living at Pembroke Castle. He was sent as ward to Lord Herbert's castle at Raglan and remained in the lord's household for many years.

Initially, Margaret Beaufort accompanied Henry Tudor to Raglan Castle. Then, in 1462, Margaret Beaufort married Sir Henry Stafford, a younger son of Humphrey Stafford, the first duke of Buckingham. This proved to be her happiest marriage, but there was no further issue and she was separated from Henry Tudor for much of the time. At the Readoption of Henry VI in 1470, Jasper returned to Wales, took back control of Henry Tudor, and took him to see Henry VI in London. Margaret visited them at court. After Tewkesbury in 1471, Jasper and Henry Tudor fled to Brittany and began a long exile. When Sir Henry Stafford died of his wounds following Barnet in 1471, Margaret married Lord Thomas Stanley, much later the first earl of Derby. Theirs was a much less happy marriage, one of convenience for both partners. In fact, Margaret took vows of chastity and ceased all marital relations with her husband. Apparently, Stanley agreed to this. It was a classic political marriage.

Margaret attended the court of Edward IV and worked to get Henry Tudor back to England. In 1483, there was an agreement that Henry could return to England with a pardon and marry one of Edward's younger daughters, but this did not happen because King Edward died. Lord Stanley was steward of the royal household for both Edward IV and Richard III. At the time of the usurpation in 1483, Margaret used Stanley's London house to communicate with Elizabeth Woodville in sanctuary and to help with organizing the Buckingham Rebellion (Gregory, 2010).

After the rebellion collapsed, Lord Stanley had to keep Margaret under house arrest in one of his northern castles, but from there she continued her conspiracy with her son Henry Tudor in exile. Richard III was suspicious of Stanley, but Stanley made sure he knew nothing of his wife's activities and proved expert at appearing to support King Richard. After Bosworth, Margaret Beaufort was a prominent member of Henry VII's court. Some claim that she displaced Queen Elizabeth York as the king's favourite family advisor.

The mother of Margaret Beaufort was Margaret Beauchamp of Bletso, who had three marriages: the first was to Oliver St John, the father of Edith St John and the grandfather of Sir Richard Pole, who married Margaret, the countess of Salisbury; the second was to John Beaufort, the first duke of Somerset, who was the father of Margaret Beaufort; and the third was to Lionel Welles, the father of Richard Welles, who was executed at Empingham in 1470, and the father of John Viscount Welles, who married Cecily Plantagenet, the daughter of Edward IV. These marriages explain the Pole and Welles half-brothers of Margaret Beaufort frequently mentioned in the literature.

Henry Tudor (1457–1509), the second earl of Richmond, was the only son of the well-known Margaret Beaufort. He was born at Pembroke Castle in Wales; his father, Edmund Tudor, the earl of Richmond, died in a Yorkist prison three months before Henry was born. Henry's paternal grandfather, Owen Tudor, was a squire of the body for Henry V; this means that he was a bodyguard. After the death of Henry V, Owen Tudor married Henry V's queen, Catherine of Valois. They had two children, Edmund and Jasper Tudor. Henry Tudor's uncle Jasper looked after Henry and his thirteen-year-old mother at Pembroke Castle. When Edward IV became king in 1461, Jasper went into exile, and Henry, with his mother, was sent to Raglan Castle under the wardship of William Herbert, the Yorkist earl of Pembroke, and his wife. Henry Tudor's maternal grandfather was John Beaufort, the first duke of Somerset. His great-grandfather was John Beaufort, the first earl of Somerset; his great-great-grandfather was John of Gaunt; and his great-great-great-grandfather was King Edward III. This made Henry a claimant to the English throne through his mother, a female of the line (see Appendix D). Although Henry's claim to the throne was widely considered weak, it can be argued that this was not so. John of

Gaunt's marriage was legitimized by the Pope, Henry's right to inherit was backed by the 1397 Act of Parliament, his claim through his mother was supported by precedent in the 1460 Act of Accord, he defeated Richard III at Bosworth, and he married the surviving Yorkist heir. By 1486, that could hardly be called a weak claim to the throne.

In 1462, young Henry Tudor's mother married Henry Stafford, which meant a long period of separation for boy and mother. At the Readoption in 1470, Jasper returned from exile and took Henry Tudor to the court of Henry VI. It is alleged that Henry VI told Henry Tudor that he would one day be king of England. Nobody at the time believed this. But maybe Henry VI saw no reason to prohibit inheritance through a female of the line, namely the young boy's mother, Margaret Beaufort. This is interesting because Henry VI's own Lancastrian claim to the throne was based on the Salic law, which prohibited claim through a female of the line. In 1469, Henry Tudor accompanied Lord Herbert to Edgecote. After the execution of Herbert, Sir Richard Corbet took Henry back to continue being looked after by the Herbert family (Higginbotham, 2013). By 1471, with the violent return of Edward IV and many Lancastrian deaths, including that of Henry VI, Henry Tudor was the last male Lancastrian claimant left alive, but few gave him any serious consideration. After Tewkesbury, Jasper and Henry Tudor escaped to Brittany to begin a long exile together. They did not return until 1485.

With the deaths of Edward IV and Edward V and the usurpation by Richard III in 1483, Henry Tudor suddenly became a very serious contender for the throne. He plotted to overthrow Richard III. His co-conspirators in 1483 were his mother, Margaret Beaufort; Dowager Queen Elizabeth Woodville; the duke of Buckingham; and others. In the Buckingham Rebellion of October 1483, Henry Tudor landed briefly on the south coast of England at Poole, but he found the rebellion in collapse amidst the violent storm and retreated back to Brittany. The plotting only continued; at Christmas 1483, at Rennes Cathedral, he promised to invade England again, to overthrow Richard III, and to marry Princess Elizabeth of York. By then, with the deaths of the princes in the Tower earlier in 1483, Henry was considered the Lancastrian heir to the throne. Along with many others, Henry Tudor was attainted by the 1484 Parliament. When Richard III almost succeeded in extraditing him from Brittany, Henry escaped in a hurry to France in June 1484. For many months, the French government would not consider supporting an invasion of England on his behalf because of domestic threats against the French Crown, but by early 1485, the French King Charles VIII, feeling safer on the French throne, considered more support for Henry Tudor.

In August 1485, Henry Tudor sailed to England with a combined force of English, Scottish, and French soldiers. After landing near Milford Haven in Wales and recruiting Welsh and English soldiers, he advanced through Shrewsbury into the Midlands of England. Despite being outnumbered, he defeated and killed Richard III at Bosworth Field and was proclaimed king as Henry VII. He had his coronation first, on 30 October 1485; then, in January 1486, he married Elizabeth of York. The Red Rose of Lancaster and the White Rose of York were combined into the hybrid Tudor Rose. Henry VII did not hold his queen's coronation until 1487 because he did not wish to emphasize her much stronger Yorkist claim to the throne. Elizabeth's claim was through Lionel of Clarence, the third son of King Edward III (see Appendix C), whereas Henry's claim was through John of Gaunt, the fourth son of Edward III (see Appendix D). There were many alive who had better genealogical claims than Henry Tudor, but none held rights of conquest and none were married to Edward IV's direct surviving heir.

The House of Neville

This famous family, a branch of the Beaufort line, was descended from King Edward III by John of Gaunt's third marriage to Katherine Swynford, through a daughter named *Joan Beaufort,* who married *Ralph Neville (1364–1425), the earl of Westmoreland,* and had no fewer than fourteen children. These included *Richard Neville, the fifth earl of Salisbury;* the often married *Lady Katherine Neville; Lady Eleanor Neville,* who married *Henry Percy, the second earl of Northumberland; Robert Neville, the bishop of Durham; William Neville, Lord Fauconberg,* Edward IV's great commander who became the first earl of Kent; *Edward Neville; Lady Anne Neville,* who married *Humphrey Stafford, the first duke of Buckingham;* and *Lady Cecily Neville,* who married *Richard, Duke of York,* and was the mother of King Edward IV and King Richard III (see Appendix E).

Lady Katherine Neville (1397–1483) was notable because she had four marriages, successively to John Mowbray, the second duke of Norfolk, Sir Thomas Strangeways, Sir John Beaumont, and, finally, Sir John Woodville. She was thus the famous dowager duchess of Norfolk who refused to part with her wealth. She outlived all her husbands, even the twenty-year-old John Woodville, who was executed in 1469 after Edgecote. By her first marriage, she was mother to John Mowbray, the third duke of Norfolk, a loyal supporter of King Edward IV, whose late arrival at Towton was decisive. Lady Katherine was grandmother to John Mowbray, the fourth duke of Norfolk, who was never one of Edward IV's favourites and who died in 1476. The fourth duke's daughter, Anne Mowbray, Lady Katherine's great-granddaughter, became the countess of Norfolk in her own right. Anne was married to Prince Richard of Shrewsbury in 1478. When she died in 1481, Edward IV took the whole Norfolk inheritance for his son Richard; by this action, the king deprived the alleged rightful heirs, Lords Howard and Berkeley, descendants of the first duke of Norfolk, both of whom had waited a long time. Berkeley had considerable debts and was paid off, but Howard was undoubtedly alienated by his loss. Edward IV knew that the transaction was doubtful, so he had Parliament make it lawful. Lord Howard was one of those who facilitated the usurpation by Richard III; by the force of his greed and ambition, he may even have been a driving force behind it (Clive, 1974). Soon after his coronation, Richard III made John Howard the duke of Norfolk. With the death of Lady Katherine, her properties probably reverted to John Howard, but it is by no means clear.

The elder Richard Neville (1400–1460) married Alice Montacute, heiress of Thomas Montacute, the fourth earl of Salisbury. When Thomas Montacute died, Richard became the fifth earl of Salisbury by right of his wife. Their ten children included Richard, John, George, Katherine, Eleanor, and Margaret Neville, and four others.

The younger Richard Neville (1428–1471) married Anne de Beauchamp, cousin and heiress of Anne de Beauchamp, the fifteenth countess of Warwick. When the young countess died at age five years, Richard Neville became the sixteenth earl of Warwick by right of his wife. As he also became the sixth earl of Salisbury and inherited the earldom of

Westmoreland, he became the most powerful magnate of his time. In this way, the family wealth was accumulated by excellent marriages.

Richard, Earl of Warwick, was the famous Kingmaker. He was killed at Barnet in 1471. He had two daughters, Isabel and Anne. The earl of Warwick detested the various Woodville marriages arranged by Queen Elizabeth Woodville and Edward IV, mostly in the years 1464–66. It was ironic that most of his own great wealth could be ascribed to marriages: his own, that of his father, the earl of Salisbury, and that of his grandfather, the earl of Westmoreland. Yet Richard Neville was largely responsible for the destruction of Queen Elizabeth Woodville's good reputation; it was considered disgraceful if the commoner Queen Elizabeth Woodville attempted the promotion of her sisters by favourable marriage arrangements.

According to J. R. Lander (1969), Warwick was the classic Machiavellian prince: first, he supported Lancaster; then, he helped York to rebel against Lancaster in 1460; then, when York would not follow his advice, he rebelled against York and reverted back to Lancaster in 1469.

John Neville (1431–1471), Baron Montagu in 1461, was made the interloper earl of Northumberland in 1465 for his suppression of the North Country rebellions, which followed the accession of Edward IV. John's son, *a younger George Neville (1461–1483),* was thought to be intellectually weak; he was later made the duke of Bedford and briefly betrothed to Princess Elizabeth. When John Neville, later promoted to be the marquis of Montagu, joined his brother Richard Neville in rebellion, Edward IV was forced to flee to Burgundy. When Edward made his spectacular return to England in 1471, both John and Richard Neville were killed at Barnet. John's son, young George, was later deprived of his title in 1478, allegedly for lack of personal wealth; but more likely it was Edward IV's continuing to express his anger against the rebellious Neville family.

The elder George Neville (1431–1476) was the Archbishop of York; he was chancellor of England from 1460 to 1467, appointed by Richard, Duke of York, the Lord Protector, following the Act of Accord. George Neville's appointment was confirmed by Edward IV. He was also briefly chancellor during the Readoption of Henry VI in 1470–71. The archbishop was imprisoned at Guînes Castle, Calais, from 1472 to 1474, on suspicion of treason; he had cooperated with George, Duke of Clarence, and the earl of Oxford during the years following Tewkesbury. Edward IV did not trust

George Neville, but he did not have enough evidence to deal with him more severely and so eventually released him.

The sisters of Richard, Earl of Warwick, all made excellent marriages. *Lady Katherine Neville,* the younger Katherine, married Lord William Hastings, the stalwart supporter of Edward IV, with a power base in the Midlands of England. *Lady Eleanor Neville* married Thomas, Lord Stanley, his first marriage. Their son, George Stanley, was held hostage by Richard III before Bosworth in vain hopes of keeping Lord Thomas Stanley's loyalty. *Lady Margaret Neville* married John de Vere, the thirteenth earl of Oxford, who was a fierce and persistent enemy of Edward IV.

The elder daughter of Richard, the sixteenth earl of Warwick, Isabel Neville (1451–1476), married George, Duke of Clarence, the younger brother of Edward IV. They were married in Calais without the permission of the king. Isabel's son was *Edward Plantagenet (1475–1499), the seventeenth earl of Warwick,* who spent much of his later life in the Tower and was executed for treason in 1499 after his attempted escape with Perkin Warbeck and his attempted overthrow of Henry VII. Isabel and George also had a daughter, *Margaret (1473–1541),* later *the countess of Salisbury* in her own right. She married Sir Richard Pole. Her first son, Henry Pole, Baron Montagu, was executed for plotting against Henry VIII in 1539; her second son, Reginald Pole, was cardinal of Rome, papal legate, and the last Roman Catholic Archbishop of Canterbury under Queen Mary Tudor. Reginald opposed the English Reformation and went into voluntary exile to escape the fury of Henry VIII. Later, Margaret was imprisoned in the Tower and brutally executed at the orders of Henry VIII, most likely because she was the mother of Reginald Pole. Her execution was disgusting, because on the scaffold she attempted physically and unsuccessfully to escape the executioner's axe. Henry VIII was worried by the public protest.

The younger daughter of Richard, the sixteenth earl of Warwick, Anne Neville (1456–1485), first married Edward of Westminster, the Lancastrian Prince of Wales, who was killed at Tewkesbury in 1471. Second, she married Richard, Duke of Gloucester, and became queen consort of England when her husband became King Richard III. Anne was the mother of *Edward of Middleham (1473–1484), the second Yorkist Prince of Wales,* who died in childhood and caused a succession crisis for the House of York. When Anne died in 1485, there was an eclipse of the sun which darkened the land. Richard was widely accused of poisoning her. Such was England's dislike for Richard III. But, more likely, she died of pulmonary tuberculosis.

The House of Stafford

The Stafford line descended from Thomas of Woodstock, the earl of Buckingham, later the duke of Gloucester, who was the sixth and youngest son of King Edward III. Thomas married Eleanor de Bohun. They had a daughter, *Anne Plantagenet (1383–1438), the countess of Buckingham,* who had three marriages. The first, to Thomas, the third earl of Stafford, was not consummated. The second was to Edmund, the fifth earl of Stafford; and the third, to William Bourchier. The above-mentioned earls of Stafford were successive sons of Hugh, the second earl of Stafford. The family tree (abbreviated) of the Staffords is shown in Appendix F.

Anne Plantagenet and Edmund, the fifth earl of Stafford, had a son, *Humphrey Stafford (1402–1460), the sixth earl of Stafford and the first duke of Buckingham,* who was chancellor of England for Henry VI after the death of Somerset. Humphrey died defending the king at the Battle of Northampton in 1460. Humphrey, the first duke of Buckingham, was married to Anne Neville, a daughter of Ralph Neville and Joan Beaufort, and together they had no fewer than ten children. These included *another Humphrey Stafford (1425–1458),* the eldest son and heir, who was severely wounded at First St Albans and died of his wounds – and possibly the plague – without inheriting. Another son, *Sir Henry Stafford (1425–1471),* married the well-known Lady Margaret Beaufort and died of his wounds soon after Barnet in 1471. Another son, *John Stafford (1427–1473),* was later made the Yorkist first earl of Wiltshire by Edward IV.

The last-mentioned Humphrey Stafford, who died without inheriting in 1458, married the less well-known Margaret Beaufort (Stafford), daughter of Edmund Beaufort, the second duke of Somerset. Humphrey and Margaret had a son, *Henry Stafford (1455–1483), the seventh earl of Stafford and the second duke of Buckingham,* who was married to Katherine Woodville as a child. Henry grew to hate his Woodville family, although his antipathy has been exaggerated. Edward IV greatly distrusted him. Henry played a large role in fostering the usurpation by Richard, Duke of Gloucester. But later, in 1483, he changed his mind, realized that he had been duped by the 1461 marriage contract invention, joined the Woodvilles, rebelled against Richard III, lost badly, and was executed for treason. His son Edward Stafford, the third duke of Buckingham, was also executed for treason in 1521.

The House of Portugal

John of Gaunt had another daughter by his first wife, Blanche. The daughter's name was Philippa. She is shown in the Lancaster family tree (see Appendix B). Philippa married John I, King of Portugal. Her descendants were successive kings of Portugal following her husband: namely Edward I, Alfonso V, and John II. In 1485, as doom approached, Richard III considered marriage to Princess Joanna (1452–1490), a royal daughter of Alfonso V. She had a bad dream about a young man's death, so she consented to the marriage if Richard was still alive. Her dream was mysteriously accurate in predicting Richard III's death.

The House of Spain

John of Gaunt had a daughter named Catherine with his second wife, Constance of Castile. With her marriage to King Henry III of Castile, Catherine had a son, King John I of Castile. John had a daughter, Isabella of Castile, who married Ferdinand II of Aragon, a marriage which laid the foundation for the kingdom of Spain. Isabella and Ferdinand had an older daughter named Isabel (1470–1498) and a younger daughter named Katherine of Aragon, who was later the queen of England. The Infanta Isabel, aged fourteen years, was considered a likely queen for Richard III, but a wedding never happened. For the purpose of producing an heir for Richard III, Isabel of Spain would have been a better choice than Joanna of Portugal. But with Richard's death, it was no longer relevant.

CHAPTER 15

The Rulers of France and Burgundy at the Time of King Edward IV

Charles VI, King of France (1368–1422); and Philip the Bold (1342–1404), John the Fearless (1371–1419), and Philip the Good (1396–1467), Successive Dukes of Burgundy

When Charles VI became king of France at the age of twelve years in 1380, there was for him a regency by his uncles. Eight years later, in 1388, the twenty-year-old king declared the regency at an end and ruled for himself. When Charles VI was disabled by a serious psychotic disorder in 1392, he attacked and killed four of his knights and had to be forcibly restrained. His queen, Isabeau of Bavaria, became regent. Her chief advisors were Philip the Bold (1342–1404), the duke of Burgundy, one of the king's uncles, and Louis, Duke of Orléans, the king's younger brother. There was intense rivalry for influence between the two men, as often happens in a regency. Philip the Bold tended to lose influence, and the young duke of Orléans tended to gain. But in 1404, Philip the Bold died. His son John the Fearless (1371–1419) took over as the duke of Burgundy and advisor to the regent. Exasperated by his rival, John the Fearless had the duke of Orléans assassinated in the streets of Paris in 1407. Charles, the new duke of Orléans, formed a league against John the Fearless, headed by Bernard, the count of Armagnac, and very soon there was open warfare between the Burgundian and Armagnac factions.

This prolonged and destructive conflict was the reason why the French were particularly ineffective when Henry V invaded France in 1415, won the famous Battle of Agincourt, and proceeded to conquer much of northern

351

France. In 1418, in the face of continued occupation by Henry V and continued incapacity by Charles VI, the dauphin Charles declared himself regent. This angered the king, who accused his son of treason. Then, John the Fearless tried to end the factional trouble by negotiating with the dauphin. But in 1419, John was assassinated at Montereau by partisan Armagnacs who were concerned that there would be an unsuitable settlement; the dauphin was present but claimed to have played no part in the murder. John's son Philip the Good, the new duke of Burgundy, continued the role of Burgundy in the government of France under Charles VI.

In 1420, Philip the Good was party to the Treaty of Troyes made between King Charles VI and the English King Henry V. Philip the Good was more than happy to support the claim of Henry V to the French throne, probably because he thought that Henry V would be a strong king. In the 1420 Treaty of Troyes, Henry V was made heir and successor to Charles VI; the dauphin Charles was disinherited on the basis of his part in the assassination of John the Fearless. The daughter of Charles VI, Catherine of Valois, was given in marriage to Henry V. But the Treaty of Troyes did not last long; by 1422, both Charles VI and Henry V were dead. The dauphin became King Charles VII in that part of France south of the River Loire, except for the Aquitaine. Northern France remained under the control of England and Burgundy, with the duke of Bedford as regent for King Henry VI. Charles VII was depressed and inactive in the face of this unfortunate situation. The French people, anxious to be rid of the English, despaired of their new king.

When Charles VI died in 1422 and was succeeded by Charles VII, it was not surprising that Philip the Good was dismissed and thereafter returned to his affairs in Burgundy. Between 1429 and 1443, Philip added considerably to his Burgundian lands by inheritance and purchase. In his long reign, he oversaw the rise of Burgundy as the pre-eminent nation state in Europe. It was the climax of commercial prosperity, wealth, and prestige. He had a splendid palace at Bruges, the centre of taste and fashion. Music and the arts flourished, and the land grew rich from international trade. It should not be forgotten that the feudal lord of the duke of Burgundy was the king of France. It was with the palace at Bruges that Edward IV later competed with his own brilliant English court.

Philip the Good had three marriages: first, to Michele, the daughter of Charles VI; second, to Bonne of Artois; and third, to Isabella of Portugal, who produced Philip's son Charles the Bold. In addition, Philip the Good had no less than eighteen illegitimate children by multiple mistresses; he made King Edward IV look chaste. Philip's surtitle obviously represented sardonic humour. Philip the Good made little attempt to stop the civil war between his own Burgundian faction and the Armagnac faction, which made considerable problems for poor King Charles VII. It was not until 1429, when Joan of Arc appeared to lead the French armies out of the quagmire that Charles VII started to make any headway in downtrodden France. In 1435, Philip the Good, acting for Burgundy, made peace with Charles VII in the First Treaty of Arras; from that point onwards, without the Burgundian alliance, the English fortune in France declined.

Philip the Good helped Edward IV by refusing to assist Queen Margaret Anjou with her campaign in the north of England in the years 1462–64 following Towton. Philip greatly valued the prosperous wool trade that was growing rapidly between England and Burgundy. Instead, Queen Margaret Anjou obtained help from Louis XI when he became king of France in 1461.

Charles VII (1403–1461) was king of France from 1422 to 1461. He supported the House of Lancaster. His sister Catherine of Valois was the widow of Henry V, and Henry VI was Charles's nephew by marriage (see Appendix A). In 1420, Charles's father, Charles VI, insinuated that he was illegitimate, as Queen Isabeau was known to have multiple sexual affairs. Humiliated by this insult from his own father, young Charles fled to Aragon, where he married Marie of Anjou and fell under the influence of his powerful mother-in-law, Yolande, the duchess of Anjou. By the time of the 1420 Treaty of Troyes, Henry V was declared heir to the king of France; in effect, Charles VI disinherited his son, the dauphin. When Charles VI died in 1422, there were three claimants: the dauphin, soon to be Charles VII; his younger brother, Charles, Duke of Orléans, a prisoner in the Tower of London following Agincourt; and King Henry VI, barely a year old, the successor of Henry V. Initially, Charles VII was king of France only south of the River Loire, with the exception that the English held the Aquitaine in the south-west. The French capital was at Chinon. England and Burgundy controlled northern France, including Paris and

Rheims. Because France was divided, subjugated, and at war with itself, Charles VII was depressed and inactive until 1429, when Joan of Arc made her miraculous appearance and inspired Charles VII, heavily supported by Yolande, the duchess of Anjou, to finally take action against the English invaders.

In 1429, under the brilliant leadership of Joan of Arc, the French lifted the Siege of Orléans, won the Battle of Patay, and, by continuous military pressure, pushed the English back in north-eastern France. In July 1429, Charles was crowned at Rheims, the traditional coronation cathedral of the Valois kings. But the wonderful Joan of Arc was captured by Burgundian partisans, imprisoned for a year, and burned at the stake by the English in 1431; they thought she was a witch. In the same year, on 16 December, the English had Henry VI crowned king of France at Notre Dame Cathedral in Paris. This was indeed a foolish procedure, as English rule in France was widely detested. Then, in 1435, France and Burgundy made peace in the First Treaty of Arras, and the English lost their all-important Burgundian support. From that time, the English star in France began to fade. In 1436, Paris fell to French forces. Soon after this, Richard, the third duke of York, arrived in Normandy to take up his position as lieutenant. While York stayed mainly in Normandy, Charles VII established his control of Paris and north-east France and continued in control south of the River Loire. The French king slowly and painfully gained the ascendancy; he continued the difficult task of uniting France and preparing sufficient forces to deal with the English occupation in Normandy, its surrounds, and the Aquitaine in the south-west.

In 1444, by the Treaty of Tours, the province of Maine was ceded to France. There was a truce which began in 1445 and was intended to last, with extensions to 1450. Henry VI married Charles VII's niece by marriage, Margaret of Anjou, in 1445. Therewith, the Aquitaine was generously allowed to remain in English hands for the time being. During the truce, Charles VII further built up his forces and prepared to expel the English from his land. When the English broke the truce in 1449, the French king progressively drove them out of his kingdom. Northern France, Normandy, Brittany, and the Aquitaine were recovered. The French had further great victories at Formigny in 1450 and at Castillon in 1453. As a result, the English held only Calais. It was plain: without Henry V,

England did not have the money, the resources, or the political will to hold France. English defeat was inevitable. The Hundred Years War in France was over by 1453, but in England there was a general despondency. The government was corrupt and the War of the Roses was about to begin.

Later in his reign, Charles VII quarrelled with the dauphin, afterwards Louis XI, who fled to Burgundy in 1456 and refused ever to return while Charles VII was alive. In 1457, at the request of his niece Queen Margaret Anjou, Charles VII sent forces to attack England at Sandwich, but not much came of it. The English people were very angry with Margaret. In 1458, Charles had a lethal diabetic ulcer, then a large tumour in his mouth, probably a teratoma, and died of a prolonged and miserable starvation in 1461. Charles VII was titled "the Victorious"; he left France reconquered, largely free of the English, and with a standing army for protection. Like Edward IV, Charles VII has been badly underrated by history, probably because of the romantic story of Joan of Arc. Both kings had to recover their kingdoms by armed force; both kings left their kingdoms infinitely better off than how they had found them.

Louis XI (1423–1483) was king of France from 1461 to 1483, corresponding closely to the reign of Edward IV in England. He was the son of King Charles VII and Marie of Anjou, and the grandson of King Charles VI. As his father was the brother of Catherine of Valois, who married Henry V, Louis was the cousin of King Henry VI, the son of Henry V. Not surprisingly, Louis XI supported the House of Lancaster and did his best to help Queen Margaret Anjou, who was the daughter of his brother-in-law René and, therefore, the king's niece (see Appendix A).

Louis XI had four major enemies: his own father, Charles VII; his brother Charles Valois, the duke of Berry; Charles the Bold, the duke of Burgundy; and Edward IV, the Yorkist king of England. He rebelled constantly against his father, Charles VII, who he regarded, mistakenly, as a weak king. Later, he fought to reduce the power of the magnates in his kingdom. This included his own brother, the duke of Berry. In so doing, he increased the power of the monarchy. He fought constantly to annex the territories of Burgundy, which he regarded as the property of France, eventually succeeding, in part, with the Second Treaty of Arras in December 1482, following the death of Charles the Bold at the Battle of Nancy in 1477 and the death of his successor, Mary of Burgundy, in 1482.

Louis XI helped the Lancastrians in Northumberland in the years following Towton, which happened in 1461. In 1464, the French king was infuriated by the collapse of the Warwick negotiations for Edward IV to marry Princess Bona of Savoy, the French king's sister-in-law. At that time, nobody considered that Edward IV was allegedly already married to Lady Eleanor Butler, apparently not even Canon Robert Stillington, who, as lord keeper of the privy seal, made no objection to the royal marriage plans of the English and French governments for King Edward IV and Princess Bona. Louis XI conspired with the earl of Warwick and Queen Margaret Anjou at Angers and Amboise and planned the overthrow of Edward IV; he equipped Warwick for his invasion of England in 1470; and he supported Margaret when she invaded England in 1471. Louis XI was the deadly enemy of Edward IV, but his admirers believed that he was also a very wise and cunning king.

When Edward IV invaded France in 1475, Louis settled with the English at Picquigny with wine, money, and song, all to Edward IV's great satisfaction. Edward's daughter Elizabeth was betrothed to the dauphin. The meeting between Edward and Louis on the bridge over the River Somme, with a protective lattice between them, must have been one of the most amusing encounters in English history. Edward did well speaking French, and Louis tried to seduce the womanizing Yorkist king with bawdy tales of his French ladies and a forgiving cardinal of Rome. The invaders went home to England without bloodshed. For those who believe that the English claims in France were a waste of time, money, and blood, the settlement was most fortunate. The king teased his daughter, calling her "Madam le Dauphin." The money the French paid to Edward allowed the English king to refrain from calling his Parliament for many years. He was able to keep general taxation low for his subjects. Louis XI regarded the money as a pension, but Edward IV called it tribute. When Louis XI reached a settlement with Burgundy in the Second Treaty of Arras of December 1482, he planned to stop paying Edward's pension, as he no longer feared an English attack. The betrothal between Edward's daughter and the dauphin was cancelled. Edward IV felt that he had been duped and considered plans to invade France again, but Edward's death supervened – and Louis XI died a few months later in the same year.

Louis XI was known as the Spider King for the web of spies that he maintained everywhere in Europe; his military and diplomatic offensives were unremitting. His spies told him what happened to King Edward V, and, before he died, Louis XI said that he blamed Richard III for the murders of the princes in the Tower. The admirers of the all-knowing Louis XI would say that the case against Richard III was closed! Commines expressed the Spider King's opinion of Richard III as follows:

> Not long after [the death of Edward IV], he [Louis XI] received letters from the Duke of Gloucester, who was made king, styled himself Richard III, and had barbarously murdered his two nephews; but our king looked on him [Richard] as an inhuman and cruel person and would neither answer his letters nor give audience to his ambassador.

But Richard III could have reasonably expected the French pension to be continued, as the Treaty of Picquigny included an extension for one year following the death of Edward IV.

Louis encouraged the power of the middle class in France, much like Edward IV did in England, and the two kings did much to encourage commerce, trade, and the accumulation of national wealth. Louis has received credit for leading France into the modern age, but Edward has been generally and unjustifiably denied such recognition by historians, in favour of the Tudor King Henry VII and his successors.

Charles the Bold (1433–1477), the duke of Burgundy from 1467 to 1477, was the son of Philip the Good and Isabella of Portugal. Charles legally took over the government of Burgundy in 1465 as his famous father grew old and died in 1467. Charles had three marriages: to Catherine, a daughter of Charles VII; to Isabella of Bourbon, who gave birth to his daughter Mary; and to Margaret of York, a sister of Edward IV, who proved a wonderful stepmother for Mary of Burgundy and a powerful force in Burgundian politics for many years.

Charles the Bold spent the rest of his life in a ferocious struggle against Louis XI, who had become king of France in 1461 following the death of Charles VII. Charles the Bold was prominent in the League of the Public Weal, a confederation of French nobles anxious to limit the growing power of the French Crown. As the duke of Burgundy, Charles had King Louis

XI as his feudal overlord, but that counted for little, as they were deadly enemies. Thanks to his father, Philip the Good, and his own efforts, Charles controlled far more extensive lands than just his duchy, which was south-east of Paris and based on the west side of the River Saône. Starting in the duchy and moving first east and then north, the dukes of Burgundy controlled the Palatine county of Burgundy on the east side of the River Saône, the duchies of Lorraine, Bar, and Luxembourg, the principality of Liege, all the land that is now Belgium, and all the land that is now Holland. Access to the North Sea ports made Burgundy a powerful factor in international trade and naval operations.

In 1465, Charles the Bold invaded France and forced Louis XI to sign the Treaty of Conflans, an agreement which attempted to limit the royal powers. In 1468, Charles made a marriage treaty with Edward IV by marrying Margaret of York, an arrangement hostile to France. There followed multiple rebellions, mainly on his eastern frontier and mostly instigated by the hostile conspiracies of the Spider King, Louis XI. There were campaigns against the Austrians, the Swiss, and the duchy of Lorraine; and Charles spent much time laying siege to towns such as Neuss, Morat, and Nancy.

Charles the Bold supported Edward IV by assisting in the naval blockade of the French coast against the earl of Warwick in 1470, then by backing Edward IV's dazzling invasion and recovery of England in 1471. He gave Edward men, money, harbour, and ships; Edward could not have asked for more from his brother-in-law. In 1471, Charles the Bold invaded France for the second time, but it came to little and he withdrew. The French were adept at not offering battle and waiting for the invaders to leave. In 1475, Charles supported Edward IV's invasion of France, but he was too busy in the east, did not join Edward as agreed, and was disappointed when Edward returned to England. The rebellions against his rule continued, and Charles was killed at the Battle of Nancy in Lorraine in the winter of 1477.

Charles was succeeded by his daughter Mary, who, badly needing protection from Louis XI, married Maximillian, the son and heir of Emperor Frederick III, on 18 August 1477. In December 1482, in the Second Treaty of Arras, territorial concessions were made to France and a temporary peace was finally agreed. King Edward IV was not happy.

Burgundy was a valuable ally, and then it was lost – and Edward's French pension was no longer to be paid. Worse, the betrothal of his daughter Elizabeth to the dauphin was broken.

Charles VIII (1470–1498) was *king of France from 1483 to 1498*. As he was only thirteen years old, his older sister, Anne of Beaujeu, was regent for him. Unlike what happened in England when Edward IV died, Anne was loyal to the new king and gave an excellent performance as regent. Anne was challenged by Louis, Duke of Orléans, and a rebellion known as the Fools' War broke out. Anne put down the rebellion and imprisoned Louis. After this temporary settlement, France was able to support Henry Tudor with his invasion of England in 1485. In 1488, the nobles again rebelled, hoping to restrict the royal power, but Anne defeated them at the Battle of St Aubin, where Sir Edward Woodville was killed. Charles VIII was betrothed to Margaret, the daughter of Maximillian, the archduke of Austria, and then to Mary, the duchess of Burgundy, but this was cancelled and Charles married Anne of Brittany in 1491, thus uniting France and Brittany. After this, Charles ruled for himself without a regency. In 1494, Charles invaded Italy with a powerful army. He intimidated northern Italy and was crowned king of Naples in 1495, but the Italian nobles raised armed resistance and drove him out of Italy in the same year. In 1498, he hit his head on a low door frame and died soon after, with what was probably a subdural haematoma, at the age of only twenty-eight years. He was succeeded by the above-mentioned duke of Orléans, who became Louis XII.

CHAPTER 16

The Supporters, Friends, and Close Associates of King Edward IV

Henry Bourchier (1405–1483), the Yorkist first earl of Essex, was a leading member of the council throughout the reign of Edward IV. His mother was Anne Plantagenet, the countess of Buckingham, the daughter of Thomas of Woodstock, who was the youngest son of Edward III (see Appendix F); this means that Henry was a great-grandson of Edward III. Henry's father was Sir William Bourchier, the third husband of Anne Plantagenet. Anne's first marriage was without issue, her second marriage produced the Stafford line, and her third marriage produced the Bourchier line.

Henry Bourchier married Isabel of York, a daughter of Anne Mortimer and Richard, Earl of Cambridge (see Appendix C). Isabel was an older sister of Richard, the third duke of York, and so Henry was an uncle by marriage to Edward IV and Richard III. A brother of Henry was Thomas Bourchier, the Archbishop of Canterbury.

After his attendance at First St Albans, Northampton, and Towton, Henry Bourchier was made the Yorkist first earl of Essex by Edward IV in 1461. He remained loyal to the king and served for a long time as the Lord High Treasurer. He was also steward of the royal household for several years.

There were eleven children of the marriage between Henry and Isabel. A son, William Bourchier, married Anne Woodville in 1466; William served under Edward IV at Barnet. Anne and William had two daughters, and in addition a son, also named Henry Bourchier, who became the second earl of Essex after his father, William, died in 1480 without inheriting, and after his grandfather Henry, the first earl of Essex, died of natural causes in 1483. The elder Henry had died on 4 April 1483, a few days before the unexpected death of Edward IV. Henry, the second earl of Essex, the son of William, attended the funeral of Elizabeth Woodville in 1492.

Among the other sons of Henry, the first earl of Essex, and Isabel, Humphrey was killed at Barnet and Edward was killed at Wakefield. This family gave much for the cause of the Royal House of York. Henry Bourchier did not live through the usurpation, but he would have disapproved of Richard III. Henry's brother Thomas, Archbishop of Canterbury, performed the coronation of Richard III, but he did not attend the coronation banquet; it is sometimes inferred that he did not wish to sit next to the Usurper King at the banquet table. His place was taken by the bishop of Durham, a prelate from the North Country who was, perhaps, more supportive of Richard III.

William FitzAlan (1417–1487) was the sixteenth earl of Arundel by 1438 during the reign of Henry VI. He was a descendant of Richard FitzAlan, the eleventh earl of Arundel, one of the lords appellant who quarrelled with King Richard II and was executed for treason in 1397. William fought on the losing Yorkist side at Second St Albans in 1461. He married Joan Neville, a sister of Richard Neville, the sixteenth earl of Warwick. A son of William and Joan, Thomas FitzAlan (1450–1524), Lord Maltravers, married Margaret Woodville and later became the seventeenth earl of Arundel. The son of Thomas and Margaret, also William FitzAlan (1476–1543), became the eighteenth earl of Arundel; and a daughter, also named Margaret, married John de la Pole, the earl of Lincoln.

John de la Pole was the heir of Richard III in 1485 after Queen Anne died. He fought on the Yorkist side at Bosworth but was reconciled with Henry VII after the battle. John later rebelled against the Tudor king, hoping to seize the crown, and died at Stoke Field in 1487. William FitzAlan was not present at Bosworth to support Richard III, but this was probably related to his advanced age. Charles Ross (1999) said that young Thomas, Lord Maltravers, Margaret Woodville's husband, was present at Bosworth to keep his feudal oath and support the last Yorkist king.

Humphrey Stafford (1439–1469) was made the interloper Yorkist first earl of Devon in 1469, a new creation by Edward IV. Humphrey represented a distant branch of the main Stafford family line; he fought on the Yorkist side at Mortimer's Cross and at Towton, both in 1461. He owned considerable property in Dorset, Wiltshire, and Somerset. For his loyal support of Edward IV, he was awarded many forfeited estates in the West Country of England, in particular the lands of the Courtenay earls of Devon, especially those of the sixth earl of Devon, who was executed after Towton. Humphrey efficiently represented the king's interests in this loyal Lancastrian area; he was a principal commissioner of justice in the region. Humphrey did not become the earl of Devon until 1469. After a disagreement about where to camp overnight, he walked out on William Herbert, the earl of Pembroke, prior to the Battle of Edgecote Moor in 1469. By the time Stafford thought better of his angry reaction and reached the battlefield the next day, it was too late. Herbert was defeated after a fierce fight; Stafford escaped the battlefield but was killed during his flight, near Bristol. Thus he held his title as earl of Devon for only a few months. By his impetuosity, he had badly let down his king. If he had lived, then this loyal Yorkist would have been consumed by regret and guilt over this unfortunate matter. The title earl of Devon became vacant until the Readoption of Henry VI, when the title reverted back to the Courtenay heir, John, the seventh earl of Devon, who soon after died at Tewkesbury.

William Herbert (1423–1469), the Yorkist earl of Pembroke, was Edward's powerful supporter in Wales and in the Welsh Marches, the borderlands of England, where he exercised the royal power effectively. Herbert fought for Edward IV at Mortimer's Cross in 1461 and marched to London in support of Edward's successful bid for the throne. With the attainder of Jasper Tudor, the Lancastrian earl of Pembroke under Henry VI, Lord Herbert was the beneficiary of many estates in Wales. The sixteenth earl of Warwick coveted these estates, so Warwick and Herbert were mortal enemies. At his reduction of Pembroke Castle in 1461, Herbert found living in the castle the boy Henry Tudor, who he sent with his young mother, Margaret Beaufort, to his castle at Raglan. Having purchased the boy's wardship from the king, he had young Henry Tudor reared by Lady Herbert. Herbert's son, also named William (1451–1491), was made Lord Dunster and married Mary Woodville in 1466. After Mary died, William would later marry Katherine Plantagenet, the illegitimate daughter of Richard III.

The senior Herbert was given the title first earl of Pembroke by Edward IV in 1468 for his reduction of Harlech Castle, the last of the Lancastrian strongholds after Towton. Finally, Lord Herbert took a fine Welsh army to Edgecote Moor to support the king in 1469, but there was a disagreement with the Yorkist earl of Devon. Herbert lost part of his force, in particular his archers. He was defeated by the rebels after a fierce fight and was then executed by Warwick, who seldom had mercy when dealing with his enemies.

The junior William Herbert succeeded his father as the second earl of Pembroke. But the second earl was not as efficient as his father and did not do well in Wales, which remained loyal to the Lancastrian cause. Young William was at Tewkesbury in 1471 when he was aged twenty years. He accompanied Edward IV to France in 1475. But despite this, in 1475, young William had to surrender the earldom of Pembroke to the Crown, in exchange for the earldom of Huntingdon. The Prince of Wales, the future Edward V, became the third earl of Pembroke in 1479. Young William later did much better than previously; it is said that he held South Wales for Richard III so Henry Tudor had to take a more northerly course through Wales when he invaded in 1485. Henry VII restored the earldom of Pembroke to Jasper Tudor in 1485, after Bosworth Field; but young William, who did not support Richard III at Bosworth, for reasons not certain, held the earldom of Huntingdon until he died in 1491.

Richard Neville (1428–1471), the sixteenth earl of Warwick, was a first cousin by marriage of Edward IV. Richard's aunt Cecily Neville was Edward's mother. Richard and Edward were also cousins by blood, as they were both descended from Edward III; Richard was a great-great-grandson and Edward was a great-great-great-great-grandson, so they were also third cousins, two generations removed. Richard led the Yorkist army on many occasions. He assisted Edward IV in gaining the throne in 1461, but he drove Edward IV out of England in 1470 and briefly restored Henry VI as king. So, Warwick is known in English history as the Kingmaker.

Richard's grandfather was Ralph Neville, the earl of Westmoreland, who married Joan Beaufort and added her extensive estates to his own. Richard's father was also named Richard, the earl of Salisbury, who married Alice Montacute, through whom he inherited his earldom. Richard himself married Anne de Beauchamp, ultimately the heiress of Richard de Beauchamp, the thirteenth earl of Warwick. The inheritance came to Richard Neville's wife when the thirteenth earl died in 1439. His son, the fourteenth earl, died in 1446, and the thirteenth earl's granddaughter, the two-year-old fifteenth countess of Warwick, died in 1448. As the direct line had died without children, the younger daughter of the thirteenth earl, Anne de Beauchamp, then inherited the earldom in her own right. Her husband, Richard Neville, became the sixteenth earl of Warwick in her right. This review reveals how important was Richard Neville's marriage, and that of his father and grandfather, for accumulating his wealth. But Warwick spent a great deal of his time criticizing the Woodville family for exactly similar but much less efficient transactions. This must be considered significant hypocrisy. Yet, Warwick ruined the reputation of Queen Elizabeth Woodville by his constant criticism, and in so doing he greatly impaired the reputation of King Edward IV, as well.

Richard Neville was knighted in 1445 during the reign of Henry VI. Richard and his father, the earl of Salisbury, supported Henry VI at first, but they gradually drifted to support York for several reasons. Richard's uncle by marriage was Richard, Duke of York. And Warwick had bitter disputes, mostly over inherited land in Glamorgan, with the Lancastrian king's favourite, the second duke of Somerset. In 1455, Warwick commanded the Yorkist forces with distinction at First St Albans, after which Richard, Duke of York, was confirmed as Lord Protector. Warwick was rewarded by York with the office of the captain of Calais.

In 1457, the French attacked Sandwich and there was general fear of a French invasion of England. Warwick was charged with patrolling the English coast and providing protection. He conducted highly successful naval operations against the ships of France, Castile (Spain), and the Hanseatic League (Germany), which made him very popular with the English people.

In 1459, he joined the Yorkists at Ludlow Bridge, but his own Calais lieutenant, Andrew Trollope, deserted the Yorkist force – and many Yorkists refused to fight against the king on the open battlefield. The Yorkist leaders had to flee without a battle. The earls of Warwick, Salisbury, and March retreated to Calais, and the duke of York fled to Ireland. In 1460, Warwick sailed to Ireland to coordinate with York; on the way home, the Lancastrian fleet, under the duke of Exeter, sighted but failed to capture Warwick, who returned safely to Calais.

Then, Warwick invaded England. He landed at Sandwich, occupied London, and defeated the king at the Battle of Northampton in 1460. His victory owed much to the fine performance of the earl of March, later Edward IV, commander of the Yorkist left battle. This Yorkist triumph was followed by the Act of Accord; and Richard, Duke of York, was made Lord Protector and heir of King Henry VI. In the Yorkist disaster at Wakefield in December 1460, the duke of York; his second son, the earl of Rutland; and Warwick's father, the earl of Salisbury, were all killed. Warwick marched north from London and was defeated at the Second Battle of St Albans by the queen's marauding Lancastrians, reinforced with fierce Scots. But Warwick and much of his force escaped. At Chipping Norton, he joined Edward, the earl of March, fresh from his decisive victory at Mortimer's Cross. Together, they entered London while the Lancastrians hesitated and Edward was proclaimed King Edward IV by the people and Parliament alike. It was not an usurpation, as some Lancastrians claimed.

Warwick played little role at Towton, sustaining an injury at Ferrybridge, but afterwards he was confirmed as captain of Calais and made Lord High Admiral of England and steward of the Duchy of Lancaster by Edward IV. Warwick and his brother John Neville then played a large part in suppressing the northern rebellions that followed in the years 1462–64.

Warwick wielded considerable power for two years, but he became alienated from Edward IV. Warwick was angry about many issues: the king's secret Woodville marriage in 1464; Edward's favouritism shown to the extensive Woodville family; the multiple other Woodville marriages in the years 1464–66; the rejection of a French marriage alliance which Warwick favoured; the close relationship Edward IV favoured with Burgundy; and, finally, Edward's failure to allow the marriage of Warwick's daughter Isabel with George, Duke of Clarence, the new king's brother. It is fair to say that during the 1463–69 period, Warwick gradually lost power and influence and was progressively replaced in the king's favour by the senior Richard Woodville and his son Anthony Woodville.

The outbreak of further northern rebellions in 1469 was almost certainly engineered by Warwick and Clarence. Warwick's forces under Sir William Conyers defeated the Yorkist earl of Pembroke at Edgecote in

July 1469, and Warwick executed the senior Richard Woodville and his son John Woodville. Very soon, Warwick's forces captured King Edward IV, who had fallen strangely depressed and inactive. The earl of Warwick ruled as dictator of England, with both kings of England, Henry VI and Edward IV, locked up in prison. But Warwick could not control the country. Disorder and rebellion broke out, so he was forced to release Edward IV from Middleham Castle in September 1469. Then, Edward, reunited with his many followers, badly mauled the rebels under Sir Robert Welles at Empingham in 1470. Warwick and Clarence, accused correctly of treason, fled to France.

After negotiations with King Louis XI and Margaret of Anjou, which was further treason, Warwick invaded England later in 1470, forced Edward to flee to Burgundy, and restored Henry VI to the throne in the so-called Readoption. For the second time, Warwick was virtual dictator of England. But again, Warwick found that he could not rule the country, such was the general level of mistrust. He could not take property or office from the Yorkists, as he needed their support, and so he could not bribe or reward the Lancastrians, who hated him anyway. Edward IV invaded England, occupied London, and sent Henry VI back to the Tower. Then, Edward destroyed the Lancastrians and killed Warwick at Barnet in 1471. Following this, Edward IV destroyed Queen Margaret Anjou and the remaining Lancastrians at Tewkesbury in 1471.

Warwick was a fine soldier but a somewhat defensive tactician; he was no match for the brilliantly aggressive Edward IV. Warwick is noted for pride, ambition, and savagery. But in his time, he was the most powerful magnate in England and was popular with the English people, mostly for his successful naval operations in the English Channel, but also for his frequent public entertainment of the London populace. His role as kingmaker has been somewhat exaggerated. Prior to Edward's accession, Warwick had left London undefended, had suffered an humiliating defeat at Second St Albans, and had barely escaped with half his army and his own life. The Mayor of London had to send three gentleladies, including Jacquetta Woodville, to persuade Queen Margaret not to pillage a defenceless London. When the people saw the handsome Edward in 1461, it was a foregone conclusion that they wanted him to be king. What is more, restoring a disabled Henry VI to the throne for six disorganized months in 1470–71 could hardly be called making a king. Nevertheless, the sixteenth earl of Warwick, even with all his faults, has remained one of the most famous men in English history.

John Neville (1431–1471), the marquis of Montagu, the younger brother of Richard, the sixteenth earl of Warwick, was made Baron Montagu soon after Edward IV assumed the throne in 1461. John Neville led the suppression of Lancaster in the north of England, with notable victories in skirmishes at Hedgeley Moor and Hexham, both in 1464. For his service, he was awarded the estates and title of the third earl of Northumberland, who had been killed at Towton in 1461. During the troubles of 1469 and 1470, John suppressed several of the northern rebellions against Edward, even though these rebellions were frequently fomented by his own brother, the earl of Warwick. After Empingham in 1470, Edward took back from John the earldom of Northumberland and restored it to the heir, young Henry Percy, the fourth earl of Northumberland, who Edward hoped would be able to pacify the northern regions of England more effectively than John Neville. In return, John Neville was elevated to the title marquis of Montagu, but at this time, he considered insufficient the Devon lands given him; he called them a "magpie's nest." His son George was created duke of Bedford and was contracted in marriage to Edward's eldest daughter, Elizabeth, the princess of York. Edward IV hoped that if he himself did not survive the rebellions, then John Neville would put young George and Elizabeth on the throne and govern England as regent (Clive, 1974). Clearly, Edward no longer favoured Warwick, but he had a high opinion of Montagu. However, these fairly reasonable rewards did not satisfy Montagu, so he followed his brother Richard, Earl of Warwick, in changing to the Lancastrian side in 1470, a decision which forced Edward IV to abandon his kingdom and flee to Burgundy. Like his kingmaker brother, the marquis of Montagu was killed at Barnet upon Edward IV's triumphant return in 1471.

Lord William Hastings (1431–1483) was a distant cousin of Edward IV. William's mother was Alice Camoys. In the same line, his grandmother was Elizabeth Mortimer, and his great-grandfather was Edmund Mortimer, the third earl of March (see Appendix C), who was also the great-great-grandfather of Edward IV. Lord Hastings and Edward IV were therefore second cousins, one generation removed. William was present at Mortimer's

Cross, at the London proclamation of Edward IV as king in 1461, and at Towton, where he was knighted. He married Katherine Neville (see Appendix E), a sister of Richard Neville, the sixteenth earl of Warwick. Katherine was previously married to William Bonville, the sixth Baron Harington, who died at Wakefield. Katherine and William Bonville had a daughter, Cecily Bonville, Hastings' stepdaughter, who later married the marquis of Dorset, the elder son of Queen Elizabeth Woodville. Hastings fled to Burgundy with Edward IV in 1470. He came back to England with the king's invasion force in 1471, recruited more troops for the king's army, and commanded at Barnet and again at Tewkesbury.

For much of the reign of Edward IV, Hastings held the important position of Lord Chamberlain, which allowed him to control access to the king. From this, he profited handsomely, as many were prepared to pay for the access. Edward IV gave him substantial estates, mostly in the Midlands of England. Hastings mistrusted the Woodvilles. He quarrelled with Thomas Grey, the marquis of Dorset, over disputed property, mostly in the Midlands; over favour with the king; and over their common mistresses, Jane Shore included. The marriage of Hastings' stepdaughter Cecily Bonville with Dorset did not seem to calm the disagreements. Hastings also quarrelled with Anthony Woodville over the captaincy of Calais. Anthony wanted the appointment and was supported by the queen, but the king gave it to Hastings – and the two men made pointless public accusations against each other.

For her part, the queen blamed Hastings for participating in many of the king's wanton misadventures and for not encouraging the king to be more careful. This is the most likely reason why Hastings disliked the queen and did not cooperate with her when Edward IV died – not until it was too late. But it was also likely that he had been listening to Warwick, Clarence, and Gloucester for too long.

It seems not unreasonable to believe that part of the succession problem in 1483 arose as a result of Edward's profligate misbehaviour, which made the false marriage contract story seem believable. The politically astute Queen Elizabeth Woodville warned both Edward IV and Lord Hastings of likely problems, but they largely ignored her. Most modern minds would think that the menfolk were gravely mistaken and conclude that the reviled Queen Elizabeth Woodville was correct in her assessment of the problem.

Hastings promised Edward before the king died that he would seek reconciliation with Dorset, but this did not happen. He may also have promised to seek reconciliation with the queen, but this did not happen, either. If Hastings had earlier supported the queen in 1483, then perhaps things might have turned out differently. When Edward IV died, Hastings promptly sent messages to Gloucester in Yorkshire, indicating Richard's appointment as Lord Protector and providing the instruction that he reach London as soon as possible. A few have suggested that Hastings might have instructed Richard to go to Ludlow and escort the new king to London, which might explain why Gloucester treated Anthony Woodville so harshly at Northampton. It is commonly believed that Hastings warned Richard about the potential hostility of the queen towards a protectorate. However, Hastings did not favour the plan of Richard, Duke of Gloucester, to usurp the throne; Hastings supported the retention of King Edward V in accordance with the dead king's wishes and the usual English custom of inheritance. He did not realize there was a problem until it was too late. On the other hand, Queen Elizabeth quickly realized there was a big problem, but she could do little to oppose Richard's plans. Were it not for his antipathy towards Queen Elizabeth, Anthony Woodville, and the marquis of Dorset, Lord Hastings might have supported King Edward V more effectively.

It is alleged that Hastings had discussions with Rotherham, Morton, and Stanley about releasing Edward V from the Tower and conducting him to safety in order to frustrate the plans of Richard, Duke of Gloucester. Hastings also maintained communication with the Woodvilles in the sanctuary for this purpose. But the plans were considered too dangerous and were never put into operation. This sequence of conversations is described by some authors as the Hastings Conspiracy (Kendall, 2002). Some even suggest that Anthony Woodville, imprisoned in the north of England, was also involved, but this is very unlikely, considering the distance and time involved. Richard, Duke of Gloucester, was probably informed by Sir William Catesby of these discussions. On 13 June 1483, at a council meeting at the Tower, Richard accused Hastings of treason; Hastings was seized at Richard's orders and executed immediately in the Tower courtyard – a shameful, illegal procedure. Some claim that the execution occurred a week after the arrest, perhaps with a judicial hearing, but most authorities say that the arrest and the execution happened on the same day. As death came suddenly, Hastings had only a short time to realize that he should have acted more quickly in defence of the boy king and the Queen Mother. But perhaps it was good that civil war was avoided.

John Mowbray (1415–1461), the third duke of Norfolk, was the Earl Marshal of England from 1432, during the reign of Henry VI. In 1450, he supported Richard, Duke of York; in 1459, he swore allegiance to Henry VI but subsequently turned back to York once more. Having lost all faith in Henry VI, he asked Edward to be king in 1461. Norfolk pleaded sickness and arrived late at Towton, but his late intervention was decisive and tipped the scales for York. As Earl Marshal, he officiated at Edward's coronation in 1461, but he truly was ill and died later that same year.

He was succeeded by his son, also John Mowbray (1444–1476), the fourth duke of Norfolk. The new duke led a constant oppression of the Paston family, usually over property, mostly over Caister Castle in Norfolk. The Paston family made frequent complaints in what are known as the Paston Letters. The fourth duke of Norfolk had one daughter, Anne Mowbray, who became the countess of Norfolk in her own right in 1476 when the fourth duke died. This is an example of how Edward IV was quite happy to allow a female to inherit if she was a direct descendant. But the king may have had an ulterior motive. The countess of Norfolk was married to the king's second son, Richard of Shrewsbury, in 1478, when the prince became the next duke of Norfolk (in title only, as the estate remained with his young wife). When Anne Mowbray died in 1481, young Richard was given the complete inheritance, title, and estate, confirmed by an act of Parliament. Those deprived of this inheritance, Lords Howard and Berkeley, were offended. Berkeley was paid off handsomely, but John Howard remained bitter and took his revenge by supporting the usurpation of Richard III when Edward IV died.

Sir John Howard (1421–1485) was the son of Sir Robert Howard and Margaret de Mowbray (1388–1459). Margaret was the eldest daughter of Thomas de Mowbray, the first duke of Norfolk, a junior member of the lords appellant, who died in exile in 1399. Sir John Howard and his Mowbray relatives upheld the Yorkist cause in Norfolk for many years. Sir John fought hard at Towton in 1461 and was knighted on the field for his service.

Howard was one of the many Yorkists who joined Edward IV after his release from Middleham Castle in 1469. He was then made Lord Howard and fought with distinction at both Barnet and Tewkesbury. He served as treasurer of the royal household under Edward IV, conducted many important diplomatic missions for the king, served in the 1475 invasion of France, and was Lord High Admiral, responsible for the successful naval attack on Scotland in 1481.

Unfortunately, John Howard supported the duke of Gloucester with his plan to usurp the throne in 1483. It is difficult to understand why Edward did not do more to retain Howard's loyalty, but the king was offended by the fourth duke of Norfolk because of all the trouble he had caused in East Anglia. When the fourth duke of Norfolk died in 1476, Howard hoped for the duchy, but the heiress, Anne Mowbray, became the countess of Norfolk in her own right and held the estate. Then, in 1478, Edward IV betrothed and married his son young Prince Richard to Anne Mowbray and had Parliament give Richard the title duke of Norfolk, at first with no estate. But when Anne died in 1481, young Richard was given all of the estate, an act confirmed by Parliament. So, in effect, Edward took the duchy of Norfolk and gave it to his son Richard. This may explain why, later, Howard did not support the boy King Edward V. When Edward IV died in 1483, John Howard led the funeral procession to Windsor Castle. Some believe that if it were not for Howard's encouragement, then Richard, Duke of Gloucester, would not have followed his disastrous course in deposing King Edward V and seizing the throne (Clive, 1474).

For Richard III, John Howard was Lord High Steward and Earl Marshal. He was created Richard's first duke of Norfolk in 1483, soon after Richard III assumed the throne. It should be noted that young Richard, Duke of Norfolk, was alive at the time and imprisoned in the Tower with his brother, Edward V. Parliament had not removed the title or declared the prince to be legally dead. Before the Battle of Bosworth Field, it is said that an anonymous note posted on his tent warned John Howard that a double-cross was in the making: "Jack of Norfolk, be not so bold, for Dickon thy master is bought and sold." It is suggested that the phrase "bought and sold" meant "betrayed" in the fifteenth century. Northumberland and the two Stanleys, Lord Thomas and Sir William, did indeed support Henry Tudor at the crucial end of the famous battle. John Howard was the only magnate killed on the side of Richard III. This may indicate that very few supported Richard III. Howard was killed by an arrow through his throat and no doubt died of suffocation; his protective bevor was earlier damaged during a clash with the earl of Oxford.

Howard was posthumously attainted by the Tudor government of Henry VII for his support of Richard III; so, the Norfolk title and estate reverted to the Crown. Thomas's son, Thomas Howard, who Richard had made the first earl of Surrey, succeeded John Howard as the second duke of Norfolk when the title was restored to the Howard family in 1514 by Henry VIII. This was after Thomas had won the great Battle of Flodden Field against King James IV of Scotland in 1513, while Henry VIII was away in France. John Howard's grandson, also named Thomas Howard, succeeded as the third duke of Norfolk. This was after the third duke's wife, Edward IV's daughter Anne, had died. The third duke was a prolonged survivor, an elder statesman during the Tudor period, and affectionately known as the Old Duke.

John Howard was the great-grandfather of Queen Anne Boleyn and, therefore, the great-great-grandfather of Queen Elizabeth I, one of England's most famous rulers. Anne Boleyn's mother was Elizabeth Howard, a daughter of Thomas Howard, the second duke of Norfolk, the victor at Flodden Field.

Walter Blount (1416–1474), Lord Mountjoy, was a follower of Richard, the third duke of York, who died in 1460. After Ludford Bridge, Blount fled to Calais with Warwick, Salisbury, and the young earl of March, later Edward IV. Blount was at Towton in 1461 and was knighted on the battlefield; as a reward, he was made the governor of Calais. Blount became Lord Mountjoy in 1465 and attended the council. He married Edward IV's aunt Anne Neville, the dowager duchess of Buckingham, the widow of Humphrey Stafford, the first duke of Buckingham (see Appendix F), a sister of Edward's mother, Cecily (see Appendix E). Mountjoy received many of the lands of Thomas Courtenay, the Lancastrian sixth earl of Devon who was executed after Towton. Mountjoy joined Edward at Pontefract when Warwick released the king from custody at Middleham Castle in September 1469, and he served the king at Empingham in 1470. At the Readoption of Henry VI, he was briefly imprisoned by the Lancastrian regime and lost all of his titles and estates. Blount rejoined the king in 1471 and fought at Barnet and Tewkesbury. He died in 1474. He was succeeded by his grandson Edward, the second Baron Mountjoy, who died a year later, and then by his younger son, John Blount (1445–1485), the third Baron Mountjoy, who continued as governor of Calais but was ailing with ill health. After Richard III usurped the throne in 1483, John Blount's brother, Sir James Blount, the commander at Hammes near Calais, deserted York and changed sides. He and his prisoner, the earl of Oxford, along with a significant number of English troops, fled to Henry Tudor and joined the gathering invasion force in France. John Blount was relieved of his office when it became known that his brother, James, had deserted. He was replaced by John of Gloucester, who was ably supported by his deputy, Lord John Dinham.

Remarkably, young James Blount's wife defended Hammes Castle against Richard's forces under Lord Dinham for weeks. John de Vere returned to Hammes to negotiate terms. They only surrendered the castle when safe passage to France for Lady Blount and her troops was guaranteed. By that time in his reign, early 1485, nothing much went right for Richard III. His forces could not dislodge Lady Blount. John Blount did not support Richard at Bosworth because he was alienated, but also, more likely, because he was terminally sick and died on 12 October 1485, soon after Bosworth.

John Lord Dinham (1443–1501) served Edward IV in the West Country after the death of Humphrey Stafford at Edgecote in 1469. Previously, he had sheltered the young earl of March after the calamitous Yorkist setback at Ludford Bridge in 1459. Also, he and his wife helped organize the escape of the three Yorkist earls to Calais by finding the necessary transport ships. Lord Dinham served on the council from 1462. He was one of the loyal Yorkist affinity who joined Edward IV at Pontefract after the king's release from Middleham Castle in September 1469. In the reign of Edward IV, he was deputy commander at Calais, a post he retained under Richard III. When Richard appointed his illegitimate son John of Gloucester as captain of Calais, the king trusted Dinham to make sure that young John did not get into too much trouble because of his inexperience. Lord Dinham was not at Bosworth to support Richard III; this is best explained by his necessary presence at Calais. John Dinham later served Henry VII as Lord Treasurer for an extended period, from 1486 to 1501.

John Tiptoft (1427–1470), the earl of Worcester from 1449, was much trusted by Edward IV. He served under Henry VI, stayed in Italy for several years studying law and Latin, and returned to England in 1461. His translations of Cicero's *De Amicitia* and other Latin works were printed by William Caxton. In the Yorkist regime, he was appointed as constable of England, and as such he administered the attainders, forfeitures, and punishments of many Lancastrian adherents, including the twelfth earl of Oxford and his eldest son, Aubrey, who were both executed in 1462.

From 1467, Tiptoft served as lord deputy of Ireland, where he had attainted in the Irish Parliament and executed Thomas FitzGerald, the seventh earl of Desmond. The Irish earl was critical of the king's marriage and made derogatory remarks about the queen. He suggested to the king that he divorce Elizabeth Woodville and find a more suitable wife. Unbelievable as it may sound to the modern mind, in those times, this alone constituted treason and was punishable by death. Queen Elizabeth Woodville responded by encouraging Tiptoft's proceedings against the earl in the Irish Parliament. The earl's loose tongue, however, was not the only problem. Desmond had preceded Tiptoft as lieutenant. During his administration, he had supported the native Irish against the king's loyal English subjects, with disastrous attacks on people and property in the Pale around Dublin. This was, of course, more treason. The Irish–English in the Parliament at Drogheda, firm supporters of Edward IV, were very hostile towards Desmond. Tiptoft hardly needed any support from the queen. In the end, Desmond was attainted and executed. But of great concern, the earl's two young sons were also allegedly executed. It would be surprising if the queen, a faithful mother, supported this – if she had known about it. Nevertheless, some authors suggest that this unfortunate episode contributed to the hostility of Richard III against Queen Elizabeth Woodville, although he did not mention her when he discussed the matter with Desmond's son (Higginbotham, 2013) and, instead, laid all the blame on the Irish Parliament.

The punishments that Tiptoft handed out were often extremely cruel, even by contemporary English standards. Some claim that Tiptoft learned to commit these atrocities from the Italian magnates at the time of the Renaissance. The judicial murder of the two Desmond boys seems to have been yet another example; Tiptoft was later called the Butcher of England.

It is doubtful that the queen had much to do with any of these judicial atrocities, let alone the execution of the Desmond sons. It would appear that Tiptoft might be described as Edward's hatchet man. In 1470, Tiptoft executed by rectal impalement twenty of Warwick's men involved in the rebellions that year; it is possible that the men were already dead when they were subjected to this grotesque procedure. At the Readoption of Henry VI, Tiptoft went into hiding, but he was arrested and tried by John de Vere, the thirteenth earl of Oxford, the new Lancastrian constable of England, for the execution of the twelfth earl of Oxford and his son. Tiptoft was found guilty and was executed at the order of the earl of Warwick, much to the pleasure of the general populace. It is said that the earl scornfully requested that the executioner deliver three blows with the axe, one blow each for the three persons of the Holy Trinity.

History's conclusion is that Edward IV may have been misguided in trusting Tiptoft, but the king never admitted it. The queen's later reputation was to suffer. While there was not a great deal of contemporary concern in 1468, in 1538, during the reign of Henry VIII, Desmond's grandson complained about the queen's role in the Desmond affair when he attempted to recover some lost property. Later historians have condemned the queen for her role in this episode. Of course, the queen was not present to defend herself, and other historians, as discussed by Arlene Okerlund (2005), have completely exonerated her. But all this did not matter much, as Richard, Duke of Gloucester, alive and biding his time, was determined not to change his low opinion of the commoner Queen Elizabeth.

Sir John Wenlock (1404–1471) was chamberlain to Queen Margaret Anjou and was knighted in 1449. As speaker of the House of Commons in 1455, he was on the Lancastrian side at First St Albans. However, he supported the Yorkists from 1455 onwards; after Ludford Bridge in 1459, he retreated with the Yorkist earls to Calais and was attainted in 1460 by the Lancastrian government. Sir John was a good friend of Warwick and gradually drifted to the side of York, for which he fought at Blore Heath, Mortimer's Cross, Second St Albans, and Towton. He was part of Edward IV's triumphant entry into London in 1461. He was made Knight of the Garter and chief butler of England. His particular skill was in diplomacy; he often represented Edward as an ambassador, and he attended the council from 1461. He is listed here as a supporter, but he was sometimes also the enemy of Edward IV.

As commander at Calais, Wenlock refused Warwick entry in 1470, after Empingham, but soon drifted back to his old friend and, with him, went to the side of Lancaster. Sir John invaded England with Queen Margaret Anjou in 1471. At Tewkesbury, he commanded the centre battle formation with young Edward of Westminster; he failed to support Somerset's near successful charge with the Lancastrian right battle against Gloucester's left-battle division. Sir John said his men could not fire on the Yorkists because Somerset's men were in the way. He also said that Somerset bungled the manoeuvre by coming out of the woods too early, so he emerged in front of Gloucester, not behind him as planned. Somerset was so angry that he killed Wenlock on the field, allegedly with a single blow of a battleaxe; he did this in front of demoralized Lancastrian troops, who soon fled the field in the face of the violent Yorkist attack. For his role in the War of the Roses, he was known as the Prince of Turncoats, which may be a little unfair as he only changed twice, for instance in 1455 and 1471. Switching sides was not uncommon during this confusing time in the history of England.

John Tuchet (1423–1490), the sixth Baron Audley, was an active supporter of Edward IV in the West Country, where his properties were located. Although considered by Lancastrians to be greedy and ruthless, he derived little benefit from his association with Edward, except for the few minor offices and appointments he was awarded. He fought for York at Mortimer's Cross, Barnet, and Tewkesbury. It would appear that John Tuchet, the sixth baron, did appear at Bosworth in support of Richard III, according to Charles Ross (1999). He should not be confused with his father, James Tuchet, the fifth Baron Audley, who commanded the Lancastrian forces at Blore Heath in 1459 and was beheaded after the Yorkist victory.

Bishop John Morton (1420–1500) was a supporter of Edward IV, but not a constant one. He was present at Towton on the Lancastrian side, fled with Queen Margaret Anjou to Scotland, and was attainted. He lived in the household of Queen Margaret in France until 1470. He participated in the negotiations between Warwick, Louis XI, and Queen Margaret, and he landed with Warwick's invasion force in 1471. After Barnet and

Tewkesbury, he made his peace with Edward IV. The king used him for diplomatic missions. Morton was one of those who negotiated the Treaty of Picquigny in 1475. He was chancellor for the Duchy of Cornwall and thereby on the king's council, sometime before he was made the bishop of Ely in 1479.

Morton was the principal executor of Edward's last will; he raised no objection to the claim that before he died, Edward IV appointed Richard, Duke of Gloucester, as Lord Protector. He had discussions with Hastings and Rotherham about releasing King Edward V from the Tower, part of the so-called Hastings Conspiracy. Morton was at the council meeting which led to the illegal execution of Lord Hastings. Other accounts differ from his; a minority opinion, favourable to Richard III, suggests that Hastings was arrested and tried before his execution. But Morton's eyewitness account of the treacherous murder has been accepted by history. Plus, there is no good reason why Morton would have lied, as there were too many other witnesses. Following the death of Hastings, Gloucester suspected Morton of treason and sent him to the Tower; but he was soon released to Brecknock Castle in Wales, under the charge of the duke of Buckingham, where he influenced the duke to rebel against Richard III. Morton corresponded with Margaret Beaufort in Lancashire, with Queen Elizabeth Woodville in sanctuary, and with Henry Tudor in Brittany. Almost certainly, this correspondence was related to the Christmas 1483 declaration by Henry Tudor at Rennes Cathedral that he had agreed to marry Elizabeth of York after his recovery of the English crown for the House of Lancaster.

When the Buckingham Rebellion failed, Morton went into hiding and escaped to Antwerp to wait out the reign of Richard III. He did not expect Richard III to last for long. Morton was offered pardon by Richard III, but the bishop rejected it. Under King Henry VII, Morton was Archbishop of Canterbury and chancellor of England. He was the mentor of Sir Thomas More, who, during his teen years, worked as a page at Morton's residence at Lambeth Palace in London. Some think it may be Morton's version of history which is recounted by Sir Thomas More (2005) in his book titled *The History of King Richard III,* but it should be noted that Sir Thomas More used quite a few other witnesses in addition to Morton. Also, Sir Thomas More was writing many years after the bishop's death. It seems confirmed that Morton was virulently against Richard III but had considerable respect for King Edward IV.

John Stafford (1427–1473), the Yorkist earl of Wiltshire, was the youngest son of Humphrey Stafford, the first duke of Buckingham – the same duke who was killed at Northampton in the year 1460 (see Appendix F). John was the uncle of Henry Stafford, the second duke of Buckingham, who rebelled in October 1483 and was executed for treason by Richard III.

John Stafford fought for York at Hexham in 1464. He was made steward of the Duchy of Cornwall in 1469, earl of Wiltshire in 1470, and chief butler of England in 1471. Stafford served Edward IV for a time as a diplomat on missions to speak with James III of Scotland. His three-year-old son Edward Stafford (1470–1499) succeeded him as the second earl of Wiltshire.

William Neville (1410–1463), Lord Fauconberg, later the first earl of Kent, cleared the Lancastrians at Ferrybridge, the skirmish which preceded the Battle of Towton, and led the Yorkist vanguard at Towton the next day. William was the second son of Ralph Neville and Joan Beaufort (see Appendix E). He was therefore a great-grandson of Edward III. He married the disabled Fauconberg heiress and took the title of Lord Fauconberg. His older brother was Richard, the fifth earl of Salisbury, and his nephew was Richard, the sixteenth earl of Warwick.

In the Hundred Years War, he served in France, where later he was imprisoned. During this time, he paid for the upkeep of Roxburgh Castle, one of his holdings, and as a result became heavily indebted. He was ransomed in 1453 and returned to England, where he was on the council during King Henry VI's second illness. Neville sided with Lancaster at First St Albans in 1455. After that, he changed sides and followed Richard, Duke of York. As he was the uncle of Richard, the sixteenth earl of Warwick, he was more naturally a Yorkist. He was Warwick's deputy commander in Calais and participated in the many military and naval operations that Warwick had undertaken from Calais in the years after 1457.

In 1460, he captured Sandwich, which was then used as a springboard for Warwick's invasion of England that year. Fauconberg led the right battle at Northampton. The other two commanders were Edward, Earl of March, on the left, and Richard, Earl of Warwick, in the centre. He returned to Calais and missed the Yorkist defeats at Wakefield and Second St Albans.

In 1461, he returned to London and joined the newly proclaimed King Edward IV. After the great Yorkist triumph at Towton, he joined the king's council and was appointed lieutenant of the north, Earl of Kent, steward of the royal household, and Lord High Admiral of England.

Lord Fauconberg died in 1463 during the Lancastrian rebellions, at the Siege of Alnwick, but possibly of natural causes. Much underrated, he was one of the most successful Yorkist commanders. His one acknowledged illegitimate son, Thomas Neville, was known as the Bastard of Fauconberg. Thomas rebelled against Edward IV in 1471, as a supplement to Queen Margaret's campaign that year, and was later executed at the orders of Richard, Duke of Gloucester, for unrelated offences.

James III (1451–1488), King of Scotland, who reigned from 1460 to 1488, could be regarded as a friend of Edward IV, but the political situation in Scotland did not make it easy. He was nine years old at his succession. His mother, Mary de Gueldres, was regent and supported Henry VI and the Lancastrian incursions into Northumberland. After Mary's death in 1463, the new regent, Bishop Kennedy, made peace with England. Henry VI had to leave Scotland and go back to England, later as a fugitive when the Yorkists recovered all the northern castles in 1464. Kennedy died in 1465. The next year, Robert, Lord Boyd, kidnapped the king and ruled as regent. In 1469, James III married Margaret of Denmark, drove the Boyd family out of Scotland, seized all their lands for the Crown, and ruled for himself, quickly confirming the peace with England. James III was hated by his nobles, first because of his interest in scholarship and the arts, second because he preferred low-born ministers in his government, and last because of his friendly policy towards England.

In 1474, James arranged the betrothal of his eldest son and heir, James, to Cecily, a daughter of Edward IV. Later, James III also tried to arrange the marriage of his sister Margaret to Anthony Woodville, but Margaret became pregnant and the plan had to be abandoned. Relations with Edward IV rapidly deteriorated thereafter. Scottish raids into Northumberland resumed in 1480, no doubt encouraged by Louis XI of France. English ships under Lord Howard destroyed many Scottish vessels in the Firth of Forth in 1481. When Gloucester invaded Scotland in 1482, the Scottish nobles refused to fight for the hated king. The fifth earl of Angus, known as Archibald "Red" Douglas, hanged many of the king's ministers at

Lauder Bridge and imprisoned the king in Edinburgh Castle. Gloucester occupied Edinburgh, extracted a partial refund of money previously paid in instalments for Cecily's dowry, captured Berwick, and returned to England, all at the instructions of Edward IV, who maintained contact by an elaborate relay of messengers on horseback. James III was not a friend of Richard III and, despite an earlier peace treaty in September 1484, sent Scottish troops to join Henry Tudor (Miller, 2003). They must have been effective at Bosworth Field. After the death of James's queen, Henry VII considered marrying Edward IV's widow, Elizabeth Woodville, to James III, as part of a marriage treaty, but the Scottish king was killed at the Battle of Sauchiburn in 1488, fighting against his rebellious lords. Henry VII's plan for Elizabeth's treaty marriage did not support the often repeated, but unlikely notion, that he thought that Dowager Queen Elizabeth was a traitor to the Tudor government.

Sir William Stanley (1435–1495), the younger brother of Lord Thomas Stanley, was a Yorkist supporter for most of his life, but not in the end. He was at Blore Heath in 1459. In 1465, he was granted the properties of Lord Clifford, who had been killed at Ferrybridge. At the Readoption of Henry VI, he did not support Warwick, so his properties were ransacked by angry Lancastrians. At the return of Edward IV in 1471, Stanley joined the king with three hundred troops at Nottingham. It would be surprising if he was not at Barnet, but there is apparently no mention of him in the accounts. He was knighted on the field at Tewkesbury in 1471. The capture of Queen Margaret Anjou after the battle, at Little Malvern Priory, is attributed to Sir William and his men. After Edward IV was dead, Stanley went along with Richard III and raised troops at the Buckingham Rebellion, most probably for the king. Richard III made him Chief Justice of North Wales. During the Margaret Beaufort conspiracy, he slowly converted to the cause of Henry Tudor, becoming convinced that the sons of Edward IV were dead at the hands of Richard III and supporting the idea that the true heir was Princess Elizabeth of York.

About a week after Henry Tudor landed in Wales, young George Stanley, held hostage by Richard III, tried to escape. When young George was recaptured, he said that Sir William was supporting Henry Tudor. This explains why Richard III officially declared Sir William to be a traitor. In the week before Bosworth, Sir William met twice with Henry Tudor, first at Stafford and second at Atherstone, but apparently gave no commitment. On the battlefield at Bosworth, Sir William remained to one side and only joined the battle when he saw that Richard III was vulnerable. His intervention was decisive in giving Lancaster the victory; it was his men who killed Richard III.

Sir William served Henry VII as Lord Chamberlain; he wanted the earldom of Chester, but Henry made no move on his behalf. In about 1493, Sir William made short statements which appeared to support Perkin Warbeck, in whom he saw suggestions of Edward IV. Sir William was executed for treason in 1495.

Lord Thomas Stanley (1435–1504) was known for hedging his bets and staying friendly to all sides during turbulent times. The original Stanley property was Tatton Park in Cheshire. Lord Thomas first married Eleanor Neville (see Appendix E), a sister of Warwick the Kingmaker, which made him brother-in-law to the famous earl. He second married Margaret Beaufort (see Appendix D), the mother of Henry Tudor, which made him the stepfather of Henry VII.

At Blore Heath in 1459, he was in the field with his forces but did not take part in the battle. It was hard to know which side he took. Complaints about him were heard in the Lancastrian Parliament, which suggests that he was expected to support Henry VI. It may be that he was for Lancaster at Northampton in 1460. That Lancastrian disaster must have made him even more cautious. In early 1461, he was the beneficiary of property transferred by Henry VI, so he still appeared to be Lancastrian.

By late 1461, he was more Yorkist. He was made Chief Justice of Chester and appeared for Edward IV at Towton. After Empingham in 1470, Warwick fled to his brother-in-law Stanley in Yorkshire, who offered no assistance in the rebellion against the Yorkist king. But later in 1470, at the Readoption of Henry VI, Stanley accompanied Warwick to the Tower of London to restore Henry VI as king. Stanley did not appear at either Barnet or Tewkesbury in 1471; he must have had difficulty deciding where his loyalties lay. In 1474, he was made steward of the royal household by Edward IV, and in 1475, he attended the king's invasion of France. In 1482, he accompanied Gloucester to Scotland. Lord Stanley commanded the right-battle division and, while Gloucester was in Edinburgh, invested Berwick and captured the citadel. In 1483, he was present at the funeral of Edward IV.

After the death of Edward IV in April 1483, it appears that Lord Stanley continued as the steward of the royal household, awaiting the pleasure of the next king, whoever that was to be. On 10 May 1483, he was present at council when Bishop John Russell was made chancellor of England and given the Great Seal. Stanley supported Edward V and took part, with Hastings, in secret discussions about releasing Edward V from the Tower, but the participants decided that the plan was too dangerous and abandoned it. On 13 June 1483, he attended the council meeting at which Hastings was executed in the Tower garden. Stanley was briefly held under house arrest on suspicion of conspiracy. He made little objection when Gloucester usurped the throne. At the coronation of Richard III, he carried the mace ahead of the king. It appeared that he had made a smooth transition. Soon, he accompanied Richard on his first royal progress.

During the Buckingham Rebellion, Stanley remained loyal. His son George, Lord Strange, had a considerable force in the field, presumably to support the king. After Buckingham was executed, Stanley became the constable of England in his place. Early in 1485, Richard had enough confidence in Stanley to give him and his brother William commissions of array to raise troops in Cheshire and Lancaster. This was a serious mistake. Stanley took leave of the court in July 1485 to attend to matters at his home. In the approach to Bosworth, Stanley met Henry Tudor at Atherstone but would not commit himself. Soon after, he sent word to Richard that he was ill with the sweating sickness and could not join the king. At Bosworth, he attended but never entered the battle; however, he sent many of his troops with Sir William Stanley to decisively defeat Richard III. When it was over, it appears likely that one of his men found Richard's crown, it is said under a hawthorn bush. Lord Stanley placed the crown on Henry Tudor's head and declared him the new king.

For his reward, he was made the earl of Derby, appointed as lord high steward of England, and confirmed as constable of England. Stanley joined Oxford and Dowager Queen Elizabeth Woodville as sponsors at the baptism of Prince Arthur in 1486; he attended the coronation of Queen Elizabeth York in 1487. Henry VII kept heaping rewards upon him. At Stoke, in 1487, Stanley had his son Lord Strange lead his royal forces, as perhaps he was feeling his age. After Stoke, he received the properties of the rebel Sir Thomas Broughton and others. When the king executed his brother Sir William Stanley for treason in 1495, Henry mollified Lord Thomas by making him Chancellor of the Exchequer. His ultimate transition from York back to Lancastrian Tudor was smooth; Lord Thomas Stanley was the master political trimmer.

Thomas Rotherham (1423–1500), Archbishop of York, was a man of humble birth. He was bishop of Rochester in 1468, bishop of Lincoln in 1472, and Archbishop of York from 1480 to 1500. He was keeper of the privy seal from 1467 to 1474, except during the Readoption of Henry VI, and Lord Chancellor from 1475 to 1483. After the death of Edward IV, Rotherham's sympathies lay with the queen; he sent the Great Seal to her in sanctuary, but then thought better and recovered it from her. This revealed his loyalty to Edward's queen. He was replaced as chancellor by Bishop John Russell on 10 May 1483. He was briefly sent to the Tower on 13 June 1483 for his part in secret discussions with Hastings and Morton about releasing King Edward V from the Tower prison, but he was soon released to the supervision of Sir James Tyrell, as Richard needed to be careful how he treated his prelates. Rotherham officiated at the celebrations in York to mark the occasion of Richard's coronation and also at the investiture of Edward, the young Prince of Wales.

John Alcock (1430–1500), Bishop of Rochester, was also a man of humble birth. He was bishop of Rochester in 1472, bishop of Worcester in 1476, and bishop of Ely in 1486. He was educated at Cambridge University and was on the council for a short time in 1470–71. In 1476, he was made the Lord President of the Council of Wales, in which capacity he was also the tutor for Edward, Prince of Wales, later King Edward V. He was removed from his position as tutor by Richard III, who seemed not to favour him. If Richard III had ever decided on a hearing by an ecclesiastical law court wherein the imprisoned king was given representation, then Alcock and Rotherham would have been excellent choices to represent young King Edward V. But this idle thought was apparently never a consideration. In 1484, Alcock was a commissioner appointed to negotiate the peace with Scotland. Alcock was briefly Lord Chancellor of England for Henry VII in 1485–87. He baptized Prince Arthur and is most famous for founding the Jesus College at Cambridge University.

Thomas Bourchier (1404–1486), Archbishop of Canterbury, was a great-grandson of Edward III through Thomas of Woodstock, Edward III's youngest son; this was so through the third marriage of his mother Anne Plantagenet, which was to William Bourchier (see Appendix F). Thomas was the brother of Henry Bourchier, the first earl of Essex. Thomas was later the Archbishop of Canterbury who crowned Elizabeth Woodville as queen of England in 1465. Obviously, he thought her marriage to the king was perfectly valid.

Thomas Bourchier, educated at Oxford, was chancellor of Oxford University from 1434 to 1437. He was dean of St Martin's Le Grand in 1427, bishop of Worcester in 1434, bishop of Ely in 1443, and Archbishop of Canterbury from 1454 to 1486. Thomas was chancellor of England from 1455 to 1456; he was appointed by Richard, the third duke of York, and left office when the duke left office at the end of his first protectorate. Thomas accompanied the Yorkist earls of Warwick, Salisbury, and March in attempts to negotiate a battlefield settlement before the Battle of Northampton in 1460, but the duke of Buckingham refused them an audience with Henry VI. The archbishop must have been much involved with the negotiations prior to passage of the Act of Accord in 1460. Thomas crowned Edward IV in 1461. In 1473, he was made a cardinal of Rome but resided in England. In 1475, he was a principal negotiator for the Treaty of Picquigny.

After the death of Edward IV in April 1483, he persuaded Elizabeth Woodville to allow Prince Richard to leave sanctuary and join his brother at the Tower. He gave his surety for the life of the prince, but he was unable to keep his promise. The prince died in the Tower, probably in early September 1483. Although he had sworn allegiance to King Edward V, Thomas crowned Richard III – but he did not attend the coronation banquet. This is often taken as a sign of his unhappiness about the usurpation. He almost certainly warned Richard III against violating the sanctuary of Elizabeth Woodville. It is strongly suspected that he conspired against Richard III during the Buckingham Rebellion, but his prelacy protected him from attainder. He crowned Henry VII and married the new king with Elizabeth of York, thus uniting the Houses of Lancaster and York. Bourchier retired to his books and roses in 1486 and died the same year.

It is a mystery why Archbishop Bourchier did not try to dissuade Richard from his unlawful course; perhaps Lord Thomas was too old, or perhaps he had too often been the peacemaker. Maybe the bishops were unsure of Richard's intentions until it was too late. The first suggestion came on 8 June 1483, but it did not appear definite until Dr Shaw spoke on 22 June 1483. That left only three days to make a momentous decision. The bishops should have told Richard that his proposal was illegal, not consistent with custom and precedent, and therefore not constitutional. They should have told Richard that an ecclesiastical law court and then a proper Parliament were needed. If they had been persistent with gentle persuasion and no threats, then they might have changed the Lord Protector's mind. Many things about Richard's character and intellect suggest that he might have listened to reason and perhaps taken a different course. But, as previously mentioned, it seems likely that Richard had already considered that approach in the ecclesiastical law courts, but had decided that he could not with certainty make his case.

Sir James Tyrell (1450–1502) was a loyal Yorkist. He may not have been a friend of Edward IV and his children, but he started with that tendency. He was knighted at Tewkesbury in 1471. Richard, Duke of Gloucester, had him escort his new mother-in-law, the countess of Warwick, and take her from the sanctuary at Beaulieu Abbey to Middleham Castle in Yorkshire in 1473. Sir James held a variety of positions: High Sheriff of Cornwall, justice commissioner in Suffolk, member of Parliament, sheriff of Glamorgan, steward of the Duchy of Cornwall, chamberlain of the exchequer, governor of Cardiff Castle, and several others – all before 1483, in the reign of Edward IV. Tyrell accompanied Gloucester to Scotland in 1482. He took custody of Bishop Rotherham after the murder of Hastings, attended the coronation of Richard III, and conducted the prisoner duke of Buckingham to Salisbury for the traitor's execution. Sir Thomas More was mistaken in suggesting in his book *The History of Richard III* that Richard III was not familiar with Sir James Tyrell.

If something nefarious needed to be done, then the king of England knew where to find his man. Sir Thomas More (2005) said that in August 1483, Sir James arranged the murder of the princes in the Tower for Richard III; but some think it was early September. In late 1484, Sir James went to Flanders on important business for King Richard III; some have suggested that this was to oversee the alleged transfer of a surviving Edward V and Prince Richard from the Tyrell estate at Gipping in Suffolk to a new, permanent residence in Burgundy. But this has never been proven and seems most unlikely. Tyrell's journey must have been for other business. In January 1485, Tyrell was made governor of Guînes Castle at Calais; at that time, he received an unusually large payment from Richard III. It is suggested by some that this was for his supervision of the princes in Burgundy, but, equally, it could also have been a late reward for his earlier murder of the princes in 1483, perhaps in fulfilment of a prior agreement, so that the deed and its reward would not appear closely associated in time.

His position at Guînes was confirmed by Henry VII. In 1486, he received two pardons from Henry VII, the first in June for his Yorkist career, and the second a month later for some unknown reason. Some say it was for a simple matter, such as erroneous paperwork for the first pardon. But others have speculated that he arranged for the murder and disposal of the princes in the Tower for Henry in 1486. There is no good evidence for this, as the princes were never seen again after August 1483 and much more likely died in the Tower.

In 1501, Tyrell was accused of treason for supporting Edmund de la Pole while the earl was visiting in Flanders. Tyrell was tricked into boarding an English warship bound for London. In the Tower, he confessed to the murder of the princes and said he followed the instructions of Richard III; this latter account is according to Sir Thomas More (2005). Tyrell was executed for treason in 1502. He paid the price for his recent Yorkist liaison; he was not executed for his destruction of the princes.

If Tyrell took the princes to Burgundy for Richard III in late 1484, then this means they had survived in England for over one year without being recognized, and for another long but unknown period in Burgundy, also without being recognized. It is not likely, especially as the duchess of Burgundy supported all attempts to put a Yorkist, any Yorkist, any pretender, back on the English throne during the reign of Henry VII. But the revisionists have not given up; they claim that Perkin Warbeck, the pretender, was the stalking horse for the real Prince Richard living unidentified in Burgundy. Duchess Margaret never made an attempt to put a real prince back on the throne of England; the obvious explanation is that she never had a real prince in her hands. That desperate theory would leave no explanation for the skeletons found in the Tower; those experts in 1674, 1933, and 1955 – and those later – must all have been wrong.

If Tyrell murdered the princes for Henry VII in July 1486, then they would have been in the Tower and not seen for nearly three years. Also, their dental ages estimated in 1933 and later would not have fit with their known chronological ages. Sir James goes down in English history as a villain; but either way, both Richard III and Henry VII appeared grateful to him. It may be that Richard III rewarded him for the well-executed secret murders in the Tower, and that Henry VII rewarded him for the fall of the Royal House of York, leaving behind no serious male heirs!

Sir Thomas More (1478–1535) was five years old at the death of Edward IV. His father, Sir John More, was a prominent London barrister and, later, a judge. At age thirteen years, Thomas was a page in the household of Cardinal Morton at Lambeth Palace. From 1492, he attended Oxford University – and later studied law at Lincoln's Inn. For some time, he lived at a monastery and followed a monkish lifestyle of prayer, fasting, and penance. He entered Parliament in 1504. In 1510, he became an undersheriff in London; in 1518, he was in the Privy Council; in 1523, he was speaker of the House of Commons; and in 1529, at the fall of Wolsey, he was Lord Chancellor. His famous book titled *Utopia* was published in 1516. Prior to and probably after that time, he was busy writing his book *The History of Richard III* based on the confessions that Sir James Tyrell and John Dighton made in 1502. Sir Thomas More had apparently found the records in the archives. This book appears not to be finished, ending with the Brecknock conversations between Morton and Buckingham in what was probably August 1483; so, it is More's version of the disqualification and death of the princes in the Tower, maybe based on his recall of Morton's testimony, but modified with the evidence given by many other witnesses interviewed for the book. The work is very detailed, but, of course, the dialogue is invented, which represents a not uncommon literary device. As it reads, it appears unfair to Richard III. Sir Thomas More may have abandoned it for this reason. But others have speculated that he may have decided that some of his vital facts were in error. Certainly, there are some minor errors – for instance, the age of Edward IV is wrong – but the king's birthdate in France may not have been as well established at that time as it is now. There is another reason why Sir Thomas More may have abandoned the book, probably a better one. He was writing during the reign of King Henry VIII, and his version of the story suggested that

Edward V or his heir should still be the king. His ruthless Tudor master might not have been pleased with him, as the Tudor kings always worried about the legality of their claim to the throne and the existence of Yorkist claimants.

Sir Thomas More resigned as chancellor in 1532, as he did not agree with the king's plan to annul his marriage to Queen Katherine. An ecclesiastical law court convened at Dunstaple Priory declared on 23 May 1533 that the king's marriage to Katherine was null and void. At the English Reformation, More refused to submit his acceptance to the March 1534 Act of Succession which made Princess Elizabeth, the daughter of Queen Anne Boleyn, the heir to the throne. Sir Thomas More was imprisoned in the Tower from 17 April 1534, but he still refused to accept that Henry VIII was the Supreme Head of the English Church, as legislated by the Act of Supremacy passed in November 1534. After a formal trial, he was executed for treason on 6 July 1535.

His manuscript for *The History of Richard III* was discovered among his papers after his death and was later published by his nephew William Rastell in 1557. The version referenced in the present text is based on the original handwritten manuscript discovered in his home; there were several other versions which were considered corrupted and not reliable. For his high opinion of King Edward IV, for his good words about Queen Elizabeth Woodville, and for his sympathy with Edward V and Prince Richard, Sir Thomas More must be considered a friend of the first Yorkist king or, at the very least, a friend of his legacy.

CHAPTER 17

The Enemies of King Edward IV

John de Vere (1442–1513), the thirteenth earl of Oxford, was a staunch Lancastrian. He married Margaret Neville, a sister of the Kingmaker, the sixteenth earl of Warwick (see Appendix E). John's father, the twelfth earl of Oxford, also a staunch Lancastrian who supported Queen Margaret Anjou, was executed at the orders of John Tiptoft, the constable of England, in 1462, along with his eldest son, John's brother Aubrey. But the thirteenth earl was allowed to assume his title and estate because Edward IV was following a policy of conciliation. Oxford acted as chamberlain to Queen Elizabeth Woodville at her coronation in 1465.

John de Vere, the thirteenth earl, was correctly suspected of disloyalty for colluding with Lancastrians and spent some time in the Tower in 1468, but he was pardoned in April 1469. Then he sided with Warwick and Clarence in the 1469 rebellion and went into exile with Warwick in 1470, after Empingham. He was present when Warwick had to kneel for so long before Queen Margaret Anjou at Angers Cathedral; the Lancastrian queen thanked Oxford graciously for his loyalty. Later, in 1470, the earl invaded England with Warwick and assisted Warwick at the time of the Readoption of Henry VI. As constable of England in the new regime, he tried John Tiptoft for the judicial murder of his father, the twelfth earl of Oxford, and had Tiptoft executed, much to the pleasure of the London crowd.

Early in the 1471 invasion by Edward IV, John de Vere evacuated Newark when the returning king threatened his forces. Oxford lost at the Battle of Barnet, through no fault of his own, and escaped to France. At this time, his lands were confiscated. After Tewkesbury, the earl conspired with George Neville and George, Duke of Clarence, against Edward IV. For Louis XI, he raided the coasts of Calais, Essex, and Cornwall in 1472. But he was captured by the Yorkists at St Michael's Mount in February 1474, imprisoned near Calais at Hammes Castle, and attainted in 1475. Some believe he tried to commit suicide after the death of Clarence by plunging into the moat at Hammes, but more likely it was a bungled attempt at escape. After a long twelve-year imprisonment, he finally escaped in October 1484, took with him the English commander at Hammes, Sir James Blount, and many English soldiers, and eventually joined Henry Tudor in France. Henry Tudor sent him back to Hammes to negotiate the escape of Blount's wife and other English soldiers who had converted to the Lancastrian side.

The earl of Oxford commanded with distinction at both Bosworth Field in 1485 and Stoke Field in 1487. After Bosworth, with the death of his friend Lord Howard, Oxford said, "A better knight could not die, but he might die in a better cause." Henry VII appointed him Lord High Admiral, Lord Chamberlain of England, and constable of the Tower. If the Yorkist princes were still in the Tower in 1486, as suggested by a few, then it must have been John de Vere or his deputy who refused to execute them. Although the earl was certainly an honourable man, this story about the princes is very likely not true. Oxford was probably the best of the Lancastrian commanders, but his victories came after Edward IV was gone. It can be said that his career, like that of Henry Tudor, was resurrected because of the usurpation by Richard III. It is reasonable to conclude that if the Yorkists had stayed with the legal succession of King Edward V and the legal protectorate of Richard, Duke of Gloucester, then there probably would have been no Lancastrian recovery of the kingdom, no Henry VIII, no Reformation, and no Virgin Queen.

Oxford's wife Margaret died in 1506; subsequently, he married Elizabeth Scrope, the widow of his good friend Lord Beaumont. The earl of Oxford was the great chamberlain at the coronation of Henry VIII in 1509. John de Vere died in 1513; his heir, also John de Vere, his nephew, became the fourteenth earl of Oxford.

The numerous *dukes of Somerset* (see Appendix D) led the Lancastrian armies at many of the battles against the House of York. They are as follows:

John Beaufort (1403–1444), the first duke of Somerset, assisted Talbot at the Siege of Harfleur in 1440. When the town was recovered and the duke of York arrived in Normandy, Somerset resigned his post and returned to England. In 1443, appointed as captain general of Guyenne, Somerset led a significant English army into Gascony but failed to restore order. This expedition took men and resources from the duke of York in Normandy, much to York's annoyance; furthermore, Somerset was paid for his failure, while York's expenses were never refunded. This may be the origin of the feud between the duke of York and the Beauforts. Somerset died soon after his return to England. History has always wondered if he killed himself because of his failure. He had married Margaret Beauchamp of Bletso in 1439; he was the father of the famous Lady Margaret Beaufort and the grandfather of King Henry VII (see Appendix D).

Edmund Beaufort (1406–1455), the second duke of Somerset, succeeded his brother John. Edmund was the infamous favourite of Henry VI. He was guilty of maladministration in England and of poor military leadership in France, where he was lieutenant from 1447, after the duke of York had left. He suffered all the ignominious losses from 1450 to 1453, as the English lost France and the Hundred Years War came to a close. Earlier, he had quarrelled with Warwick over estates in Glamorgan, which may help explain why Warwick supported the duke of York. Edmund was an uncle of the well-known Lady Margaret Beaufort. Richard, the third duke of York, bitterly hated Edmund and wanted him replaced as the king's favourite. Twice, the duke of York, as Lord Protector, sent Somerset to the Tower, but each time, Queen Margaret released him. Earlier, Edmund was considered a possible heir to Henry VI, which may also explain the antipathy of Richard, Duke of York. The Yorkists claimed that he was the real father of the Prince of Wales, Edward of Westminster, which was a terrible insult to Queen Margaret Anjou and Henry VI. When war between the factions in England became inevitable, Somerset was killed at the First Battle of St Albans in 1455.

Edmund's son, *Henry Beaufort (1436–1464), the third duke of Somerset,* led the Lancastrian forces at Wakefield in 1460, at Second St Albans in 1461, and at Towton later, in 1461. After his defeat at Towton, Henry Beaufort escaped to Scotland, but he returned to lead the northern rebellions against Edward IV in 1462. Edward IV greatly admired Henry; Edward tried to befriend him and turn him to the side of York. After being captured in Northumberland, Henry submitted to Edward, in March 1463. The two ate, drank, and hunted together; it is even alleged that they shared the king's bed, a not uncommon practice in those days, without inference of homosexuality. On a visit to Northampton, Henry was attacked by a mob which blamed him for burning Northampton before the battle in 1460; so, Edward sent him to Wales under guard for his own protection. But later, Somerset escaped and arrived back at Bamburg Castle in December 1463. All of Edward's efforts came to naught as Henry resumed in rebellion. Henry was defeated at Hedgeley Moor in 1464 and again in the same year at Hexham, where he was captured. At the orders of Warwick, he was executed. Edward has been criticized for this example of poor judgement, but the incident reflects how seriously the Yorkist king tried to reconcile with his subjects.

The younger brother of Henry Beaufort, *Edmund Beaufort (1438–1471), the fourth duke of Somerset,* was not present at Barnet, as he had no respect for Warwick. Instead, he waited for Queen Margaret's invasion force on the south coast of England, and he commanded at Tewkesbury, later in 1471. Edmund made the famous charge in the woods with the right battle, but he emerged from the tree cover too early, which placed him in front of the Yorkists, not behind them as planned. His forces were destroyed by Richard, Duke of Gloucester, and King Edward IV. Edmund blamed Wenlock for not supporting him, but the old soldier argued that Edmund had bungled the manoeuvre and placed his men where Wenlock could not provide support with cannonade. Never mind that Somerset killed Wenlock in front of his own men, after which the demoralized Lancastrians soon fled. Somerset claimed sanctuary in Tewkesbury Abbey, but Edward claimed that there was no sanctuary for treason. The Yorkists dragged him out at dagger point. Two days later, he was tried and executed. He was the last of the direct Beaufort male line. Edward IV has been much criticized for the savagery at Tewkesbury, but, in the face of constant rebellion, Edward had no choice. His critics had never walked in Edward's shoes. His patience with the rebels was, in fact, truly remarkable.

Sir Ralph Percy (1425–1464), a younger son of Henry Percy (1393–1455), the second earl of Northumberland, took part in the northern rebellions following the accession of Edward IV in 1461. Sir Ralph was hardly considered someone who could be easily persuaded to support the Yorkist side. His father was killed at First St Albans in 1455; an older brother, Thomas, Lord Egremont, was killed at Northampton in 1460; and his oldest brother, Henry, the third earl of Northumberland, was killed at Towton in 1461. Yet, Edward IV tried to turn him to the House of York by leaving him in his commands and giving him positions of trust in Northumberland. This conciliation was not successful, as Sir Ralph Percy was largely responsible for surrendering the Northumberland castles to Queen Margaret in 1463. He was killed fighting for Lancaster at Hedgeley Moor in 1464. If all his attempts at conciliation are considered, then it is hard to know how Edward IV gained his reputation for savagery.

Margaret of Anjou (1430–1482), a beautiful princess of France, was queen consort of England when she married Henry VI in 1445, as arranged by the Treaty of Tours in the previous year. Her father was René of Anjou, a brother-in-law of King Charles VII. Henry VI was the son of Catherine of Valois, a daughter of Charles VI, and a sister of Charles VII (see Appendix A). Margaret was, through her paternal grandfather, the great-great-granddaughter of John II, King of France; and Henry VI, by blood, was the great-great-grandson of John II. Their relationship was at the four degrees of affinity, which meant that a papal dispensation for their marriage was obtained.

Margaret fought with bitter determination, first to defend her husband's throne against the House of York, and later to defend the inheritance of her son Edward of Westminster, born in 1453. The Yorkists mounted a huge propaganda campaign against her, claiming that her son was not legitimate or, alternatively, that her son was a birth-room changeling. This reflected the Yorkist disdain for Henry VI. Accusations of bastardy were a common political ploy in the Middle Ages, as we have seen during the short reign of King Edward V. As Henry VI was disabled by insanity, it was a long time before Queen Margaret and her council could have Henry acknowledge her son as his own. While this may have supported the Yorkist suspicions, it was unfair. In the meantime, in 1454, the Parliament made the duke of

York the Lord Protector. Margaret was not pleased with the events at First St Albans in 1455.

In 1456, Margaret moved the court of Henry VI from London to Coventry and recruited more support for Henry VI against Richard, Duke of York. She persuaded the king to dismiss the Lord Protector. She must have remained extremely sceptical of the king's attempts at reconciliation between the parties in 1458 on the so-called Love Day. Her victory, and that of her husband the king, at Ludford Bridge in 1459, forced the flight of the duke of York to Ireland and of the Yorkist earls of Warwick, Salisbury, and March to Calais.

Naturally, Margaret bitterly opposed the Act of Accord in 1460 following the Lancastrian defeat at Northampton because it disinherited her son Edward of Westminster. She fled to Scotland and returned with a large Scottish force paid with permission for the Scots to plunder England, but only south of the River Trent; of course, this did not endear her to the English people. Her failure to occupy London, after the Lancastrian victories at Wakefield in the last days of 1460 and at Second St Albans in early 1461, allowed Edward IV to enter London after his smashing victory at Mortimer's Cross and take the throne in 1461. Margaret was not well liked in England; her Scottish troops caused widespread destruction north of London. She did not understand the English people's xenophobic antipathy for both Scotland and France. She planned to cede Calais to France and Northumberland to Scotland, which was tantamount to treason in English eyes. People in London were tired of the ineffective Henry VI, his greedy Lancastrian supporters, and his French queen. Parliament considered that Henry VI had broken the terms of the Act of Accord and was glad to recognize Edward, the seventh earl of March, as the legal heir and the new king of England.

After Towton in 1461, the queen fled again to Scotland. She invaded Northumberland with French help in 1462 and, for a while, held all the major castles of Northumberland in 1463. But following the Yorkist victories in 1464 and Edward IV's intense diplomatic offensive, she could not obtain additional support from Scotland, Burgundy, or France. So, she eventually settled her court in France (Lorraine) at Kœur-la-Petite. In 1470, despite her hatred of Warwick, she was finally persuaded by King Louis XI of France, her cousin, to join forces with the turncoat earl. Her bitter confrontation with the kneeling Warwick at Angers Cathedral is one of the most famous interpersonal scenes in English history.

She invaded England in support of Warwick in 1471 but was badly delayed by storms in the English Channel and arrived too late to be of any assistance to Warwick at Barnet. At the shocking news of Edward IV's great victory at Barnet, she wanted to return to France but was persuaded by Edmund, the fourth duke of Somerset, to try joining with Jasper Tudor in Wales. She was finally demoralized after the shattering defeat of her forces at Tewkesbury in 1471 and the battlefield death of her son Edward of Westminster. She was imprisoned in London, in the Tower at first, but later under reasonably comfortable conditions at Windsor and, later, at Wallingford Castle, which was near her friend Alice, the dowager duchess of Suffolk, widow of William de la Pole, the first duke of Suffolk. At Picquigny in 1475, she was ransomed by Louis XI for ten thousand crowns; on her arrival back in France, the king took all her French estates, presumably in return for the ransom paid. She died in a state of abject poverty in France in 1482. She might have been happier had she remained in England.

Edward of Westminster (1453–1471), the Lancastrian Prince of Wales (see Appendix B), invaded England with his mother, Queen Margaret Anjou, in 1471, and was killed during the headlong flight at Tewkesbury. Earlier in his life, when he was only eight years old, the two Yorkist knights who famously protected Henry VI at Second St Albans were beheaded at his orders. This unchivalrous behaviour was disgraceful and reflected badly on both mother and son, but mainly on his mother, as Edward was so young. Edward was intensely arrogant and opinionated; reports indicate that he was obsessed with making war and beheading people. The English people can probably be thankful that he never achieved the throne. On 13 December 1470, he married Anne Neville, daughter of Warwick, while the earl and Queen Margaret were in France plotting to invade England. But the queen would not allow the marriage to be consummated. We are not told how she managed this, but it indicates how little she trusted Warwick. Perhaps this explains why some authors claim that Anne and Edward were never truly married, only betrothed.

Some claim that, at Tewkesbury, the prince was taken prisoner first and then subsequently murdered by Gloucester and others, rather than killed during the battle. This appears not to be true, but it is perhaps considered an attempt by later Tudor historians to further despoil the already ruined reputation of Richard III. Sir Clements Markham (1906) had a high opinion of the Lancastrian Prince of Wales. He considered Edward to be a fine student and a brave knight. Markham's tender description of Edward's death reflected his admiration. His description was based on a drawing, then in Bruges, made by a witness at the battle. During the wild pursuit, there was a death blow from behind, the horse with rider went down, and the prince's golden Plantagenet hair tumbled across the horse's mane. That is stuff that Hollywood would love.

Sir John Fortesque (1394–1479) was educated in law at Exeter College, Oxford University, and from 1442 was Chief Justice of the King's Bench under Henry VI. Prior to the Act of Accord of 1460, he supported the Lancastrian position, arguing that Philippa, a granddaughter of Edward III, was not legitimate at her birth. He later admitted he was wrong (see Appendix C). He was at Towton in 1461 and fled with Henry VI to Scotland; and later, in 1464, he fled with Queen Margaret Anjou into exile in France. He was attainted by Edward IV's first Parliament. He wrote the treatise *De Laudibus Legum Angliæ,* a commendation of the laws of England, for the benefit of Edward of Westminster, admittedly with only limited effect on the young prince. This early, Sir John set forth what was later known as the Blackstone Formulation: "that it is preferable for twenty guilty people to escape justice, rather than for a single innocent person to suffer execution at law." Fortesque returned to England in 1471 with Queen Margaret; he was captured at Tewkesbury, but he was not executed because he had shown constant loyalty to Henry VI. He submitted to Edward IV and was pardoned. He wrote another treatise, *The Difference between an Absolute Monarchy and a Limited Monarchy,* for Edward IV; it was later published as *The Governance of England.* He believed that in France, the king made the law, but in England, Parliament made the law and the king executed it. In retrospect, we can conclude that this was only approximately true; if Richard III had agreed and not cancelled the planned Parliament of King Edward V, then English history might have been different.

The numerous Courtenay earls of Devon were initially committed Lancastrians, as the first two included in this text fought against Edward

IV. But it was not so simple, as the next earl (Edward) supported Edward V and hated Richard III, and the last three included William, Henry, and young Edward, who were possible Yorkist kings. The author has left the last four on the list of enemies, but as a practical matter they probably would have been more likely supporters of King Edward IV.

Thomas Courtenay (1432–1461), the Lancastrian sixth/fourteenth earl of Devon, was a staunch supporter of Queen Margaret Anjou. Thomas had a reputation for brutal internecine warfare. He was executed at York after the Battle of Towton in 1461 and was posthumously attainted. Most of his Devon properties, but not the title of earl, were distributed between the Lord Mountjoy and Humphrey Stafford, strong supporters of Edward IV. The title was held vacant. Thomas Courtenay's younger brother, *Henry Courtenay,* who also lost properties when his older brother was attainted, plotted against the Yorkist regime. He was tried in 1468 and executed for treason in 1469; he never held the title earl of Devon. Another younger brother, John Courtenay, would later be restored to the title at the Readoption of Henry VI.

John Courtenay (1435–1471), the Lancastrian seventh/fifteenth earl of Devon, was awarded the earldom by the earl of Warwick in 1470, in the name of the readopted Henry VI. He was the brother of Thomas, the sixth earl. But when King Edward IV made his spectacular return, John was soon after killed at the Battle of Tewkesbury in 1471 and posthumously attainted. After extinction, the earldom was restored in 1485, following Bosworth. The new King Henry VII rewarded John's distant cousin, one of Henry Tudor's most loyal supporters, Edward Courtenay.

The earls of Devon had confusing numerics, making it often difficult to identify them correctly and causing confusion. The ancient title began in 1141 (first creation) and was held in the De Redvers family; there followed eight generations, ending with Isabel de Redvers, the eighth countess of Devon, who died without an obvious heir in 1293. In 1335, late in his life, Hugh de Courtenay (1276–1340), a distant cousin of the countess, was declared the ninth earl of Devon by inheritance, but alternatively he was the first Courtenay earl of Devon in a second creation. There were seven such Courtenay earls of Devon, ending with John, the seventh/fifteenth earl of Devon, who was killed at Tewkesbury in 1471 and attainted. The title was then vacant except briefly when Henry Stafford was the interloper Yorkist earl of Devon for a few months in 1469 until his death at Edgecote.

Edward Courtenay (1453–1509) became (by way of Henry VII) the first earl of Devon in 1485 (a new third creation) after Bosworth in 1485. In relation to John Courtenay, the seventh/fifteenth earl of Devon, Edward was a second cousin, one generation removed. Edward's birth year above is an estimate; he was made Knight of the Garter by Edward IV. He was a fierce opponent of Richard III after the usurpation; it could be concluded that he supported the legacy of Edward IV. He gave his support to Henry Tudor and assisted Margaret Beaufort's secret correspondence with Dowager Queen Elizabeth Woodville regarding the marriage plans for Henry Tudor and Princess Elizabeth York. Edward joined the Buckingham Rebellion. When it failed, Edward escaped to Brittany and served Henry Tudor. Edward was attainted in 1484 by Richard III's only Parliament. Despite his attainder, he acted in the dangerous role of secret courier between the conspirators in England and France. He was with Henry Tudor at Bosworth Field; he was made the earl of Devon and served in the Tudor government.

Edward had an older cousin, *Peter Courtenay (1432–1492),* who was part of another branch of the Courtenay family. Peter studied law at Oxford, Cologne, and Padua, served Henry VI at the Readoption, and, later, was secretary to Edward IV. He was bishop of Exeter in 1478. He joined the October Rebellion against Richard III. When the rebellion failed, he fled with his brother Walter Courtenay to Henry Tudor in Brittany. Peter was made the bishop of Winchester in 1487 during the reign of Henry VII.

William Courtenay (1475–1511) was the son and heir of Edward Courtenay, Henry VII's first earl of Devon. William married Katherine Plantagenet, a younger daughter of Edward IV, so he was a possible Yorkist king of England in right of his wife, which explains why Henry VII was wary of him. William was involved with the exiled Edmund de la Pole, a nephew of Edward IV, a Yorkist claimant to the throne who planned an abortive invasion of England. For this association, William Courtenay was attainted in 1504 and did not inherit the title earl of Devon when his father, Edward, died in 1509. However, the title was restored to William by Henry VIII just before William himself died in 1511. So, briefly, for a month, *William Courtenay was the first earl (by way of Henry VIII) of Devon (a new, fourth creation).*

Henry Courtenay (1498–1539), the (Henry VIII) second earl of Devon (in the fourth creation), was the son of William Courtenay and Katherine, so he was a grandson of Edward IV. Later, he was made the *marquis of Exeter,* by which name he is better known. Henry Courtenay was arrested in 1538 and executed in 1539 for his part in the Exeter Plot. A possible aim of this plot was to put Exeter on the throne in place of Henry VIII. Others have suggested that, more likely, the object was to put Cardinal Reginald Pole on the throne along with Princess Mary. This would have represented a Catholic restoration. Pole was the son of Sir Richard Pole and Margaret, the countess of Salisbury, the daughter of Edward IV's brother George, the duke of Clarence.

The eleven-year-old son of Henry Courtenay, *young Edward Courtenay (1527–1556),* a great-grandson of King Edward IV, was imprisoned in the Tower with his father in 1538 because of his involvement in the Exeter Plot. Edward was released from the Tower in 1553, made a Knight of the Bath, and restored as earl of Devon by Queen Mary Tudor. *He was titled the (Queen Mary) first earl of Devon (fifth creation).* He was effectively exiled and died at Padua in 1556. He, too, was a potential Yorkist king of England. At one point, it was suggested that he marry Princess Elizabeth Tudor and assume the throne, which was the objective of the Wyatt Rebellion against Queen Mary. This explains why Queen Mary Tudor never allowed him to return from exile, especially since she did not wish to execute him. He was the son of her very close friend Gertrude Blount Courtenay. There was never any thought that young Edward was not legitimate; nobody believed what was in the 1484 Titulus Regius.

Jasper Tudor (1431–1495), the Lancastrian earl of Pembroke, was the second son of Owen Tudor and Catherine of Valois, the widow of Henry V. Thus, Jasper was the half-brother of Henry VI through the former Queen Catherine Valois. Jasper's elder brother, Edmund, Earl of Richmond, married the twelve-year-old Margaret Beaufort in 1455. Their son was Henry Tudor, the future Henry VII, born in 1457. As Edmund died three months before Henry was born, Jasper looked after Henry, who became the second earl of Richmond at birth. Jasper was made the earl of Pembroke in

1453 and lived frequently at the court of Henry VI. He was responsible for holding Wales against the Yorkist forces of Sir William Herbert.

When Queen Margaret Anjou, with Scottish help, invaded England in 1461, Jasper and his Lancastrian forces entered England proceeding east and attempted to join her advance south on London. After his shattering defeat at Mortimer's Cross in 1461, Jasper escaped to Scotland, leaving behind his father, Owen Tudor, who was executed. Soon, with the succession of Edward IV in 1461, Jasper was attainted and then fled to France. Edward IV sent Henry Tudor to the care of Sir William Herbert and his wife at Raglan Castle. During the following years, Jasper made several guerrilla-style attacks on Yorkist outposts in Wales. In 1468, with French help, Jasper invaded Wales, sacked Denbigh Castle, and attempted to relieve the Siege of Harlech Castle by Sir William Herbert. When, despite his best efforts, Harlech fell, Jasper fled back to France to be with Queen Margaret.

In 1470, Jasper invaded England with Warwick, then immediately departed for Wales and recruited forces for the Lancastrian cause. He was at neither Barnet nor Tewkesbury. After the shattering Lancastrian defeats, he fled with Henry Tudor to Brittany in 1471, which marked the start of a long exile. In 1485, he invaded England with Henry Tudor and commanded under the earl of Oxford at Bosworth Field. What little Henry Tudor knew about war, he learned from his uncle Jasper. Henry VII restored Jasper to his earldom of Pembroke in 1485, and in 1488 made him also the duke of Bedford.

After Bosworth, Jasper married Katherine Woodville, the sister-in-law of Edward IV, the widow of the executed Henry Stafford, the second duke of Buckingham. Katherine was a Woodville, attractive and charming, who frequently landed on her feet. She was titled the duchess of Pembroke and the duchess of Bedford.

Henry Percy (1421–1461), the third earl of Northumberland, was the son of Henry Percy (1393–1455), the second earl of Northumberland, who was killed at First St Albans in 1455. The third earl was the grandson of Henry "Hotspur" Percy (1366–1403), who rebelled against Henry IV and was killed at the Battle of Shrewsbury in 1403. The third earl was the great-grandson of Henry Percy (1341–1408), the first earl of Northumberland, who also rebelled against Henry IV and died at the Battle of Bramham

Moor in 1408. Through his mother, Eleanor Neville, the third earl of Northumberland was the grandson of Joan Beaufort and Ralph Neville, and hence a descendant of King Edward III (see Appendix E). Despite his close Neville family relations, the third earl remained a committed Lancastrian. He was present at Wakefield in 1460 and commanded at Towton in 1461, where he was killed in the battle and posthumously attainted. His son, not surprisingly also called Henry Percy and usually referred to as young Henry, the fourth earl of Northumberland, was not such a committed Lancastrian and is perhaps better described as a friend of Edward IV.

Henry Percy (1446–1489), the fourth earl of Northumberland, when he was only fifteen years old, was imprisoned in the Fleet Prison after Towton in 1461. With the death and attainder of his father, the third earl, the earldom of Northumberland was forfeited to the Yorkist Crown. In 1464, the young Henry Percy was transferred to the Tower, still without his title and estate. In 1465, the earldom was given to John Neville for his suppression of the northern rebellions against Edward IV, which occurred in 1462–64. In 1469, presumably after negotiations, Edward IV released young Henry Percy from the Tower. Henry joined Edward after the king's release from Middleham Castle later in 1469; and Edward restored him to his earldom of Northumberland after Empingham in 1470. Edward hoped that the young Henry Percy would keep the Lancastrian north of England more peaceful than had John Neville.

As compensation for the loss of the earldom, Edward made John Neville the marquis of Montagu, a much better title than Baron Montagu. Even though he held the Courtenay estates in Devonshire, the loss of the great Northumberland properties alienated John Neville, who turned against Edward IV. There were disastrous consequences when Richard Neville, Earl of Warwick, invaded England in 1470. Edward IV was caught between the advancing hostile forces of Warwick and Montagu. He decided, wisely, that his chances were small, and so he fled England to exile in Burgundy. Edward calculated that it was better to stay alive and fight another day. He should have passed that advice to his younger brother Richard III, who might have recalled the advice as victory at Bosworth Field slipped away in 1485.

At first, it appeared that Edward had gained little by his restoration of young Henry Percy, the fourth earl of Northumberland, but when Edward IV invaded England in 1471, young Henry Percy made no move against Edward, even though the king was so vulnerable from lack of support in the north of England. Henry did not want to side with Warwick, as the latter might restore his brother John Neville to the earldom of Northumberland. But Henry could not openly support Edward IV, either, as he knew that his north men would not fight for the Yorkist king, likely because the memories of Towton were still festering. So, young Henry Percy did nothing and allowed Edward to gather strength in the north. In the end, the restoration of Henry Percy was helpful to Edward's cause. After Tewkesbury, the fourth earl of Northumberland put down the incipient northern rebellions against Edward IV and saved Edward the trouble of having to go farther north. The fourth earl played little role in the government of Edward IV, except that he was important in keeping the peace in the north of England and cooperated with Richard, Duke of Gloucester, who, later as king, made Northumberland the great chamberlain of England. The fourth earl of Northumberland and Sir Richard Ratcliffe were in charge at the Pontefract executions of Anthony Woodville and his companions in 1483. There was possibly a brief hearing, but the prisoners were not allowed to speak for themselves.

Richard III appointed the young earl of Lincoln as the president of the Council of the North, to assist the fourth earl in controlling Northumberland. Young Henry may have resented this, which may explain his behaviour at Bosworth. The fourth earl of Northumberland commanded the Yorkist rearguard reserve at Bosworth Field (see Appendix I–K), but he did not enter the battle. He deprived Richard III of a large part of his force and watched from a distance as the Usurper King was defeated and killed. Henry VII imprisoned young Henry Percy for a while because of his seeming support for Richard III, but he soon thought better of it and restored him to his title. Young Henry Percy was murdered during a minor tax rebellion in Yorkshire in 1489, some say by Yorkist partisans, as vengeance for his treachery against Richard III.

Henry Holland (1430–1475), the third duke of Exeter, was an unrepentant Lancastrian. He was a great-grandson of John of Gaunt, who had a daughter by his first wife, Blanche of Lancaster. This daughter's name was Elizabeth, and she was Henry Holland's grandmother. Elizabeth is shown in the Lancastrian family tree (see Appendix B). Elizabeth married John Holland, the first duke of Exeter. They had a son, also named John, who became the second duke of Exeter and was Henry Holland's father. The third duke was therefore in the direct Lancastrian line for the English throne and probably considered, mistakenly, that he had a better claim than Richard, the third duke of York, who died in 1460. The Exeter line was not involved in the usurpation by Henry IV in 1399. The first duke of Exeter was the maternal half-brother of Richard II and remained loyal to Richard II throughout the usurpation debacle at the end of the fourteenth century.

Henry Holland, the third duke of Exeter, was the constable of the Tower, where he developed the torture rack nicknamed "the Duke of Exeter's daughter." In 1447, he married Anne Plantagenet, sister of Edward IV, but remained staunchly Lancastrian. As she was a loyal Yorkist, their marriage was doomed. They had a daughter named Anne Holland.

Henry commanded at Wakefield in 1460 and at Second St Albans in 1461. He commanded the left battle at the Lancastrian disaster of Towton in 1461. He then escaped to Scotland, and then to France with Queen Margaret. For his role at Towton, he was attainted. His Yorkist wife legally separated from him in 1464; his title and estates were settled on Anne in her own name in 1467. His attainder was lifted and he recovered his title and many of his properties at the Readoption of Henry VI in 1470. Exeter commanded again at Barnet, where he was severely wounded and left for dead on the battlefield; but he miraculously recovered, reached sanctuary at Westminster, and was later sent to the Tower. After his attainder was renewed by Edward IV, his title and estates were again settled on his wife, Anne, in her own name, in 1471. The duchess, ever faithful to Edward IV, succeeded in divorcing Henry in 1472. Henry accompanied Edward IV to France in 1475. It is unlikely that he volunteered for this campaign, given that he was released from the Tower for the purpose. On the way back to England, it is alleged that he was pushed overboard by partisan Yorkists and drowned at sea; his body was recovered in the waves at Dover.

There is some confusion about who was the duke of Exeter during this period of English history. The title was created by Richard II in 1397 (first creation) for Henry Holland's grandfather John Holland, the first duke, who was executed in 1400 for treason against the Usurper King Henry IV, at which time the title became vacant. In 1416 (second creation), the title was given to Thomas Beaufort (see Appendix D), a son of John of Gaunt by Katherine Swynford. But when Thomas died without issue in 1426, the title was again vacant. In 1439 (first creation again), John, the son of the first duke, was restored to the title and became the second duke of Exeter. Henry Holland, the third duke (same first creation), inherited Exeter when his father, the second duke, died in 1447.

James Butler (1420–1461), the Lancastrian first earl of Wiltshire and the fifth earl of Ormonde, was a staunch Lancastrian who served terms as lord lieutenant of Ireland and Lord Treasurer of England under Henry VI. James Butler bitterly hated Richard, the third duke of York, for his claim to the throne. He fought at Mortimer's Cross, Wakefield, Second St Albans, and Towton; he was captured and beheaded soon after Towton and posthumously attainted, when the title became vacant. In 1470, Edward IV gave the title to John Stafford (see Appendix F), a younger son of Humphrey Stafford, the first duke of Buckingham.

Mary de Gueldres (1434–1463), mother of James III, King of Scotland, was regent of Scotland for her son from 1460 to 1463. She supported Queen Margaret Anjou and the Lancastrian King Henry VI. After Towton in 1461, she sheltered the Lancastrians and aided their subsequent incursions into Northumberland in 1462. After her death in 1463, Bishop Kennedy of St Andrews became regent of Scotland and made peace with Edward IV. This forced Henry VI to return to Northumberland, where he resided in the castles which, by treachery, had been surrendered to the Lancastrians. When the Yorkists regained control of the castles in 1464, Henry VI became a fugitive in the North Country, but he was captured in 1465 and imprisoned in the Tower of London.

Henry Stafford (1455–1483), the second duke of Buckingham, is listed as an enemy of Edward IV, but he was more an enemy of Edward's successor, the young King Edward V. Buckingham was a great-great-great-grandson of Edward III; some consider that he later planned to claim the crown for himself (see Appendix F).

After his father, Humphrey Stafford, died of the plague in 1458 without inheriting, Henry was the heir of Buckingham. When his grandfather, the first duke of Buckingham, was killed at Northampton in 1460, Henry became the second duke of Buckingham at the age of five years. His grandmother Anne Neville, the dowager duchess of Buckingham, held his estate (see Appendix F). In early 1464, Edward IV purchased his wardship and handed custody to his elder sister, Anne, Duchess of Exeter. But in early 1465, his custody was transferred to Queen Elizabeth Woodville. Soon after, as a child of ten years, Henry was betrothed and married to the seven-year-old Katherine Woodville, the young sister of the queen. At the coronation of the queen on 26 May 1465, the young duke and duchess were carried by their attendants so they could see better.

It was alleged that Henry hated his Woodville family and complained bitterly of his marriage, but relations between the Woodville and Stafford families were usually cordial. With the attractive Katherine, the duke of Buckingham had five children, so, apparently, he did not spend all his time complaining. As described by Susan Higginbotham (2010), the marriage was often happy. At sixteen years of age in 1471, Henry may have been at Tewkesbury. He was certainly present at the king's triumphant entry into London soon afterwards. Henry accompanied Edward IV in the 1475 invasion of France. Edward IV did not trust him and gave him little power or responsibility. Henry did, however, become seneschal of England, and in that capacity he pronounced the death sentence on George, Duke of Clarence, in 1478.

After Edward IV died in 1483, Henry sent his most trusted agent, Humphrey Persivall, to assure Richard, Duke of Gloucester, of his enthusiastic support. Persivall carried back to Buckingham the request that the two dukes combine forces at Northampton on 29 April 1483. It seems likely that following this, Persivall made the appropriate arrangements with Anthony Woodville, after which the dukes were able to take control of the new king, Edward V, on 30 April 1483.

The duke investigated for Gloucester the attitude of senior members of the council concerning the proposed seizure of the throne and may have warned Gloucester of Hastings' loyalty to King Edward V. This was followed by the murder of Hastings on 13 June 1483. On 16 June 1483, the duke was part of the delegation which persuaded the Queen Mother to release young Prince Richard from the sanctuary at Westminster Abbey and send him to the Tower Palace to be with Edward V. The duke gave eloquent speeches at the Guildhall, Westminster Hall, and Baynard Castle (later, in June 1483), helping to persuade the magnates to support Richard, Duke of Gloucester, as king. Henry was persuasive, but the reception was not always enthusiastic. Richard III appointed him constable of England, Chief Justice of Wales, and, later, great chamberlain.

Henry Stafford played a pivotal supportive role in the usurpation of the throne by Richard III, but he eventually turned against Richard III, for reasons probably related to Henry's feeling that he had been deceived about the validity of Edward IV's marriage. No doubt, his Woodville wife Katherine would have told him the marriage was valid; possibly, the guilt-ridden Richard III confirmed this in late July 1483. There is also no doubt that Bishop Morton would have told him in August 1483 that Edward IV's marriage was valid. Stafford joined the Woodvilles in backing Henry Tudor, led the disastrous rebellion of October 1483, and was executed for treason at Salisbury, outside the Blue Boar Inn. Probably, he contemplated seizing the throne himself but rejected the idea; he understood that a marriage between Henry Tudor and Princess Elizabeth York would be a better dynastic solution. It is believed that he was buried at the nearby Greyfriars Cemetery; it is unlikely that Richard III would have permitted his burial at Salisbury Cathedral, which some accounts suggest as his final resting place.

CHAPTER 18

The Arch-Villain of This Sad Tale: The Greatest Enemy of Edward IV's Legacy

Robert Stillington (1420–1491), Bishop of Bath and Welles, played a central role in the marriage contract invention. He could be considered an enemy of Edward IV, but he was more an enemy of the Woodville faction, and only after Edward IV died. He was certainly an enemy of the boy King Edward V and, therefore, an enemy of Edward IV's legacy. Both Stillington and Gloucester probably considered Edward V to be more Woodville than Plantagenet.

Although most authorities say that Stillington was born in 1420, the records at Oxford University suggest that he was born before 1410 and therefore was older than stated. After 1445, Stillington was appointed to many church offices, including archdeacon of Colchester and archdeacon of Taunton. In 1458, he was appointed as the dean of St Martin's Le Grand in London; and in 1465, he was appointed as the bishop of Bath and Wells. In 1460, after the Act of Accord, he was made keeper of the privy seal in the Yorkist government while Henry VI was still king and while Richard, the third duke of York, was briefly Lord Protector.

Stillington continued to hold high government office throughout much of Edward IV's earlier reign. He remained Lord Privy Seal until 1467 and was Lord Chancellor from 1467 to 1473, except for the six months of the Readoption of Henry VI (Hicks, 2008). Never once did he say anything about a serious problem with the royal marriage. As Stillington graduated from Oxford University with a doctorate in civil and canon law, he could well have advised the king if he thought there was a problem, yet he did not.

After Lady Eleanor Butler died in 1468, and while Stillington remained chancellor of England, a solution could have been found if one was really needed. A secret annulment of any alleged prior contract, which means it never happened, could well have solved the problem – if there ever was one. All such a plan needed was a letter to the Pope requesting assistance. Such a letter would have remained in the Vatican archives undisclosed, more or less forever. Alternatively, the bishops could have done the same thing in secret and only informed the Pope later, if at all. It should be recalled that, when questioned by his mother, Cecily, the king did not state that there was any earlier marriage contract; in fact, the king denied any marriage contract with anyone. If he said that, then that means there was no consent, which means there was no 1461 marriage contract.

When he was dismissed from office in 1473, Stillington remained resentful towards the king. The Croyland Chronicler (1854) said the bishop had become elderly and ineffective. Despite his age, Stillington continued to represent the king on several peace commissions. Also, he officiated at an important embassy with the French ambassador in January 1479 (Ross, 1997). Stillington was in the Tower for three months, from 6 March 1478 to sometime in the following June, when he was pardoned and released after paying a large fine. The reason for his imprisonment was his close association with the treacherous Clarence and unidentified "words uttered prejudicial to the king."

If Stillington had said that the king's Woodville marriage was bigamous, then he would have been locked in the Tower and never released. Edward and Elizabeth would not have tolerated such a threat to the succession. Some partisans believe that Edward was naive enough to release Stillington after he made public allegations about the invalidity of the king's marriage. They claim that Stillington informed Clarence about the alleged 1461 marriage contract between Edward IV and Lady Eleanor Butler. It is not difficult to imagine the effect that this knowledge would have had upon the treacherous Clarence. He would have shouted it from one end of Christendom to the other. And yet he did not.

But the duke's criticism of the king's marriage was that Elizabeth Woodville was a widow; mistakenly, he thought that made the royal marriage invalid. If Stillington held any valid information that threatened the royal marriage or the royal succession, as this was treason, then it is very unlikely that Edward IV would ever have released him from the Tower; only his prelacy would have saved him from execution. It would not be unreasonable to assert that Stillington, like Henry VI before him, while imprisoned in the Tower, would have been permanently eliminated by just means or by foul. Edward was a merciful king, but he was not a fool.

It is far more likely that Stillington supported the sorry old tale about Edward's alleged illegitimate birth, which did not concern the king, as there was no evidence that his father had ever denied his legitimacy. Even if his mother had really denied Edward, legally it would have been up to his father to give his agreement, and that had not happened. As it was, Clarence was executed in 1478 for his repeated acts of treachery and treason in the period 1468–1477 (and his repeated attacks on Edward IV's legitimacy), not for anything to do with any 1461 marriage contract. Nobody heard about that until five years later, in 1483.

Philippe de Commines, the Burgundian chronicler writing in 1493, alleged that the bishop of Bath (Stillington) was present when Edward IV and an English lady were contracted and had then formally married Edward IV and the English lady (Lady Eleanor Butler) prior to Edward's marriage with Elizabeth Woodville. Sir George Buck repeated the same story 130 years later, but nobody came up with any believable evidence. Buck also claimed that Lady Eleanor's family pressured Stillington in 1483 to inform Richard, Duke of Gloucester, about the marriage contract, but this was more unsubstantiated conjecture. The Talbots had done nothing earlier (since 1464) and nothing before Edward IV died. It is interesting to speculate: if the 1461 marriage contract story was indeed true, then why did Stillington *not* give the information to Clarence? After all, Stillington was out of office after 1473 and remained resentful of the king, and Clarence was in desperate trouble for treason, in great danger for his life. Clarence could have used the information to blackmail the king and save himself from execution. This would be one more bit of support for the suggestion that Stillington invented the 1461 marriage contract story only later, much later, after Edward IV died and when Gloucester was looking for a pretext for the usurpation.

The bishop probably assisted Buckingham in devising the petition to Richard, Duke of Gloucester, which was presented on 26 June 1483 at Baynard Castle. Stillington drew up the scurrilous Titulus Regius in early 1484, declaring Richard to be the rightful king and setting out the proposed reasons. In those speeches and documents and in the rumours that followed, Commines, writing in 1493, found the story about Stillington witnessing the marriage contract and, later, performing the formal marriage. It is noteworthy that in the Titulus Regius it was not claimed that supportive evidentiary proof for the 1461 marriage contract was available; it was simply not mentioned. Offers to provide evidence clearly referred to other charges in the statute, namely those of sorcery, as previously discussed. And no evidence for even that was ever provided.

Despite his efforts on behalf of Richard III, Stillington was not rewarded by the king, who probably remained sceptical of the marriage contract story and probably suffered from very persistent regret and guilt over the matter. Richard greatly preferred the argument that Edward IV was not the son of Richard, the third duke of York, despite his mother's anger about it.

Henry VII sent Stillington back to the Tower for a short time immediately after Bosworth, allegedly because of his association with the marriage contract story and his authorship of the contemptible Titulus Regius of 1484. Henry needed to reverse the declared invalidity of Edward IV's marriage as part of his plan to marry Princess Elizabeth, Edward's daughter. Elizabeth was widely considered the proper heir after Edward V and his younger brother, Richard, were murdered in 1483. The people of England simply did not consider her to be illegitimate. Henry VII's new act of Parliament accused Stillington of "horrible and haneous [heinous] offences" against King Edward IV. Nevertheless, Stillington was pardoned on 22 November 1485. After all, Henry VII would never have been king without the collapse of the House of York induced by Stillington's story, and Henry needed to lay the matter to rest and move on to more pressing matters, as his position as king was far from well established.

Stillington was never happy with his continued loss of influence under Henry VII. He was accused of being involved with the rebellion of Lambert Simnel in 1487 and thereafter sought protection at Oxford University, but he was soon returned yet again to prison, this time at Windsor, where he died of natural causes in 1491. He was buried in the cathedral at Wells. During the reign of Queen Elizabeth I, his grave was rudely invaded to recover the lead which lined the coffin in which he was buried.

Bishop Robert Stillington must go down in English history as a villain. As a bishop, he must have been aware that an ecclesiastical law court was required to properly decide the matrimonial matters of validity and legitimacy; he must have known that his unsubstantiated accusation would require proper documentary proof at such a hearing; and he must have known that a second witness to the alleged contract was required under the canon law (Helmholz, 1974). It is obviously surprising that an ordained bishop did not recommend an ecclesiastical law court hearing. By failing to keep proper evidence, if his allegations were true, and failing to give Richard, Duke of Gloucester, sensible advice under the circumstances, Stillington facilitated the tragic deposition of the boy King Edward V. His shameful lies were inevitably followed by several judicial murders, several criminal murders, a monstrous usurpation, a secret regicide, and open rebellion. There followed a very short and unhappy reign, with the ultimate overthrow of King Richard III by armed force. The last Yorkist king is now, forever in English history, branded as an usurper. With his far too clever invention of a believable but unsupported fabrication, the bishop of Bath, more than any other confederate of Richard III, was responsible for ultimately bringing down the grand Royal House of York. And, in the process, he very nearly destroyed the magnificent legacy of King Edward IV.

APPENDICES

APPENDIX A

The Abbreviated Family Tree of the Kings of France at the Time of King Edward IV

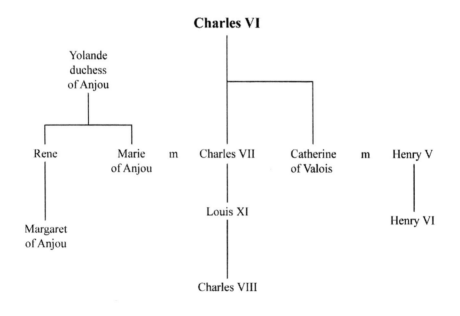

Kings of France

APPENDIX B

The House of Lancaster

The family tree is modified and abbreviated to show the straightforward line of inheritance and succession. The Lancastrians were descended from John of Gaunt, the fourth son of Edward III. Note also that the Lancastrians were descended from the first marriage of John of Gaunt, which made them higher in the line of succession than the Beauforts, who were descended from Gaunt's third marriage.

Edward III

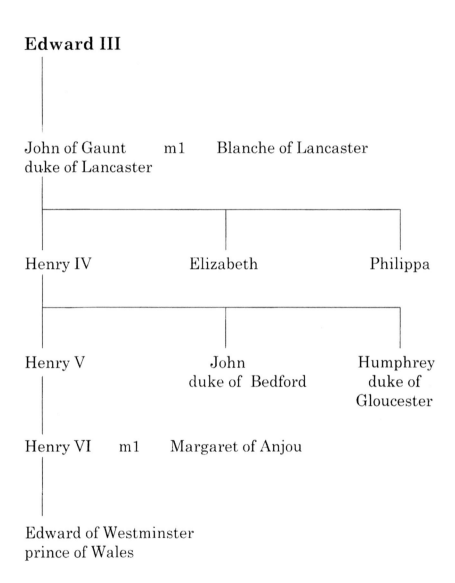

John of Gaunt   m1   Blanche of Lancaster
duke of Lancaster

Henry IV   Elizabeth   Philippa

Henry V   John   Humphrey
                     duke of Bedford   duke of
                                         Gloucester

Henry VI   m1   Margaret of Anjou

Edward of Westminster
prince of Wales

House of Lancaster

APPENDIX C

The House of York

The family tree is modified and abbreviated to show the straightforward line of inheritance and succession. The direct line was from the duke of Clarence, the third son of Edward III, into which line the House of Mortimer married. The York inheritance came by way of marriage into the Clarence line by a descendant of a younger son of Edward III, namely Edmund, Duke of York, the fifth son. The Yorkists, descended from the third son of Edward III, were higher in the succession than the Lancastrians, the Beauforts, and the Nevilles, who were descended from John of Gaunt, the fourth son of Edward III.

Edward III

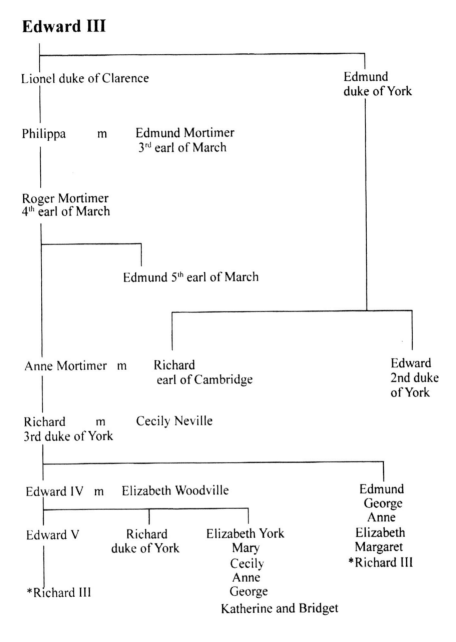

Lionel duke of Clarence

Edmund duke of York

Philippa   m   Edmund Mortimer
3rd earl of March

Roger Mortimer
4th earl of March

Edmund 5th earl of March

Anne Mortimer   m   Richard
earl of Cambridge

Edward
2nd duke
of York

Richard   m   Cecily Neville
3rd duke of York

Edward IV   m   Elizabeth Woodville

Edmund
George
Anne

Edward V   Richard   Elizabeth York   Elizabeth
                  duke of York   Mary   Margaret
                                      Cecily   *Richard III
                                      Anne
                                      George
*Richard III   Katherine and Bridget

House of York

APPENDIX D

The House of Beaufort

The family tree is modified and abbreviated to show the straightforward line of inheritance and succession. The Beauforts were descended from the third marriage of John of Gaunt, the fourth son of Edward III, which placed them lower in the line of succession when compared with the families of York and Lancaster.

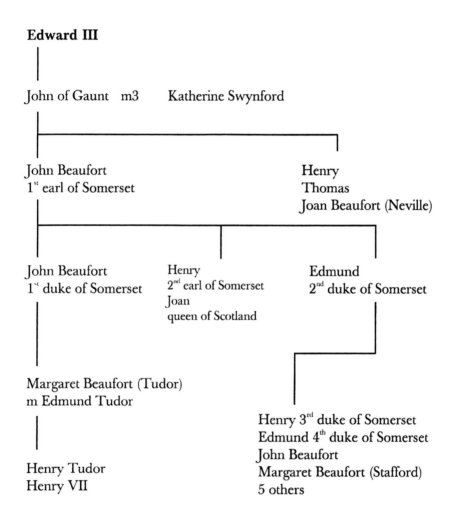

Edward III

John of Gaunt   m3   Katherine Swynford

John Beaufort
1st earl of Somerset

Henry
Thomas
Joan Beaufort (Neville)

John Beaufort
1st duke of Somerset

Henry
2nd earl of Somerset
Joan
queen of Scotland

Edmund
2nd duke of Somerset

Margaret Beaufort (Tudor)
m Edmund Tudor

Henry 3rd duke of Somerset
Edmund 4th duke of Somerset
John Beaufort
Margaret Beaufort (Stafford)
5 others

Henry Tudor
Henry VII

House of Beaufort

APPENDIX E

The House of Neville

The family tree is modified and abbreviated to show the straightforward line of inheritance and succession. The Nevilles were a branch of the Beaufort line descended from the third marriage of John of Gaunt, the fourth son of Edward III.

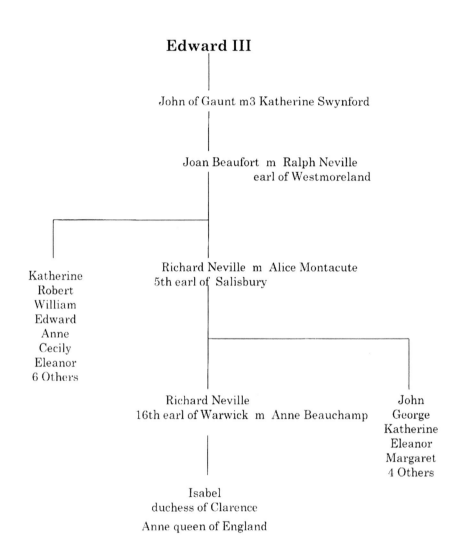

Edward III

John of Gaunt m3 Katherine Swynford

Joan Beaufort m Ralph Neville
earl of Westmoreland

Katherine
Robert
William
Edward
Anne
Cecily
Eleanor
6 Others

Richard Neville m Alice Montacute
5th earl of Salisbury

Richard Neville
16th earl of Warwick m Anne Beauchamp

John
George
Katherine
Eleanor
Margaret
4 Others

Isabel
duchess of Clarence

Anne queen of England

House of Neville

423

APPENDIX F

The House of Stafford

The family tree is modified and abbreviated to show the straightforward line of inheritance and succession. The Staffords were descended from the second marriage of Anne Plantagenet; she was descended in the line of the sixth son of Edward III, namely Thomas, Earl of Buckingham, which made the Staffords lower in the line of succession.

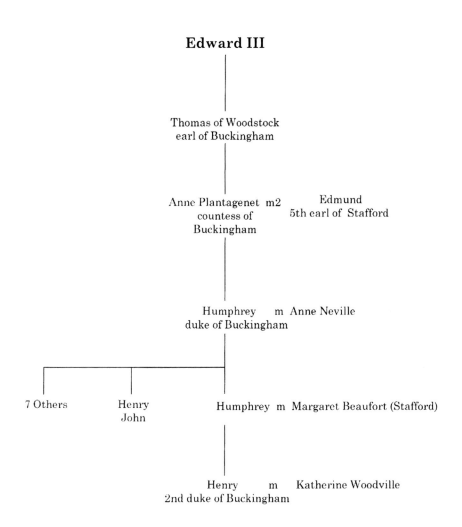

Edward III

|

Thomas of Woodstock
earl of Buckingham

|

Anne Plantagenet m2   Edmund
countess of   5th earl of Stafford
Buckingham

|

Humphrey   m Anne Neville
duke of Buckingham

7 Others   Henry   Humphrey m Margaret Beaufort (Stafford)
John

Henry   m   Katherine Woodville
2nd duke of Buckingham

House of Stafford

APPENDIX G

The Battle of Barnet on 14 April 1471

North is top of the page; the diagram is not to scale; the forces were initially arranged on an east–west alignment facing north–south, with the Lancastrians to the north and the Yorkists to the south. For Lancaster, the Exeter division was at (1), the Warwick division was to the rear at (2), the Montague division was at (3), and the Oxford division was at (4). For York, the Hastings division started near (B) but was routed by Oxford and fled south to the position shown in the diagram at (A). The Edward IV division was at (B), and the Gloucester division was at (C). At the start, the Yorkists were shifted to the east, so Oxford (4) outflanked Hastings (A), and Gloucester (C) outflanked Exeter (1). The Hastings division (A) was overlapped, was defeated, and fled south, pursued by Oxford (4), as shown in the diagram. But when Oxford (4) returned to the main field in heavy fog, he was mistakenly attacked by friendly forces under Montagu (3). Gloucester (C) overlapped and forced Exeter (1) back. With all these changes, the alignment shifted to near north–south, as shown in the diagram. Edward IV (B) attacked hard in the centre, and the Lancastrians were defeated.

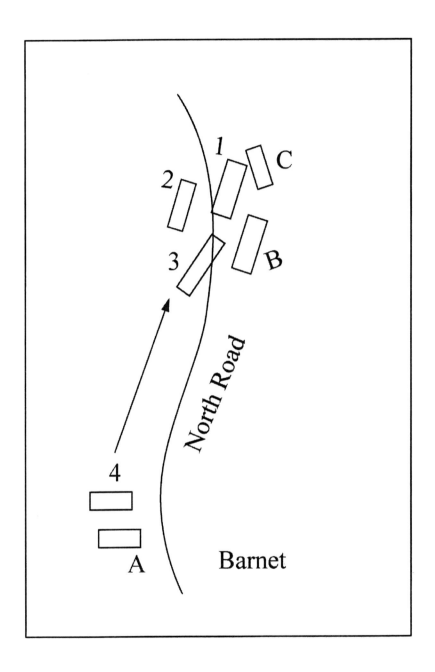

APPENDIX H

The Battle of Tewkesbury on 4 May 1471

North is top of the page; the diagram is not to scale; the forces were arranged on an east–west alignment facing north–south, with the Lancastrians to the north and the Yorkists to the south. For Lancaster, the commanders were Somerset at (1), Wenlock at (2), and Devon at (3). For York, the Gloucester division was at (A), Edward IV was at (B), and Hastings was at (C). Edward had additional forces in the trees to the west. Somerset made his charge in the same trees but emerged too early and failed to get behind Gloucester as planned. Gloucester attacked Somerset to the north, the additional forces from the trees attacked Somerset on the west, and Edward wheeled part of his battle and attacked Somerset on the east. With Somerset defeated, Edward IV wheeled back and attacked hard to the north. The defeated Lancastrians fled north, some to the abbey, but most to the Bloody Meadow, where there was considerable loss of life.

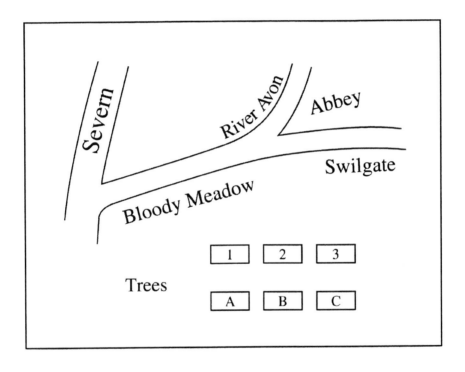

APPENDIX I–K

The Battle of Bosworth Field on 22 August 1485

North is top of the page; the diagram is not to scale. This is the more modern description, as recent metal-detection methods have placed the battle about two to three kilometres to the south-west of Ambien Hill, near a swampy area at the old Roman road known as Fenn Lane. The location of the various forces appears not to be settled at the present time, but the diagram follows approximately the suggestions of Peter Foss (1998). The Norfolk division was at (1), the main royalist division was at (2), and Richard III was behind his men at (3) on higher ground. The rebel army under Oxford was at (4); Henry Tudor was at (5). Among those of doubtful loyalty to York, Northumberland was at (6), Sir William Stanley was at (7), and Lord Thomas Stanley was at (8). Oxford attacked Norfolk relentlessly, forcing his division back; Henry Tudor moved south towards the Stanleys. Richard III caught sight of Henry Tudor on the move and made his famous, heroic, and nearly successful charge; but the king was unhorsed when he was bogged down in swampy ground (as shown by the elongated oval shape with dashes). Sir William Stanley attacked Richard III from the south, and Richard III was killed. The Yorkists soon gave up the fight, and Henry Tudor was crowned the victor. This diagram is an adaption, and may need further modification as more evidence is discovered.

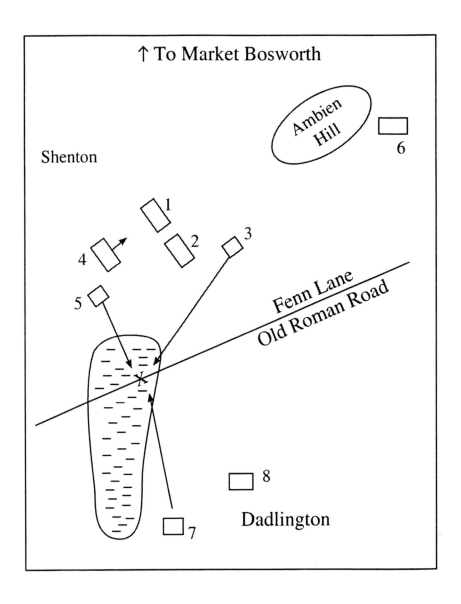

Sources

Ashdown-Hill, John, *Eleanor, the Secret Queen* (Gloucestershire: History Press, 2010).

_____, *The Last Days of Richard III* (Gloucestershire: History Press, 2011).

Bacon, Sir Francis, *Bacon's History of the Reign of King Henry VII* (Cambridge: Cambridge University Press, 1889).

Baldwin, David, *Elizabeth Woodville, Mother of the Princes in the Tower* (Gloucestershire: Sutton Publishing Limited, 2002).

"Blaming the Dead Guy," *Edward V 1483* [website] (2008). <http://edwardv1483.com/index.php?p=1_31_Blaming-the-Dead-Guy> accessed 9 June 2014.

Board, Ernest, "King Edward IV and His Queen, Elizabeth Woodville[,] at Reading Abbey, 1464," *BBC* [website] (2012). < http://www.bbc.co.uk/arts/yourpaintings/paintings/king-edward-iv-and-his-queen-elizabeth-woodville-at-readin41580> accessed 6 June 2014.

Brereton, Humphrey, *The Most Pleasant Song of the Lady Bessy* (London: Richard Taylor, 1829).

Britain's Real Monarch, Jones, Michael (dir.) (London [BBC documentary], 2004).

Brooke, Christopher, *The Medieval Idea of Marriage* (Oxford: Oxford University Press, 1989).

Bryce, Tracy, "Titulus Regius: The Title of the King," *Cogeco.com* [website] (2008). <http://home.cogeco.ca/~richardiii/Titulus%20Regius.htm> accessed 6 June 2014.

Churchill, Winston, in H. S. Commager (ed.), *History of the English Speaking Peoples* (New York: Barnes and Noble Books, 1995).

Clive, Mary, *This Sun of York: A Biography of Edward IV* (New York: Alfred A. Knopf Publishing, 1974).

Coogan, Michael D. (ed.), *The New Oxford Annotated Apocrypha* (New York: Oxford University Press, 2010).

Commines, Philippe de, *The Historical Memoirs of Philippe de Commines Containing the Transactions of Louis XI, Charles VIII, Edward IV, and Henry VII* (London: Military Chronicle Office, 1817).

_____, *Memoirs, the Reign of Louis XI, 1461–1483,* tr. Michael Jones (London: Penguin Books, 1972).

Coote, Leslie, review of Jonathan Hughes, *Arthurian Myths and Alchemy: The Kingship of Edward IV* (Stroud, Sutton Publishing, 2002), in *Reviews in History* [online journal] (June 2003). <http://www.history. ac.uk/reviews/review/335> accessed 6 June 2014.

Croyland Chronicler, *Ingulph's Chronicle of the Abbey of Croyland, with the Continuations by Peter of Blois and Anonymous Writers,* tr. Henry T. Riley (London: Renaissance Books, 1854).

Dean and Chapter of Westminster, "Edward V," *Westminster Abbey* [website] (2012). <http://www.westminster-abbey.org/our-history/ royals/burials/edward-V> accessed 6 June 2014.

Drewett, Richard, and Redhead, Mark, *The Trial of Richard III* (Gloucester: Alan Sutton Publishing Limited, 1984).

"Edward IV of England," *Wikipedia* (last updated 3 July 2014). <http:// en.wikipedia.org/wiki/Edward_IV_of_England> accessed 6 July 2014.

Ellis, Henry; Grafton, Richard; and Hall, Edward, *Edward Hall's Chronicle* (containing the history of England during the reign of Henry IV and succeeding monarchs to the end of the reign of Henry VIII, in which are particularly described the manners and customs of those periods, carefully collated with the editions of 1548 and 1550) (London: J. Johnson and others, 1809) (Weidenfeld and Nicolson, 1981).

Fields, Bertram, *Royal Blood: Richard III and the Mystery of the Princes* (New York: Regan Books, 1998).

Foss, Peter, *The Field of Redemore: The Battle of Bosworth Field, 1485* (Leicestershire: Kairos Press, 1998).

Green, Richard Firth, "Historical Notes of a London Citizen, 1483–1488," *English Historical Review* 96 (1981), 585–90.

Gregory, Philippa, *The Red Queen* (New York: Simon and Schuster, 2010).

_____, *The White Queen* (New York: Simon and Schuster, 2009).

Hammond, Peter, *Richard III and the Bosworth Campaign* (Yorkshire: Pen and Sword, 2010).

Helmholz, R. H., "The sons of Edward IV: a canonical assessment of the claim that they were illegitimate," in P. W. Hammond (ed.), *Richard III: Loyalty, Lordship and the Law* (London: Yorkist History Trust, 1986).

_____, *Marriage Litigation in Medieval England* (Cambridge: Cambridge University Press, 1974). (The statements relevant to this book are to be found on pages 41 and 62.)

Hicks, Michael, "Robert Stillington," *Ingilby History* [website] (2004–08). <http://ingilbyhistory.ripleycastle.co.uk/ingilby_4/Stillington%20 Robert%20(d1491).pdf> accessed 6 June 2014.

Higginbotham, Susan: "Did the Woodvilles Raid the Royal Treasury?" *The History Files* [website] (2011A). <http://www.thehistoryfiles.com/did-the-woodvilles-raid-the-royal-treasury/239/> accessed 6 June 2014.

_____, "Edward IV and Elizabeth Woodville's Wedding Date," *The Unromantic Richard III* [blog] (2008). <http://unromanticrichardiii. blogspot.com/2008/09> accessed 6 June 2014.

_____, "Myths about Elizabeth Woodville," *Susan Higginbotham* [website] (2011B). <http://www.susanhigginbotham.com/subpages/ elizmyths.html> accessed 6 June 2014.

_____, *The Stolen Crown* (Naperville, Illinois: Sourcebooks, Inc., 2010).

_____, *The Woodvilles: The Wars of the Roses and England's Most Infamous Family* (Gloucestershire: History Press, 2013).

"Jacquetta of Luxembourg," *Wikipedia* (last updated 4 April 2014). <http://en.wikipedia.org/w/index.php?title=Jacquetta_of_ Luxembourg&printable=yes> accessed 9 June 2014. (This site gives as its source Richardson, Douglas, *Plantagenet Ancestry: A Study in Colonial and Medieval Families* [London: Royal Ancestry, 2011]).

Kendall, Paul Murray, *Richard the Third* (New York: W. W. Norton, 2002).

Kingsbridge, Charles Lethbridge (ed.), letter to Sir William Stonor dated 9 June 1483, "The Stonor letters and papers, 1290–1483 (# 330)," *University of Michigan Digital Library* [website] (2006). <http://quod. lib.umich.edu/c/cme/ACA1723.0001.001?rgn=main;view=fulltext> accessed 9 June 2014.

Lander, J. R., *Conflict and Stability in Fifteenth-Century England* (London: Hutchinson, 1969).

Leslau, Jack, *Richard III, HolbeinArtworks.com* [website] (revised 9 January 2001). <http://www.holbeinartworks.org/efaqssevenkrichardiiitwentyone.htm> accessed 6 June 2014.

Levine, Mortimer, "Richard III, Usurper or Lawful King?" *Speculum* 34 (1958): 391–401.

"List of Parliaments of England," *Wikipedia* (last updated 5 May 2014). <http://en.wikipedia.org/wiki/List_of_Parliaments_of_England> accessed 9 June 2014.

Mancini, Dominic, *The Usurpation of Richard III* (tr. C. A. J. Armstrong) (Gloucester: Sutton Publishing Limited, 1989).

Markham, Sir Clements, *Richard III: His Life and Character* (New York: Russell and Russell, 1906).

"Mary of York," *Digiplanet* [website] (2012). <http://www.digplanet.com/wiki/Mary_of_York> accessed 9 June 2014.

Maurer, Helen, "Who Killed the Princes in the Tower?" *iVillage* [website] (2005). <http://www.ivillage.com/forums/pregnancy-parenting/hot-topics/hot-debates/general-discussions/who-killed-princes> accessed 9 July 2014.

Miller, Michael D., "King Richard III," *Wars of the Roses* [website] (2003). <http://www.warsoftheroses.co.uk/chapter_72.htm> accessed 9 June 2014.

More, Thomas, *The History of King Richard III* (London: Hesperus Press Ltd., 2005). (Note: This is a modern copy of the 1513 version.)

Myers, A. R., *The Household of Edward IV: The Black Book and the Ordinance of 1478* (Manchester: Manchester University Press, 1959).

Norwich, John Julius, *Shakespeare's Kings* (London: Scribner, 1999).

Okerlund, Arlene, *Elizabeth Wydeville: The Slandered Queen* (Gloucestershire: Tempus Publishing Limited, 2005).

O'Regan, Mary, "The pre-contract and its effect on the succession in 1483," *The Ricardian* 4 (1976): 2–7.

Payne, Henry Arthur, *Plucking the Red and White Roses in the Old Temple Gardens* (1908), *Pinterest* [website] (2013). <www.pinterest.com/pin/97601516895649835> accessed 9 June 2014.

"Plantagenet of York, Edward V," *English Monarchs* [website] (2013). <http://www.englishmonarchs.co.uk/plantagenet_13.htm> accessed 9 June 2014.

Potter, Jeremy, *Good King Richard? An Account of Richard III and His Reputation, 1483–1983* (London: Constable and Company Ltd., 1983).

"Richard's Rebels" (a list of those involved in the Buckingham Rebellion), *Edward V 1483* [website] (2008). <http://edwardv1483.com/index.php?p=1_7_Richard-s-Rebels> accessed 9 June 2014.

Richardson, Douglas, *Plantagenet Ancestry: A Study in Colonial and Medieval Families* (ed. K. G. Everingham) (Salt Lake City, Utah: Royal Ancestry Series, 2011).

"Richard III," article on the College of Arms website, 2013. <http://www.holbeinartworks.org/efaqssevenkrichardiiitwentyone.htm> accessed 26 July 2014.

Ross, Charles, *Edward IV* (New Haven, Connecticut: Yale University Press, 1997).

_____, *Richard III* (New Haven, Connecticut: Yale University Press, 1999).

Routh, E. M. G., *Lady Margaret: A Memoir of Lady Margaret Beaufort* (London: Oxford University Press, 1924).

Santiuste, David, *Edward IV and the Wars of the Roses* (Yorkshire: Pen and Sword Books Limited, 2010).

Smith, Anne Easter, *The King's Grace* (New York: Simon and Schuster, 2009).

Smith, George Barnett, *History of the English Parliament* (London: Ward Lock Bowden Co., 1894).

Sutton, A. F., and Visser-Fuchs, L., "A Most Benevolent Queen; Queen Elizabeth Woodville's Reputation, Her Piety and Her Books," *The Ricardian* 10 (1995): 214–45.

St Aubyn, Giles, *The Year of Three Kings* (London: Faber and Faber, 1983).

Tanner, L. E., and Wright, W., "Recent investigations regarding the fate of the Princes in the Tower," *Archaeologia* 34 (1934): 8–26.

Tey, Josephine, *The Daughter of Time* (New York: Macmillan Company, 1951).

Vergil, Polydore, *Three Books of Polydore Vergil's English History, Comprising the Reigns of Henry VI, Edward IV, and Richard III* (ed. Sir Henry Ellis) (London: Camden Society, 1844).

Walpole, Horace, *Historic Doubts on the Life and Reign of King Richard III* (Stockbridge, Massachusetts: Hard Press, 2013).

Wavrin, Jean de, *Chroniques d'Angleterre* (late fifteenth century), *Luminarium: Anthology of English Literature* [website] (2005). <www.luminarium.org/encyclopedia/edward4marriage.jpg> accessed 9 June 2014.

Weir, Alison, *Lancaster and York* (London: Vintage Books, 1995).

———, *The Princes in the Tower* (London: Folio Society, 1999).

Wroe, Ann, *The Perfect Prince* (New York: Random House, 2003).

"Year Book of Henry VII: De Termino Hillarii Anno Primo Regni Regis Henrici Septimi," *Boston University School of Law* [website] (2010). <http://www.bu.edu/phpbin/lawyearbooks/page.php?volume=11&first_page=50&last_page=50&id=11050> accessed 6 June 2014.

INDEX

30, 51, 222, 351–52, 357–59

Butler, Lady Eleanor, biographical information, 192, 195–96, 205–6, 317–20. *See also* marriage contract story

Butler, James, 404

Butler, John, earl of Wiltshire, 20, 24

Butler, Thomas, 318

C

Cade, Jack, 7

Calais, relationship with England, vii–viii, 13–14, 36, 354–55, 390, 394

Campeggio, Cardinal, 326

Canon Law, 203–17

Castillon, battle of, 9, 230

Catesby, Sir William, 140, 147, 148, 201, 211–12

Catherine (daughter of John of Gaunt), 350

Catherine of Valois, 5, 341, 343, 352

Caxton, William, 219, 277, 288

Cecily Neville, duchess of York
    allegiance to Edward IV, 4, 38, 216
    biographical information, 239–41
    marriage controversy and, 81, 201
    Richard III and, 116–17
    stripped of power, 71–72
    will of, 241

Cecily Plantagenet of York (daughter of Edward IV), 70, 305–7

Charles IV, king of France, vii

Charles the Bold, duke of Burgundy
    biographical information, 353, 357–59
    death of, 57

Edward IV and, 39
    marriage to Margaret Plantagenet, 249–50
    political alliances, 29–30, 37, 286

Charles V, Holy Roman Emperor, 331

Charles VI, king of France, 5, 351–52, 353

Charles VII, king of France, 6, 7, 11–12, 352–55

Charles VIII, king of France, 129–30, 359

Cheney, Sir John, 147

chivalry, tradition of, 274

Churchill, Sir Winston, 117, 132, 225

Church of England, 205, 209, 304, 326–30

civil rights, under Edward IV, 226

civil service, 234, 301

Clarence. *See* George Plantagenet, duke of Clarence

Clement VII, Pope, 326

Clifford. *See* John, ninth Lord Clifford; Thomas, eighth Lord Clifford

Clive, Mary, 53–54, 103–4, 149, 228

cohabitation, marriage and, 204–5

Collingbourne, William, 136

commerce, under Edward IV, 219–20

Commines, Philippe de
    Edward IV and, 39, 60–61, 225
    Louis XI on Richard III, 357
    on marriage contract story, 76–78, 408
    on princes in the Tower, 132–33
    on Stillington, 200

commoners, vs. nobility, 301

Commonplace Book, 133

conciliation policy, of Edward IV, 224–25

Conflans, Treaty of, 358

Constance of Castile, 350

Convention Parliament, 101

Conyers, William. *See* Robin of Redesdale

Cook Thomas, 274–75

Coote, Leslie, 228

Cork of Carlyle, 27

council, of Edward IV, 65–67, 71

Council Meetings. *See also* Great Council
  1456 (Coventry), 11–12
  10 May 1483, 73
  June 1483, 78–84
  London Guildhall, speech given at, 94–97

Council of the North, 131

Courtenay, Edward (d.1556), 399

Courtenay, Edward, first earl of Devon, 126, 128, 265, 313–14, 333–34, 397, 398

Courtenay, Gertrude Blount, 333

Courtenay, Henry (brother of Thomas), 30–32, 224

Courtenay, Henry, marquis of Exeter, 314–15, 332–34, 397, 399

Courtenay, John, 43, 45, 397

Courtenay, Peter, 126, 128, 139, 398

Courtenay, Thomas, sixth earl of Devon, 30, 397

Courtenay, Walter, 126, 128

Courtenay, Sir William, 313, 314, 332, 398–99

Coventry, 11, 41

Cranmer, Archbishop Thomas, 327

Cromwell, Lord, 43

Cromwell, Thomas, 326–27, 329, 333

Croyland Chronicler
  about, 59
  in court of Edward IV, 218
  on Elizabeth, 67, 274, 278
  on legitimacy of Edward V, 86
  on marriage contract story, 81, 102
  on Parliament of 1484, 130, 179
  on princes in the Tower, 119
  records preserved by, 173, 182
  on Richard III, 111–12, 114, 140, 163–64
  on speech at Westminster Hall, 99
  on treasure of Edward IV, 72

custom duties, under Edward IV, 221

D

Darnley, Lord Henry, 324

Dartford, confrontation at, 8–9

de Brézé, Pierre, 12, 25, 27

de la Pole, Edmund, third earl of Suffolk, 259–60

de la Pole, John, earl of Lincoln
  appointments of, 129
  biographical information, 248–49, 258–59
  at Bosworth Field, 148
  claim to throne, 84, 92, 190, 256, 361

de la Pole, John, second duke of Suffolk, 234, 248

de la Pole, Richard, fourth earl of Suffolk, 260–61

de la Pole, Sir William (d. 1539), 261

de la Pole, William, first duke of Suffolk, 6, 248

dental remains, analysis of, 159–162, 170

Howard, Lord John
  biographical information, 370–72
  death of, 146
  military actions, 36
  as supporter of Edward IV, 233,
    309
  support of Richard III, 84, 115,
    127–28, 143
Howard, John, 312, 346
Howard, Katherine, 313
Howard, Thomas, first earl of
  Surrey, 147–48, 149, 311–12
Howard, Thomas, second earl of
  Surrey, 115, 146, 311, 312–13,
  372
Humphrey, duke of Gloucester, 5
Hundred Years War, vii–viii, 351–55
Hungerford, Sir Walter, 144

I
Ibsen, Michael, 247
illegitimacy of Edward IV, claims of,
  3–4, 91–94, 174, 200–201, 240,
  335
impersonators. *See* pretenders, as
  Edward IV's heirs
inheritance, laws of, 235. *See also*
  succession
Isabeau of Bavaria, 351, 353
Isabella, queen of Spain, 50, 350
Isabel of Castile, 141

J
James I, king of England, 325, 337.
  See also James IV, king of Scotland
James II, king of Scotland, 11, 14
James III, king of Scotland, 14, 56,
  137–38, 281, 379–80
James IV, king of Scotland, 321,
  323, 325, 337. *See also* James I,
  king of England

James V, king of Scotland, 323–24
James VI, king of Scotland, 324–25
Joanna of Portugal, 141, 350
Joan of Arc, 5, 353, 354
John, duke of Bedford, 5, 268
John, Lord Scropes, 24
John, ninth Lord Clifford, 23, 247
John I, king of Castile, 350
John I, king of Portugal, 350
John II, king of France, vii
John of Gaunt, 18, 92, 181, 339,
  350
John of Gloucester, 142, 252–53
John the Fearless, 351
Jones, Michael, 77
judicial system, under Edward IV,
  227

K
Katherine, duchess of Buckingham,
  116–17
Katherine of Aragon, 263, 304,
  325–26, 350
Katherine Plantagenet (daughter of
  Richard III), 252–53
Katherine Plantagenet of York
  (daughter of Edward IV), 70,
  313–15
Knight, John, 158

L
Lambert Simnel Rebellion, 259,
  262, 281–82, 297
Lancaster, duchy of, 18–19, 25
Lancaster family tree, 416–17
Lancastrians
  claim to throne, 11–12, 15–16
  under Edward IV, 228–29
  emblem of, 18
  in War of the Roses, 10, 149
  Woodville marriages and, 300

447

Mowbray, John, second duke of
Norfolk, 309, 346
Mowbray, John, third duke of
Norfolk, 24, 370
Mowbray, John, fourth duke of
Norfolk, 234, 370
Mowbray, Margaret, 310
Mowbray, Thomas (d.1405), 309
Mowbray, Thomas, first duke of
Norfolk, 309
Murray Kendall, Paul, 86, 95–97
Myers, A. R., 218

N

naval policy, of Edward IV, 231
Nesfield, John, 135
Neville, Anne. *See* Anne Neville,
Queen
Neville, Cecily. *See* Cecily Neville,
duchess of York
Neville, Charles, 33
Neville, Lady Eleanor, 348
Neville, George, Archbishop of
York, bishop of Exeter
as archbishop, 31
biographical information, 347–48
as chancellor, 14, 24, 38, 233
Edward IV and, 33
imprisonment of, 50
negotiations with France/
Burgundy, 26, 30
rebellion role, 32–33, 47
Neville, George (d.1483), 347
Neville, George, duke of Bedford,
367
Neville, house of, 345–49, 422–23
Neville, Sir Humphrey, 33, 224
Neville, Isabel, 30, 31, 36, 52–53,
347, 348
Neville, John, Baron Montagu
alienation from Edward IV, 35,
401
biographical information, 347,
367
military actions, 26, 30–31,
33–34, 37, 40, 42–43
Neville, Lady Katherine, duchess of
Norfolk, 346
Neville, Katherine (wife of William
Hastings), 348, 368
Neville, Margaret, countess of
Salisbury, 29, 348
Neville, Lady Margaret (wife of John
de Vere), 348
Neville, Ralph, 339
Neville, Richard, fifth earl of
Salisbury, 10, 12–15, 19, 346, 363
Neville, Richard, sixteenth earl of
Warwick
alliance with George Plantagenet,
39
biographical information, 346–
47, 363–67
conflict with Henry VI and
Margaret, 11–12
death of, 43
as dictator of England, 32, 37–43
Edward IV and, 29–30, 33, 34–
35, 78–81, 365
estates, settlement of, 48–50
French marriage treaty, 28, 79
Louis XI and, 356
marriage contract story and, 97,
198, 199
military actions, 10, 21, 26,
35–38, 266
rebellion role, 31–33, 365–66
resentment of Woodville family,
285, 289, 294, 295, 299–301
Neville, Thomas, 36, 40, 48
Neville, William, Lord Fauconberg,
233, 378–79

450

marriage to Elizabeth
Plantagenet, 138–40
mock trials of, 212–16
negotiations with Queen
Elizabeth Woodville, 133–36
plots/rebellions against, 118–19,
125–30, 165
princes in the Tower and, 132,
162, 163–66
reign of, 131–34
reputation of, 95–97, 136–44,
201, 256–57
supporters of, 84
use of marriage contract story,
201
Richard Plantagenet, duke of
Gloucester. *See also* Richard III
biographical information, 252–55
children of, 252–53, 255, 258
confirmation as duke, 24–25
Edward's conciliation with, 33
in Edward's return invasion, 40
exile of, 37
Hastings and, 369
as Lord Protector, 60, 66–75,
82–84, 86–89, 186–90
military actions, 56
rivalry with George, 48–50, 54
usurpation plans, 84–85
Woodville family and, 287–88,
299–301
Richard Plantagenet of Eastwell (son
of Richard), 253
Richard Plantagenet of Shrewsbury
(son of Edward IV). *See also*
princes in the Tower
biographical information, 308–
11, 370, 371
claim to throne, 90
Elizabeth's effort to protect, 74
murder of, 70, 131–34, 150–57

surrendered to soldiers, 87–88
titles awarded to, 52, 58
Robin of Holderness, 30–31
Robin of Redesdale, 30, 31, 32
Rochefort, William de, 132, 172
Roper, John, 153
Roper, William, 153
Ross, Charles, 104, 143, 176, 186,
220, 225–26
Rotherham, Thomas, Archbishop of
York, 61, 73, 85, 126, 233, 383
Rous, John, 194
Royal Library, 219
Russe, Robert, 118
Russell, Bishop John, 59, 73, 89, 98,
142, 164, 233. *See also* Croyland
Chronicler

S
Salic Law, 17, 50
sanctuary
custom of, 45–46
sought by Elizabeth, 278, 279
Sanctuary Plot, 118–19, 182
Sandwich, hostilities against, 12, 14,
378
Savage, Sir Thomas, 144
Say, Lord William, 37, 43
Scales, Elizabeth, 21
Scotland
1463 truce with, 26
planned invasion of, 137–38
relationship with England, 11,
56–57, 144, 230
Scrope, Ralph, 306
Scropes, Lady, 38
Settlement, Acts of, 115, 130
Seymour, Edward (elder), 332
Seymour, Edward (younger), 332
Seymour, Lady Jane, 328–29
Seymour, Thomas, 332

CPSIA information can be obtained at www.ICGtesting.com
Printed in the USA
LVOW12s0808030215

425374LV00001B/5/P